Money and the morality of exchange

Money and the morality of exchange

EDITED BY

J. PARRY and M. BLOCH

CAMBRIDGE
UNIVERSITY PRESS

Published by the Press Syndicate of the University of Cambridge
The Pitt Building, Trumpington Street, Cambridge CB2 1RP
40 West 20th Street, New York, NY 10011–4211, USA
10 Stamford Road, Oakleigh, Melbourne 3166, Australia

First published 1989
Reprinted 1991, 1993

Printed in Great Britain by Athenæum Press Ltd. Newcastle upon Tyne

British Library cataloguing in publication data

Money and the morality of exchange.
1. Monetary systems
I. Parry, Jonathan, 1943–
II. Bloch, M.
332.4

Library of Congress cataloguing in publication data

Money and the morality of exchange/edited by J. Parry and M. Bloch.
    p.   cm.
ISBN 0-521-36597-X. – ISBN 0-521-36774-3 (pbk.)
1. Exchange – Cross-cultural studies.
2. Money – Special aspects – Cross-cultural studies.
3. Economic anthropology.
I. Parry, Jonathan P.
II. Bloch, Maurice.
GN450.M66 1989
306′.3 – dc19   88-37709 CUP

ISBN 0 521 36597 X hard covers
ISBN 0 521 36774 3 paperback

CE

Contents

vi   Contents

Contributors

Maurice Bloch obtained his PhD from Cambridge University. At present he is Professor of Social Anthropology at the London School of Economics. His latest book is *From blessing to violence*, Cambridge University Press. Together with J. Parry he edited the volume *Death and the regeneration of life*.

Janet Carsten obtained her PhD at the London School of Economics and is currently a Research associate in the Department of Anthropology at the University of Cambridge and a Fellow of Clare Hall. She is the author of a number of articles on Malaysia.

Chris Fuller obtained his PhD from Cambridge University. At present he is a Reader in Social Anthropology at the London School of Economics. His latest book is *Servants of the goddess*, Cambridge University Press.

Olivia Harris studied at Oxford and the London School of Economics. She is currently Senior Lecturer at Goldsmith's College, University of London. She is the author of various articles on the Laymi of Bolivia.

David Lan obtained his PhD at the London School of Economics. As well as being an anthropologist he is a successful playright. He is the author of *Guns and rain* (Currey/University of California Press).

Johnny Parry obtained his PhD at Cambridge University. Currently he is a Reader in the Department of Anthropology at the London School of Economics. He is the author of *Caste and kinship in Kangra*. Together with M. Bloch he edited *Death and the regeneration of life*, Cambridge University Press.

Mike Sallnow obtained his PhD from Manchester University. Currently he is Senior Lecturer in Anthropology at the London School of Economics. He is the author of *Pilgrims of the Andes*, Smithsonian Institution Press.

Jock Stirrat obtained his PhD from Cambridge University. Currently he is Lecturer in Anthropology at Sussex University. He is the author of *On the Beach*, Hindustan Publishing Corps.

Christina Toren obtained her PhD from the London School of Economics. She has taught at the University of Manchester and at the School of African and Oriental Studies of the University of London. At present she is preparing two books, one on the learning of symbolism in Fiji and the other on anthropology and psychology.

1

Introduction: money and the morality of exchange

MAURICE BLOCH and JONATHAN PARRY

This collection is concerned with the way in which money is symbolically represented in a range of different societies and, more especially, with the moral evaluation of monetary and commercial exchanges as against exchanges of other kinds. The focus, then, is on the range of cultural meanings which surround monetary transactions, and not on the kinds of problems of monetary theory which have conventionally preoccupied the economist. There is now a very large literature on so-called 'primitive money', but this does not centrally concern us here since all the chapters in this volume deal principally either with state-issued currencies which act as a general medium of exchange, or – as in our two Andeanist contributions – with the symbolism of precious metals and their relevance to Andean ideologies of production and exchange.

The first thing these essays collectively emphasise is the enormous cultural variation in the way in which money is symbolised and in which this symbolism relates to culturally constructed notions of production, consumption, circulation and exchange. It becomes clear that in order to understand the way in which money is viewed it is vitally important to understand the cultural matrix into which it is incorporated. This may seem a bland enough lesson, but it is one which has often been forgotten by anthropologists writing about money – and less culpably also by historians and sociologists. As a result they have commonly fallen into the trap of attributing to money in general what is in fact a specific set of meanings which derive from our own culture.

At another level, however, our essays reveal a unity which underlies all of the apparently diverse examples they consider. This is to be found neither in the meanings attributed to money nor in the moral evaluation of particular types of exchange, but rather in the way the totality of transactions form a general pattern which is part of the reproduction of social and ideological systems concerned with a time-scale far longer than the individual human life. It is only when these total patterns are

1

compared that we can begin to go beyond the conclusion that the variable symbolic elaboration of money and monetary exchange is yet another illustration of the way in which different cultures see things differently. Each of our case studies, we argue, reveals a strikingly similar concern with the relationship between a cycle of short-term exchange which is the legitimate domain of individual – often acquisitive – activity, and a cycle of long-term exchanges concerned with the reproduction of the social and cosmic order; and in each case the way in which the two are articulated turns out to be very similar. This suggests something very general about the relationship between the transient individual and the enduring social order which transcends the individual.

Thus in the first part of this introduction we are centrally concerned with the way in which our own cultural discourse about money has inhibited a proper appreciation of the variability in its cross-cultural construction. In the second part we try to develop the thesis that once we move to the wider, more encompassing, level of the total system of exchange some important continuities begin to emerge.

The revolutionary implications of money in Western discourse

One particularly prominent strand in Western discourse, which goes back to Aristotle, is the general condemnation of money and trade in the light of an ideal of household self-sufficiency and production for use. The argument goes something like this. Like other animals, man is naturally self-sufficient and his wants are finite. Trade can only be natural in so far as it is oriented towards the restoration of such self-sufficiency. Just as in nature there may be too much here and not enough there, so it is with households which will then be forced to exchange on the basis of mutual need. 'Interchange of this kind is not contrary to nature and is not a form of money-making; it keeps to its original purpose – to re-establish nature's own equilibrium of self-sufficiency' (Aristotle 1962: 42). Profit-oriented exchange is, however, unnatural; and is destructive of the bonds between households. Prices should therefore be fixed, and goods and services remunerated in accordance with the status of those who provided them. Money as a tool intended only to facilitate exchange is naturally barren, and, of all the ways of getting wealth, lending at interest – where money is made to yield a 'crop' or 'litter' – is 'the most contrary to nature' (Aristotle 1962: 46).

Aristotle's writings re-surfaced in the Western world in the thirteenth century and were taken up by Thomas Aquinas through whom they achieved a new renown. His influence on the economic thought and attitudes of the Middle Ages was, as Polanyi (1971: 79) observes, quite as great as that which Smith and Ricardo were to exercise on the thinking of a subsequent epoch; and his authority was invoked in support of the Church's profound disquiet about material acquisition. Some of the ideological reasons for this medieval unease about money – especially money as representative of the merchant's profit and the usurer's interest – are briefly reviewed in Parry's contribution to this volume. Here we may simply note that one of the major problems was that the merchant apparently created nothing, while the usurer earned money even as he slept. 'The labourer is worthy of his hire', but it was not at all clear that the merchant and the money-lender laboured. It was essentially this idea of material production as the source of value (Le Goff 1980: 61) which prompted Tawney (1972: 48) to remark that 'the true descendant of the doctrines of Aquinas is the labour theory of value. The last of the Schoolmen was Karl Marx.'

Our own intellectual tradition, however, also contains another very different kind of discourse about money and monetary exchange which sees it as a far more benign influence on social life, for the conclusion to be drawn from Mandeville's *Fable of the bees* and from the 'many advantages' Adam Smith put down to man's propensity 'to truck, barter and exchange' was that the happiness and prosperity of society was founded on the individual pursuit of monetary self-gain. In fact as Hirschman (1977) points out, and we return to his argument below, this theory goes back much further than either of these writers and originally took the form of condoning money-making as a comparatively harmless and gentle vice that could be positively harnessed to the commonweal as a curb on other 'passions' of a more dangerous and disruptive kind.

Between these two radically opposed views of money there are, of course, a very large number of intermediate positions. Simmel (1978), for example, saw in it an instrument of freedom, and a condition for the extension of the individual personality and the expansion of the circle of trust; but at the same time as a threat to the moral order. But what all these different strands in our cultural tradition appear to agree about is that – whether for good or ill – money acts as an incredibly powerful agent of profound social and cultural transformations. Regardless of cultural context and of the nature of existing relations of production and exchange, it is often credited with an *intrinsic* power to revolutionise society and culture, and it is sometimes assumed that this power will be recognised in the way in which the actors themselves construct money symbolically. The essays collected here cast some doubt on both these propositions. Money, we believe, is in nearly as much danger of being fetishised by scholars as by stockbrokers.

Marx and Simmel on the social corollaries of money

This 'fetishism' appears in different degree in the work of two highly influential writers on money, to whom we have already referred: Marx and Simmel.

For Simmel (1978), money was of major significance for the development of the cognitive world we now inhabit since it helped to promote rational calculation in social life and encouraged the rationalisation characteristic of modern society; while in the same vein others have seen money as the basis for an abstract system of thought (cf. Frankel 1977: 7). More than a reflection of other structural features of a modern economy and society (as Dalton [1965] would represent it), Simmel saw money as an active agent which constitutes 'the major mechanism that paves the way from *Gemeinschaft* to *Gesellschaft*. Under its aegis, the modern spirit of calculation and abstraction has prevailed over an older world that accorded primacy to feelings and imagination' (Coser 1977: 194). Encapsulating the modern spirit of rationality, calculability and anonymity, it represents a privileged instance for investigating the whole.

Unlike Simmel, who sees money itself as the principal catalyst for the transformation of social life, Marx's treatment links it to the (for him) more fundamental phenomenon of production for exchange – this being what ultimately creates the need for an abstract money medium. For both writers, however, money is associated with, and promotes, the growth of individualism and the destruction of solidary communities.

Like Aristotle, Marx's condemnation of money and market exchange reflects a certain romantic nostalgia for a world in which production was for use and the interdependence of the human community had not been shattered by exchange. However exploitative the old order, it was not – as capitalism is – based solely on explicit, relentless, egotistical calculation. If the labour theory of value invited a critique of capitalism (and of the abstract money medium with which it is associated) on grounds of equity, the new mode of production also gave rise to a grave misgiving – shared also by many non-Marxist writers – that it denied those moral 'bonds which unite men one with another' which Durkheim emphasised as the basis of all social solidarity. Exchange (by which Marx meant *market* exchange) begins with the exchange of surpluses between communities. But once objects have become commodities in external trade, they inevitably tend to become commodities within the community and to dissolve the bonds of personal dependence between its members. Independent communities become dependent, and dependent individuals become independent (Roberts and Stephenson 1983: 13). Exchange and the abstract money form from which it is inseparable, thus stand condemned as agents of individualisation (cf. Marx 1964: 96) and of the dissolution of the communal bonds which obtained in the world of production for use.

When, Marx argues, the direct labour a medieval serf owed to his lord was commuted into a rent-in-kind and then (more significantly) into a money-rent, a contractual relationship replaced the bonds of personal dependence between them and many peasant holdings were expropriated, while some serfs managed to buy themselves free from their rent obligations and become independent peasants with property rights in the land (Roberts and Stephenson 1983: 20–1).

Simmel traces a rather similar evolution but emphasises the advance in human freedom which results.

The lord of the manor who can demand a quantity of beer or poultry or honey from a serf, thereby determines the activity of the latter in a certain direction. But the moment he imposes merely a money levy the peasant is free, in so far as he can decide whether to keep bees or cattle or anything else (Simmel 1978: 286).

While money erodes older solidarities, for Simmel it also promotes a wider and more diffuse sort of social integration. In the case of barter, trust is confined to the parties directly concerned in the transaction; but monetary exchange extends this trust to an enormously expanded social universe. 'Now each,' as Frankel puts it (1977: 31–2), '[is] no longer dependent only on his relation to the other but also on relations to the economic circle which, in an abstract and indefinable way, guaranteed the functioning and acceptability of the money they made use of.'

Not only is it claimed that money changes the way in which people think, and dissolves bonds between persons based on kinship and other ascriptive criteria, it is also held to effect that separation between persons and things which, as Mauss (1966) stressed, is denied by many primitive and archaic societies. Money permits possession at a distance. Only in the form of money can profits be easily transferred from one place to another, allowing for a spatial separation between the owner and his property which 'enables the property to be managed exclusively according to objective demands while it gives its owner a chance of leading his life independently of his possessions' (Simmel 1978: 333). While the gift of a specific object always 'retains an element of the person who gave it', exchange relationships tend to be 'more completely dissolved and more radically terminated by the payment of money . . .' (ibid. p. 376; cf. Mauss 1966).

Notwithstanding Marx's insistence that property is really a relationship between people masquerading as a relationship between persons and things, there is a sense in which he too represents money as driving a wedge between persons and things in that it appears to sever the relationship between the producer and his product. The worker has no access to the means of production and is paid a wage for his labour. As a result his product is held to belong to somebody else, and is alienated on the market in an absolute way as if it had no connection with him. The commodity comes to appear as though it has 'a "natural price", a relation to money and other commodities independent of the human factors involved' (Ollman 1976: 196). While in the feudal world the lord and his serfs were inseparable from the land in which they had rights, with private property freely exchangeable against money a man's individuality is not conflated with his property in the same way (ibid. p. 208–9).

The impersonality and anonymity of money, it is argued, lends itself to the impersonal and inconsequential relationships characteristic of the market-place and even to a complete anonymity in exchange. Destructive of community, money depersonalises social relations. 'The indifferent objectivity of money transactions is in insurmountable conflict with the personal character of the relationship . . . The desirable party for financial transactions . . . is the person who is completely indifferent to us, engaged neither for us nor against us (Simmel 1974: 227).

Anonymous and impersonal, money measures everything by the same yardstick and thereby – it is reasoned – reduces differences of quality to those of mere quantity. It is in its denial of the unique, and in the fact that it may easily come to be regarded as the means to *all* ends so that its possession confers an almost god-like power, that Simmel locates its most dangerous potential. Similarly Marx (1961: 132) speaks of money as 'the radical leveller, that . . . does away with all distinctions' – not even the bones of the saints being able 'to withstand this alchemy'.

In the light of such arguments it is tempting to conclude that money acts as a kind of acid which inexorably dissolves cherished cultural discriminations, eats away at qualitative differences and reduces personal relations to impersonality. It is only to be expected, then, that those 'traditional' cultures which must for the first time come to terms with it will represent money as a dark satanic force tearing at the very fabric of society.

It is not only in such a world, however, that money is credited with a mastery over men. Though in the ideology of fully fledged capitalism no longer an agent of some evil empire, money is nevertheless credited with a life-like power. Indeed, as Marx saw it, this fetishism of money as the pre-eminent example of the fetishism of commodities is inseparable from capitalism. Here money itself is endowed with fecundity. Money 'breeds' money much – Marx ironically observed – as 'it is an attribute of pear trees to bear pears . . .' Money as capital is ideologically transformed into the source of production, reducing the workers to mere appendages, making it appear only right and proper that capital should reap its 'just reward'. Moreover money as a generalised standard of value misrepresents production by making the value of a commodity expressed in money terms appear as an intrinsic quality of the commodity itself – like one of its physical properties – rather than of the labour which went into its production, which now becomes lost from sight. Relations between people masquerade as relations between things.

Non-monetary: monetary :: 'traditional' : 'modern'?

Given that money is held to have the kind of profound impact on society and culture to which we have alluded above, it is hardly surprising that there is a tendency to postulate a fundamental division between non-monetary and monetary economies (or even *societies*). By the process of slippage which Harris describes in her contribution (chapter 10), it is also easy to see how this opposition gets elided with a series of other dichotomies – 'traditional' and 'modern', pre-capitalist and capitalist, gift economies and commodity economies, production for use and production for exchange – with money acting as a major catalyst of the 'great transformation' between them, or at least as a telling index of it. The effect of this has been to blind a number of writers to the importance of money in many 'traditional', pre-capitalist economies.

Fuller's chapter makes this point with devastating effect in reference to anthropological discussions of what has inappositely been called the 'Hindu jajmani system'. What he shows is how this so-called 'system' has been used to exemplify a radical opposition between 'traditional' and 'modern' economic systems and ideologies and how, in the service of this objective, anthropologists (and others) have managed to ignore the overwhelming historical evidence for the importance of monetary exchanges and market integration in the 'traditional' Indian rural economies to which their models purport to refer. This is true of a whole range of commentators from those nineteenth-century writers for whom the moneyless world of the jajmani 'system' was part of a picture of the village community as a 'little republic' sufficient unto itself, to Wiser who perpetuates this stereotype, to Dumont who is concerned to demolish the idea of the village as a sociologically meaningful isolate but who nevertheless contrives to downplay the significance of market exchange in the pre-British era. What implicitly seems to underlie this misre-presentation is a deeply entrenched notion about the transformative potential of money such that its presence becomes an index of a 'modern' society, with the corollary that in a 'traditional' one it can only be of peripheral significance. But whatever the cause of such blindness, its effect was to encourage Marx in the formulation of his highly question-able theory of an unchanging 'Asiatic mode of production', and Dumont in his overdrawn contrast between the political economy of pre-British and British India, and perhaps also between *Homo hierarchicus* and *Homo aequalis*.

More generally, Fuller's argument should alert us to the possibility that the significance of money and market exchange has been similarly under-estimated in the ethnographic description and analysis of pre-capitalist economies elsewhere in the world, and to the fact that the extent of monetisation is not a reliable index of the atrophy of the 'moral economy'. As Bayly (1985: 286) has concluded from the Indian historical record, the expansion of the cash economy 'did not . . . dissolve the relations of dominance that arose from the interplay between the norms of caste and the structure of the petty kingdoms'. Even within the domain of the market

buyers and sellers were constrained by obligations that required that they purchase certain things at certain times, in certain markets. The widespread existence of markets, money-lenders, and double-entry account books was not incompatible with the persistence of pre-capitalist mentalities in material culture . . . money of itself could not transform relationships . . . (ibid. p. 316)

Gifts and commodities

A further opposition in this sequence on which several of our chapters have some bearing is that between gift and commodity exchange. In Gregory's (1982) neat formulation the first is based on an exchange of *inalienable* objects between *interdependent* transactors; the second an exchange of *alienable* objects between *independent* transactors. It is, moreover, often assumed that this radical opposition between the principles which underlie the two types of exchange will be reflected in an equally radical contrast in their moral evaluation. Stirrat's chapter, however, reminds us that there are commodity contexts in which the alienable object is transacted between conceptually interdependent persons; while in the case which Parry describes the *gift* is alienated as radically as possible and must never return to the donor, for it is held to embody his sins (cf. Parry 1986) – and this is so regardless of whether it is in cash or kind. Here money is clearly far from being a purely depersona-lised instrument. Like the gift in kind it contains and transmits the moral qualities of those who transact it.

As this suggests, the idea that the very impersonality of money makes it of questionable appropriateness as a gift (except significantly in charitable contexts where the relationship between donor and recipient is similarly impersonal) seems to be a peculiarity of our own culture – a peculiarity which is explored in some detail in the chapter by Bloch (see also Wolfram (1987). The gift, as Schwartz (1967) has noted, imposes an identity on both the donor and the recipient, and reveals 'the idea which the recipient evokes in the imagination of the giver'. But gifts of money do not impose an identity in the same way, and in this respect its abstract impersonality dissolves the giver's authority. The problem seems to be that *for us* money signifies a sphere of 'economic' relationships which are inherently impersonal, transitory, amoral and calculating. There is therefore something profoundly awkward about offering it as a gift expressive of relationships which are supposed to be personal, enduring, moral and altruistic. But clearly this awkwardness derives from the fact that here money's 'natural' environment – the 'economy' – is held to constitute an autonomous domain to which general moral precepts do not apply (cf. Dumont 1977). Where it is not seen as a separate and amoral domain, where the economy is 'embedded' in society and subject to its moral laws, monetary relations are rather unlikely to be represented as the antithesis of bonds of kinship and friendship, and there is consequently nothing inappropriate about making gifts of money to cement such bonds.

The radical opposition which so many anthropologists have discovered between the principles on which gift and commodity exchange are founded derives in part, we believe, from the fact that *our* ideology of the gift has been constructed in antithesis to market exchange. The idea of the purely altruistic gift is the other side of the coin from the idea of the purely interested utilitarian exchange (Parry 1986), and we cannot therefore expect the ideologies of non-market societies to reproduce this kind of opposition (cf. Strathern 1985). In his contribution to this volume Parry discusses a series of cases which exemplify a whole range which runs from a situation in which the (supposedly) morally unproblematic sphere of gift exchange is opposed to morally perilous commodity exchange, to one in which it is gift exchange which represents a dire moral peril while commodity exchange is distinguished from it by its moral neutrality, to a context from which this kind of opposition in moral evaluation appears to be largely absent.

While those who write in the Marxian tradition stress the mystification which accompanies commodity exchange, they tend by antithesis to treat the world of gift exchange as non-exploitative, innocent and even transparent. An instance of this romantic idealisation of the world of gift exchange is Taussig's otherwise highly suggestive discussion of the way in which the peasantry of the Cauca valley in Columbia have symbolically constructed the world of commodity relations (Taussig (1980). By contrast the chapters by Sallnow and Bloch in this volume show just how far from being politically innocent such non-commodity exchanges often are, while Parry argues that in Hindu India it is not commodity exchange which is ideologically problematic and loaded but rather what is often made to stand for innocence in Marxist writing – the exchange of gifts.

How misleading it may be to imply that there is universally some kind of unbridgeable chasm between gift and commodity exchange is illustrated by Hart's recent discussion of exchanges of fish for yams and vegetables between coastal and inland villages in the Trobriands. Sometimes these exchanges take the form of ceremonial prestations (known as *wasi*) between community leaders; sometimes of barter between individual households (*vava*). Hart argues that the first reflects:

high social distance and weak political order, bringing big men and corporate organization into play. Informal interpersonal haggling reflects low social distance and strong political order. The issue is whether individuals belonging to different groups feel free to risk the conflict inherent in barter without invoking all the danger, magic, prestige and hierarchy that go with ceremonial exchange. Thus one form is a temporary social framework created in the relative absence of society; the other is an atomised interaction predicated on the presence of society (Hart 1986).

The essential point for our purposes is that Hart's approach allows him to emphasise the dynamic aspects of these institutional arrangements, for it is easy to see how a breakdown in political relations between coastal and inland villages would effect a shift from barter to ceremonial exchange, and their reestablishment a move back in the other direction. Here at any rate the opposition between 'gift exchange' and 'commodity exchange' looks rather less absolute than is often implied, for it seems that one may evolve rather easily into the other.

We are similarly somewhat sceptical of the radical opposition between 'gifts' and 'commodities' implied by the notion of 'fetishism' to which we have previously referred, and of the enormous significance attributed to money in the creation of such phantasmagoric constructions.

For Marx there is a crucial distinction – though it is not always consistently maintained – between money as capital when it is exchanged for labour power, and money as mere money when it is exchanged for the products of labour. Since surplus labour is the source of capital accumulation, and since it is only in capitalism that labour power is routinely exchanged for money, it may be argued that it is only here that money will generally appear to have the self-expanding value implied by the notion of fetishism – that it becomes an aspect of the nature of money that it 'breeds' more money. At any rate Marx writes as though, in the absence of commodity exchange mediated by money, the products of labour are recognised for what they really are. In the pre-capitalist world, relations do not take this 'abstract' form but rather the form of concrete personal relations. In the Middle Ages, for example, the personalised nature of economic relations meant that there was no necessity for labour and its products to assume a fantastic form different from their reality. They take the shape, in the transactions of society of services in kind and payments in kind. Here the particular and natural form of labour, and not, as in a society based on production of commodities, its general abstract form is the immediate form of social labour. Compulsory labour is just as properly measured by time, as commodity producing labour; but every serf knows what he expends in the service of his lord is a definite quantity of his own personal labour power . . . the social relations of individuals in the performance of their labour appear at all events as their own mutual personal relations, and are not disguised under the shape of social relations between the products of labour (Marx 1961: 77).

Or again, we have the more general formula that:

the whole mystery of commodities, all the magic and necromancy that surrounds the products of labour so long as they take the form of commodities, vanishes therefore, as soon as we come to other forms of production (ibid. p. 76).

What such statements would seem to suggest is that in the pre-capitalist world the products of labour are *not* surrounded by 'magic and necromancy' – a proposition which is difficult to square with Mauss's characterization of the gift in primitive and archaic societies, which he describes – in terms reminiscent of Marx's description of the commodity – as 'not inert' but 'alive and often personified' (Mauss 1966: 10). Moreover, Mauss's evidence (ibid. pp. 43–4) suggested that the ceremonial 'coppers' which were exchanged in the potlatches of the northwest-coast American Indians are represented as 'begetting' other coppers (Mauss 1966: 43–4), much as money is said to 'breed' money. On the face of it, then, it would seem that the objects of exchange are as likely to be fetishised in a pre-capitalist economy as in a capitalist one (cf. Comaroff 1985: 72–3; Josephides 1985: chap. 9).

It is, however, possible to argue that the magical halo acquired by the objects of exchange have quite different origins in the two cases. It might, for example, be said that the fetishism of commodities derives from the separation between the product and the producer, which confers on the commodity the appearance of a quasi-independent existence, while – following Mauss – that of the gift would derive from the lack of separation between persons and things, which gives it the appearance of being animated by the personality of the donor (Taussig 1980: 36–7). Or, again, one might distinguish between the 'fetishism' or 'objectification' characteristic of capitalism, where for the most part persons are spoken of as though they were things, and the 'personification' characteristic of pre-capitalist economies where things acquire the attributes of persons (cf. Gudeman 1986: 44). Such distinctions smack, however, of a certain arbitrariness and special pleading. 'Money talks' in a capitalist economy; persons are sometimes transferred in a remarkably 'thing-like' manner in some pre-capitalist ones, while (to give but one example) 'the history of cloth in India also shows how things could retain the quality of the people who fashioned and exchanged them, even in a fully monetized economy' (Bayly 1986). It is therefore quite unclear to us that there is any simple divide between the kind of mystical aura which surrounds the objects of exchange in capitalist and pre-capitalist economies, or that it can be money which explains the (alleged) difference.

The impact of money on 'traditional' worlds

The dominant notion which we have identified in our own cultural discourse about money – that it represents an intrinsically revolutionary power which inexorably subverts the moral economy of 'traditional' societies – has often, we believe, been taken over somewhat uncritically by the anthropologist. The effect of this has been to misrepresent the real complexity of the causal factors at work in the transformations experienced by many cultures as they are sucked into the world of the capitalist market. It is perhaps worth pausing over two particularly striking examples of this kind of misrepresentation.

Probably the best-known discussion of the impact of Western money on a previously non-monetary subsistence economy is Bohannan's account of the case of the Tiv of northern Nigeria (Bohannan 1955, 1959; Bohannan and Bohannan 1968). The 'traditional' Tiv economy contained three distinct ranked spheres of exchange: a lowest ranking sphere of subsistence goods transacted mainly by market exchanges in which people tried 'to maximize their gains in the best tradition of economic man' (1968: 227); a sphere of prestige goods in which brass rods served as a medium of exchange, standard of value and means of payment; and the highest ranking sphere of rights in human beings and, in particular, of rights in marriageable women. Small localised agnatic lineages formed ward-sharing groups in which rights in the daughters of the group were vested. The elder men of the group were the guardians of one or more girls whom they exchanged with outsiders for a wife for themselves or for one of their close agnates – the only entirely acceptable recompense for the gift of a girl being the return of another.

The vast majority of exchanges were what Bohannan calls 'conveyances' *within* the sphere, and these were morally neutral. But under certain circumstances 'conversions' between spheres were possible, and these were the focus of strong moral evaluations – grudging admiration for the man who converted 'up', scorn for the one who converted 'down'. Conversions between the subsistence and the prestige spheres occurred, for example, when an individual was forced by an acute scarcity of subsistence products to exchange brass rods for food. Conversions between the prestige sphere and the sphere of rights in women occurred, for example, when a man managed to contract a *kem* marriage which did not involve giving a ward in return, but which did involve a payment of brass rods for the wife's sexual and domestic services and a subsequent payment for the rights of a father over any of the children she bore him. Since such a wife had been acquired without obligation to the ward-sharing group, they had no claim in her daughter whom the father could allocate in marriage as he chose. He had in effect converted brass rods into rights over people.

Central to Bohannan's analysis is the importance he attaches to the introduction of Western money in subverting Tiv spheres of exchange and converting this 'multicentric' economy into a 'unicentric' one. Other factors, like external trade, are acknowledged to be of significance, but Bohannan's main emphasis is on the new medium of exchange which provided a common denominator which allowed all commodities to be compared against a single measure and made them immediately exchangeable. 'It is in the nature of a general-purpose money that it standardizes the exchangeability value of every item to a common scale. It is precisely this function which brass rods, a "limited-purpose money" in the old system, did not perform.' 'Money', he concludes, is 'one of the shatteringly simplifying ideas of all time, and like any other new and compelling idea, it creates its own revolution' (1959).

This, we believe, considerably overstates the case for it is not *a priori* obvious that *by itself* money does indeed reduce everything to a common measure, or make it impossible for the Tiv to deny that certain things can be bought for money – as we deny that academic and political honours, marriage partners, sexual favours and so on can legitimately change hands against a money payment. Nor is it clear that such a reduction has in fact occurred to the extent which Bohannan's more general statements imply. At the time of his fieldwork, for example, there was little evidence that land was becoming a commodity. The idea of renting or selling it was regarded as thoroughly immoral, and as tantamount to renting or selling one's genealogical position (1969: 90–2). Nor could it be exchanged against anything else at all – not even another plot of land – and all this in spite of the fact that for various reasons there was now increasing pressure on what was already a scarce resource.

This is not, of course, to claim that nothing has changed – only that the transformation of Tiv economic behaviour may not have been quite as radical as Bohannan implies. But more importantly we would argue that the introduction of Western money does not account for these changes, and that other factors are of far greater significance. The first of these was an expansion of the 'economic frontier', in significant measure as a result of the *Pax Britannica*, and the penetration of an external market into Tivland – money being one index of this penetration though incorporation into the wider market meant far more than the introduction of a 'general-purpose' medium of exchange. What it meant above all was that Tivland became a market for significant numbers of Ibo traders who paid cash (essential to the Tiv for the payment of tax) for agricultural produce which they then exported – driving up prices and creating shortages in Tivland itself. It is small wonder, then, that the Tiv claim that the Ibo 'spoil a market' and try to exclude them from it. What's more, these outside traders had no commitment to the moral economy of the Tiv, and were presumably quite ready to trade prestige goods for cash – thus effectively destroying the barriers to conversion between the prestige and subsistence spheres.

At the other end of the scale the British effectively destroyed the impermeability of the highest sphere by legislative fiat. Traditionally what had inhibited the conversion of prestige goods into rights over women was the institution of exchange marriage which meant that normally the only way to obtain a wife was to offer a girl in exchange. But under missionary pressure and 'what appeared superficially to be popular demand' (Bohannan and Bohannan 1968: 248) the colonial authorities managed – with surprising success – to outlaw such exchange marriages. The result was that instead of brides being exchangeable only for daughters and sisters, they now became freely available on payment of brass rods. The effect of this seems to have been to deprive the lineage elders of much of their power, for they had clearly wielded influence over the young men by controlling their access to women. Unable to convert the fruits of their labour into marriage payments, the young men had traditionally been beholden for wives to the elders of the ward-sharing group. 'Popular demand' to do away with exchange marriage was not perhaps so 'superficial' after all. At any rate it would seem to be a reasonable inference that Tiv spheres of exchange buttressed a system of 'gerontocratic' authority, and their subversion posed a direct threat to that authority.

It is not surprising, then, that when Bohannan writes about the Tiv's mistrust of money it always seems to be the *elders* who are deploring the situation. Although we can find no direct evidence that the young men invoked a different discourse about money, we rather doubt that they were so unanimous or unequivocal in their condemnation. It is, however, clear that Tiv elders talk about money in the way that *we* are apt to do – they make it into a condensed symbol of market relations, fetishise it by attributing to it an innate force independent of human will, and blame it for all the woes of their world.

Our second, and more recent, example of this tendency to represent money as *the* crucial agent of social and economic transformation is Kopytoff's (1986) rich and fascinating paper on 'The cultural biography of things', in commenting on which we confine ourselves exclusively to that part of his argument which bears most directly on our central theme and with which we have the greatest difficulty.

For Kopytoff, the crucial attribute of a commodity is its exchangeability, and commodity exchange is a feature of *all* societies. A perfectly commoditised world would be one in which everything is exchangeable for everything else; while in a completely decommoditised one everything would be singular, unique and unexchangeable. Neither, of course, is conceivable in practice and all real world situations fall somewhere between the two poles – exactly where depending on the balance struck between two opposing tendencies towards an expansion of the field of commoditisation and its restriction. While a radical movement in the first direction denies cognitive discrimination, and thereby culture itself, a trend towards complete 'singularisation' would make exchange – and thereby social life – progressively impossible.

The natural world must therefore be arranged into value classes for exchange, and these value classes – which necessarily exist in *every* society – constitute what anthropologists have conventionally called 'spheres of exchange'. Acknowledging the difficulties involved in the labour theory of value, Kopytoff notes its relevance for an understanding of these separate exchange spheres. Produce and items of manufacture, say, yams and pots, can be compared by reference to the labour which went into their production, but no such common standard is available in the case of, say, pots and ritual offices, or yams and wives, and it is the absence of any obvious measure of equivalence which forms 'the natural basis for the cultural construction of separate spheres of exchange' (p. 72).

The problem, then, as Kopytoff sees it, lies not in explaining why the Tiv had separate spheres of exchange but rather in explaining why they had only three spheres and not more. His answer – and this brings us to the heart of our disagreement with him – lies in the technology of exchange, for commoditisation is pushed to the limits which the relatively inefficient exchange technology of the Tiv allowed.

One perceives in this a drive inherent in every exchange system toward optimum commoditization – the drive to extend the fundamentally seductive idea of exchange to as many items as the existing exchange technology will comfortably allow. Hence the universal acceptance of money whenever it has been introduced into non-monetized societies and its inexorable conquest of the internal economy of these societies, regardless of initial rejection and of individual unhappiness about it – an unhappiness well illustrated by the modern Tiv. Hence also the uniform results of the introduction of money in a wide range of otherwise different societies: more extensive commoditization and the merger of the separate spheres of exchange. It is as if the internal logic of exchange itself pre-adapts all economies to seize upon the new opportunities that wide commoditization so obviously brings with it (p. 72).

Consistent with this, Kopytoff goes on to claim that the expansion of the field of commoditization which accompanies capitalism is not a consequence of capitalism itself, but of the exchange technology with which it is associated and which places 'dramatically wider limits to maximum feasible commoditization' (p. 72). In every economy, we are told, there is an inherent drive – restrained only by the cultural need to discriminate – toward 'the greatest degree of commoditisation that the exchange technology permits'; and in small-scale societies this drive is critically inhibited by 'the inadequacies of the technology of exchange' (p. 87).

As will be clear from what has gone before, we are extremely sceptical of this kind of technological determinism, and would instance Barth's (1967) Darfur study as one example which clearly shows that it cannot be the inadequacies of the technology of exchange alone which provides the basis for spheres, for here we find both. Moreover, if money is really such a 'fundamentally seductive idea' it is perhaps strange that the colonial powers in Africa should have repeatedly found that they needed to tax people in order to draw them into the wider economy. It is also surprising that a great many societies failed to borrow the idea of a generalised medium of exchange from more astute neighbours. One might have expected Kapauku or Tolai ingenuity to spread like wildfire. The main point we want to stress, however, is that by coupling money to capitalism in his suggestion that it was money – and not capitalism with which money was associated – that was responsible for a dramatic expansion of commoditisation, Kopytoff ignores the existence of money as we know it in many pre-capitalist economies. He does not say exactly when he believes the 'dramatic expansion' occurred, but it is surely clear that widespread monetisation considerably pre-dates the dominance of a capitalist sector, while experience elsewhere in the world would suggest that the existence of money does not inexorably result in wholesale commoditisation (and rather seldom in the commoditisation of land and labour). As we have previously argued, in the Tiv case at any rate there seem to be grounds for reversing Kopytoff's proposition: the expansion of commoditisation owed far more to an expansion of the market sector than it did to the introduction of Western money. In the 'inexorable conquest of the internal economy' of this previously non-monetised economy, the heavy armour was not money but the new set of exchange relations with which the Tiv were forced to come to terms.

Money and the end of evil

Another assumption which runs through much of the literature we have reviewed, and is marked in the work of both Marx and Simmel, is that money gives rise to a particular world view. It occurs in a particular form in a recent paper by Macfarlane (1985), on which we comment in order to signal a more general doubt.

As a broad cross-cultural generalisation, Macfarlane suggests that a strong sense of evil is undeveloped in hunter-gatherer societies; is a dominant aspect of the value system of the densely populated agrarian 'peasant' societies of China, India, parts of South America and Catholic Europe; and has largely disappeared from 'modern' society. His central problem is to account for this (alleged) disappearance, and this he does in terms of a contradiction between two different ideological currents. The first of these is encapsulated in St Paul's warning that 'the love of money is the root of all evil'; the second in Adam Smith's hard-nosed observation that 'it is not from the benevolence of the butcher, the brewer, or the baker that we expect our dinner, but from their regard to their own self-interest' (Smith 1904: 16). Avarice, the root of all evil, becomes the foundation of society; Publick Benefit derives from Private Vice; the good of the collectivity is served by the evil propensities of the individual. In the face of this contradiction, Macfarlane argues, the absolute distinction between virtue and vice is eroded, and it becomes impossible to sustain an overpowering sense of unmitigated evil.

While this ideological double-bind might seem to be culturally highly specific, at various points Macfarlane couches his argument in more general terms. Echoing Simmel's observation that money is subversive of 'moral polarities', for example, he writes that:

'Money', which is a short-hand way of saying capitalist relations, market values, trade and exchange, ushers in a world of moral confusion . . . [it] complicates the moral order, turning what was formerly black and white into greyness . . . it is money, markets and market capitalism that eliminate absolute moralities . . . (p. 72).

Burridge's discussion (1969) of the preoccupation with money in the symbolism of Melanesian cargo cults is cited in support of this general proposition that 'money disrupts the moral as well as the economic world.'

Interesting though Macfarlane's argument is, we believe it to be seriously flawed – both in its specific application to Western Europe and in its more general form. With regard to the latter, it is abundantly clear from the different chapters in this volume that money and market exchange are central features of the political economy of many peasant agrarian societies of the type in which, in Macfarlane's view, an ideology of evil is most likely to flourish. To cite Bayly (1985: 316) once more:

What is striking [in India] is the way in which the formal apparatus of markets and a monetized economy molded themselves to and were accommodated by mentalities that still viewed the relationships between men, commodities, and other men in terms of good (pure) and evil (polluting).

Not only is it entirely illegitimate to conflate money with capitalist relations and market values, but the extent to which either money or the capitalist market 'ushers in a world of moral confusion' is culturally extremely variable, and depends – as our collection repeatedly shows – on the nature of the system they confront and on the mechanisms it is able to develop for 'taming' and 'domesticating' them. Contrary to Macfarlane's assumption, the concern with money we find in many Melanesian cargo cults is not – Parry's chapter argues – a concern with its morally perilous nature or its subversive quality, but merely with discovering the secret of its fecundity, of making it multiply; a possibility which appears quite 'natural' in a world in which traditional valuables regularly attract an increment in exchange.

As for its specific application to Western Europe, what we find surprising about Macfarlane's argument is its curiously ahistorical nature. He writes as though St Paul's condemnation of avarice were a constant and unchanging value in Western civilisation. But while it may well be true that an unswerving pursuit of riches has been widely frowned upon at all times, it is clearly the case that the extent to which money-making and money-mindedness have been seen as a moral peril has undergone considerable shifts of emphasis. Little (1978:34), for example, notes how it was at the end of the thirteenth or beginning of the fourteenth century that 'the pictorial theme of men and also apes defecating coins made its appearance in the margins of gothic manuscripts', and explicitly contrasts the mentality that produced these drawings with 'the one that, in the ninth and tenth centuries, used depictions of royal and imperial coins to decorate sacred books'. It was during the eleventh (Little 1978: 36), or perhaps the twelfth (Duby 1982: 322), century that avarice supplanted pride as the vice *par excellence*, and this period saw a burgeoning of satires on the theme of money (Murray 1978: 72). The timing is significant since this was a period of rapid urban growth and of a major expansion of market trade. In other words, the attention devoted to money, trade and avarice as a moral peril grew with the significance of the money economy. So far from a general erosion of the sense of evil, as Macfarlane's thesis would suggest, what we really seem to witness is a *heightening* of the sense of evil inherent in money.

What happened in the West, we would argue, is not that money subverted a sense of evil, but rather that *one* discourse (amongst others) *about* money made money-making more and more marginal to the devil's domain, and almost (but never quite) succeeded in wresting it from him entirely. Hirschman (1977) traces the fascinating story of how, from the later Middle Ages on, the sin of avarice becomes in official ideology less and less heinous, and is eventually removed from the category of 'passions' to become an 'interest'. Crucial to this transformation is the theory that one 'passion' can be set to tame another; that 'greed, avarice, or love of lucre, could usefully be employed to oppose and bridle such other passions as ambition, lust for power, or sexual lust' (ibid. p. 40) which were seen as more socially disruptive. The notion that Publick Benefit derives from Private Vice was a theory about statecraft before it became a justification for market capitalism, for money-making was seen as a more enlightened way of conducting affairs than 'passions' of a more bellicose nature. With Dr Johnson's pronouncement that 'there are few ways in which a man can be more innocently employed than in getting money', it becomes a positively harmless pastime. Indeed, as the most dogged and persistent of passions, it ceases to be a vice at all and becomes a legitimate 'interest' of the individual, opposed to his 'passions' by its very predictability and rationality; and a society in which men freely pursue their interests is contrasted to 'the calamitous state of affairs that prevails when men give free reign to their passions' (ibid. p. 32). The paradox, however, was that:

as soon as capitalism was triumphant and 'passion' seemed indeed to be restrained and perhaps even extinguished in the comparatively peaceful, tranquil, and business-minded Europe of the period after the Congress of Vienna, the world suddenly appeared empty, petty, and boring and the world was set for the Romantic critique of the bourgeois order as incredibly impoverished in relation to earlier ages – the new world seemed to lack nobility, grandeur, mystery, and, above all, passion' (ibid. p. 132).

The meanings of money

While writers like Simmel and Macfarlane see money as giving rise to a particular world view, what we would like to emphasise is how an existing world view gives rise to particular ways of representing money.

As our two Andeanist chapters suggest, it is Taussig's (1980) failure to give due weight to this cultural template that vitiates much of his re-interpretation of Nash's (1979) ethnography on the folklore and ritual practices of Bolivian tin-miners. According to this folklore, Tio – 'the devil' – controls the fertility of the mine, claims the miners' lives when he is not properly reciprocated for his gifts of ore by appropriate sacrificial offerings, and enables some individual miners to enrich themselves by entering into a secret pact with them. As Taussig interprets it, such beliefs represent an indigenous reflection on the power, danger and immorality of the new capitalist economy, and on the perils which result from the fact that what is extracted as a gift from the spirit guardians of the mine is then transformed into a commodity. This makes mining very different from the traditional peasant economy of production for use in which there is an unproblematic and undisrupted reciprocity between the peasants and the supernatural sources of fertility.

What Harris's chapter shows, however, is that peasants too may be said to owe their riches to a pact with the 'devils', and it is therefore implausible to interpret the belief in such 'devil contracts' as a commentary on the evils of proletarianisation and capitalist relations of production. Neither in symbolism nor in ritual are agriculture and mining opposed. The fertility of the mines is ritually restored in a strikingly similar way to the fertility of the fields and flocks; minerals are held to grow in the mines like potatoes, and it is said that – like land – a mine should be left to lie fallow to recuperate its fertility. As Sallnow points out, it is only in mining that death at the hands of the spirits is a permanent occupational hazard, but this is only an extreme variant of the requirement of a sacrificial spilling of blood in Andean agricultural ritual. Since Andean peasants have long been incorporated into the market, and market relations do not represent a comparable supernatural danger, it is clearly not commoditisation itself which constitutes the problem. Rather the real explanation for the mystical danger of mining lies in ideas about the cosmological significance of precious metals as supreme commodities, the proper use of which is to flow upwards as tribute to the state. This tribute reproduces an ordered relationship between the state and the local community – a relationship which is the source of the latter's fertility and prosperity, and which is threatened by any individual appropriation of gold and silver that would disrupt this flow. Hence the dangers of mining derive not from the fact that the ore:

is extracted as a gift and disposed of as a commodity – that is, from the imperfect articulation between the dictates of capitalism and the norms of Andean culture – but rather from within the culture itself . . . The supernatural perils of gold-mining [and by association of all mining] are a consequence not of the ultimate commoditisation of the product, but of the cultural logic in which it is initially embedded.

When the argument that money brings about a radical transformation of society is extended by the proposition that it must therefore lead to revolutionary and *specifiable* changes in world view, it is easy to further assume that money means what money (supposedly) does. Regardless of culture, it will always tend to symbolise much the same kinds of things.

But seen as set, what the authors in this volume appear to show is that the meanings with which money is invested are quite as much a product of the cultural matrix into which it is incorporated as of the economic functions it performs as a means of exchange, unit of account, store of value and so on. It is therefore impossible to predict its symbolic meanings from these functions alone.

At first sight, however, it might seem that such relativism is called into question by several of the cases discussed by our contributors who document cases where money does indeed appear to carry the kind of symbolic load with which we are familiar from our own tradition. The Shona spirit mediums described in Lan's chapter, for example, avoid and reject European goods as incompatible with the sacred domain of ancestral authority. Similarly, Stirrat reports that the Sri Lankan fishermen with whom he worked associate money with disorder and a disruption of the proper hierarchical order of caste; and Toren that the Fijians talk of the world of money as the antithesis of the ordered moral world of chiefs and kinship.

In fact, however, these apparent similarities with our own cultural discourse are largely illusory. Though Shona mediums must avoid all contact with Western commodities like soap, petrol and Coca-Cola, we unexpectedly find that there is no such prohibition on money – in part because it is symbolically assimilated to a traditional item, hoes. Unlike these other items, money does not stand in opposition to the realm of the sacred. Again, the seeming familiarity of the Sinhalese case turns out to reflect an entirely different set of meanings, for the fishermen's distaste for money has far less to do with an hostility towards commoditisation and the market than it has to do with the fact that here the control of money is in the hands of women. The Fijian example is also a case of false familiarity, but one which suggests a rather different kind of difficulty with those traditional arguments which attribute to money a specific significance regardless of context: a difficulty which derives from a misunderstanding of the nature of symbolism itself.

The Fijian opposition between money (standing for anti-social acquisitiveness) and *yaqona* drinking (standing for community) does at first sight indeed seem redolent of our own opposition between commerce and instrumentality on the one hand, and kinship and morality on the other. What Toren makes clear, however, is that this opposition has as much to do with the contrast between cross-cousins and other kinsmen as it has to do with the contrast between the market and the pre-monetary economy. At this point not only does what is seemingly familiar from our own culture begin to look very much less familiar, but it becomes apparent that we are not dealing with a simple opposition of irreconcilables, but rather with interconnected concepts which are part of a transformative discourse.

This is easiest to appreciate when we consider the kinship aspect of the Fijian contrast which opposes an image of society as ordered by a fixed hierarchical pattern of consanguinity, affinity and chiefship represented in the ritual of *yaqona* drinking, to an image of the ephemeral, egalitarian, sexual and chaotic relations of unmarried cross-cousins. The relationship between these two orders is not, however, one of static and absolute opposition, for one side of the contrast is continually being transformed into the other in a way which, far from being threatening, actually represents an image of the successful reproduction of the community. This is because cross-cousins should become spouses, and hence the chaotic world which is partly conjured up by money is the necessary precursor to the world of ordered hierarchy conjured up by *yaqona*. What we therefore have is a continuing dialectic in which cross-cousins who are opposed are then united by marriages which belong to the domain of hierarchical kinship, but these in turn renew the opposition through the birth of children who are again opposed as cross-cousins. This synthesis is represented in the ritual of 'drinking cash' by the combination of the symbolism of money and of *yaqona* drinking. In the first part of the ritual the subversive creativity of cross-cousins assumes the form of monetary competition, but in the second part this chaotic behaviour is harnessed to the reproduction of the ordered *yaqona* drinking community when the result of the cash rivalry becomes a beneficial social fund. This type of transformation is – as we shall see – in no way exceptional.

Not only does money mean different things in different cultures, but – as this example suggests – it may mean different things within the same culture. Sometimes represented as subversive of the most valued social relations, it can also be viewed as an instrument for their maintenance. While in one context life 'in the manner of money' is the antithesis of the 'Fijian way', in another, money is morally neutral or even positively beneficial. Again the ambiguity is by no means unusual. What the Fijian example also demonstrates therefore is the misleading nature of the assumption that symbolic meanings can be precisely specified. As Lévi-Strauss (1958: 147–80) has argued is the case with symbolism in general, the Fijian symbolism of money and *yaqona* drinking are continually being combined in creative ways to express processes and transformation. It is consequently not only impossible to say what money will 'mean' irrespective of cultural context, it is even misleading to presuppose that it will have any fixed and immutable meaning in a given context – a point which is also suggested by Appadurai's (1985) astute comments on the typically antagonistic interests of merchants (as champions of unfettered equivalence in exchange) and the political elite (as champions of regulation and control) in a world in which the status hierarchy is protected by sumptuary laws. What money means is not only situationally defined but also constantly re-negotiated.

Transactional orders

We must, therefore, shift our focus from a consideration of the meanings of money to a consideration of the meanings of whole transactional systems and to the kind of transformative process we have identified for the Fijian case. When we do this a very different kind of picture emerges. What we then find are significant regularities which strongly qualify the highly relativistic conclusions to which a consideration of money in isolation has led us in the first part of this introduction. A particularly clear instance of the kind of regularity we have in mind is provided by Carsten's chapter in this volume.

As in the Fijian case, the Malay fishermen she describes symbolically transform money from a subversive and threatening force into something moral and socially positive. As in our Sri Lankan case, there is an intimate connection between the symbolism of money and the symbolism of gender, but there the similarity ends. Unlike Stirrat's Sinhalese, the Malay fishermen of Langkawi are quite willing to engage in commercial exchanges, though they can only legitimately do so with comparative strangers, for such relations are seen as incompatible with the moral bonds of kinship. Once the money has been earned, however, the men hand it over to the women who remain uncontaminated by contact with the amoral domain of market transactions. The women can then, as it were, 'de-contaminate' the money they receive, transforming it into a morally admissable resource which sustains the household and the community. This they do by analogy with the way in which they transform raw food into a cooked meal, the eating of which is one of the strongest Malay symbols of solidary relations. Women, Carsten argues, symbolically 'cook' the money, and thereby convert it into something which can be safely incorporated into – and will nourish – the household.

The fishermen of Langkawi are thus involved in two different transactional orders: a world of fishing and commerce in which men engage with strangers in a myriad of short-term transactions and where individual competition, if not sharp practice, is acceptable; and a world which is oriented towards the longer-term goals of reproducing the household, which in Malay ideology provides the model for representations of the wider community.

The crucial and more general point is that, as for the Malays, in one form or another, each of the cases discussed in this volume reveals a similar pattern of two related but separate transactional orders: on the one hand transactions concerned with the reproduction of the long-term social or cosmic order; on the other, a 'sphere' of short-term transactions concerned with the arena of individual competition.

Amongst the Shona, the long-term transactional order is symbolically constructed in terms of an image of an immortal chiefdom which is represented by the spirit mediums who embody the ancestral rulers, who in turn dispense fertility to their descendants in return for obedience, respect and tribute. In both our Andean cases, it again revolves around a sacred and enduring polity which is represented as the source of the prosperity and increase which flows down to the local community as long as tribute flows up. Again, in Fiji, exchanges of *yaqona* between chiefs and the people construct an idealised image of an unchanging hierarchical order; while in the Sri Lankan case the predictable long-term order of caste with which the men identify is opposed to the short-term amoral sphere of the market in which the women assume the crucial roles. With the Merina of Madagascar, we similarly find an image of the eternal descent group symbolised by the immobile stone tomb, which is seen as opposed to – but also as partially dependent on – individualistic transactions of a short-term acquisitive nature. Finally, in India, gifts to the Benares Brahmans are concerned with the reproduction of the cosmic and social order and – by ridding him of his sins – with restoring the pilgrim's place within it. In each case this long-term transactional order is concerned with the attempt to maintain a static and timeless order.

In each, however, cultural recognition is also explicitly given to a cycle of short-term exchanges associated with individual appropriation, competition, sensuous enjoyment, luxury and youthful vitality. This is variously the world of commerce, wage-labour or brigandage, and is often identified with exchanges between strangers. In the Merina case, for example, such transactions are concerned with *harena* – movable goods which are individually acquired through competitive activities like war and trade. In life a legitimate source of sensual enjoyment, *harena* must at all costs be dispersed before death for they are firmly rooted in a transient world which defies and negates the image of a permanent and collective ancestral essence embodied in the tomb.

As this might lead one to expect, there is a close association between Merina funerary practices and the two transactional orders, and an explicit connection is made between ancestral body-substance and inherited wealth on the one hand, and between the vital substance of the living and *harena* on the other. The case is instructive for it seems to reveal something more general about the relationship between the two cycles of exchange. The short-term individualistic transactions concerned with *harena* are morally acceptable so long as they remain subordinated to, and do not compete with, the long-term restorative cycles which focus on the undifferentiated collectivity of the ancestors. Indeed such activities are particularly desirable when the goods they yield are used to maintain this over-arching order – as, for example, when individually acquired wealth is employed to restore the tombs or fund the ceremonies associated with them.

But, of course, all this is extremely similar to what we have already said about the Fijian and Malaysian cases where the morally equivocal money derived from short-term exchange cycles is transformed by a simple symbolic operation into a positively beneficial resource which sustains the ideal order of an unchanging community. Much the same pattern emerges once more from Parry's Indian example, where even wealth acquired through the most devious means by merchants, bandits and kings is unproblematic so long as a proportion of it is gifted to Brahmans as part of the long-term cycle of cosmic purification. Again, in Sri Lanka we find that money ceases to be dirty and becomes a legitimate interest of men when it is used in consumption to maintain the solidarity and class identity of the fishing village and to reproduce the household; and this kind of conversion is also graphically illustrated by Harris's vignette of impoverished Bolivian peasants pouring away their wealth in libations to the sacred earth, and down their throats to produce holy drunkenness.

What we consistently find, then, is a series of procedures by which goods which derive from the short-term cycle are converted into the long-term transactional order – procedures which include the 'drinking' of cash in Fiji, the 'cooking' of money in Langkawi, and the 'digesting' of the pilgrims' gifts by the Brahmans of Benares. And of course it is no accident that such transformations should so often be expressed in an alimentary idiom, for everywhere this is one of the most powerful of all possible metaphors for transformation. It is not that what is obtained in the short-term cycle is a kind of ill-gotten gain which can be 'laundered' by being converted into socially approved channels of expenditure and consumption. It is rather that the two cycles are represented as organically essential to each other. This is because their relationship forms the basis for a symbolic resolution of the problem posed by the fact that transcendental social and symbolic structures must both depend on, and negate, the transient individual.

It is widely argued that outside the ideological ambit of the capitalist market, the economy is seen as being 'embedded' in society, that the relentless individual pursuit of material self-gain is generally discountenanced, and that collective goals are normally accorded primacy over those of the individual. Much of the so-called 'formalist–substantivist' controversy turned on the issue of whether maximizing man exists, either in fact or theory, in the pre-capitalist world; and – though Polanyi himself was a creditable exception (see, for example, Polanyi 1971) – the answers provided have generally tended to take the form of a straightforward 'yes' or 'no'. What we believe our discussion illustrates, however, is that all these systems make – indeed *have* to make – some ideological space within which individual acquisition is a legitimate and even laudable goal; but that such activities are consigned to a separate sphere which is ideologically articulated with, and subordinated to, a sphere of activity concerned with the cycle of long-term reproduction. The relationship between the politico-economic domain of *artha* and the moral order of *dharma* in Hindu theory provides an almost paradigmatic case of this kind of relationship between the two cycles. We therefore find it strange that Dumont (1970) should see the world renouncer as more or less the sole representative of the values of individualism in Indian society, and should apparently deny any role to such values in the sphere of *artha*.

That this ideological space should exist is, we believe, inevitable – for the maintenance of the long-term order is both pragmatically and conceptually dependent on individual short-term acquisitive endeavours. Not only do the latter in fact provide much of the material wherewithal necessary for the reproduction of the encompassing order, but it also has to be acknowledged that this order can only perpetuate itself through the biological and economic activities of individuals. What we claim to be describing then is an extremely general set of ideas about the place of the individual in a social or cosmic order which transcends the individual.

The articulation between the two spheres is, however, by no means unproblematic. If the long-term cycle is not to be reduced to the transient world of the individual, they must be kept separate – witness the Malay preoccupation with insulating the domestic domain against commercial transactions. But if the long term is to be sustained by the creativity and vitality of the short-term cycle, they must also be related – hence the concern with the kinds of transformative processes of which the 'cooking' of money in Langkawi is just one example.

The possibility of conversions between the two orders also has much to do with their moral evaluation. While the long-term cycle is always positively associated with the central precepts of morality, the short-term order tends to be morally undetermined since it concerns individual purposes which are largely irrelevant to the long-term order. If, however, that which is obtained in the short-term individualistic cycle is converted to serve the reproduction of the long-term cycle, then it becomes morally positive – like the cash 'drunk' in Fiji or the wealth given as *dana* in Hindu India. But equally there is always the opposite possibility – and this evokes the strongest censure – the possibility that individual involvement in the short-term cycle will become an end in itself which is no longer subordinated to the reproduction of the larger cycle; or, more horrifying still, that grasping individuals will divert the resources of the long-term cycle for their own short-term transactions.

The nightmarish spectre of this last eventuality is illustrated by our two Andean cases. Sallnow vividly evokes the extreme danger and secrecy with which Peruvian peasants associate the mining of precious metals. The reasons for this are complex, but one way of unravelling its logic is to start from Harris' report that – though infinitely more valuable – precious metals are seen as growing in the earth like tubers or potatoes. Fertility and increase of all kinds is a blessing of the mountain spirits, and normal crops – like potatoes – require the normal reciprocation of libations and an occasional blood offering. One who obtains precious metals, however, is obtaining a kind of super crop, for which the only possible return is the life of the miner himself. But the temptation of course is to try to conceal the appropriation and thus avoid the debt; though such a stratagem is thoroughly anti-social since the mountain spirits will then extract their return at random. A renegade of this sort who threatens to permanently divert the resources of the long-term cycle to his own short-term advantage, is the antithesis of the paragon who liberally pours libations on to the earth or into his body in order to transcend, through drunkenness, his calculating individualist self. Through his self-abnegation the latter ensures that what he derives from the long-term cycle has been returned to it even before it has been given.

Similarly in the Benares case, the Brahman who receives *dana* but fails to pass it on *in toto* is in effect diverting wealth destined for the long-term cycle for his own short-term ends. The consequence is not only that he himself will rot with leprosy and suffer the torments of hell, but that – since he is blocking the channels of purification which flow in the opposite direction to *dana* – he also brings sin and misfortune to his unwitting donors. But when the munificent merchant confers *dana* on the Brahmans he is doing exactly the opposite. He is converting wealth accumulated in short-term acquisitive activity into a long-term cycle concerned both with a whole chain of purification and elimination of sin, and with the support of Brahmans whose ritual activities sustain the cosmos.

Equally, our ethnography also illustrates the other horrendous possibility that the individual will become so embroiled in the short-term cycle that he will ignore the demands of the long cycle. It seems to be this danger with which Merina notions about tree-planting are concerned. Since the tree outlasts the individual who planted it, it represents a kind of illicit immortalisation of the type of wealth that should be dispersed before death. This anti-social attempt to perpetuate his own individuality amounts to a denial of the claims of the long-term cycle associated with the undifferentiated collectivity of the dead, and is therefore liable to be punished by the ancestors.

Again, for the Sri Lankan case, Stirrat documents the existence of two different 'spheres of consumption': one concerned with reproducing the basic viability of the household and marking its equivalence to all other households within the community; the other concerned with an intensely competitive expenditure between households. Though both kinds of consumption are positively valued, expenditure in the second sphere of competitive conspicuous consumption is most fully justified when it is directed at social reproduction through marriage; but it becomes distinctly immoral when it jeopardises the viability of the household and thereby subverts the long-term order. Much the same considerations, we suggest, lie behind the tirade of Toren's Fijian teacher against 'the world of money'. In other circumstances Fijians regard money as morally unproblematic, but what the old man bewails is that it tends to take people over and encourage them to neglect chiefship and kinship. When the short-term cycle threatens to replace the long-term cycle then the world is rotten. It is in such circumstances that a morally indeterminate instrument becomes something morally opprobrious.

Money and the two transactional orders

We have argued, then, that money is accorded quite different meanings in different cultures, but that once we focus on the broader patterning of transactions some rather significant regularities begin to emerge. With hindsight, however, this conclusion is what we might have expected to start with, for the symbolism of money is only one aspect of a more general symbolic world of transactions which must always come to terms with some absolutely fundamental human problems. One of these is the relationship between the individual human life and a symbolically constructed image of the enduring social and cosmic order within which that life is lived; a relationship also discussed in our introduction to *Death and the regeneration of life* (Bloch and Parry 1982), with which the argument of the previous section is very much in line.

The obvious corollary of our relativistic conclusion about the meanings of money is that it is quite impossible to penetrate these meanings without an understanding of the ways in which they are informed by the wider symbolic and social orders, a point which is admirably demonstrated by Martin's (n.d.) discussion of the contrasting significance of money in Taiwan and the United States. Such superficial similarities which do emerge in the meanings given to money in different cultures is, we would suggest, a kind of epiphenomenon of regularities which exist at a deeper level. That is, they are a consequence of regularities in the way in which the transactional world as a whole is symbolically constructed in terms of what we have called long and short-term cycles. Both in Madagascar and in the Andes, certain forms of money are closely identified with the long-term order of exchange. Because of the instrumental uses to which money lends itself, the more familiar case however is for it to be most closely associated with the short-term order (as, for example, in our Fijian and Malaysian cases), and it may even become a condensed symbol of that order. Such similarities in symbolic construction as exist, we are arguing, derive from similarities in the way in which this order is constructed by different cultures.

It is, as we have seen, a commonplace assumption that money gives rise to a specific world view and to particular kinds of social relationship, but this is very dubious. The further implication of our discussion however is that – within rigorously circumscribed limits and with or without money – the vast majority of cultures make some space for exchanges which display many of the features which are sometimes, as in our own society, associated with monetary exchange (a degree of impersonality, considerable scope for individual gratification and a concern for pure instrumentality, for example). Those writers who credit money with the paternity of these features are therefore constructing a false history in which what is actually an extremely general contrast *within* cultures between the domains of the long and short-term orders becomes a contrast *between* cultures – and it is on this basis that the notion of a 'great divide' between the monetary and pre-monetary worlds has rested. In one way or another the chapters by Fuller, Harris, Lan and Bloch which follow all make reference to this kind of historical falsification.

We do not, of course, intend to imply that everything is everywhere the same, or to downplay the great variety of symbolic systems documented in this volume. Nor do we wish to suggest that the kind of scheme we have outlined is either universal or eternal. While we believe the pattern we have identified as common to all our case studies is typical of a wide range of societies, it is arguable that the mature ideology of capitalism would be an example of something entirely different. By a remarkable conceptual revolution what has uniquely happened in capitalist ideology, the argument would run, is that the values of the short-term order have become elaborated into a theory of long-term reproduction. What our culture (like others) had previously made room for in a separate and subordinate domain has, in some quarters at least, been turned into a theory of the encompassing order – a theory in which it is *only* unalloyed private vice that can sustain the public benefit.

What is also possible, however, is that the conceptual shift has been rather less radical, and that what has really happened – as Mauss's essay on the *The Gift* implied long ago – is rather that Western ideology has so emphasised the distinctiveness of the two cycles that it is then unable to imagine the mechanisms by which they are linked. One of the merits of this formulation would be that it suggests a way of understanding the quite contradictory representations of money – as devilish acid or as instrument and guarantor of liberty – to which we are heirs. What, in other words, these two different discourses would reflect is the radical divorce between the two cycles, each discourse deriving from the perspective of one side of the dichotomy alone.

These are issues which we cannot properly tackle here, however, for the central focus of this collection is on ideologies which have been largely developed outside the centres of capitalism. The general comparative lesson of which they provide a timely reminder is that the specificity of the particular symbolic system, the similarities in the solutions which different cultures provide to the same fundamental problems of human existence, *and* the way in which historical forces act on and transform an existing cultural template, all have to be taken into account if we are to begin to understand the meanings of money. The lesson is also one which we need to take to heart if we are to understand our own representations of exchange.

References

Appadurai, A. 1986. 'Introduction: commodities and the politics of value', in *The social life of things: commodities in a cultural perspective*, pp. 3–63, Cambridge: Cambridge University Press.
Aristotle 1962. *The politics*, Harmondsworth: Penguin Books.
Barth, F. 1967. 'Economic spheres in Darfur', in R. Firth (ed.), *Themes in economic anthropology*, pp. 149–74, London: Tavistock Publications.
Bayly, C. A. 1986. 'The origins of swadeshi (home industry): cloth and Indian society. 1700–1930', in A. Appadurai (ed.), *The social life of things: commodities in cultural perspective*, pp. 295–321, Cambridge: Cambridge University Press.
Bloch, M. and Parry, J. (eds.) 1982. *Death and the regeneration of life*, Cambridge: Cambridge University Press.
Bohannan, P. 1955. 'Some principles of exchange and investment among the Tiv', *American Anthropologist*, 57: 60–9.
    1959. 'The impact of money on an African subsistence economy', *The Journal of Economic History*, 19 (4): 491–503.
Bohannan, P. and Bohannan, L. 1968. *Tiv economy*, London: Longmans.
Burridge, K. 1969. *New heaven, new earth: a study of millenarian activities*, Oxford: Basil Blackwell.
Comaroff, Jean 1985. *Body of power, spirit of resistance*. Chicago: University Press.

Coser, L. 1977. *Masters of sociological thought: ideas in historical and social context* (2nd edition), New York: Harcourt Brace Jovanovich, Inc.

Dalton, G. 1965. 'Primitive money', *American Anthropologist*, 67: 44–65.

Duby, G. 1982. *The three orders: feudal society imagined* (trans. A. Goldhammer), Chicago: Chicago University Press.

Dumont, L. 1970. *Homo hierarchicus: the caste system and its implications*, London: Weidenfeld and Nicolson.

1977. *From Mandeville to Marx: the genesis and triumph of economic ideology*, Chicago: University of Chicago Press.

Frankel, S. H. 1977. *Money: two philosophies*, Oxford: Basil Blackwell.

Gregory, C. 1982. *Gifts and commodities*, London: Academic Press.

Gudeman, S. 1986. *Economics as culture: models and metaphors of livelihood*, London: Routledge and Kegan Paul.

Hart, K. 1986. 'Heads or tails? Two sides of the coin', *Man*, 21 (4): 637–56.

Hirschman, A. O. 1977. *The passions and the interests: political arguments for capitalism before its triumph*, Princeton: Princeton University Press.

Josephides, L. 1985. *The production of inequality: gender and exchange among the Kewa*, London: Tavistock Publications.

Kopytoff, I. 1986. 'The cultural biography of things: commoditization as process', in A. Appadurai (ed.), *The social life of things: commodities in a cultural perspective*, Cambridge: Cambridge University Press.

Le Goff, J. 1980. *Time, work and culture in the middle ages*, Chicago: Chicago University Press.

Lévi-Strauss, C. 1958. *Anthropologie structurale*, Paris: Plon.

Little, L. 1978. *Religious poverty and the profit economy in medieval Europe*, London: Paul Elek.

Macfarlane, A. 1985. 'The root of all evil', in D. Parkin (ed.), *The anthropology of evil*, Oxford: Basil Blackwell.

Martin, E. (forthcoming). *The meaning of money in China and the United States* (1986 Lewis Henry Morgan Lectures, University of Rochester.).

Marx, K. 1961. *Capital*, vol. 1, Moscow: Foreign Languages Publishing House.

1964. *Pre-capitalist economic formations*, London: Lawrence and Wishart.

Mauss, M. 1966. *The gift: forms and functions of exchange in archaic societies* (trans. I. Cunnison), London: Cohen and West Ltd.

Murray, A. 1978. *Reason and society in the Middle Ages*, Oxford: Clarendon Press.

Nash, J. 1979. *We eat the mines and the mines eat us: dependency and exploitation in Bolivian tin mines*, New York: Columbia University Press.

Ollman, B. 1976. *Alienation: Marx's conception of man in capitalist society* (2nd edition), Cambridge: Cambridge University Press.

Parry, J. P. 1986. '*The gift*, the Indian gift and the "Indian gift"', *Man*, 21 (3): 453–73.

Polanyi, K. 1971. *Primitive, archaic, and modern economies: essays of Karl Polanyi*, ed. G. Dalton, Boston: Beacon Press.

Roberts, P. C. and Stephenson, M. A. 1983. *Marx's theory of exchange, alienation, and crisis*, New York: Praeger Publishers.

Schwartz, B. 1967. 'The social psychology of the gift', *The American Journal of Sociology*, 73 (1): 1–11.

Simmel, G. 1978. *The philosophy of money*, London: Routledge and Kegan Paul.

Smith, Adam 1904. *An inquiry into the nature and causes of the wealth of nations*, ed. E. Cannan, 2 vols., London: Methuen.

Strathern, M. 1985. 'Kinship and economy: constitutive orders of a provisional kind', *American Ethnologist*, vol. 12.

Taussig, M. 1980. *The devil and commodity fetishism in South America*, Chapel Hill: The University of North Carolina Press.

Tawney, R. H. 1972. *Religion and the rise of capitalism*, Harmondsworth: Penguin Books.

Wolfram, S. 1987. *Inlaws and outlaws; kinship and marriage in England*, Beckenham: Croom Helm.

2

Misconceiving the grain heap: a critique of the concept of the Indian jajmani system

C. J. FULLER

The exchange of produce, goods and services within the Indian village community, executed without the use of money, has long featured prominently in the literature of economic anthropology. It has served as a clear example of a socio-economic institution that is not subject to the operation of market forces, but is instead regulated by customary rights and privileges as these are expressed and enforced by the hereditary caste division of labour. From the nineteenth-century reports of British administrators in India to the modern literature of anthropology, the enduring symbol of this moneyless institution has been the grain heap divided into shares on the village threshing floor.

In the contemporary ethnography of India, the village exchange system is usually referred to as the 'jajmani system'.[1] Few of the more perceptive writers on this topic have confined themselves to empirical description alone. They have looked too at the morality or values associated with exchange within the jajmani system and, especially in the work of Dumont, the argument has been powerfully put that these values, characteristic of 'traditional' Indian society, are fundamentally different from those of modern, Western society, dominated by its monetised, capitalist market economy. In other words, the village jajmani system has exemplified the radical opposition between traditional and modern economic systems and ideologies. Moreover, the argument has often been extended so that the pre-colonial Indian economy as a whole has also – if not always explicitly – been firmly consigned to the traditional side of the dichotomy.

To this dichotomous picture, in which shares in the grain heap stand ideologically opposed to monetised transactions in the marketplace, the evidence on money in India – and much more besides – is embarrassing. As I shall show, it is virtually impossible to fit that evidence into the conventional wisdom about the traditional Indian economy. The grain heap has been a powerful but misleading image and anthropologists in

33

particular have been too readily beguiled by it. One result, I shall argue, has been the construction of an anthropological fiction, the jajmani system itself, which has had serious implications for understanding – or misunderstanding – the economy and exchange relations in India. A re-examination of the jajmani concept will also, as I shall show in my conclusion, raise some pertinent questions about the comparative analysis of economic systems and the phenomenon of money in general.

The jajmani system in anthropological literature

In this section, I am principally concerned with the jajmani system as portrayed in general anthropological accounts, which in turn have often found their way into textbooks. One of the clearest general accounts is by Kolenda; it was first published in 1963 and reprinted in the very popular anthology, *Tribal and peasant economies*. Kolenda's paper, which reviews the literature up to 1963, includes a straightforward summary of the jajmani system, which I now quote in slightly abbreviated form.

Briefly, the *jajmani* system is a system of distribution in Indian villages whereby high-caste landowning families called *jajmans* are provided services and products by various lower castes such as carpenters, potters, blacksmiths, watercarriers, sweepers, and laundrymen. Purely ritual services may be provided by Brahman priests and various sectarian castes, and almost all serving castes have ceremonial and ritual duties at their *jajman's* birth, marriages, funerals, and at some of the religious festivals. . . . The landowning *jajmans* pay the serving castes in kind, with grains, clothing, sugar, fodder, and animal products like butter and milk. Payment may amount to a little of everything produced on the land, in the pastures, and in the kitchen. Sometimes land is granted to servants, especially as charity to Brahman priests. In this system, the middle and lower castes either subscribe to each other's services in return for compensations and payments, or exchange services with one another (1967: 287).

The key points here are that there is indeed a system, later stated to be 'integrated on a local basis' (ibid.: 330), that this system exists within villages, that it is constituted of relations between high-caste landowning families and their clients, that it covers both ritual and non-ritual services, and that payment is made in kind. The rates of payment, as Kolenda explains, are not however inevitably fixed by custom, but may be susceptible to pressures of supply and demand (ibid.: 326–9).

I wish to argue that the system so well described by Kolenda is largely a figment of the anthropological imagination.[2] But before I do so, some further discussion is required. In the 1950s and 1960s, there was an extensive debate – thoroughly evaluated by Parry (1979: 74–83) –

about whether the jajmani system was integrative or exploitative, based on consensus or coercion. Advocates of the exploitative position eventually lost the argument, mainly because they relied upon a concept of exploitation – of clients by landowning patrons – which was not employed convincingly in analysing the ethnographic data. Through the work of Dumont, the integrative position largely triumphed.

In *Homo Hierarchicus* (1970a), Dumont develops his analysis of the jajmani system into a wider discussion of the ideologies of market and non-market economies, a theme taken up again in *From Mandeville to Marx* (1977). His argument partly builds upon a paper by Pocock (1962), who wants the term 'jajmani' to be restricted to relationships between patrons and properly religious specialists: priests, but also washermen and barbers who remove pollution and have crucial roles at rites of passage. Relationships with artisans and unskilled labourers, mainly agricultural, are not truly jajmani, although these relationships (particularly with labourers) are, 'by an extension of the ideology of caste' (1962: 92), akin to true jajmani relationships.

Dumont, contending that so-called economic facts are encompassed within the religious ideology, suggests that Pocock has missed the point: 'strictly jajmani' relationships 'serve as a model for the others' (1970a: 107). He writes: 'Were we to travel in our imagination to a threshing floor in traditional India, we would see there the farmer measuring one after the other the King's share, that of the person who is found to have a superior right over the land, then the shares of the Brahman who serves as domestic priest, the barber, and so on, until perhaps he reaches the untouchable ploughman' (ibid.: 104). These shares are not defined by the market and the distribution of grain is not strictly an economic phenomenon; rather, the whole distribution takes place within the religious order. 'The needs of each are conceived to be different, depending on caste, on hierarchy, but this fact should not disguise the entire system's *orientation towards the whole*' (ibid.: 105). The 'hierarchical collectivity' is the referent to which the system is oriented and the division of the harvest displays interdependence. 'An economic phenomenon presupposes an individual subject; here on the contrary everything is directed to the whole . . . This view of an ordered whole, in which each is assigned his place, is fundamentally religious' (ibid.: 107).

It is significant that Dumont does include the king, and the whole to which he refers is not congruent with the village community *per se*, a vital point to which I shall return. Further on in *Homo Hierarchicus*, Dumont comes back to the division of the harvest, noting that it does not express exclusive rights in land, but rather: 'The interdependence of the castes is expressed here by the existence of complementary rights, where that of the king and that of the cultivator are only the main links in a chain which was sometimes complex' (ibid.: 157) – a reference to the intermediaries often present in the agrarian system between cultivator and king. Hence, Dumont argues, the values of caste are antithetical to those of modern property rights: 'In short the caste system is strongly contrasted to what we call land ownership' (ibid.: 158). Property rights, directly connected with the conversion of land and labour into marketable commodities, only developed fully during the period of British rule and only then did 'a distinct sphere of activity which may properly be called economic' come into being (ibid.: 165). In traditional India, the political encompassed the economic, and the politico-economic was itself encompassed within the religious (ibid.: 165).

At this point, the above summary of Dumont's analysis will suffice, although I shall return to it later. I now turn to three specific issues: the distinction between jajmani and baluta systems; the question of whether there is any *system* in the full sense of that term; and (in most detail) the material on the state and revenue payments.

Jajmani and baluta

It is normally assumed in the anthropological literature that the jajmani system is defined by relationships between landowning patron (*jajman*) and client (*kamin, praja*, etc.) households (or sometimes client castes as a whole): see, for example, Kolenda (quoted above), Dumont (1970a: 98) or Mandelbaum (1970: 161–2). This was indeed how Wiser described the system in a north Indian village in his book, *The Hindu jajmani system*, first published in 1936 and usually cited as the first competent study. Most nineteenth-century sources, though, describe something rather different, the so-called 'village establishment': each village having its permanent complement (ideally twelve) of hereditary officials (headman, accountant, etc.) and servants (carpenter, barber, washerman, etc.). The classic descriptions (usefully summarised by Wilson (1855: 52–6)) come from western India and the system was often called the 'baluta' (or 'balute') system, the name that it has in the Maratha region. Such a system is described, for example, in the famous passage from the *Fifth Report* of 1812 that was quoted by Marx in his discussion of the Indian village community.[3] In the baluta system, in contrast to the jajmani system as defined above, officials and servants are not the clients of patron households, but are attached to the village as a whole or to a division of it, and the remuneration which they receive at harvest time from the cultivators is made on behalf of the entire village or division (except for the often excluded Untouchables).

Lest it be thought that the older sources are unreliable, I should emphasise that the ethnographic evidence is not in doubt, even though the number of detailed modern studies of baluta systems happens to be less than those of patron–client jajmani systems. Orenstein (1965) gives the most exact account of a baluta system in a Maharashtrian village and his data plainly support his argument that there is a 'generalized village [to] servant relationship' (1965: 214), and that conceptually the tie is between a *bālutedār* clan and the village as a whole, and not between households or castes (ibid.: 216, 230). Orenstein's ethnography is in these respects consistent with Fukuzawa's data on the baluta system in eighteenth-century Maharashtrian villages, which also show the servants to be linked to the village as a whole – the one significant exception being the domestic priest serving only his *jajman* (1972: 26–40; 1982: 252; see also Schlesinger 1981: 243–4, 263–3). Other material, especially from south India, shows a pattern closer to the Maharashtrian baluta system than to the patron–client jajmani system, but an ethnographic review is not required here, since it is the analytical implications on which I want to focus.

My initial point is straightforward. It is clear that the patron–client jajmani system and the baluta system are conceptually distinct; it is therefore inaccurate to treat them as one, as Fukuzawa (1972) rightly argues. Dumont, for instance, asserts that the older descriptions of baluta 'were already dealing in fact with what is here called *jajmānī*' (1970a: 292, n. 42d; cf. 1970b: 118), while Mandelbaum simply states: 'In some parts, especially in the Maharashtrian region, the artisan and service families maintain jajmani relations with a segment of the village rather than individual families' (ibid.: 163). The problem here is not so much one of nomenclature – the ill-advised extension of the term 'jajmani' from one type of system to another – but rather the conflation occurring on the analytical level.[4]

One consequence of this conflation is the false assumption of geo- graphical uniformity. According to Dumont (ibid.: 102): 'The universa- lity of the [jajmani] system has been contested, though with little foundation.' This criticism is addressed to Harper (1959), who describes a Malnad (Karnataka) village with significant cash-cropping and wide- spread monetary payments, which clearly does not have a jajmani system, notwithstanding Dumont's unconvincing attempt (following Pocock 1962: 80–5) to argue otherwise. It may be noted, too, that evidence from Bengal (although sparse) suggests the general absence there of any significant jajmani or baluta relationships (Raychaudhuri 1983: 10; Schwartzberg 1968: 110). In any case, even from the limited evidence presented here, it is clear that there is no pan-Indian jajmani system of the patron–client type and therefore no justification for generalising about the Indian village economy on that basis. In reality, patron-client-type jajmani systems – or the best approximations to them – appear to be particularly, though not exclusively, concentrated in an area of northern India stretching from western Uttar Pradesh to Rajasthan, Haryana and Punjab, approximately the northwest quadrant of the country. Commander, who draws attention to this fact, suggests that it is connected with the existence in the region of 'predominantly small-holding peasant husbandry' (1983: 287); his interesting observation deserves more systematic investigation by anthropologists and historians, although Krause (n.d.) has already questioned the accuracy of Commander's correlation.

The issues raised by Commander and Krause cannot be pursued here. I only need to stress the point that a particular type of jajmani system can only occur under particular historical circumstances. By contrast, the conventional anthropological view presumes a kind of historical (or, rather, ahistorical) uniformity, on which I shall have more to say later. In fact, however, there is evidence of change from one type of system to another. For medieval south India, Stein (1980: 424–5) shows that village officers and servants (*ayagar*, Kannada equivalent of Marathi *balutedar* (Wilson 1855: 41)) appear to have been paid by dominant peasant patrons in earlier times, but later received specified income shares (in granted land, grain or cash) from the village as a whole. Stein links this change to the increased administrative penetration of the villages under Vijayanagara rule, although Baker (1984: 41, 47, 53–5), repeating earlier interpretations, writes that the village officers and servants were actually appointed by warrior chiefs settled in the countryside by the Vijayanagara or later Nayaka states. Their disagreement may be ignored here, because the key point is the alteration in response to external political pressure. In Gough's Thanjavur village, an alteration in the reverse direction appears to have occurred in the early nineteenth century, when 'the British made most village servants the private responsibility of the landlords' (1981: 204; cf. 181–3, 204–6, 265–85 for details on village servants, etc.). Other similar modifications associated with administrative action by states could undoubtedly be found, and more intensive research would probably reveal some of the general conditions under which, for example, patron–client jajmani systems are transformed into village-service baluta systems, and *vice versa*. This, in turn, when linked with further investigation of the kind begun by Commander and Krause, could lead to a better understanding of the connection between different types of village economic system and structures of local and supra-local political power.

Because the distinction between the two types of system is conceptual, it is quite possible that there may be no absolute certainty whether village servants are linked to the village as a whole or to individual patron households. Something akin to this appears to be reported by Gough (ibid.: 266) and also by Mayer (describing a Malwa village), who states – in relation to artisan and servant caste *kamins* – that: 'Services for payments in kind . . . are partly performed for the cultivators, and are partly village service.' The cultivators pay on behalf of the whole village and, writes Mayer, 'One could thus say that the *kamin* are more the servants of the cultivators (i.e. those with ploughs) than of other villagers' (1960: 71). This imprecision, I suggest, is not so much Mayer's, as his informants', operating a system that is itself conceptually betwixt and between.

To close this section, let me reiterate the following points. Disguised by contemporary anthropological use of the term jajmani are at least two conceptually distinct systems: patron–client jajmani and village-service baluta. Quite possibly, further distinct variants should also be isolated, building upon Harper's article (1959). Plainly, it is incorrect to assume that there really is a uniform village economic system of the type conventionally labelled jajmani existing throughout rural India, now or at any time in the past. Further, until this unwarranted assumption is abandoned, serious investigation into regional and historical variation will be impossible, as Kolenda (1967: 288) does in fact observe.

Is the jajmani system a system?

The second major issue is whether the jajmani system (to revert to the one term) is properly describable as a *system*. That is to say, is the system in question really a systematic, integrated entity, as has regularly been assumed? In Lewis's judgement: 'It is greatly to Wiser's credit that he was able to characterise *jajmani* relations *as a system*' (1958: 55–6). Arguably, however, nothing has promoted more misinterpretation than Wiser's ostensible breakthrough. Pocock rightly drew attention to this issue (1962: 78–9 and *passim*), but he has been ignored by many writers, who seem to have taken it for granted that the system is indeed a system in the full sense of that term.

Consider first the terminology. The Hindi term *jajmān* derives from the Sanskrit *yajamāna*, 'patron of the sacrifice', for whom the *purohita*, the priest, carried out the ritual act itself. The term's original sacrificial referent is crucial to Dumont's argument that the entire jajmani system is fundamentally religious (1970a: 97–8).[5] In parts of northern India, however, the term *jajman* has been extended to cover 'patron' in a more general sense, so that not only a (Brahman) priest, but also a carpenter, a washerman, etc. refers to his patron as a *jajman*. Wiser (1969: xx), for example, who worked near Delhi, describes this usage clearly, and

40   C. J. Fuller

Wilson (1855: 226) noted it as early as 1855. Such an extensionist usage is vital to Dumont's argument that strictly jajmani relationships are the model for all others: that all are 'expressed *in the same language*' (1970a: 98).

In fact, however, the linguistic extension is not universal, even in north India. To quote but three examples: Miller (1975: 83), who also worked near Delhi, specifically states that only a priest refers to his patron as a *jajman*; Berreman (1972: 57–8) says the same about his Garhwal villagers; and Parry (1979: 59) reports, for his Kangra villagers, that a *jajman* is only the patron of a Brahman, a barber or a funeral priest. Equally significantly it appears to be rare, if not unheard of, for a single term to be used for the priest and all other specialists. Wiser (1969: xx), for instance, states that the priest is known by the honorific term *pandit* ('religious scholar') and the lower-ranking servants by the rather demeaning term *kam karnewala*, translated as 'worker'. Similar distinctions are ubiquitously recorded. Parry (1979: 59–71) shows in detail how Kangra villagers distinguish between priests and (in ritual contexts) barbers (*purohit*), who are remunerated with gifts, craftsmen (*kamin*), whose remuneration is 'explicitly a payment', and a third category of beggars who rely on alms. Berreman (1972: 57–8) notes that the Brahman receives 'gifts', but the patron of an artisan is a *gaikh*, 'one who purchases the service of another', and Mayer's informants distinguish between payments to servant and artisan *kamins*, as opposed to alms to *mangats*, literally 'beggars' but also including priests (1960: 63–72).

Starting from a different point, Good (1982: 24–31), discussing a south Indian village, particularly stresses that the categories of prestations made at harvest time to clients and village servants (in a system plainly approximating to the baluta model) are not exclusive to this one context. Prestations referred to by the same terms and understood by informants as identical in kind are also made on other occasions, for example at rites of passage, when they are made between members of the same caste. Consequently, Good argues, there is no isolable sphere of so-called jajmani relationships that is independent of other, non-jajmani relationships. And this argument too undoubtedly has general, if not universal, applicability.

These distinctions in terminology and in categories of remuneration, as well as the use of the latter categories in diverse contexts, all point towards the same conclusion: that there is in the Indian village no discrete, isolable jajmani system in the full sense of that term, either in informants' conceptions or in empirical fact. The system, so-called, is neither internally integrated nor isolable from a wider set of exchanges. Indeed, it is noteworthy that some careful ethnographers, such as Mayer or Parry, precisely avoid the term 'system' in describing their material, whereas two recent ethnographers, Good and Gaborieau (1977: 66) (who describes a Nepalese case), flatly deny that there is a single system in their respective regions. Commander's careful study of nineteenth-century north Indian material is even more devastating for the notion of a jajmani 'system'. He refers to 'the fragmented and rather partial sense in which the *jajmani* structure can be found to be functioning' (1983: 307) and concludes that '*jajmani* bore, for the most part, a very dim resemblance to the pure model' (ibid.: 310). Only a historian's caution, perhaps, prevents him from stating unequivocally that the jajmani 'system' is a complete misnomer, since this, I suggest, is what he plainly shows to be the case.

In my opinion, it is now time that the notion of a jajmani *system*, with its distinctive functionalist overtones, was abandoned once and for all. As this assertion could easily be misunderstood, let me stress that I am not disputing the ethnographic evidence, only its interpretation. The evidence certainly shows that, in many Indian villages, there do exist relationships between patrons and clients, or village and servants, of the type labelled 'jajmani' or 'baluta', in which customary payments in kind are made. However, these relationships and payments cannot all be subsumed within a single analytical category and they do not, even when taken together, define or constitute an integrated *system*. Sets of jajmani or baluta relationships there may be, but jajmani or baluta systems – in the strong sense of that term – there are not. Through this chapter my use of the term 'system' should be taken to refer only to such sets. Moreover, to assume in advance the form or structure of these sets, let alone their systemic integration, effectively precludes proper analysis and interpretation. Ideally, perhaps, the term 'jajmani system' would be discarded altogether, but realistically I doubt if this will ever happen. Probably we must resign ourselves to using a term which can only be silently modified as 'so-called' in recognition of the fact that a fictional system is denoted.

The state and revenue payments

The third issue concerns the state and revenue payments. This material will clearly demonstrate the impossibility of isolating the village exchange system from its wider context (cf. Fuller 1977: 107–8), a point particularly well made by Wolf (1966: 47–57), whose textbook *Peasants* provides a much better account of the importance of revenue payments for the local-level economy in pre-colonial India (and elsewhere) than do most introductory works focusing on India alone. Although the material I shall present all derives from published sources, none of it to my knowledge has ever been properly considered in anthropological discussions of the jajmani system or traditional Indian economics.[6]

I return to the threshing floor in traditional India to which Dumont has already taken us. Certainly, throughout pre-British India from the most ancient times, the revenue due to the ruler from the land was conceived of as a share of the harvested crop. Hence it can in principle be sharply distinguished from a fixed monetary tax on the land itself. Although Dumont does not specifically discuss the use of money, the phraseology of his account consistently implies that the king's share was taken in grain. In some parts of India, even as late as the nineteenth century, a simple division in kind (*batai, bhaoli*) did still occur. Thus, for example, Tod (quoted in Baden-Powell (1892: 270–1)) describes the scene at the threshing floor in villages in the kingdom of Udaipur (Rajasthan) in the early nineteenth century. He states that the crop was divided into heaps, each of a standard volume, which were then cut into four equal parts. From each heap fixed amounts were taken to be handed over to the village headman, accountant, watchman, messenger, carpenter, blacksmith, potter, washerman, shoemaker and barber. Altogether, these shares totalled one of the quarter heaps. The second quarter went to the king, and the last two quarters to the cultivator himself, after further shares had been taken for the king's heir. Small shares for the royal family were also removed from the grain handed over to the village servants. The net result was that the king's share actually totalled three-tenths, not one quarter. Most probably, Tod's description is a generalised one, not an account of a specific village that he visited, but there is no doubt that the system was broadly as he portrayed it, and certainly there were many other regions of India in which a similar distribution of the grain was effected.

However, it appears to have been far more common, in the eighteenth century and earlier, for kings, chiefs and other political dominators enjoying a right or power over cultivators to take their shares in cash, not kind. In the simplest system, which was widespread, the share was calculated in grain on the threshing floor, as in Tod's description, but taken in the form of cash by immediately commuting the value of the grain at the prevailing market rate (or at a rate fixed to his advantage by the revenue-collector). An example may be quoted from a report of 1819 on Masulipatam district (modern Andhra Pradesh), which came under British control in 1759.[7] In that area, revenue was collected by the local chiefs known as *zamindars*. As harvest time approached, the *zamindars* sent their servants to the villages to prevent illicit cutting of the grain and to estimate probable yields. Inspectors stood on the threshing floor and affixed their seals to the piles of grain, and then supervised carefully the measurement of shares. The shares due to the village servants were deducted from these piles and the remainder was divided fifty-fifty between the *zamindar* and the cultivator. The *zamindar*'s share was then immediately handed over to the cultivator and its value taken from him in cash.[8]

In practice, payments in kind or cash were not mutually exclusive. Throughout south India, for instance (as the *Fifth Report* extensively documents: e.g., 1969 reprint, 1: 219, 223), it was common for revenue from wet land to be paid in kind but from dry land always in cash, and in some areas the British government continued with this system in the early nineteenth century (Kumar 1983: 220). In the Delhi region in the sixteenth century, payment in cash reverted to payment in kind during a period of extremely low prices, possibly caused in part by a severe shortage of money (Habib 1982: 67). Such a change may also have occurred on other occasions when specie was in short supply. The persistence of payment in kind does not, however, affect the crucial point to be made here that revenue payment in cash was very widespread and almost certainly more common than payment in kind throughout most of India by the eighteenth century and indeed earlier.

Since economic anthropology sometimes gives the impression that money is a modern phenomenon (overlooking the huge numismatic collections housed in every major museum), it should be emphasised that regular minting of coins by rulers had begun in India by the second century BC. This early money was not state-regulated legal tender and the extent of monetisation in this early period is unclear, but certainly money-lending was sufficiently widespread to require the attention of Hindu lawgivers nearly two millennia ago (Basham 1971: 222–4). Detailed evidence on currency is only available from more recent times and in the medieval period, the coinage of the various kingdoms was frequently debased and its production erratic. However, during the Mughal period (sixteenth–seventeenth centuries), a century or two before the British Raj, the empire, according to Habib, 'could well boast of one of the finest coined currencies in the contemporary world, a tri-metallic currency of great uniformity and purity' (1982: 360). At the empire's many mints, coins with standard gold, silver or copper content were produced and debasement was fairly effectively controlled. In the same period, bills of exchange rapidly grew in importance for the settlement of large transactions.[9]

Cash payment of land revenue in northern India is recorded from as early as the end of the thirteenth century (Habib 1982: 61), although – according to Ghoshal (1929: 227) – it was widespread in eastern India by the ninth century. However, it was in the Mughal period, principally during the reign of the emperor Akbar, in the late sixteenth century, that pre-colonial India's most sophisticated, cash-based revenue system was developed. Akbar expanded the empire to include all of what is now north India, Pakistan and Bangladesh, and much of this enormous territory – from Lahore to Allahabad – was largely covered by his new revenue system, which I shall now outline relying on Habib (1963: ch. 6; 1982: ch. 9, 1).

Already, possibly by the fourteenth century, a system (*kankut*) had been introduced which relied on making estimates of the harvest beforehand, so that the royal assessors did not need to visit each and every village to collect their dues at harvest time. This system was therefore administratively rather more sophisticated than that being operated by Masulipatam chiefs in the eighteenth century. Nonetheless, *kankut* had disadvantages, notably that the amount of revenue was still directly dependent on harvest yields, and these were sought to be overcome by the *zabt* system, whose final form was developed by Akbar's ministers. Surveys were carried out in order to discover average yields, prices and areas under cultivation in the empire's various provinces. Using this information, revenue rates were fixed in cash for each crop in each revenue district, and these were applied every year irrespective of price fluctuations from season to season (though provision was made for crop failure). By these means, the imperial treasury was assured of a reasonably constant revenue which did not require a vast complement of officials to measure lands and harvests each year, or to visit each village to inspect the actual harvest. All that was needed was an effective system to force the cultivators to pay when the revenue collectors arrived in their villages, and this was achieved, if necessary, by severe methods.

Obviously, the Mughal revenue system, despite its sophistication, did not work like a perfect bureaucratic machine and Habib (1963: 214) notes its 'loopholes', especially in respect of fraudulent measurement by petty officials. The revenue rates were also generally very high and undoubtedly often oppressively so, especially in areas where revenue collection was assigned to *jagirdars*, the aristocratic 'revenue farmers', granted the right by the emperor to collect revenue in a specified region. Nor did the *zabt* system in its complete form ever entirely displace other methods of revenue assessment and collection, and it did of course collapse along with the breakdown of the Mughal administration in the late seventeenth century. Nonetheless, elements of the system survived into later years (ibid.: 223) and similar systems, depending on assessment of surveyed lands and collection in cash, were also employed by other regimes, such as the Marathas in western India (Fukuzawa 1982: 257; 1983: 181). However, the defects in the operation of the *zabt* system and its disintegration are not the most vital points here. Much more important is the unmistakable evidence, first, that the majority of cultivators in most of India had been paying their land revenues in cash, not kind, long before the onset of colonial rule, and, second, that during the sixteenth and seventeenth centuries, millions of cultivators in northern India did so according to an assessment system which in practice (if not in its originating logic) had ceased to depend on shares in the actual harvest at all.

The historical evidence summarised above shows how misleading is Dumont's description of division on the threshing floor. The same applies to Neale's presentation, which takes its cue from the evocative assertion by Benett (a nineteenth-century British revenue officer) that: 'the basis of the whole society [was] the grain heap, in which each constituent rank had its definite interest' (quoted in Neale 1957: 224; cf. Commander 1983: 288, 299). It is true, as already stated, that Dumont and Neale do at least recognise the king's importance in the distribution of the harvest in the village, unlike so many anthropologists (cf. Fuller 1977: 102). At the same time, it is also true (as it is of my own earlier approach (ibid.: 100–3)) that this emphasis on the division of grain on the threshing floor totally fails to give due weight either to the importance of money in the pre-colonial revenue systems, or to the degree to which the most sophisticated of these systems had been detached from the actual harvest. Even if we look only at the matter of money itself, we can see that it was plainly an indispensable element in the politico-economic system within which pre-colonial Indian cultivators were located. It is therefore entirely mistaken to characterise the pre-modern rural Indian economy as non-monetary, as so much anthropological writing – coloured by the bucolic symbol of the grain heap – tends to do.

In order to pay the cash revenue, the cultivators evidently had to sell the requisite portion of their crop, and this they did to traders and merchants, many or most of whom belonged to specialised trading castes and communities. Grain was generally sold in small rural markets, which were in turn connected to larger urban markets. Grain, though, was not the only village product to be sold in these markets; cash crops like indigo, other foodstuffs and animals, as well as manufactured goods such as textiles and metalware, were also important. Overwhelmingly, according to Raychaudhuri, the flow was from countryside to town and, he writes, in pre-eighteenth-century India: 'The collection of revenue in cash generated a pressure to sell; the towns, providing the necessary demand, were dependent on the villages for the supply of not only primary products but most of the manufactured goods they consumed' (1982: 327). In other words, the demand for cash revenue was a major factor serving to integrate villages into a wider monetised economy.

The vast scale of pre-colonial India's long-distance trade, both national and international, and the financial sophistication of its merchants, are well-known. In this sector of the Indian economy, the existence of an active market mechanism is clear (Chaudhuri 1979: 146). But there is a problem about whether such a mechanism can also be found at the village level. Raychaudhuri, for example, assumes that in general it cannot. Writing about rural artisans, he argues that: 'There is little reason to doubt that the bulk of the rural manufacturers in [the Mughal] period, as earlier and later, were produced by the hereditary artisan castes bound to the dominant agricultural castes by traditional ties of the client–patron relationship and collectively maintained, like their fellow service caste-groups' (1982: 279), and he specifically states that the system was that now described as 'jajmani' by anthropologists.[10] At the same time, he cites evidence that, 'By the seventeenth century, if not much earlier, exchange [on a cash basis] had made significant inroads into the subsistence-oriented system of manufacture by collectively maintained artisans' (ibid.: 280), and he also notes that peasant farmers did produce for the market. Habib refers to a wide range of cash crops grown during the Mughal period, even if not so extensively as in modern times (1963: 39–57), and he strikingly remarks that: 'In fact we find cultivation responding closely, almost desperately, to market demand' (ibid.: 81). Also important here is Habib's evidence (ibid.: 75–81) that there was considerable trade between village and town, and even between villages, a fact that cannot be squared with the tendency to treat the revenue demand as the *only* significant path along which peasants could be pulled into the wider cash economy.

Some recent historical work develops this point further and challenges more powerfully the assumption that villages largely remained outside the domain of monetary exchange and the market economy. Bayly, writing about northern India in the seventeenth to nineteenth centuries, criticises the assumption that the pre-colonial state was 'little more than a machine for extracting tribute from entrenched local communities, and that surface political changes hardly affected the conduct of rural life' (1983: 37), and that the peasant farm 'made its own production decisions in isolation from the interference of outside elites, excepting demands for rent or revenue' (ibid.: 38). 'We have come to accept too rigidly the distinction between revenue management and agricultural production' (ibid.: 40), he remarks. And he also concludes, after a survey of evidence from the Baiswara region (in Oudh) and the Benares kingdom, that there was already – before the British gained control there – a pattern of commercial development which arose within the agricultural society and then linked up with growing urban demand produced by the emergence of the new [post-Mughal] kingdoms' (ibid.: 106). In other words, the actions of the state and non-rural elites could directly draw farmers and other villagers into a wider economic system which displayed the unmistakable signs of market-oriented development. Perlin also criticises the assumption that revenue payment alone linked villages into the wider economy: 'taxation is frequently cited as a major indicator of integration, forcing the peasantry into the market place, but in fact the explanation of the effects on the medieval countryside of a heavy tax-demand in cash requires much more empirical research and more elaborate analysis' (1978: 195). In a number of papers, he has begun this work and in particular (as mentioned in note 9) he reveals a striking amount of money use and monetary exchange in pre-colonial Maharashtra, at all levels of society (1983: 60–79). Perlin's work is part of a broader endeavour to show how his 'characterization of the last centuries of pre-colonial history conflicts sharply with the hallowed images of old order India' (ibid.: 79). To these images, as he rightly observes, anthropology has made a major contribution and this paper is also intended to help break them down. Here, however, I must concentrate on the specific point at issue and I cannot fully assess the work of Perlin and other historians.

It is true that the implications of the historical evidence on money use remain open to debate.[11] For example, cultivators could meet a cash revenue demand without handling money at all if money-lenders or traders, having received the grain from the cultivators, made themselves responsible for actually paying the revenue. In such a case, money itself might be hardly found inside villages or, even if it were, might be conceptualised as a kind of 'special-purpose' money connected only with revenue payment and not used in other transactions (cf. Schlesinger's comments on money in a modern Indian village (1981: 264)). Either of these situations could occur even if historical data unambiguously showed that villages were subject to a cash revenue regime. Certainly it is premature to jump to conclusions in this area. Nevertheless, it still appears reasonable to conclude that the extent to which villages in pre-colonial India were integrated into the wider economy and were penetrated by a market mechanism mediated by monetary exchange has probably tended to be underestimated. That 'customary', non-market exchange in kind dominated each village's economic system is clearly an assumption, present in many anthropological descriptions, which is incompatible with the weight of historical evidence.

Property rights in the pre-colonial period

In considering the impact of British rule on India, the question of land revenue is central. As Stokes explains, certain basic assumptions underlay the various revenue systems which the East India Company state sought to set up in the late eighteenth and early nineteenth centuries. Amongst them was the belief that any system

required the revenue demand to be fixed, and the remaining produce of the soil recognized as private property in the full legal sense. Absolute precision and security for private property were obtainable if the fiscal demand of the State were to be guaranteed against all future enhancement, and if the tax were to be levied as a definite monetary sum on the land and not as a fixed share of the produce.

Further, the demand could not be too heavy, because:

a tax which absorbed so much of the produce as to leave no more than the bare expenses of cultivation would deprive land of all saleable value. . . . Only by limiting the land tax so as to leave a private rent could saleable property rights be established (1959: 82).

At first sight, a revenue system guided by such doctrines would appear to have ushered in a revolution. The new government would not take a share of the harvest but tax the land, and would at the same time convert land into a commodity in a capitalist market system. In reality, the revolution was altogether less dramatic. Naturally, a vast gap existed between the set of assumptions outlined concisely by Stokes and the practicalities of revenue settlement as dealt with by British settlement officers and Indian cultivators on the ground. But in any case, there is now serious doubt about the meaningfulness of this innovatory ideology of property creation. For the late eighteenth and early nineteenth centuries, Washbrook flatly states that:

In spite . . . of its frequent avowals to the contrary, the Company state was not bent on creating a free market economy sustained by the rule of law. It did not, at least willingly or consciously, dismantle the ancien régime's revenue system and institutions of economic management. Indeed, it worked them more intensively than they had ever been worked before.

And he continues:

[the Company's] elaboration of a legal system which treated and protected landed property as if it existed at a remove from the state, as a private subject's right, was pure farce (1982: 665).

Washbrook's language may be more trenchant than usual, but his scepticism about any radical impact on Indian institutions (particularly relating to agrarian relations) in the early colonial period now seems to be broadly shared by other modern historians (ibid.: 661; Baker 1984: 52–76; Stokes 1978: chs. 1 and 3). An abrupt historical discontinuity, brought about when the British gained decisive dominion in India, is now seen to have been a mirage.

This assessment is reinforced if the evidence on pre-colonial revenue systems is recalled. As we have seen, the systems based on estimated yields, notably *zabt*, had in practice already departed far from a simple division of the harvest. In terms of a formal description of their workings, the *zabt* system did not actually differ all that much from the land revenue systems of the British, even if the latter were ideally designed to be taxes on the land itself.

Attention must now be given to the question of property in pre-colonial India. The local chiefs known as *zamindars* in northern India had a right to take a part of the peasant cultivators' produce, and in the eyes of the Mughal administration they came to be regarded as equivalent to local revenue collectors serving the state. Habib, in particular, shows plainly that the *zamindari* right to take a part of the produce (or to collect revenue) from the cultivators was a species of private property.

Zamindari . . . did not signify a proprietary right over land. It co-existed with other rights and claims on the product of the soil. It is important, at the same time, to note that *zamindari* in itself (not the land under *zamindari*) had all the hall-marks of an article of private property. It was inheritable and could be freely bought and sold (1963: 154; see also 1982: 246).

To establish the matter 'beyond doubt or question', he cites numerous cases of *zamindari* sales (1963: 157–8, 162–3) and also notes that the right was leasable (ibid.: 159). Disputes over *zamindari* rights could be dealt with by the courts, which regarded them as private property (ibid.: 179). Hence there seems to be no doubt, as Raychaudhuri writes, that: 'Amidst the complex welter of rights in land, one emerging tendency can be discerned quite clearly: the growth of "property" rights and of a market in these' (1982: 176).[12] Because of the size of the *zamindari* class, there was 'a large and active market in properties' and later, in the dying phase of the empire, 'the tendency to convert claims to a share of the produce into an absolute proprietary right over land appears to have been general' (ibid.: 177).

Nor was the north Indian *zamindari* the sole example of proprietary rights in pre-colonial India's agrarian system. In western and southern India, too, the hereditary superior cultivator's right known as *miras* was widely bought and sold for centuries before British rule became established (Kumar 1983: 210). To give but one illustration, an example may be quoted from Fukuzawa's work on medieval western India. There, we learn:

Village officers used to own more or less large *mirās* . . . land and be allowed by the government to have some *inām* [tax-free] . . . land as well. Moreover, they were entitled to enjoy certain rights and privileges . . . to receive some amount of produce from peasants and village artisans. Their office and accompanying *inām* land as well as privileges were called *watan* . . . which was not only heritable but saleable and transferable with acknowledgement of state authorities and village assembly (1982: 250–1).

And a number of other examples of proprietary rights are instanced by Fukuzawa at the same place in the text.

Any attempt at cataloguing the various kinds of agrarian proprietary rights existing in pre-British India is impossible here. Instead, the important fact to reiterate is the certain existence in pre-colonial India of agrarian, private property rights and an extensive market in them. It is true, as we have seen, that these proprietary rights rarely amounted to a proprietary right in the soil itself. Indeed, this continued to be so in the early period of British rule, since many so-called land sales were actually sales of revenue-collecting rights (Stokes 1978: 3). Land itself, therefore, had not generally become a 'fictitious commodity' in Polanyi's terms, and it would clearly be inaccurate to suppose that 'landed property' in the full, capitalist sense of that phrase existed on any widespread scale in pre-colonial India.

However, it would be equally wrong to deny the significance of the property right by trying to fit these data into a scheme primarily characterised by the coexistence of multiple rights or shares in a non-market, 'redistributive' system. (Polanyi's (1957) term is used without any comment on its appropriateness.) It is a vital aspect of such a redistributive system that it is held together by a set of exchanges different in kind from those found in a market economy and that it is governed by a different logic. In Dumont's terms (1970a: 157), the logic is determined by the values of interdependence expressed through complementary rights, which do not permit any claim to exclusive proprietary ownership. At one level, the *zamindari* (or similar) right did remain one component in a redistributive system, since it did not amount to an exclusive right over land itself. However, to end discussion there is to suppress a central feature. The very fact that the right was a species of alienable property shows that this redistributive system incorporated *within itself* a type of right which, being private and exclusive, stands as the antithesis of complementary interdependence.

It is true that even if this last point were conceded, it would not be decisive as it stands. It could still be argued that *zamindari* ownership was encompassed or dominated by complementary interdependence or re-distributive exchange, so that any claim to exclusive ownership qualified only marginally the collective orientation of the total system. A proprie-tary *zamindar*, for instance, could still act as a traditional lord, concerned to maximise power and prestige (for example, by acquiring a host of clients) rather than profit (for example, from rental income), and he could continue to do so – and be regarded as doing so – even if the lordship itself were a marketable commodity. More generally, the existence of proprietary rights in pre-colonial India does not by itself demonstrate any significant displacement of the logic of interdependence as defined above.

However, there is other evidence which has to be recalled here; see above, mainly citing Habib, Bayly and Perlin. That evidence shows that peasant cultivators were *not* insulated from the effects of the market, even if they recognised their *zamindars*, like other local chiefs, as lords with whom they maintained relationships not governed by the values of market exchange. Cultivators had to respond to market demand as producers and revenue payers; cultivators and other villagers had to buy and sell all manner of produce and goods in local markets, and had to deal with merchants and money-lenders; and the 'elite groups could, and did, seek to penetrate into agricultural production and management through control of the revenue system' (Bayly 1983: 40).

Proprietary *zamindari* and similar rights therefore have to be seen in the context of other evidence about the market, monetary exchange, cash revenue systems and agricultural production. When all this is taken together, it becomes impossible to treat it all as marginal, as if it had no significant bearing on the characterisation of the pre-colonial Indian economy. Of course, as already stated, it is undeniable that non-market relationships of the jajmani or baluta type were and are important in Indian villages. But the importance of these relationships has to be assessed within a context in which proprietary rights, market exchange and so on were, even in pre-colonial India, also major features of the economic system as a whole. The whole cannot be properly understood if one side of the coin is split from or accorded definitive priority over the other.

To put it another way, my submission is that the historical evidence shows that – by the standards of normal anthropological definitions – pre-colonial India simply does not fit the model of a 'traditional' or 'archaic' economy. It also shows that it is wrong to assume that the establishment of British rule was the only begetter of 'modern' economic features, as many writers (including myself in an earlier article (1977)) have tended to suggest. The anthropological model of a 'traditional' India only really shaken by British rule has been a grossly distorting lens through which to view the Indian economic evidence. One distorted image has been the concept of the jajmani system, hypothetically located in a traditional economic universe which, in reality, did not historically exist. Since the general question of 'history' and 'tradition' is, I believe, critically relevant here, even for the singular instance of the jajmani system, I now want to give it some attention.

History, timelessness and the 'traditional' economy

That the concept of the jajmani system is linked to that of the 'traditional Indian village' – jajmani being the economic system of such villages – is plain enough. Dumont's article on the 'village community' (1970b: ch. 6) is rightly regarded as a major contribution to the demolition of a myth which played such an important role in functionalist studies of villages (and their jajmani systems). In his essay, Dumont is especially concerned to show that the village was never isolated from the wider political system (1970b: 119), and, as seen above, he does correspondingly include the king in his analysis of jajmani. He also argues, in greater detail, that the importance of hierarchy in the village has been consistently overlooked, from nineteenth-century writers onwards. Dumont's essay does not, however, examine and criticise the attribute of 'traditionalism' – timelessness, stability – which is also part and parcel of the concept of the village community, and this aspect will now be investigated.

Because Marx is considered in some detail by Dumont and because his argument is of interest in itself, I shall begin with him. Marx held that pre-colonial India had no history: 'What we call its history, is but the history of the successive intruders who founded their empires on the passive basis of that unresisting and unchanging society' (1969: 132).[13]

Marx's explanation of this situation varied somewhat between his different writings (Anderson 1974: 473–83), but a famous passage from *Capital*, in which he describes the Indian village, is certainly important;

Those small and extremely ancient Indian communities . . . are based on possession in common of the land, on the blending of agriculture and handicrafts, and on an unalterable division of labour . . . The chief part of the products is destined for direct use by the community itself, and does not take the form of a commodity. Hence, production here is independent of that division of labour brought about, in Indian society as a whole, by means of the exchange of commodities. It is the surplus alone that becomes a commodity, and a portion of even that, not until it has reached the hands of the State, into whose hands from time immemorial a certain quantity of these products has found its way in the shape of rent in kind (1954: 337).

There then follows Marx's summary of the village service (baluta) system. He continues:

The whole mechanism discloses a systematic division of labour; but a division like that in manufactures is impossible, since the smith and the carpenter, &c., find an unchanging market . . . The law that regulates the division of labour in the community acts with the irresistible authority of a law of Nature . . . The simplicity of the organisation for production in these self-sufficing communities that constantly reproduce themselves in the same form . . . this simplicity supplies the key to the secret of the unchangeableness of Asiatic societies, an unchangeableness in such striking contrast with the constant dissolution and refounding of Asiatic States, and the never-ceasing changes of dynasty. The structure of the economic elements of society remains untouched by the storm-clouds of the political sky (ibid.: 338–9).

The empirical inaccuracy of much of Marx's description of the village has often been noted. But I want to draw attention to the sentence referring to the state's revenue as 'rent in kind'. Elsewhere in *Capital*, in the discussion of ground rent, Marx reiterates that rent in kind 'is quite adapted to furnishing the basis of stationary social conditions as we see, e.g., in Asia' (1959: 796), and India was clearly in his mind.

There is a curiosity here. Rent in kind corresponds directly to crop-sharing of the type described by Tod for the Rajasthani villages, as quoted above, and it would appear as if Marx believed that this was the normal pattern of revenue payments in pre-colonial India. However, Marx cites Campbell's *Modern India* (1852) in connection with his description of the village in *Capital* (1954: 338, n. 1). Campbell's discussion of villages is in the same chapter as his account of revenue systems, which correctly states that payment was normally taken in cash, not kind, and also describes the Mughal *zabt* system (1852: 96–102). Hence Marx could hardly have been ignorant of the facts, even if Campbell's book had been the only source available to him. However, if he had incorporated those facts adequately into his argument he could not, given his general theory on ground rent and the consequences of money rent, have continued consistently to argue that Indian society was static, incapable of significant internal development and devoid of history.[14]

That Marx's idea of unchanging Asia contains contradictions – as in his discussion of the state's revenue – has been adequately shown already by, for instance, Avineri (1969) and in more detail Anderson (1974: 484–95). Moreover, they both point out (and Anderson demonstrates in detail) that Marx's denial of the possibility of significant indigenous historical development in India (and Asia generally) only continued a strong European tradition. Referring to the passage on the village from *Capital* quoted above, Anderson writes: 'The mature Marx of *Capital* itself thus remained substantially faithful to the classical European image of Asia which he had inherited from a long file of predecessors' (ibid.: 481). As Anderson in particular shows, that image cannot be justly sustained and the 'Asiatic mode of production', with which the idea of unchanging Asia is intimately linked, should 'be given the decent burial it deserves' (ibid.: 548).

If we now return to Dumont, we find that not only does he not criticise Marx's ideas about Indian stability (as remarked above), he actually largely endorses them and thus aligns himself firmly with 'the classical

European image of Asia'. Arguing that 'the idea of the individual is closely linked with a certain idea of time and history' (1970b: 142) and that the 'individual' is absent in traditional India, he concludes that 'with limitations', 'India has no history, Indian civilization being un-historical by definition' (ibid.: 143). Apparently agreeing with Marx, he states that Marx's 'strict idea of History and his perception of a fundamental difference as compared with the modern West leads him to see not a development, but a stagnation. In some manner, India is kept out of history as he understands it' (ibid.: 144). If there are new arguments here – about individualism and an alleged absence of 'time-consciousness' in Indian culture – the conclusions are nevertheless old and entirely consistent with the view (also Marx's) that only British rule set real historical change in motion. 'No doubt there is in India today a distinct sphere of activity which may properly be called economic, but it was the British government which made this possible', writes Dumont (1970a: 165). And the emergence of the 'economic', Dumont argues at greater length in *From Mandeville to Marx* (1977), is accompanied by the development of individualism and the breakdown of holism, characteristic of traditional societies in general and India in particular. His interpretation of jajmani as expressive of an 'orientation towards the whole' is thus inseparable from the premise of India's stability and exclusion from history. As I hardly need to repeat, I believe that the premise is untenable. The empirical evidence (which Dumont scarcely refers to) on pre-colonial India's economy and the relative absence of any discontinuity accompanying the establishment of British rule, plainly shows that a static, 'traditional' economy did not actually exist. Market exchange was in fact an important feature and, most crucial in this context, there were significant internal developments, notably the changeover to cash revenue systems and the emergence of proprietary rights.

Of course, it is possible that these internal developments were not historically accompanied by any real shift in values or ideology. Historical evidence on this kind of question is exceptionally difficult to interpret.[15] It does not easily reveal whether, for instance, seventeenth-century proprietary *zamindars* and those subordinate to them began to conceptualise their relationship with each other, and with the soil and its produce, in a manner different from that of their ancestors a century or two before. But there is, by the same token, little reason to assume that there was no alteration, and uncertainty about it provides no support for the thesis that significant change did not occur. The ahistorical premise cannot be validated by gaps in the historiography.

I have sought to draw attention to the continuing importance of the old idea that India had no history in Dumont's interpretation of Hindu society, including the jajmani system which, for him, demonstrates the absence of 'modern economic' values in this so-called economic institution. I have also tried to show that Dumont's argument is consistent with and in places draws upon Marx's writings about India, and further that Marx's assertions about India – particularly in relation to revenue paid to the state – are empirically invalid and incompatible with his more general thesis. The amount of attention I have paid to Dumont and, partly because of him, to Marx, reflects the importance of Dumont's theories for Indian anthropology in general, and the sophistication of his analysis of jajmani in particular. It is in Dumont's analysis, more than anyone else's, that the contrast between holistic interdependence, said to characterise jajmani, and individualist exclusive rights, characteristic of capitalist market systems, is most subtly developed into a comparison of opposed value systems.

The more empirical, Anglo-American tradition of ethnography which engendered the conventional notion of the jajmani system does, however, require separate consideration. I have already noted that the strong functionalist tendency of this school, particularly during the 'village studies' phase of the 1950s and 1960s, was a factor in the predisposition to see jajmani relations as constituting a system in the full sense of that term. The antipathy to historical research which was then widespread also undoubtedly contributed to the persistence of the concept of 'traditional village India', which not only served to obscure change over time but also indirectly deflected attention from regional variation. To be quite blunt too, simple ignorance of the historical evidence also played a major part.

In addition to these (and other factors), the importance of the overall framework of economic anthropology, within which the concept of the jajmani system was developed, also needs to be recognised. Since the stress has always been on the way in which jajmani relations contrast with those found in market exchange systems, analysis of jajmani has generally followed the tenets of 'substantivist', rather than 'formalist', economic anthropology, and the basic paradigms of substantivism can reasonably be said to underlie most analyses of jajmani systems.

Starting principally from Polanyi, the central premise of substantivist theory is an axiomatic dichotomy between 'modern' and 'traditional' economies. There is of course a convergence between Polanyi's approach and Dumont's, as the latter recognises (1970a: 313, n. 75a; 1977: 6; cf. Parry 1974: 102–7). Modern economies are those which have undergone the 'great transformation', the rise of industrial, market capitalism in Western Europe and North America, in which market exchange has become the uniquely pervasive mode of economic integration. Traditional economies are those which have not undergone this transformation and although this category is often divided into 'peasant' and 'tribal', or 'archaic' and 'primitive', the fundamental divide is still between modern and traditional, however it may be labelled by different writers. The contrast in broad terms – between opposed ideal types – is certainly real enough. However, it also needs to be recognised that the dichotomy is asymmetrical; it has a thesis: 'modern' – and an antithesis: 'traditional'. The concept of the traditional economy has been generated as the negative of the modern by isolating and defining the traits which are *not* characteristic of modern economies, or rather those which are *not* susceptible to interpretation by Western economic theory. Such a procedure is exemplified by Dalton's seminal paper of 1961, as LeClair correctly points out in his critique (Dalton 1968; LeClair 1968: 189). The concept, in other words, also originates in the modern economy; as Cook (1974: 358) observes, 'orthodox economics and its unorthodox variants [such as substantivism] are common creatures of western European thought. Both traditions had their birth in the capitalist society.'

Because the category 'traditional economy' has been generated in this way, there is no *a priori* reason to believe that different traditional economies have positive common features (LeClair 1968: 189, 205). However, the comparative method seeks them out and Indian villages may, for example, be quoted alongside African villages as directly comparable instances of communities characterised by non-market exchange. From certain angles, such comparisons no doubt have some validity, but they also tend to disguise as much as, if not more than they reveal. First, although it is generally admitted that market exchange is rarely wholly absent in traditional economies, the very definition of the category tends to underplay its importance, so that the interaction between market and non-market exchange in any one economic system is lost sight of when comparative generalisations about non-market exchange are made. Secondly, the comparative method completely ignores the patent fact that there is no historical unity between, say, Indian and African local economic systems, in contrast with the genuine unity that does exist amongst modern economies, all products of an interconnected transformation into an international, industrial market system. The method therefore tends to smother examination of sequential change within particular traditional economies precisely because uncontrolled and unhistorical parallels are repeatedly being drawn.

In any case, however, assessment of indigenous historical change is largely precluded by the fundamentally ahistorical character of the grand dichotomy itself. Although originally defined by an historical event, the rise of industrial, market capitalism, the two categories – modern and traditional – have been turned into atemporal absolutes and the only movement deemed significant or 'structural' is across the one dividing line. There is no place in the scheme for genuine change *within* the traditional category, since no such change could replicate the great transformation, by definition the sole begetter of significant structural development in the economic domain. Traditional economies have therefore only really begun to change as western market systems have impinged upon them as a result of colonialism and capitalism's expansion; the possibility that structural change could actually have occurred in pre-colonial societies is effectively ruled out. In the end, therefore, economic anthropology (especially in its substantivist form) reproduces yet again the classical European view of Asiatic stasis, but extrapolated to the whole non-western, pre-colonial world.

Underpinning the conventional ethnographic concept of jajmani, there therefore lurks the assumption that the system is 'traditional', the economic institution of villages falsely assumed to have remained static for uncounted previous centuries. Consequently, but equally falsely, all evidence of cash payments, sales of rights, responsiveness to market forces, etc. tends to be explained uncritically as the result of very recent pressures now breaking down the old economic order. In addition, the jajmani concept has tended to prevent genuinely comparative analysis of different types of exchange in India, and of their different moral connotations. Revenue payments, gifts, grants, alms, wages and so on – and each of these gross categories answers to a range of indigenously differentiated forms – have all too often been swallowed up by a monolithic category of non-market, jajmani exchange, and thereby accorded a distorting uniformity which needs to be dissolved anew.[16]

My conclusion is that the concept of the jajmani system, whether we look at its development in ethnographic studies or at the more sophisticated analysis of it produced by Dumont (and those influenced by him), is predicated upon a combination of historical inaccuracy and the ahistorical premise of unchanging, 'traditional' India. Even a brief examination of Indian economic history like that provided in this chapter reveals major inaccuracies, which in turn show that the ahistorical premise is untenable. I am aware that my conclusions do not confront directly a range of very difficult theoretical questions which are implicitly raised, notably the relation between anthropological and historical research, and the problem of whether the dichotomous paradigm of 'modern' market versus 'traditional' non-market exchange must inevitably constrain analysis in this field. But I shall not pretend to resolve these problems. Instead, I offer this chapter as a critical deconstruction of the jajmani concept in the hope that it will help to clear the path to more productive analysis of forms of exchange in Indian society, including those which centre on the grain heap, as well as to better comparative understanding of money and the market.

58   C. J. Fuller

Notes

For their critical and encouraging comments on an earlier draft, I must particularly thank Maurice Bloch, Tony Good, Britt Krause, Johnny Parry, Lee
Schlesinger, Burton Stein and David Washbrook, as well as those who offered
comments when I presented a version of this chapter at seminars at the London
School of Economics, the Universities of Madras, Durham, Chicago and
Pennsylvania, and New York University. This chapter was written in conjunction
with a project, 'A pilot study of agrarian relations and caste in South Asia', for
which the International Centre for Economics and Related Disciplines at the
LSE made a grant to Parry and myself.

 1 I do not italicise 'jajmani' (except when quoting others who do), because it
   has now become an anthropologist's technical term, which corresponds only
   questionably to an indigenous concept (Good 1982: 31–3). For the same
   reasons, the term 'baluta' (see below) will also not be italicised.
 2 It has not, of course, been exclusively the *anthropological* imagination at
   work here, because anthropological research has been carried out within a
   wider intellectual framework. Administrative and political idealisation of the
   traditional village and its economic autarchy has clearly had a reciprocal
   influence on scholarly discussion of jajmani, although this complex issue
   cannot be discussed here.
 3 'The British rule in India', *New York Daily Tribune* article, 25 June 1853
   (1969: 92–3), quotes the *Fifth Report*'s description of the south Indian village
   with only minor alterations, except that after 'astrologer' Marx omits the rest
   of its list (cf. *Fifth Report . . .*, 1969 reprint, 1: 157–8). Campbell's quotation
   (1852: 84–5) from the *Report* is shorter than Marx's and therefore could not
   have been the latter's source (*contra* Avineri's footnote). Marx's letter to
   Engels of 14 June 1853 (1969: 455–6) contains parts of the *Report* and parts of
   Wilks's description of 1810, as Dumont (1970b: 124, n. 24) notes; cf. Wilks
   (1869: 73–5). The description in *Capital* (1954: 337–8) is in Marx's own words
   and is slightly closer to the *Report* than Wilks, although Wilks is cited as the
   source by Marx, who also recommends Campbell. In *Capital*, Marx does note
   (perhaps following Campbell) that 'the constitution of these communities
   varies in different parts of India', but then ignores the point. Marx does not
   refer to 'baluta' by name, although he does mention that there are 'a dozen'
   persons in the village.
 4 Dumont's position is consistent with his argument that the dominant caste,
   not the village, is a sociological reality (1970a: 160–7). Older descriptions of
   baluta saw in that system evidence of the 'village community', which Dumont
   argues against. Patron–client relationships testify to the primacy of the
   dominant caste's role; compare Pocock's statement that jajmani relationships
   'are organized around one institution, the dominant caste of a given area'
   (1962: 79). But Dumont takes a shortcut; baluta systems *are* conceptually
   premised on ties to the village unit and the question (not discussed here) is
   how this conceptual fact combines with the institution of dominance in
   baluta-type villages.

5 Reiniche pushes this argument to the limit in proposing that there is a fundamentally religious unity to all jajmani relationships. The prototypical relationship is between *yajamana* and Brahman *purohita*, whose remuneration is the *daksina*. But all work 'est conçue implicitement sur le modèle d'un rite, porte en elle les implications d'un rite' (1977: 95), and the remuneration of service castes is, like *daksina*, 'la retombée . . . de l'activité sacrificielle', while the threshing ground 'signifie aussi la salle du sacrifice' (ibid.: 96). Fundamental to the jajmani notion is the relationship between high-status Brahman, mediating dominant-caste jajman and low-status servant, a relationship between three terms which models society and has its origins and expression in sacrificial, ritual action (ibid.: 98–103). Subtle and interesting though Reiniche's argument is, it still relies on the proposition that the *yajamana–purohita* relationship is the model for all others. The data I present supports neither that proposition, nor (though I cannot discuss it fully here) the more general one that all work is 'implicitly conceived' as ritual activity.

6 The use of historical material in the following pages is specifically intended to make a point about *anthropological* writings, and does not pretend to be a contribution to historical research. Nor does it aim at comprehensiveness, or anything close to it, since that is not required for the argument I seek to make.

7 *Minutes of evidence*, 1832, Appendix no. 89, p. 363.

8 Whitcombe (1972: 42–3) gives a more detailed quantitative summary of the *zamindars*' claims in nineteenth-century Bahraich (modern Uttar Pradesh), where a division in kind still took place. Elsewhere in the region, however, *zamindars* normally collected their shares in cash equivalents. She also gives a summary of the payments made by cultivators to village artisans, servants, etc. in Bareilly (ibid.: 37–8), and her discussion rightly treats as a whole all the payments due from the cultivators.

9 Perlin's work reveals a much greater use of money, in the shape of metallic coins and also 'humble currencies' (cowries, etc.), in pre-colonial western India than has usually been assumed by historians, and he argues that money use and monetisation were much more widespread than has previously been recognised (1983: 60–79; 1984).

10 But these conclusions are not reinforced by what Raychaudhuri writes elsewhere: 'Oddly enough, the Persian records of the seventeenth and eighteenth centuries do not mention the "jajmani system" . . . but the continuity of the system till modern times, however, suggests its unbroken existence down the centuries, and there is no reason to doubt its extensive prevalence in the period under discussion' (1983: 9). In the light of what I have said above about jajmani in anthropological analysis, Raychaudhuri's lack of dubiety is clearly unjustified.

11 I owe this point to Lee Schlesinger.

12 'Property' remains between inverted commas 'because the ownership was by and large confined to particular rights over land and not yet fully articulated as an alienable and unrestricted claim over land' (Raychaudhuri 1982: 176).

13 'The future results of British rule in India', *New York Daily Tribune* article, 8 August 1853.

14 Money rent in its simplest form is a mere modification in which the monetary equivalent of the produce is handed over to the landlord. However, argues Marx, although money rent is originally only a modification of rent in kind, it has profound consequences: it 'presupposes a considerable development of commerce, of urban industry, of commodity-production in general, and thereby of money circulation' (1959: 797). Money rent is the antithesis and dissolution of earlier types of ground rent and it must lead either to peasant freeholding or capitalist tenant farming. 'With money-rent prevailing, the traditional customary legal relationship between landlord and subjects . . . is necessarily turned into a pure money relationship fixed contractually in accordance with the rules of positive law' (ibid.: 798). Inevitably, it also leads to the development of agricultural wage-labour, capitalist leasing of land (ibid.: 798–800), and the alienability and alienation of land (ibid.: 802). On Marx's own logic, therefore, pre-colonial India's advanced systems of money rent should have been accompanied by these structural transformations.

15 The general problem of interpretation is succinctly described by Dirks, who asks how the historian is 'to elicit meaning from the past . . . how to identify and select structural features for consideration and how then to evaluate differing interpretations as to their significance *in the absence of explicit and directly germane cultural statements* (1979: 172, my italics). Dirks is probably right that historians have tended to be insensitive to the Indian cultural context, but his own interpretation of the *inam* grant as 'a system of exchange and redistribution' (ibid.: 176) draws heavily on some of the anthropological approaches I am criticising here and he assumes in passing the unproblematic status of the jajmani concept (ibid.: 177). Bayly is also concerned to give due weight to indigenous concepts of 'sharing and redistribution' in eighteenth-century north India (1983: 51), but in so doing he proposes that 'whole kingdoms . . . can be seen as extended sets of *jajmani* relations' (ibid.: 50), an extrapolation of the jajmani concept that is even more unreasonable than normal anthropological usage, as Commander (1983: 301, n. 105) remarks.

16 A random, short list of recent work which does attempt to investigate seriously indigenous cultural concepts in this domain includes Dirks (1979), Galey (1982), Good (1982), Parry (chapter 3 in this volume); relevant too is the Sanskritists' debate about *daksina*, the gift/payment made to a priest (Heesterman 1959; Malamoud 1976: 167–83). Work of this kind, disparate though it is, is vital for the positive task of making sense of forms of exchange obscured by the jajmani concept.

References

Anderson, P. 1974. *Lineages of the absolutist state*, London: NLB.
Avineri, S. 1969. Introduction. In *Karl Marx on colonialism and modernization*.
Baden-Powell, B. H. 1892. *The land systems of British India*, vol. 1, Oxford: Clarendon Press.
Baker, C. J. 1984. *An Indian rural economy, 1880–1955: The Tamilnad country-side*, Delhi: Oxford University Press.
Basham, A. L. 1971. *The wonder that was India*, London: Fontana.

Bayly, C. A. 1983. *Rulers, townsmen and bazaars: North Indian society in the age of British expansion, 1770–1870*, Cambridge: Cambridge University Press.

Berreman, G. D. 1972. *Hindus of the Himalayas*, Berkeley: University of California Press.

Cambridge Economic History of India, vol. 1, c. *1200–c. 1750*, T. Raychaudhuri and I. Habib (eds.), Cambridge: Cambridge University Press.

Cambridge Economic History of India, vol. 2, c. *1757–c. 1970*, D. Kumar and M. Desai (eds.), Cambridge: Cambridge University Press.

Campbell, G. 1852. *Modern India: a sketch of the system of civil government*, London: John Murray.

Chaudhuri, K. N. 1979. 'Markets and traders in India during the seventeenth and eighteenth centuries', in *Economy and society: essays in Indian economic and social history*, K. N. Chaudhuri and C. J. Dewey (eds.), Delhi: Oxford University Press.

Commander, S. 1983. 'The *jajmani* system in North India: an examination of its logic and status across two centuries', *Modern Asian Studies*, 17: 283–311.

Cook, S. 1974. 'Structural substantivism': a critical review of Marshall Sahlins' *Stone age economics*, *Comparative Studies in Society and History*, 16: 355–79.

Dalton, G. 1968. 'Economic theory and primitive society', in *Economic Anthropology*, E. E. LeClair and H. K. Schneider (eds.), New York: Holt, Rinehart and Winston.

Dirks, N. B. 1979. 'The structure and meaning of political relations in a south Indian little kingdom', *Contributions to Indian Sociology* (n.s.), 13: 169–206.

Dumont, L. 1970a. *Homo Hierarchicus: the caste system and its implications*, London: Weidenfeld & Nicolson.

1970b. *Religion, politics and history in India*, Paris: Mouton.

1977. *From Mandeville to Marx: the genesis and triumph of economic ideology*, Chicago: University Press.

Fifth Report from the Select Committee of the House of Commons on the Affairs of the East India Company, London, 1812, reprinted: New York: Augustus M. Kelley, 1969.

Fukuzawa, H. 1972. 'Rural servants in the 18th-century Maharashtrian village – demiurgic or jajmani system?' *Hitotsubashi Journal of Economics*, 12 (2): 14–40.

1982. 'Agrarian relations and land revenue: the medieval Deccan and Maharashtra', ch. 9, pt. 2, in *Cambridge History of India*, vol. 1.

1983. 'Agrarian relations: western India', ch. 2, pt. 3, in *Cambridge Economic History of India*, vol. 2.

Fuller, C. J. 1977. 'British India or traditional India? An anthropological problem', *Ethnos*, 42: 95–121.

Gaborieau, M. 1977. 'Systèmes traditionnels des échanges de services spécialisés contre rémunération dans une localité du Népal central', *Puruṣārtha*, 3: 1–70.

Galey, J-C. 1980. 'Le créancier, le roi, la mort: essai sur les relations de dépendance dans le Tehrī-Gāṛhwal (Himalaya indien)', *Puruṣārtha*, 4: 93–163.

Ghoshal, U. N. 1929. *Contribution to the history of the Hindu revenue system*, Calcutta: University Press.

Good, A. 1982. 'The actor and the act: categories of prestation in south India', *Man* (n.s.), 17: 23–41.

Gough, K. 1981. *Rural society in southeast India*, Cambridge: Cambridge University Press.

Habib, I. 1963. *The agrarian system of Mughal India (1556–1707)*, Bombay: Asia.

    1982. 'Northern India under the Sultanate: agrarian economy; Agrarian relations and land revenue: north India; Monetary system and prices', chs. 3, pt. 2; 9, pt. 1; 12, in *Cambridge Economic History of India*, vol. 1.

Harper, E. B. 1959. 'Two systems of economic exchange in village India', *American Anthropologist*, 61: 760–78.

Heesterman, J. C. 1959. 'Reflections on the significance of the *dakṣiṇā*', *Indo-Iranian Journal*, 3: 241–58.

Kolenda, P. M. 1967. 'Toward a model of the Hindu *jajmani* system', in *Tribal and peasant economies*, G. Dalton (ed.), Garden City, NY: American Museum of Natural History.

Krause, I-B. n.d. 'A pilot study of agrarian relations and caste in South Asia', Report to ICERD, 1985.

Kumar, D. 1983. 'Agrarian relations: south India', ch. 2, pt. 4, in *Cambridge Economic History of India*, vol. 2.

LeClair, E. E. 1968. 'Economic theory and economic anthropology', in *Economic Anthropology*, E. E. LeClair and H. K. Schneider (eds.), New York: Holt, Rinehart and Winston.

Lewis, O. 1958. *Village life in northern India*, Urbana: University of Illinois Press.

Malamoud, C. 1976. 'Terminer le sacrifice', in *Le sacrifice dans l'Inde ancienne*, M. Biardeau and C. Malamoud, Paris: Presses Universitaires de France.

Mandelbaum, D. G. 1970. *Society in India*, Berkeley: University of California Press.

Marx, K. 1954. *Capital*, vol. 1, Moscow: Progress Publishers.

    1959. *Capital*, vol. 3, Moscow: Progress Publishers.

    1969. *Karl Marx on colonialism and modernization*, S. Avineri (ed.), Garden City, NY: Anchor Books.

Mayer, A. C. 1960. *Caste and kinship in central India*, London: Routledge & Kegan Paul.

Miller, D. B. 1975. *From hierarchy to stratification*, Delhi: Oxford University Press.

Minutes of evidence taken before the Select Committee on the Affairs of the East India Company, vol. 3, *Revenue*, Parliamentary Papers, London, 1832.

Neale, W. C. 1957. 'Reciprocity and redistribution in the Indian village: sequel to some notable discussions', in *Trade and markets in the early empires*, K. Polanyi, C. M. Arensberg and H. W. Pearson (eds.), Glencoe: Free Press.

Orenstein, H. 1965. *Gaon: conflict and cohesion in an Indian village*, Princeton: University Press.

Parry, J. P. 1974. 'Egalitarian values in a hierarchical society', *South Asian Review*, 7: 95–121.

1979. *Caste and kinship in Kangra*, London: Routledge & Kegan Paul.

Perlin, F. 1978. 'Of white whale and countrymen in the eighteenth-century Maratha Deccan: extended class relations, rights, and the problem of rural autonomy under the old regime', *Journal of Peasant Studies*, 5: 172–237.

1983. 'Proto-industrialization and pre-colonial south Asia', *Past and Present*, 98: 30–95.

1984. 'Growth of money economy and some questions of transition in late pre-colonial India', *Journal of Peasant Studies*, 11 (3): 96–107.

Pocock, D. F. 1962. 'Notes on *jajmāni* relationships', *Contributions to Indian Sociology*, 6: 78–95.

Polanyi, K. 1957. 'The economy as instituted process', in *Trade and markets in the early empires*, K. Polanyi, C. M. Arensberg and H. W. Pearson (eds.), Glencoe: Free Press.

Raychaudhuri, T. 1982. 'The state and the economy: the Mughal empire; Non-agricultural production: Mughal India; Inland trade', chs. 7, pt. 1; 10, pt. 1; 11, in *Cambridge Economic History of India*, vol. 1.

1983. 'The mid-eighteenth-century background', ch. 1, in *Cambridge Economic History of India*, vol. 2.

Reiniche, M-L. 1977. 'La notion de 'jajmānī': qualification abusive ou principe d'intégration?', *Puruṣārtha*, 3: 71–107.

Schlesinger, L. I. 1981. 'Agriculture and community in Maharashtra', *Research in Economic Anthropology*, 4: 233–74.

Schwartzberg, J. E. 1968. 'Caste regions of the north Indian plain', in *Structure and change in Indian society*, M. Singer and B. S. Cohn (eds.), Chicago: Aldine.

Stein, B. 1980. *Peasant state and society in medieval south India*, Delhi: Oxford University Press.

Stokes, E. 1959. *The English Utilitarians and India*, Oxford: Clarendon Press.

1978. *The peasant and the Raj*, Cambridge: Cambridge University Press.

Washbrook, D. A. 1981. 'Law, state and agrarian society in colonial India', *Modern Asian Studies*, 15: 649–721.

Whitcombe, E. 1972. *Agrarian conditions in northern India*, vol. 1, *The United Provinces under British rule, 1860–1900*, Berkeley: University of California Press.

Wilks, M. 1869. *Historical sketches of the south of India*, vol. 1. Madras: Higginbotham.

Wilson, H. H. 1855. *A glossary of judicial and revenue terms*, London: W. H. Allen & Co.

Wiser, W. H. 1969. *The Hindu jajmani system*, Lucknow: Lucknow Publishing House.

Wolf, E. R. 1966. *Peasants*, Englewood Cliffs, NJ: Prentice-Hall.

3

On the moral perils of exchange[1]

JONATHAN PARRY

Anthropologists – as indeed their informants – often stress that gift exchange and commodity exchange are premised on fundamentally opposed principles. In Gregory's neat formulation, for example, gift exchange is seen (following Mauss) as presupposing the interdependence of the parties to the exchange and the inalienability of the gift; while commodity exchange is seen (following Marx) as presupposing the reciprocal independence of the transactors and the alienability of the commodity (Gregory 1982).

This radical contrast between the principles which underlie the two types of exchange is commonly reported as being associated with an equally radical contrast in their moral evaluation. A particularly striking example is provided by Taussig's discussion (1980) of the folklore of the Christianised Black peasantry of the Cauca valley in Columbia. Some peasants who work as wage-labourers on the big sugar plantations are supposed to enter into a pact with the devil by which they increase their production and earn a better wage; but this can only be spent on consumer goods and luxuries, for such money is barren and cannot be productively invested – though some say that it can be made over to friends who can use it for productive ends. Even the cane fields cut by one who has contracted with the devil are rendered infertile. For this reason it is believed that devil contracts are made only by male wage-labourers. Peasants working their own plots would not be prepared to lay waste their land by such a deal, while the value women place on fertility and the nurture of children also relieves them of the temptation to make terms with the devil. The man who does succumb is destined for a painful and premature end.

Taussig interprets all this as saying that capitalist relations of production are regarded by his informants as the work of the devil. They are an inherent evil, productive of death and barrenness. This privileged insight is possible because their victims still have one foot in a traditional

64

economy based on household production for use and on the reciprocal exchange of gifts between households. While in the mature capitalist economy market relations appear as part of the natural and unquestionable order of things, in Cauca the new economy is represented as neither natural nor good, for it can be questioned from the standpoint of the premises underlying a different economic order.

Beliefs about the baptism of banknotes reveal similar moral doubts about the new regime. At the time of baptism an unscrupulous godparent conceals a peso note in his or her hand, and it is the banknote rather than the child which is baptised. The first effect is that the child will be condemned to eternal purgatory when he or she dies; the second is that the godparent is effortlessly enriched at the expense of others, for the banknote endlessly returns to its sponsor with increment. This, then, provides the indigenous explanation of how capital accumulates, of how money 'breeds' money. But unlike the developed form of commodity fetishism where this process is regarded as being as natural – in Marx's image – as pears growing on pear trees, it is here revealed as something which can only occur with the aid of supernatural forces, and which involves a corruption of the most sacred social relationships.

Broadly similar symbolic constructions are hinted at elsewhere in the ethnographic record: in, for example, the Bakweri witchcraft belief that those who grow rich through market exchange do so by turning their kinsmen into zombies who toil for them on a distant mountain, beneath which, perhaps not fortuitously, is a spirit market from whence new monies enter the human world. When Frenchmen needed zombie labour to construct a deep-sea harbour, money was left lying around the Bakweri villages to entice them to the waterside (Ardener 1970). Here – as in Cauca – commodity relations appear to be a domain of dark and dangerous supernatural forces and a moral peril for those who must engage in them; and in the Cauca case at any rate such perceptions are rooted in a conviction of the moral righteousness of their antithesis, the world of use-values and gift exchange. Gift exchange is safe and good; commodity exchange is threatening and bad.

Much of this chapter concerns an ethnographic context in which the moral evaluations of exchange are so different that they might at first sight appear to be a straightforward inversion of the attitudes of the Cauca peasantry. Here it is, *par excellence*, gifts which embody evil and danger, and it is the money derived from such gifts which is barren, good only for a prodigal and futile consumption and productive only of death and damnation. By contrast, commercial profits and market transactions are generally seen in a much more benevolent light. On closer examination, however, it becomes clear that this picture must be qualified, for neither gift exchange nor commodity exchange constitute morally homogeneous and undifferentiated categories. A dire moral peril attaches only to certain kinds of gifts, while a limited range of commercial exchanges become the focus of a very similar symbolic elaboration. My first objective, then, is to try to specify the kinds of exchange in which a moral peril resides, and the kinds of exchange from which it is largely absent. The second is to begin to explore some of the factors which might account for these disparate moral evaluations.

The poison of the gift

The context referred to is the sacred north Indian pilgrimage city of Benares.[2] Many hundreds of thousands of Hindu pilgrims visit Benares each year and, of these, a substantial proportion come with the aim of performing some part of the rites associated with the dead – the cremation of the corpse, the immersion of the cremated ashes in the Ganges, the pacification and transformation of the malevolent ghosts of the unincorporated dead (*preta*), or the ritual offerings to the incorporated ancestors (*pitars*). Others are there to attain some immediate boon, or to expiate some specific sin (like cow-slaughter). The vast majority, however, come simply for the generalised merit of the pilgrimage. A large number of priestly Brahmans cater to the moral and material needs of the pilgrims: specialist ritual technicians known as *karam khandis*, hereditary pilgrimage priests (*tiratha-purohits/Pandas*), temple priests (also *Pandas*), Funeral Priests (Mahabrahmans) and so on. As a class these specialists have a not altogether undeserved reputation for a grasping rapacity and an utter ruthlessness in the extortion of gifts from the pilgrims. Though there are no comparable figures for the present day, Bayly (1983: 126) reports that at the beginning of the nineteenth century there were more than 40,000 Brahmans in the city living off religious gifts, that is between 17 and 20 per cent of the total population.

Such gifts rate as *dana*, and – notwithstanding the reputation of the priesthood – the ideology of *dana* is that of the 'pure gift'. It is a voluntary and disinterested donation made without ostentation or expectation of *any* kind of *this*-worldly return, whether material or immaterial. Not even the most trivial reciprocation can be accepted without detracting from its merit. Even the desire for *other*-worldly rewards is regarded with equivocation, so that paradoxically the full quotient of merit is held to redound only to the donor who gives without thought for his spiritual harvest. The merit acquired, in spite as it were of the ideal donor's disinterest, is proportionate to his or her means – the widow's mite being in theory the equal of the jewel-encrusted treasures of the prince.

In most, though not all, contexts the appropriate recipient of *dana* is a person of superior status; paradigmatically it is a Brahman. Every rite of passage – as well as many other rituals presided over by a Brahman priest – should be accompanied by a *dana*, without which the whole perform-ance would be completely worthless. But in north India wife-taking affines – *par excellence* the husbands of one's daughter and sister – are also the regular recipients of *dana*, which is consistent with the fact that in this hypergamous milieu they too are persons of superior status. Along with her dowry a girl is transferred in marriage as *kanya dana* (the gift of a virgin), and throughout the marriage this asymmetry persists with the *dana* flowing unilaterally from wife-givers to wife-receivers. Gifts to priests and gifts to affines – these then are the preeminent examples of *dana*. I shall consider them in turn.

Despite their proverbial cupidity, or perhaps because of it, the priests talk obsessively about the moral peril which their receipt of *dana* entails. Now it is true that some kinds of *dana* are worse than others; especially virulent, for example, are the gifts given to rid oneself of evil planetary influences, or those offered in the name of the malevolent ghost (*preta*) before its transformation into a benevolent ancestor (*pitar*) at the mortuary rites conducted on the twelfth day after death. But all *dana* is dangerous and all priests are compromised by its acceptance. 'There is no such thing as good *dana*,' they say. 'It is all vile (*nikrist*); whoever takes it burns his hand.'

From this point of view it is quite irrelevant whether the gift is in cash or kind. *Dana* is often given in monetary form, though nearly every cash payment is an explicit surrogate for goods of one kind or another – a cow, a bed, or a set of clothes, for example. Generally, such a payment represents only a fraction of the purchase price of the object for which it stands: Rs 5 for 'the gift of a cow' (*gau-dana*) when a real cow would cost many times that amount. Specially affluent and fastidious pilgrims and mourners tend, however, to regard it as more seemly and appropriate to donate the specified items rather than their cash equivalent. These are either bought in the shops or supplied out of the priest's own stocks; that is, he will 'sell' his cow (or whatever) to the pilgrim and then receive it back in *dana*. Though the fact that the same cow may have been gifted to the same priest several hundred times over is commonly the occasion for caustic comment on the spirit of the times, the priests themselves welcome this arrangement; and in general *they* prefer cash to kind since the goods they receive are generally surplus to requirements, of poor quality and difficult to dispose of at a reasonable price. Indeed the homes of some of the larger *Pandas* have the musty air of delapidated ware-houses for substandard beds, cooking utensils, umbrellas and other household paraphernalia.

The essential point here, however, is that from a moral point of view there is nothing to choose between gifts in cash and kind.[3] In whichever form, the gift embodies evil and represents a peril, and the reason for this is that it is held to embody and transmit the sins of the donor to the priestly recipient, who is likened to a sewer through which the moral filth of his patrons is passed. In an ideal world, it is true, he would be able to 'digest' the *dana* and evacuate the sin by dint of an extraordinary ritual fastidiousness involving the daily repetition of *mantras* and the perform-ance of elaborate rituals of expiation, and, above all, by giving away *with increment* all that he has taken in *dana*. In the real world, however, all this is regarded as a sheer impossibility. Quite apart from the inexorable fact that they can afford to give away little of what they receive if they are to live, most priests will frankly admit that they are ignorant of the correct ritual procedures, and would have neither the time nor the resources to get through them all even if they were not. As a result they see themselves as endlessly accumulating sin. The sewer becomes a cess-pit.

The consequences of accepting *dana* that cannot be 'digested' are that the priest contracts leprosy and rots; he dies a premature and terrible death vomiting excrement, and then faces the torments of hell. His children inherit the sins, and with them an evil disposition; and his descent line dies out in two or three generations. The priest's intellect is enfeebled, his body gets blacker and blacker and his countenance loses its 'lustre' with every gift received.

'Look,' said my friend Pahalvan Pande (a corpulent ex-champion wrestler and now a prosperous wholesaler of coal),

look at my boy Bhima. See how healthy and strong he is, for he has eaten grains which are pure and bought with the money of hard work [*mehnat*]. My elder brother [a priest] was once just as good-looking and even stronger than I. But now that ill-begotten money has turned his face as black as the coal I sell, and you see how thin he is. Yet every day he is performing *rudrabhishek* and *gayatri jap* [in expiation]. 'What, [he rhetorically concluded,] 'of those who do not [do even that]?'

The only gloss that it is necessary to add is that the priestly elder brother is generally regarded as the most knowledgeable and ritually fastidious member of their community, and that from the point of view of its commercial ethics the coal trade is as notoriously grubby as its product. Yet hardly anybody I think – least of all his elder brother – would radically dissent from the contrast Pahalvan was drawing between the spiritual dangers of their two occupations.

I say 'spiritual dangers', but more accurately they are both physical and spiritual. The sin emerges as excrement vomited at death; it causes the body to rot with leprosy, seeps into the hair (which is why it is necessary to be tonsured on many ritual occasions), and on death it makes the corpse particularly incombustible. When the corpse of the Chief Minister of Bihar was brought to the main cremation *ghat* in March 1983, it burnt only with the greatest difficulty despite the size of the pyre and the liberality of the *ghee* and resin applied to it – all on account, said my friends, of the enormous burden of sin accumulated with his corrupt earnings. Sin, then, is a bio-moral phenomenon which manifests itself in quite tangible and material ways. It is something which can be transferred from one person to another. It is 'in the money' offered in *dana*. You can give it and take it. The real difficulty is in eliminating it, this giving rise to what Shulman (1985) has neatly characterised as the 'hot potato' view of Indian social dynamics. The most obvious thing to do is to pass it on.

Nor are the dangers entirely on the recipient's side. *Dana* may only be given to a Brahman of unimpeachable character, for – in theory at least (that is, priestly theory) – the donor becomes responsible for the sins committed with the money he gives even though he cannot possibly know of the recipient's evil intentions or proclivities. 'A Brahmana,' warns Manu (IV: 190), 'who neither performs austerities nor studies the Veda, yet delights in accepting gifts, sinks *with the (donor* into hell) . . . ' It is as if from a moral point of view the donor and recipient are metamorphosed by the gift into Siamese twins.

This notion that the donor shares responsibility for any misuse of his gift should give him pause for thought, for it is almost in the nature of such money that it is misused. I have, for example, heard priests say – in tones which suggest that it could hardly be otherwise – that all the money taken in *dana* by the big Benares Pilgrimage Priests is rapidly disbursed in fees to lawyers, doctors or prostitutes. But what is universally proclaimed is that the money is never of lasting benefit. Were the ideal theory actually followed it would remain forever in high velocity circulation resting nowhere long enough to represent investment capital. But even though this ideal is totally subverted, the money can never be put to productive use. 'There is no abundance in it (*barkat nehin hoti*),' they say. 'It does not bear fruit (*phalta nehin*)', 'it is never fructified (*phalibhut*)'. Nor can it be hoarded, for when it is put by it is eaten by white ants. It comes and goes, flowing through the priest's hands like some foul liquid. One day he is so poor he eats his food off stones; the next he receives a munificent *dana* and lights his hearth with new cloth. 'The money is like that' they say – speaking as though it squandered itself.

It is true that in reality a few priestly families have managed to use the offerings made by their pilgrims to establish successful commercial enterprises of a secular kind. But for every new business that succeeds, scores fail – thus 'proving' the theory that the money itself is barren.

There is, however, an important asymmetry here. While the profits from *dana* cannot be productively utilised in commerce, it would seem that commercial profit can be transmuted into *dana and thereby increased*. People often talk as though the business ventures of a magnanimous merchant who unstintingly gives to worthy Brahmans are sure to be rewarded with success on account of the merit he accrues. Though for the wrong reasons they may well be right, for studies of Indian traders in general and of Benares merchants in particular (Bayly 1983), suggest that a reputation for piety is a hard commercial asset essential for establishing a merchant's credit-worthiness. 'One story has the great merchant prince Kashmiri Mull [a Khatri from Benares] visiting his rival, the austere and orthodox Manohar Das, as the latter mucks out his cow-sheds. "Watch out for your shoes" cries Kashmiri Mull; "Watch out for your accounts", responds the other, implying a relationship between piety, frugality and mercantile success' (ibid. p. 379).

'Money', said the Emperor Vespasian apropos his tax on public latrines, 'has no smell' – even though it is 'made from urine.' Benares people, by contrast, often talk as though the money transacted in *dana is* tainted. Does it, then, retain this taint when it is exchanged for commodities, and can it – like the proceeds of Taussig's devil contract – be utilised by others for productive investment if it is passed on to them in a different transactional mode?

Some of my evidence would suggest that such money does indeed retain the odour of sin when it enters into a different transactional sphere – as it certainly keeps its character when it is passed on to others as *dana*. I have, for example, heard it said that the businesses of those who have taken an interest-free loan from a priestly friend or kinsman never prosper until the money is repaid; and that a clerk who accepts 'the money of expiation' from a priest as a sweetener for some bureaucratic favour courts misfortune and illness. But this is not to say that the shopkeeper from whom the priest buys provisions is likely to have any qualms about the transaction, or to give a second thought to the origins of his profit. Looked at from the priest's point of view, though, the provisions which he has purchased with such money are certainly contaminated. It is as if the sin which inheres in the gift is transferred to the commodity for which it is exchanged. As I interpret the evidence, then, the basic notion is that it is only in those cases where the exchange is a unilateral one without proper reciprocation that the money of *dana* transmits its taint when transacted in a different mode. But when a balance is struck, as in the case of the shop-keeper, the sin can safely be assumed to remain with the priest.

What I hope to have conveyed, then, is a sense of the moral peril which the priests experience in relation to the offerings on which their livelihood depends. Such a livelihood is continually denigrated by the priests themselves as dependent on a combination of callous extortion and obsequious sycophancy (*ji hazuri*), and – in opposition to money earned by the honest sweat of one's brow (*khare pasina ki kamai*) – as constituting an unearned income. Though in fact the amount of effort devoted to eliciting *dana* may be quite considerable, in ideological terms *dana* is a *gift* and *not* a remuneration for priestly services, which are rewarded, as we shall see, by a separate emolument known as *daksina*. However hard the actual work by which *dana* is obtained, the money of *dana* is not 'the money of hard work'. In many cases, moreover, the intended recipient of the gifts they appropriate is a god, a ghost or an ancestor (for whom the priest stands in), and there is therefore a sense in which they can be seen as living parasitically off offerings to others (see Derrett 1966) – and sometimes distinctly dubious others to boot.

It is not therefore surprising that those who can afford to, often renounce their hereditary calling and repeatedly cite the demeaning nature of *dana* as their reason for doing so.[4] Now the interesting thing about such individuals is that they appear to have few misgivings about going in for trade. It is not money or the material world that they claim to renounce – few become ascetics. It is the proceeds of *dana*.[5] On his death-bed the medieval merchant of Cologne instanced by Tawney (1972: 49–50) directs his sons to pursue a less spritually perilous occupation than trade, and one can well imagine him recommending the priesthood. In similar circumstances the Benares priest cautions his sons against the priesthood, and one can well imagine him recommending trade.

That which is taken in *dana* must – as we have seen – be given away in *dana*, thus implying the generalised exchange of sin within the priesthood. But this injurious circulation cannot remain confined within purely priestly circles, for the wife-taking affines of priestly families are the most important recipients of their donations and they are by no means always priests themselves. Even the affinal prestations of non-priestly families (irrespective of caste) are somewhat problematic for – although such gifts have not been subject to the same snow-ball effect – they too are imbued with the sins of the immediate donors. 'In "the gift of a virgin" there is also sin and expiation' my informants would say when I asked whether the axiom that all *dana* is dangerous applies even to marriage. Gifts to priests and gifts to affines are again equated in the general complaint that nowadays the groom's people tend to be quite as ruthless and importunate in their dowry demands on the bride's family as priests are in their dealings with pilgrims. This intrinsically equivocal nature of the marriage gift re-emerges, I suggest, in the ideas of the lower castes about spirit possession.

Bhuta-preta are the spirits of people who have died a 'bad death' (the results of bad *karma*), or whose mortuary rites have been inadequately performed. Either way, they are the product of sin. Such spirits cause a whole range of misfortunes; but amongst the several symptoms which are likely to be listed in any given case, one of those most persistently cited is that although the family earns well, the money – like the money of *dana* – just seems to melt invisibly away. *Bhuta-preta* are most likely to molest members of their own family and lineage; but are also said to travel between affinally related households in the same direction as women and gifts (cf. Planalp 1956: 643). That is, they go from wife-givers to wife-receivers. By contrast, ghosts never *spontaneously* go 'against the grain' by transferring themselves to wife-giving affines.[6] In a number of the cases I recorded the spirits had moved across more than one link in the chain of affinity. That is, they had originally belonged, not to the afflicted household's immediate wife-givers, but to *their* wife-givers – to the affines of affines. As women and gifts flow asymmetrically from lineage A to lineage B to lineage C, so the *bhuta-preta* follow the same path, possessing as they go not only the girl with whom they came but also any other vulnerable member of her husband's household. But why should this be so? My informants say that the *bhuta-preta* 'follow the money'. They 'remain attached to it' and therefore 'come on top of it'.

What I am suggesting, then, is that such predominantly low-caste notions about the likely behaviour of malevolent ghosts reveal an underlying fear that the gifts given in marriage entail very much the same kinds of consequences as the gifts made to the priest. Both rate as *dana*, both should be purely unilateral transactions, and both are saturated with the evil consequences of the donor's conduct, or of the conduct of those closest to him. The sin is 'in the money' donated to the priest; and the unsatisfied spirits whose sad fate is a consequence of their sins 'follow the money' donated in marriage. For both kinds of recipient the result is suffering and misfortune, though both can hope to pass the problem on down the line to their own recipients. Consistent with all this, the belief that the money donated to the priest is barren and cannot be used for productive purposes is paralleled by the idea that the money given in marriage may be accompanied by a ghost, who ensures that that money will never yield sufficiency and that the family fortunes of its recipient will never prosper. I conclude therefore that whether we have to do with prestations to priests, or prestations to affines, the oriented gift of *dana* is seen as highly problematic and as containing evil and dangerous mystical influences.

Now I must immediately concede that it might be argued that my picture of both is altogether too bleak. It is, for example, undeniable that in certain contexts a bride is also represented as Laksmi – the goddess of wealth – who brings prosperity, fertility and increase to her husband's line. By the same token, it is also true that gifts to priests are commonly represented as positively productive of merit (*punya*). That not all *dana* is seen as an expiation (*prayiscitta*) of sin and evil would also seem to be suggested by the fact that the occasional informant will distinguish between 'bad *dana*' (*kudana*) which is given 'with desire' (*sakama*) in order to atone for a sin, counteract a malign planetary influence or win a boon from a deity, and which was likened to a bribe (*ghus*); and 'good *dana*' (*sudana*) which is given to 'worthy vessel' (*supatra*) 'without desire' (*nishkama*) for any specific reciprocation. In full measure at least, merit can only be the fruit of the latter.

With regard to 'the gift of a virgin' I do not of course deny this conflicting, more comforting and better known side of the picture; but it is nevertheless clear that in many contexts the most salient feature of affinal prestations is that they are threatening and hazardous in a way which invites direct comparison with the gift to the priest. This is consistent with the fact that the bride herself is stereotypically represented as the source of division and conflict within the joint family into which she has married; while the gifts which accompany her are patently the source of incessant wrangling and bitter recrimination. As for gifts to the priesthood, we need to distinguish between the ideal theory and people's perceptions of practice. If 'good *dana*' is given without desire to a perfect donee then in the degenerate conditions of the *Kali Yuga* – our present world epoch – there is no such thing, as there are no wholly disinterested donors and (more importantly) no really worthy recipients. The latter would be the accomplished Brahman ritualist who is learned in the Veda and who gives away more in *dana* than he receives, or – failing that – the one who resolutely refuses to take *dana* at all. The reality, then, is that the only 'vessels' who are actually available to accept *dana* are by definition more or less unworthy to receive it (*kupatra*). Ergo all *dana* is more or less bad.

I must also concede that not all transactions which anthropologists would conventionally gloss as 'gifts' rate as *dana*; and that other types of gift do not constitute a comparable moral peril. Unlike *dana*, most such gifts are governed by an explicit ethic of reciprocity. If, for example, I go to somebody's house taking fruit or sweets for the children, or if I give my wrist-watch to a friend who admires it, then that is *bhent* not *dana* and is part of the regular 'give and take' that exists between us. The *bhiksha* (or *bhikh*) given in alms to an ascetic (or beggar), and the *chanda* donated towards the upkeep of a monastery, represent exceptions to this rule of reciprocity; but neither of them is said to contain the sins of the donor or place him in jeopardy if the recipient of his charity misuses his gift for sinful purposes.

This clear-cut contrast between the poisonous nature of *dana* and the essentially benign character of other gifts is blurred only by the somewhat ambiguous category of *daksina*. Sometimes *daksina* is described as a supplement to *dana*, a gift added to the *dana* to make up for any deficiencies in it. So, for example, if I donate a cow to a Brahman, then I must add a small sum of money to my gift to top it off. This *daksina* 'consecrates' (*pratishta karna*) the *dana*, which without it 'bears no fruit'. At other times, however, informants use the term to refer to a fee paid to a Brahman priest for his ritual services. When, for example, a well-to-do patron employs a specialist *karam khandi* to perform a particular ritual which his hereditary household or pilgrimage priest is incompetent to conduct, the *karam khandi* receives *daksina* as a fee for performing the ritual; but the *dana* (which is significantly greater in value) is given to the hereditary priest who sat idly by throughout the ritual. What complicates the matter, however, is that in such a case the *dana* which goes to the latter is also accompanied by a (nominal) *daksina*; and it would clearly be possible to interpret this either as a gift which supplements the *dana*, or as a 'fee' for the ritual labour involved in accepting it. This essentially ambiguous nature of *daksina* – as 'gift' or 'fee' – is reflected in my informants' equivocation over whether or not it embodies the dangers of *dana*. Many stories suggest that it does, though equally often this is denied.

Leaving the difficult case of *daksina* aside, it is clear that it is in *dana* – and not in other kinds of gift – that a dire moral peril resides. Why, then, should this be so?

One view of the problem here would be to see it in terms of the ambiguous position of the priest in relation to a Brahmanical ideal moulded by the values of asceticism. The ideal Brahman should as nearly as possible approximate his life-style and behaviour to that of the world-renouncer, but the problem with *dana* is that the priest's acceptance of it irretrievably compromises this ideal of ascetic autonomy and inextricably enmeshes him in the material and social order. It is the Brahman's ascetic transcendence of the world which qualifies him as a 'worthy vessel' for the gifts of the pious; but the paradox is that his receipt of such gifts inevitably endangers this very transcendence. Following Heesterman (1971), I have argued elsewhere that this is a crucial aspect of the difficulty (Parry 1980). But if for no other reason than that its focus on the perspective of the priesthood fails to shed much light on the similarly problematic nature of the *dana* offered to affines, it seems clear that it is far from being the whole story.

Another way of approaching the problem might be to focus on the fact that *dana* embodies something of the bio-moral substance of the donor – something nasty at that – in a way and to an extent that other forms of gift do not. This is consistent with its ideological roots in sacrifice. *Dana* is explicitly said to be a surrogate for sacrifice appropriate to our degenerate epoch (cf. Manu I: 86; Biardeau 1976: 27). Just as the victim stands for the person of the sacrificer, so the gift stands for the donor. An extreme case of this identification is *tula dana*, where the donor is weighted against some valuable commodity which is thus equated with his 'gross body' (and is consequently said to contain his blood, marrow, and excrement), and which is then gifted in *dana*. But whether the gift contains the blood and excrement of the donor, or merely his 'sins', it is clear that its acceptance entails incorporating into the self the inferior essences of others. In an hierarchical world, such a transfer is bound to be problematic and even subversive of the hierarchy itself. If people of different strata are beings of different species, the gift becomes a kind of miscegenation. It is hardly surprising, then, that it assumes the form of a moral peril.

This notion that the gift transmits, and is therefore capable of removing, sin, not only tends to subvert its own ethic of disinterested generosity, but also presupposes that ritual – and indeed financial – reparation can be made for moral transgressions. Such attempts to dispose of ethical burdens by ritualistic means are a central preoccupation of Hindu religiosity; though the idea that this can be done does not go unchallenged in the tradition at large. Certainly the ethic of intention completely repudiates any notion that atonement for sin can be simply purchased. It might, then, be possible to interpret these beliefs about the mystical dangers of *dana* as part of the inevitable backlash against offering ritual solutions to moral problems, and as expressing a deep unease that this is an ultimately futile and fraudulent endeavour. When the gift is transformed into a purchase price for salvation – as it inevitably is – this endeavour becomes all the more problematic. Danger lies in the moral deception in which both of the parties to the exchange collude, and it is this which explains what is in a comparative perspective the most striking feature of the ideology: that here the gift is liable to demean the donor as well as the recipient.

It might further be argued that what gives this problem a special poignancy in the Benares context is that the sanctity of the city largely derives from the belief that all who die – or, according to some, all who are cremated – within its precincts automatically attain salvation or liberation from the cycle of rebirths (*moksa* or *mukti*). Now clearly the priesthood has a considerable interest in upholding this dogma on which the religious preeminence of the city – and hence their own livelihood – is founded. But equally clearly this same notion places the significance of their sacerdotal function in question, for the rituals at which the Brahman officiates become an irrelevance to the salvation prospects of many of their patrons. For those who have had the good fortune to die or be cremated in Benares, the conduct of the mortuary rituals and ancestral offerings is a mere formality quite irrelevant to the fate of their souls; for all who confidently anticipate such a death, the whole gamut of priestly rituals are arguably deprived of this ultimate significance (cf. Parry 1981). Moreover, the ideology of *bhakti* – which has exercised a profound influence on modern Hinduism and according to which devotion to a personal god is sufficient for salvation – reduces the Brahman to a similar irrelevance.[7] Thus, in the all-important matter of one's ultimate destiny, the mediating function of the priest is subverted from two different directions at once, and by ideas to which the priests themselves will more or less readily assent. It is not altogether surprising, then, that they should have a somewhat uneasy conscience about their earnings from an occupation which a part of their own belief system declares redundant.

What is, I believe, *the* most problematic aspect of *dana* concerns, however, the fact that it is an unreciprocated gift. Certainly the priests themselves commonly attribute their degradation and relative inferiority to other Brahmans to their (exaggerated) view of themselves as purely unilateral receivers of gifts. Amongst the six conventionally enumerated duties of the Brahman is to receive *and give dana*. Direct reciprocity (even as we have seen in the form of the *quid pro quo* of priestly services) is, of course, entirely contrary to the whole spirit of *dana*. But so too is the notion that the immediate recipient is the final terminus of the gift – which must at all costs be passed on to another worthy recipient. The root of the problem, however, is that in the real world the professional priest is constrained to retain most of what he receives – and the greater the disproportion between receipts and disbursements the greater the burden of accumulated sin. It is the money and goods which are siphoned out of the flow of exchange by being retained which are really barren, and which infect the family fortunes with their evil sterility. 'When you give seventeen annas having taken sixteen, then that is auspicious (*shubha*). From this no shortage will result. But if you do not give (in this way), then there will always be a continual decline (*hamesha ghatta rahega*).'

Now it is true that it might be argued that the gift is in fact reciprocated by the liberation from sin which the donor receives *in direct exchange* for his material prestations. But on the one hand the ideology denies that the gift made out of such interested motives is a 'true' gift at all; while on the other it is widely held that the Brahmans of today – or at least those who are prepared to soil their hands with *dana* – are so fallen and unworthy that, far from releasing the donor from sin, he is more probably dragged down into hell by the bonds which the gift creates between them. In short, the profligate priesthood cannot deliver on its side of the bargain and the gift *is* therefore unreciprocated.

It is also true that the *bhiksha* offered in alms to an ascetic is an unreciprocated gift, but in no way entails the kind of moral difficulties associated with *dana*. The crucial point here, I suggest, is that such prestations are given to the *renouncer*, with whom no relationship is possible since he is outside the social world. What is threatening about *dana* is that it is donated to people who have at least one foot within a social order founded on reciprocity, but from whom no return is received. The man-in-the-world belongs within a conceptual order in which all are both givers and receivers, all castes perform their allotted function on behalf of the collectivity and nobody gets anything for nothing. The mystical dangers of *dana* express the uncomfortable recognition that there are some who do.

But, of course, the whole theory insists that *dana* must be given *without* expectation of any immediate return, or any form of *quid pro quo* from the recipient. Insofar as a reciprocation is entailed this is effected through the impersonal mechanism of *karma* and consists of 'unseen fruits' (*adrstaphala*) to be plucked in another existence. The theory, as Trautmann (1981: 279) puts it, is a 'soteriology, not a sociology of reciprocity . . . ' Yet the social world in which men actually live is inescapably founded on what Gouldner (1960) called the 'moral norm of reciprocity'. There is therefore an inherent tension – even a contradiction – between a soteriology which denies reciprocity and a social order which is premised on it. This tension, I suggest, finds eloquent expression in the moral ambiguity of the gift itself – the soteriological orientation of which repudiates the moral basis of society.

The innocence of commerce

I turn now to the other side of my original dichotomy, to the realm of market exchange.[8] Here we may start by noting that the traders of Benares are celebrated for their eagle-eye for quick profits and their dubious commercial practices. They are widely supposed to use the most sophisticated techniques of adulteration; are credited with a magician's ability to pass off substandard goods and a wily canniness in manipulating the bureaucracy for licences and permits; and are commonly charged with creating artificial shortages to drive up prices. As much, and no doubt more, would be said of the businessmen of any Indian city. Yet the remarkable thing is that although everybody would agree that such practices are morally reprehensible, their condemnation generally seems to lack a real sense of outrage.

This is not, of course, to imply that the merchant is always liked or trusted. 'If you meet a snake and a Marwari (trader)', says the proverb, 'kill the Marwari.' But the rapacity of the merchant is somehow part of his *jati-dharma*, of the code of conduct which is an aspect of his nature, and one might as well get morally indignant over the propensity of scorpions to sting. Certainly nothing I have ever heard would suggest that trade is regarded as *intrinsically* bad, or that traders see themselves as confronted by the kind of moral peril which is so strongly internalised by the priests. Nor is a sense of such peril conveyed by the literature on Indian traders; and I can think of no ethnographic or historical evidence for a conception of trade remotely comparable to that of the philosopher–theologians of medieval Europe whose attitude to commerce was – as Tawney (1972: 47) put it – 'that of one who holds a wolf by the ears'.

Again, in Hinduism it is by no means easy to find parallels for such Biblical notions as the love of money being 'the root of all evil', or as camels having an easier time getting through needles' eyes than rich men getting to heaven. Incarnations of the gods do not roam about chasing money-lenders out of the temples, and not even 'the most vile of merchants' sells the Son of God for thirty pieces of silver. In a positively encyclopedic work on the origins of evil in Hindu mythology, O'Flaherty (1976) shows how Hindu thought has elaborated almost every conceivable explanation for suffering and evil. Yet by comparison with our own cultural heritage the striking thing is that the book contains hardly a mention of money and avarice. Indeed the whole thrust of the most characteristically Indian solution to the problem of theodicy – the doctrine of *karma* – is that the rich deserve and have earned their good fortune.

Nor do I find much to suggest that money is regarded as an inherently dangerous and polluting medium. It is not, as in the margins of gothic manuscripts, represented as filthy and disgusting waste defecated by demons and apes (Little 1978: 34). Far from being an outsider to society, as was the Jew in medieval Christendom, the financier tends rather to be a paragon of religious orthopraxy. Priestly rights are bought and sold with complete equanimity, and there is no Hindu equivalent of the deep unease of the Christian Church over simony. Unlike the medieval friar or the Buddhist monk, the Hindu ascetic has few qualms about handling money, and both temples and monasteries have often been engaged in large-scale trade and money-lending (Cohn 1964; Spencer 1968; Mines 1985: 26, 42). What Hindu St Francis would ever require a disciple who accepted a coin in offering to take it between his teeth and deposit it in a dung-heap? It is, of course, true that for the renouncer *any* infatuation with the world is reprehensible, but money is not singled out for special obloquy, or made to act as a condensed symbol for all such attachments.

Nor, despite often extremely high rates of interest, has money-lending ever been condemned by Hindu thought with any of the vehemence of Aristotle or St Bernard. Manu (X: 115–16) lists lending at interest among the seven acquisitions of wealth consistent with *dharma*; and as among the ten means by which a distressed Brahman may legitimately maintain himself. If it, of course, possible to find texts which deprecate its practice (Kane 1973: 3: 417–18), but what is for the most part discountenanced is merely an excessive rate of interest (ibid. p. 419–21). Certainly nothing suggests the severity with which medieval thought judged usury (as equivalent to sodomy in its opposition to natural increase), or the usurer who was to be refused communion, absolution or burial in consecrated ground (Tawney 1972: 48; Little 1978: 211). On the contrary, he is often seen as a public benefactor (Dubois 1906: 656; Darling 1925: 201–2; Parry 1979: 323); money-lending on a small scale is widely practised by well-to-do members of all respectable castes, and I know priestly families who regularly lend at interest without hinting at any of the moral doubts they so commonly voice over *dana*. In the past even the Maharajas of Benares acted as money-lenders (Bayly 1983: 373–4). In terms of the ethical evaluation of finance and trade, then, it might seem that 'the spirit of capitalism' had fewer obstacles to surmount in India than it did in Europe, where even Calvin dealt with usury 'as an apothecarie doth with poyson' (Tawney 1972: 144).

This is not, of course, to imply that all commercial transactions are equally unproblematic. Such fragmentary information as came my way on the topic of bribery, for example, would suggest that although those who demand bribes commonly represent them as a legitimate perquisite of office (employing such euphemisms as *daksina* or *haq*, meaning 'right'), the *excessively* rapacious official is seen as liable to much the same fate as the priest who lives off *dana*. It was on account of his corrupt earnings that the Chief Minister's corpse refused to burn – and I could cite a number of other examples which convey the same message.

The most striking exception to the moral neutrality of commercial profits, however, concerns the profits derived from death. The wood merchant's proceeds from the wood he sells on the cremation ground, the takings of the shopkeeper who specialises in shrouds and other mortuary paraphernalia, the fees of the burning-ground barber and of the exorcist who deals with the spirits of the malevolent dead, all carry much the same taint as *dana* and entail similar consequences. 'The money of cremation ground', people say, 'will never allow anybody to prosper.'

Because of such money one wood-seller's family was decimated within a generation, while their wife-taking affines fell to murdering each other over the dowry provided out of the profits of the sale of wood for the pyres. A young man I knew well, whose family owns one of the shops which specialises in the goods used for cremation, has a similar story to tell. Most of the time he himself works as one of the city's numerous commission agents (*dalals*) or 'guides', showing foreign tourists around the city and taking a cut on any purchases they can be persuaded to make. These sometimes include narcotics, and one day I met Bhola in jubilant mood after he made Rs 17,000 (about £1,000) on a sale of morphine. Despite the fact that he had many times told me of the terrible misfortunes his family have suffered as a result of selling the goods required for cremation, he displayed not the slightest concern about transactions such as these. Public opinion in the area, it is true, was concerned about this particular deal. The reason, however, was not because of the commodity it involved, but because the bargain had been struck with a customer who had first been contacted by another guide. The latter had therefore established a right over the commission on any purchases made by 'his foreigner'. Bhola was forced to hand over half his takings in order to avoid a violent confrontation in which the moral majority would have sided wholly with his adversary. It is clearly not profit, but the profit of death which is problematic.

At this juncture it is necessary to back-track a moment to my earlier discussion of the gift. Given that all transactions associated with death are perilous, it might on the face of it appear that my problem was misconceived, and that it is not *dana* but death which constitutes the real difficulty. Now clearly the obvious answer to this is that it is *all dana* – and not just that which is given during the mortuary rites – which is evil. The point is one to which Fuller (1984: 67f) has accorded due recognition, but – as he notes – the fact remains that in the major north Indian pilgrimage cities like Benares it is death which dominates the religious field (in a way that it does not in the temple towns of the South). It might therefore be argued that in the specific context I describe the prototypical *dana* is the *dana* of death, which – by a kind of halo effect – contaminates all other gifts and renders them problematic. The difficulty with this, however, is that Fuller himself cites a number of sources which clearly show that even in the South similar ideas about gifts (other than those made in connection with death) are by no means absent; while – as Raheja (1985) clearly demonstrates – they certainly exist in a highly elaborated form in certain *rural* areas of the north where death cannot be said to have the ideological preeminence it is given in sacred centres like Benares or Gaya.

My bold contrast between the moral perils inherent in *dana* and the moral neutrality of commercial transactions demands one further qualification. The acquisition of commercial wealth is a legitimate and laudable objective, but it is one which is ultimately justified by the generosity with which it is then disbursed. 'Let [the merchant] exert himself to the utmost in order to increase his prosperity in a righteous manner,' recommends Manu (IX: 333), 'and let him zealously give food to all created beings.' Here it is clearly the zealous giving which justifies these utmost exertions, notwithstanding Manu, even to the extent of condoning a manner of appropriation which is not unequivocally righteous. Many myths and legends tell of the hero who resorts to highway robbery in order to defray the costs of renovating a temple, or supporting the Brahmans (e..g. Dirks 1982). The traditional Indian king is recognised as having much in common with the bandit (Shulman 1980); and it is by violence, conquest and plunder that he is supposed to fund the sacrifice, or the gifts which replace it (Heesterman 1959). The merchant's plunder in the market place is clearly a less glorious and heroic mode of acquisition, but it is nonetheless one which need not trouble a sensitive conscience so long as the proceeds are dispensed as *dana*.

If not as *dana*, then at least in generous hospitality and unstinting support for indigent dependants. The model affectionately recalled in Benares is the *rais*, the monied aristocrat of the city's past, of whose eccentrically profligate expenditure a limited repertoire of admiring anecdotes is endlessly repeated. The miserly and tight-fisted are contemptuously dismissed with the maxim *sala, sanph banega* – 'that wife's brother' (i.e. that low-grade bastard) 'he'll become a snake' – a maxim which calls on the notion that one who dies with buried treasure will be reborn as a snake which is condemned to keep constant guard over its hoard. The more general point here is illustrated by an exchange in E. M. Forster's novel *A Passage to India* where Dr Aziz says,'If money goes, money comes. If money stays, death comes. Did you ever hear that useful Urdu proverb?' to which Fielding responds that his proverbs include, 'A penny saved is a penny earned', and on such the British empire rests. So while at one level there is marked contrast between the dangers inherent in commercial profit and the dangers inherent in *dana*, at another level both kinds of acquisition are united in their subordination to the same cultural imperative: that the objects of exchange must be kept in continual circulation. Not only, I would add, does this apply to gifts and commodities, for as I have argued elsewhere (Parry 1985a), a central preoccupation of much Hindu ritual discourse is the proper circulation and transformation of both food and the souls of the dead, and it is this process of circulation which maintains the cosmic and social orders.[9]

Nor, of course, is my contrast intended to imply that attitudes to money and commercial profit are entirely profane and matter-of-fact. To the contrary, here too it is surrounded by 'magic and necromancy'. Precious metals are sometimes said to multiply if they are offered in front of an image of Laksmi, and the beneficence of the goddess is invoked at the festival of Divali when the merchant worships his account books. Money 'breeds' money, though in the domain of ritual discourse it does so through the mediation of the divine power of the goddess, and not by virtue of its intrinsic fecundity. Again, there are certain benign ghosts who sometimes enter into a secret pact with a living person, whom they reward with handsome munificence for some trivial daily service. But this is no more like Taussig's devil contract than the worship of Laksmi is like the baptism of the banknote. Though, as in Cauca, what these examples suggest is that wealth is acquired with the aid of supernatural forces, these forces are not the work of the devil and are not productive of death and damnation. The world of money and the world of commodities is not intrinsically evil.

Some moral evaluations of the market

The comparison with medieval Europe which I have invoked invites the question of how we might account for this kind of variation in moral evaluation. A satisfactory solution to this problem would clearly need to take account of a whole range of factors, not least amongst them considerations of a material order. Here I can only begin to touch on certain aspects of the wider *ideological* context which seem to me to shed some light on the contrast.

One of the most persistent criticisms levelled against the medieval merchant was that he sold something which he could not possess, for his 'profit implied a mortgage on time, which was supposed to belong to God alone' (Le Goff 1980: 29). Labour, which the theologians of an earlier age had represented as a punishment for the Fall, had by the twelfth or thirteenth centuries acquired a new dignity as an activity which glorified and enjoyed the blessing of God; a re-valuation marked by the appearance in iconography of such themes as Noah's construction of the ark, or the building of the Tower of Babel (Gurevich 1985: 264–5). Since man was made in the image of God, his work should emulate God's work'– *creation*. The problem with the merchant, however, was that he created nothing, and his profit was therefore fraudulent, as was that of the usurer who accumulated money even as he slept. 'Medieval ideology,' as Le Goff (1980: 61) observes, 'was materialistic in the strict sense. Only the production of matter had value. The abstract value defined by capitalist economy eluded its grasp, disgusted it, and was condemned by it.'

In the Hindu context such ideas seem wholly alien. The gods are bound by time like men, and certainly do not own it. Physical labour is not on the whole highly esteemed; far less is it represented as an emulation of cosmogony. Vishnu's creation of the universe is not some kind of prodigious feat of engineering: it is the product of prolonged austerities and sacrifice. Nor, above all, is work preeminently a question of the production and transformation of matter. For the most part Hindu thought has rejected the kind of thoroughgoing materialism to which Le Goff refers, and which provided the medieval world with such a powerful ideological basis for its condemnation of commerce.

An even more important aspect of the matter concerns, I suggest, the way in which the moral and the politico-economic orders are held to be related to each other. As is well known, Dumont (1970) argues that Hindu thought posits a radical separation between the realm of *dharma* over which the Brahman presides and the realm of *artha* under the jurisdiction of the king. While unequivocally preeminent in terms of ritual status, the Brahman is unashamedly dependent in politico-economic terms. The distinction is therefore far stricter than that which medieval Christianity drew between the spiritual and temporal domains, for 'in the Indian case, there is no attempt to reintroduce a univocal or unilinear rank order as in medieval Roman Catholicism where the Church and the Pope claimed supremacy in temporal matters' (Dumont 1971: 69).

The term *artha* refers not only to the realm of politico-economic power which is the third of the four conventionally enumerated goals of human existence, but more generally also has the sense of 'means'. Thus *artha*, as material and coercive power, is the 'means' by which man may attain the sensual delights of *kama* and sustain the moral order of *dharma*. What Hindu thought rejects is that these means should become an ultimate end. *Artha* must be pursued in conformity with the hier-archically superior dictates of *dharma* (Malamoud 1981; Shah 1981). The explicit implication of Dumont's discussion, however, is that the strict disjunction between the two realms – and the thoroughgoing ideological subordination of the politico-economic domain – cuts it loose from its moral moorings and deprives it of real meaning. 'In traditional India, significance is attached exclusively to the immutable model of society and the truth, the model of *dharma*; as a result everything else, devoid of sense, can change at will' (Dumont 1970: 196). Denied 'the slightest value or intellectual interest', almost anything goes; and to a significant extent it is this devaluation which has condemned the Indian polity to perpetual instability. By only a slight extension of the same argument, we can see that commerce suffers a similar semantic impoverishment, and the condemnation of its abuses is consequently robbed of real force. Emptied of moral content it cannot be a major source of moral peril.

What is also possibly relevant here is the radically different nature of the rural–urban division in the two contexts. In Europe the city early on became the main centre of manufacture and locus of exchange, and the hostility to money and commerce was closely associated with an hostility to urbanism in general (Duby 1982: 220; Little 1978: 35). The expansion of the urban centres, and of the commercial economy they harboured, prompted a strident backlash against both in which townspeople were identified with money-lenders as the spawn of the devil (Gurevich 1985: 272). In pre-colonial India, by contrast, manufacture remained – as Raychaudhuri notes (1983: 22) – a predominantly rural activity, and the same kind of division 'of economic functions between town and country . . . did not emerge'. Market exchange, and money as the means of exchange, were not consequently damned by their association with an alien urban environment.

In Western Europe, the urban and commercial expansion of the later Middle Ages entailed, of course, a progressive subversion of what has been called the 'closed estate economy' (Pirenne 1967), and of the autarky of the village community where production was primarily for use and for exchange within the local community, where those who visited the market for the purchase of essential items were not really integrated into it (Braudel 1985: 55), and where the distribution of prestige goods between distant communities was as likely to be effected by gift and plunder as by trade (Grierson 1971; Geary 1986). Calling on the authority of Aristotle, whose writings penetrated Christendom in 1240 and were given currency by Thomas Aquinas (Braudel 1985: 560), medieval theorists criticised money and the trade from the standpoint of this disappearing world of self-sufficiency and production for use.

For Aristotle, the distinction between householding (*oikonomia*) and commerce (*kapelike*) is a distinction between natural and unnatural economic activity. Trading for gain is 'contrary to nature'; trade can only be 'natural' in so far as it is a requirement of self-provisioning, and in this 'natural economy' money produces no offspring. Prices should therefore be set so as to exclude profit; the ruling principle of exchange should be one of equality and mutual benefit, and of all the ways of getting wealth lending at interest is the most perverted (Aristotle 1962; Polanyi 1971). The Greek god Hermes – a trickster and thief whose career begins as the god of boundary stones – evolves logically in the deity of those professional boundary-crossers and swindlers, the merchants, recalling that in the Middle Ages the merchant was supposed to carry a thief's thumb as a talisman and that the two professions shared St Nicholas as their patron saint (Curtin 1984: 6). In both cases commerce and larceny are seen as having a natural affinity, and in both cases this judgement derives from a firm ideological commitment to an order premised on the values of autarky and production for the use of the producers. Similarly, Marx's mistrust of money and (market) exchange was nourished by a certain nostalgia for the world of use-value and self-provisioning. Exchange and the abstract money medium from which it is inseparable were condemned by Marx as agents of individualisation and of the dissolution of the communal bonds which had obtained when production was for use (see the Introduction to this volume).

It is also out of this same ideological commitment to a traditional householding economy oriented towards self-sufficiency that many peasant communities have condemned production for exchange. This was the situation which Taussig described, and Gudeman's account of the erstwhile economy of a Panamanian village suggests something strikingly similar. The household was the primary unit of production and consumption, some goods and labour being traded within the community, though this was seen in terms of the exchange of equivalents and was unproblematic. Profit in rural/urban exchanges, however, was considered mysterious and morally equivocal; and commodities purchased for cash on the market were classified as 'luxuries' and 'vices', seen as a dangerous drain on subsistence needs, vaguely imbued with evil and sometimes said to be obtained only by submitting to the influence of the devil (Gudeman 1986: 12–13).

The argument which I would like to propose here is that by contrast with the self-image of autarky and of production for the use of the producer which we encounter in all these cases, the caste order is founded on the fundamentally different premise of a division of labour between castes and their interdependence. Production is not for direct use; and neither the household, nor the caste, nor even the local community is an ideally self-sufficient entity. Despite the best endeavours of nineteenth-century British administrators to discover it, the village as a 'little republic' sufficient unto itself does not, and did not, exist – neither in practice nor in ideology. Nor can such a unit be specified at any level. My contention, then, is that the absence of any outright antipathy to money and commerce has to be understood in the context of the absence of an ideology of autarky from which this antipathy has so often drawn its force.

The point might be generalised by reference to Melanesian ethnography, where we often encounter in extreme form this quite different kind of ideological world in which society sees itself as constituted by exchange.[10] Here, one might suppose, the moral evaluation of modern money and market exchange is likely to be very different from that characteristic of the autarkic worlds to which I have just referred, and the evidence seems to suggest that this is indeed the case.

The fear which preoccupied the Kaliai of West New Britain in 1971 was that the independence of Papua New Guinea would bring the rule of money before they were ready for it, though in principle they looked forward eagerly to the new dispensation (Counts and Counts 1977). At that time the expectation was that existing social relations would be replaced by monetary ones. This expectation was largely self-fulfilling, and the ethnographers describe how over a period of only ten years even food and labour became commodities for which a monetary payment was *legitimately* demanded from close kin and affines – even from a spouse. For the Highlands of New Guinea, Strathern (1978, 1979b) similarly documents the enthusiasm with which Hageners took to commercial agriculture and incorporated money – the super-valuable of the White Man and the source of his enviable power – into their ceremonial exchange system.

In exchange systems of this sort, of course, the gift is expected to return to its donor with increment. Far from being naturally barren, exchange almost automatically attracts a 'profit' or 'increment'.[11] By contrast with the set of ideas which could condemn the medieval merchant for creating nothing, no similar charge of parasitism could possibly be levelled here at those who control the realm of exchange – for transactors *are* producers when exchange *is* production, an apparently inexhaustible source of increase. In such a world the propensity of money to breed more money must indeed appear as natural as pears growing on pear trees. Anything traditional valuables can do, the modern super-valuable can surely do better.

It might, I recognise, be objected that by emphasising the continuity between incremental exchange systems of the *moka* variety and Marx's general formula of capital accumulation, I am ignoring a fundamental contrast which emerges from Gregory's (1982) synthetic view of Melanesian exchange systems: the contrast between gift exchange systems of this kind in which the objective is to maximise net outgoings (to out-give), and commodity exchange in which the objective is to maximize net receipts or profits (to out-take). This contrast, however, is surely greatly over-drawn for if – as Gell (n.d.) points out – it were literally true the Big Man would tend to seek out 'rubbish men' as exchange partners, and ply them with gifts in the confident expectation that they would never be repaid. Of this there is, of course, no evidence and gifts are generally given to those from whom there is every expectation of an incremental return. As a consequence experience shows that with sound financial management capital grows. Moreover, in many traditional Melanesian societies commodity exchange in the form of barter relations with trade partners on the periphery of one's social universe does not seem to possess a radically different character from many gift exchange relationships firmly within that universe. In both cases (and again I am indebted to Gell) an enduring bond is established, and in both the objects exchanged seem to be definitively alienated. Gregory's neat opposition between inalienable gifts exchanged between mutually dependent transactors, and alienable commodities exchanged between reciprocally independent transactors, does scant justice to these very real continuities.

But if money breeding money appears as natural, and I suggest as innocent, as the pears on the tree, it is clearly not as easily intelligible or manageable. Hence the many cargo cults which focus centrally on this problem (cf. Burridge 1969). Take the Red Box money cult, for example, which was concerned with ensuring a self-generating supply of money for the future and 'clearly expressed [not only] a desire for inordinate amounts of cash, to make Hageners equal if not superior to Europeans, [but] also a wish to know money's true origins and so to manage its supply for themselves' (Strathern 1979a). No moral qualms here about the self-expanding nature of money as capital; only the problem of how to accomplish it. And significantly the postulated solution almost invariably involves the agency of essentially helpful supernatural beings like God or the ancestors, while the cult's failure to propagate money magically is likely to be attributed to the moral failures of its followers (Morauta 1974: 43–5).

Stent's (1977) discussion of a cargo cult concerned with the miraculous manufacture of money in Maprik sub-district in the early 1970s brings all this out with admirable clarity, and with this we return to the baptism of the banknote with which I began. The aim of the cult was to multiply silver coins, by a magical process sometimes described as 'baptism', in a so-called *faktori* constructed for this purpose. An alternative rite took place in a graveyard, where God would be called on to bless a banknote inserted between the leaves of a Bible, and where quantities of money would subsequently be found lying around on the ground. Throughout these magical rites 'traditional practices associated with (the increase of) yams were taken over and modified. The old spells, which called upon the spirits, were replaced by prayers to a new God, and the magical stones and relics . . . were replaced by the Bible.' Clearly no devil contract here, the magical increase occurs with the blessing of God, through the power of Christ and in full view of the ancestors in the graveyard. What's more, the sums so far alleged to have been produced were regarded as *samting nating*, mere petty cash. Real abundance would flow, it was said, when everyone in the community participated. The contrast with Cauca could hardly be more marked. Rather than satisfying the greed of a rapacious and anti-social individual, here the baptism of money is not only sanctioned by God but works only to the full when it is for the benefit of the whole community.

Having begun with Cauca where the radical opposition in the moral evaluation of gift and commodity exchange is of a sort familiar from much in our own cultural background, and having focused in some detail on a case which in certain ways strikingly inverts these evaluations, we end here I believe in a world from which this kind of opposition in moral loading is largely absent. When some anthropologists insist on the fundamental discontinuity between gift and commodity exchange (e.g., Gregory 1982), while others emphasise their fundamental continuity (e.g., Firth 1973), we might be well advised to keep this kind of cultural variation in mind.

Underneath such variation, however, I think it is undeniable that there are a limited number of extremely broad principles in terms of which most cultures are likely to judge exchanges of different kinds.[12] In almost every society, for example, there are some values which cannot – or should not – be exchanged at all. Moral peril consequently attaches to attempts to make them into objects of transaction. Similarly, with exchanges which are supposed to be governed by what Sahlins (1972) calls 'generalised' reciprocity but which are treated as a matter of 'balanced' or 'negative' reciprocity. Condemnation, that is, attaches to transactions in which the *quid pro quo* element is properly implicit, long-term and not subject to precise calculation but which are conducted in such a way as to make this element overt and explicit. Finally, and allowing for considerable cultural variation in the definition of these terms, any exchange is likely to be judged by whether it is 'equitable' and 'fair' – and by definition those which are not are condemned when they occur within the boundaries of the moral community (however defined).

While medieval Europe and the Hindu context I have considered can be contrasted in terms of the *type* of exchange which most obviously represents a dire moral peril (commodity or gift), it must be recognised that at another level it is common considerations of this order which inform these evaluations. Both the medieval merchant and the Benares priest are condemned for 'selling' something that is only dubiously regarded as an object of exchange at all: time which belongs to God alone in the first case, salvation and atonement for sin in the second. While according to the teachings of Aristotle trade should be conducted only on the basis of 'balanced' reciprocity, the profits of the medieval merchant seemed to represent a naked instance of 'negative' reciprocity. More radically, the Hindu priest (and the wife-taking affines who demand exhorbitant dowries) are seen as subverting the ethic of the 'pure' gift by treating such transactions as a species of commerce. In each instance a transaction which should serve other ends (whether this is the reproduction of the self-provisioning community or salvation) has become a mere matter of egotistical calculation and short-term individual advantage. 'Negative' reciprocity has replaced 'generalised' or 'balanced' reciprocity; ruthless self-seeking the solidarity and interdependence of those who are party to the transaction. But above all, the exchanges both of the merchant and the priest stand condemned on grounds of equity. The priest is tainted by the suspicion that in reality he is getting something for nothing and merely parasitically appropriates offerings primarily intended for others; the merchant by the suspicion that he created nothing and his profit was therefore fraudulent. In neither case is it absolutely clear that those who most demonstrably benefit by the exchange have actually contributed anything at all.

Notes

1 I gratefully acknowledge various extremely helpful comments on earlier drafts of this paper from André Béteille, Maurice Bloch, John Comaroff, Chris Fuller, Murray Milner, Gloria Raheja, Tom Trautmann and Peter van der Veer. Thanks are also due to David D'Avray and Janet Nelson for guidance on the literature on medieval Europe; to Lisette Josephides for some cautionary remarks on the Melanesian material, and to Alfred Gell for permission to cite his splendidly incautious unpublished paper.

2 Fieldwork in Benares was carried out between September 1976 and November 1977 (supported by the Social Science Research Council) and in August 1978, August–September 1981 and March–April 1983 (supported by the London School of Economics and Political Science). I am deeply obliged to Virendra Singh for his language instruction, and to him and Om Prakash Sharma for their research assistance.

3 Certain items – like gold, an elephant, horse, water-buffalo, emeralds and sesame seeds – are sometimes said to be especially dangerous to the recipient, but specie is never listed among them. With the exception of sesame seed, all of these things are distinguished by their high value; but others of equal value are not generally mentioned. I am only able to offer a series of more or less *ad hoc* explanations for the items regarded as a particular peril. Elephants, for example, are preeminently associated with royalty, and the textual sources endlessly emphasise how the gifts of the king represent a special danger for the Brahman. Sesame seed, I was told, should be included amongst the worst kinds of *dana* because it is given in the name of the deceased, and in the expectation that each grain prolongs his or her residence in heaven by a day. Since it is explicitly given 'in exchange' (*badle men*), it is especially 'bad *dana*' (*kudana*).

4 In view of van der Veer's (1985) recent criticism of my earlier discussion (Parry 1980), I would like to reassert this last point with particular emphasis.

5 This contrast between the proceeds of *dana* and the proceeds from other occupations is endlessly reiterated by my informants. Two further brief illustrations must suffice. The first concerns the wife's brother of a Benares priest who had come to visit from Allahabad and to whom I was one day introduced. That same evening my new acquaintance came to see me with an extremely pressing invitation to finance a shop he proposed to start. He confirmed that his family controlled lucrative priestly rights in Allahabad, but indignantly denied that he himself would ever exercise them or be willing to utilise such money to fund his commercial ambitions, for – as he emphatically explained – 'I do not like to beg.' The second example is that of a priestly

informant who dabbles as a part-time freelance journalist and derives a small and irregular income from the somewhat scurrilous pieces he contributes to the local press. If his articles yield Rs 50 in the month that money remains with him, he repeatedly told me; whereas the much larger amounts he obtains from the exercise of his priestly rights go god only knows where. Though it never struck me that these journalistic earnings (or indeed the profits of the coal-seller mentioned earlier) were particularly hard-earned, they were incessantly contrasted with the money of *dana* as *khare pasina ki kamai*.

6 The only circumstance in which they move back in this direction is when an exorcist diagnoses that an affliction emanates from such a source, and coerces the troublesome spirit to return to where it had come from.

7 I am indebted here to a helpful comment from David White.

8 I have not myself done any systematic research on mercantile activity in Benares and my evidence is largely impressionistic. I am convinced, however, that the basic contrast I draw between the moral dangers of *dana* and the relatively neutral moral aura of commerce is a valid one.

9 For a discussion of the similar ideological premium placed on passing on knowledge, see Parry 1985b.

10 More accurately, one should perhaps speak of an ideological world in which *men* see society as constituted by exchange. The extent to which women share this vision is open to question, which is not surprising given that the effect of this ideological elaboration of exchange is a radical devaluation of women.

11 I recognise that 'increment' and 'profit' are not the same thing: one sustains the relationship and (re-)creates a debt; while under most circumstances the other does not. My central point nevertheless stands – in exchange systems of this sort valuables appear to have a self-expanding character.

12 I am particularly indebted here to Murray Milner whose criticisms of an earlier draft have forced me to acknowledge these continuities.

References

Ardener, E. 1970. 'Witchcraft, economics, and the continuity of belief', in M. Douglas, ed., *Witchcraft confessions and accusations*, London: Tavistock Publications.

Aristotle 1962. *The politics*, Penguin Books, London.

Bayly, C. 1983. *Rulers, townsmen and bazaars: north Indian society in the age of British expansion, 1770–1870*, Cambridge: Cambridge University Press.

Biardeau, M. 1976. 'Le sacrifice dans l'Hindouisme', in M. Biardeau and C. Malamoud, *Le sacrifice dans l'Inde ancienne*, Paris: Presses Universitaires de France (Bibliothèque de l'école des hautes études, sciences réligieuses, vol. 79).

Biersack, A. 1984. 'Paiela ('women-men'): the reflexive foundations of gender ideology', *American Ethnologist*, 10: 118–38.

Braudel, F. 1985. *The wheels of commerce* (vol. 2 of *Civilization and capitalism*), London: Fontana Paperbacks.

Burridge, K. 1969. *New heaven, new earth: a study of millenarian activities*, Oxford: Basil Blackwell.

Cohn, B. S. 1964. 'The role of the Gosains in the economy of eighteenth and nineteenth-century Upper India', *Indian Economic and Social History Review*, 1 (4): 175–82.

Counts, D. and Counts, D. 1977. 'Independence and the rule of money in Kaliai', *Oceania*, 48: 30–9.

Curtin, P. 1984. *Cross-cultural trade in world history*. Cambridge: Cambridge University Press.

Darling, M. L. 1925. *The Punjab peasant in prosperity and debt*, London: Oxford University Press.

Derrett, J. D. M. 1966. 'The reform of Hindu religious endowments', in Donald E. Smith ed., *South Asian politics and religion*, Princeton: University Press.

Dirks, N. 1982. 'The pasts of a *Palaiyakarar*: the ethnohistory of a South Indian little king', *Journal of Asian Studies*, 41 (4): 655–83.

Dubois, Abbé J. A. 1906. *Hindu manners, customs and ceremonies*, Oxford: Oxford University Press.

Duby, G. 1982. *The three orders: feudal society imagined*, Chicago: University of Chicago Press.

Dumont, L. 1970. *Homo hierarchicus: the caste system and its implications*, London: Weidenfeld & Nicholson.

   1971. 'On putative hierarchy and some allergies to it', *Contributions to Indian Sociology*, (n.s.), 5: 58–78.

Firth, R. 1973. *Symbols public and private*, London: George Allen and Unwin Ltd.

Fuller, C. 1984. *Servants of the goddess: the priests of a South Indian temple*, Cambridge: Cambridge University Press.

Geary, P. 1986. 'Sacred commodities: the circulation of medieval relics', in A. Appadurai, ed., *The social life of things*, Cambridge: Cambridge University Press.

Gell, A. n.d. 'Inter-tribal commodity barter and reproductive gift exchange in Old Melanesia', unpublished ms.

Gouldner, A. W. 1960. 'The norm of reciprocity', *American Sociological Review*, 25: 161–78.

Gregory, C. A. 1982. *Gifts and commodities*, London: Academic Press.

Grierson, P. 1971. 'Commerce in the Dark Ages: a critique of the evidence', in G. Dalton, ed., *Studies in economic anthropology*.

Gudeman, S. 1986. *Economics as culture: models and metaphors of livelihood*, London: Routledge and Kegan Paul.

Gurevich, A. J. 1985. *Categories of medieval culture*, London: Routledge and Kegan Paul.

Heesterman, J. C. 1959. 'Reflections on the significance of the Daksina', *Indo-Iranian Journal*, 3: 241–58.

   1971. 'Priesthood and the Brahmin'. *Contributions to Indian Sociology* (n.s.), 5: 43–7.

Kane, P. V. 1973. *History of Dharmaśastra*, vol. 3, Poona: Bhandarkar Oriental Research Institute.

92   J. Parry

Le Goff, J. 1980. *Time, work, and culture in the Middle Ages*, Chicago: University of Chicago Press.

Little, L. 1978. *Religious poverty and the profit economy in Medieval Europe*, London: Paul Elek.

Malamoud, C. 1981. 'On the rhetoric and semantics of purusartha', *Contributions to Indian Sociology* (n.s.), 15 (1 & 2): pp. 33–54.

The Laws of Manu: 1886, translated from Sanskrit into English by Georg Buhler (Sacred Books of the East Series, 25), Oxford: Clarendon Press.

Mines, M. 1985. *The warrior merchants: textiles, trade and territory in South India*, Cambridge: Cambridge University Press.

Morauta, L. 1974. *Beyond the village: local politics in Madang, Papua New Guinea*, London: Athlone Press.

O'Flaherty, W. 1976. *The origins of evil in Hindu mythology*, Berkeley and London: University of California Press.

Parry, J. P. 1979. *Caste and kinship in Kangra*, London: Routledge and Kegan Paul.

——— 1980. 'Ghosts, greed and sin: the occupational identity of the Benares funeral priests', *Man* (n.s.), 15 (1): 88–111.

——— 1981. 'Death and cosmogony in Kashi', *Contributions to Indian Sociology* (n.s.), 15: 337–65.

——— 1985a. 'Death and digestion: the symbolism of food and eating in north Indian mortuary rites', *Man* (n.s.), 20 (3): 612–30.

——— 1985b. 'The Brahmanical tradition and the technology of the intellect', in J. Overing, ed., *Reason and morality*. London: Tavistock Publications.

Pirenne, H. 1967. 'Aspects of Medieval European economy', in G. Dalton, ed., *Tribal and peasant economies*, New York: The Natural History Press.

Planalp, J. 1956. *Religious life and values in a north Indian village*, Cornell University Doctoral Dissertation (University Microfilms: Ann Arbor).

Polanyi, K. 1971. *Primitive, archaic and modern economies: essays of Karl Polanyi*, ed., George Dalton, Boston: Beacon Press.

Raheja, G. 1985. *Kinship, caste, and auspiciousness in Pahansu*, University of Chicago PhD.

Raychaudhuri, T. 1983. 'The mid-eighteenth century background', in Dharma Kumar, ed., *Cambridge Economic History of India*, 2: 3–35, Cambridge: Cambridge University Press.

Sahlins, M. 1972. *Stone age economics*, Chicago: Aldine.

Shah, K. J. 1981. 'Of artha and the *Arthasastra*', *Contributions to Indian Sociology* (n.s.), 15 (1–2): 55–73.

Shulman, D. 1980. 'On South Indian bandits and kings', *Indian Economic and Social History Review*, 17, 3.

——— 1985. 'Kingship and prestation in South Indian myth and epic', *Asian and African Studies*, 19: 93–117.

Spencer, G. W. 1968. 'Temple money-lending and livestock redistribution in early Tanjore', *The Indian Economic and Social History Review*, 3: 277–93.

Stent, W. R. 1977. 'An interpretation of a cargo cult', *Oceania*, 47: 187–219.

Strathern, A. 1978. '"Finance and production" revisited: in pursuit of a comparison,' in G. Dalton, ed., *Research in economic anthropology* (vol. 1), pp. 73–104.

1979a. 'The red box money-cult in Mount Hagen 1968–71', *Oceania*, 50 (2): 88–102; (3): 161–75.

1979b. 'Gender, ideology and money in Mount Hagen', *Man*, 14 (3): 530–48.

Taussig, M. 1980. *The devil and commodity fetishism in South America*, Chapel Hill: The University of North Carolina Press.

Tawney, R. H. 1972. *Religion and the rise of capitalism*. London: Penguin Books.

Trautmann, T. R. 1981. *Dravidian kinship*. Cambridge: Cambridge University Press.

van der Veer, P. 1985. 'Brahmans: their purity and their poverty. On the changing values of brahman priests in Ayodhya', *Contributions to Indian Sociology* (n.s.), 19 (2): 303–21.

4

Money, men and women

R. L. STIRRAT

One of the themes running through much recent work in economic anthropology has been the utility or otherwise of a distinction between two types of exchange. A recent and succinct definition of this distinction is that given by Chris Gregory. 'Commodity exchange', he writes, 'is an exchange of alienable things between transactors who are in a state of reciprocal independence', whilst 'non-commodity' or 'gift exchange' is an 'exchange of inalienable things between transactors who are in a state of reciprocal dependence' (Gregory 1982: 12). In many ways, Gregory's distinction is similar to that made by the substantivists between 'market' and 'non-market' economies, and has its roots in such nineteenth-century distinctions as that made by Maine between 'Status' and 'Contract' or Tonnies' distinction between *Gemeinschaft* and *Gesellschaft*.[1]

The problem with such a distinction, however, is that although its generality makes possible the generation of 'grand theory', its generality also prevents us from recognising that there are significant differences between the various phenomena lumped together under such headings as 'the gift economy' or 'the profit economy' or whatever. This has been remarked upon by a number of writers. MacCormack, for instance, writes of the 'somewhat baffling mist of uncertainty' (1976: 89) which surrounds such terms as 'reciprocity', and goes on to distinguish a number of ways in which the term 'reciprocity' has been used by anthropologists. Similar problems exist when one starts using the concept of 'commodity' or 'commodity exchange'. I must say that I find the concept of the 'commodity' as mist-enveloped as that of 'reciprocity' or 'the gift', but provisionally, by 'commodity' I shall mean an article or a service which is produced for exchange, where exchange is between 'universal others', independent and autonomous operators, who have no relation with each other except in so far as they exchange these commodities.[2] It seems to me that what is crucial here is the *form* of exchange. 'Trade' or 'sale' are not always organised in the same way, and

94

how 'trading' or 'selling' is organised has crucial effects on the organisation of production and class formation.

In this chapter I shall look at certain aspects of 'commodity exchange'. More precisely, I shall examine one particular way in which commodity exchange can be organised and the social implications of this *particular* way of organising commodity exchange in a local setting. On one level this will take me into the field of consumption, an area which is at least as problematic as that of exchange and one often neglected by anthropologists.[3] On another level it will involve the discussion of gender relations in a particular Sinhalese village. And on a third level it will involve some comparison of the implications of different ways of organising commodity exchange.

The sexual division of labour and female control over money

The primary focus here is 100 fishing households in a village called Ambakandawila on the northwest coast of Sri Lanka.[4] Ambakandawila is no pre-capitalist community dragged screaming into the horrors of the capitalist world. Rather it was created as a moment in the spread of capitalism in the late nineteenth century. With the extension of the Sri Lankan estate economy, particularly the commercial exploitation of the coconut, the demand for food led to the growth of a string of fishing villages on what were the previously deserted beaches of the northwest coast of Sri Lanka. The first permanent settlers seem to have arrived in Ambakandawila in the 1880s. From the start these fishermen were involved in production for the market and were generally full-time fishermen not involved in any other sort of productive activity.[5] When I lived in Ambakandawila, besides fishing households, there were also about forty non-fishing households in the village. These households relied on such activities as teaching, jobs in the local town or labouring in the coconut estates. There were few economic ties between them and those households which depended on fishing.

Fishing in Ambakandawila was carried out by men using small rafts known as *theppans* which carry crews of one or two men. Prior to the 1960s these rafts were powered by paddles or sails, whilst cotton nets made by the fishermen and their families were used to catch the fish. From around 1963, the cotton nets began to be replaced by nylon nets and outboard motors began to be used to power the *theppans*. In the period with which I am concerned here, mainly 1969–75, all the fishermen used nylon nets and about half used outboard motors.[6] Entry into *theppan* fishing was relatively easy, an old *theppan* and a few nets costing very little. It was also relatively easy for a fisherman to build up his stock of gear in small units. There were no major discontinuities in the investment function except for the 'lumpiness' involved in the purchase of outboard engines. In Ambakandawila all households owned their own gear and in general there was little co-operation in production or in the ownership of gear between households. Where there was co-operation it was rare and short-lived. I will say more about it later.

Fishing in Ambakandawila was men's work. Unlike many other fishing communities there were no ritual restrictions on women coming into contact with fishing gear or even going on short trips by *theppan* or boat, but women did not fish. The men said that the women did not have the physical strength or knowledge to fish; the women said that they had no intention of fishing and no desire to spend up to twelve hours a day at sea. In the past, both men and women were involved in making or mending nets, but – with the introduction of nylon nets – by 1970 the only point at which they generally co-operated in the production process, was in taking fish out of the nets after the *theppan* had been beached. From then on, the disposal of the fish was the responsibility of women, the mothers or wives of the men who caught the fish. The way in which the fish was sold had important effects both on the role of women and on relations between households in Ambakandawila. On the one hand it gave women rather than men control over cash, and on the other, through the women, the highly competitive ideology of the market place was conveyed into the village where it generated in a particularly acute form competitive relations between households.

Almost all the fish caught from Ambakandawila was sold in Chilaw market about three miles away. The women took the fish to market by bus where it was sold to petty traders, most of whom transported the fish into the interior on bicycles or in small vans. Each woman sold her own fish to the highest bidder, women competing with other women and with the traders to maximise their prices. The market looked chaotic, a few hundred women from Ambakandawila and other villages in the area selling to an equally large number of small traders. The result approximated to the ideal of a free commodity market, prices fluctuating from minute to minute depending primarily on the supply of fish, the demand function being relatively constant. Relations between sellers and buyers in Chilaw market were highly antagonistic and often openly aggressive, the fishwomen having a well-deserved reputation for the virulence of their language and the belligerence of their behaviour. All transactions were settled immediately for cash. No long-term relationships were built up between sellers and buyers, and it was rare for fishwomen and the fish buyers even to know each others' names. In other words, in terms of Gregory's definition, exchange in Chilaw market took the form of 'commodity exchange'.

This division of labour was simply a 'taken for granted' in Ambakandawila, and just as there were no ritual or religious barriers on women going to sea, so too there were no formalised barriers on men selling their fish. Rather, it was argued that men did not have the time to sell the fish and that they lacked the necessary trading skills. Even on those few occasions when small traders by-passed the market and came to the village, men stood back and let the women do the selling. This was also the case when members of the small non-fishing population of Ambakandawila came to the beach to buy fish. For two or three months of the year some of the Ambakandawila fishermen beached their *theppans* by the market, but even then it was the women who did the selling. In one peculiar case a wife refused to sell her husband's fish and in desperation he started taking his fish to market himself. But his attempts at selling the fish were disastrous and he had to persuade his mother to sell the fish until his wife relented.

The result of this division of labour was economic interdependence between male and female, husband and wife. Households without a fishing male or a fish-selling female were in trouble and, in general, each household formed an autonomous economic unit based upon its owner-ship of the means of production and the division of labour between male and female members of the household. Everyone in Ambakandawila was Roman Catholic, and the ideology of the family promulgated by the Church only reinforced tendencies towards the dominance of the nuclear family as the basic unit of society in the village.

One obvious effect of this division of labour was that wives controlled access to the cash generated through the sale of fish. What cannot be stressed too strongly is that fishing households in Ambakandawila were fully integrated into the market economy. They were, in current jargon, 'simple commodity producers' or 'petty commodity producers'. Almost everything they consumed, almost everything that was needed for fishing, was bought through the market economy. They even bought up to 30 per cent of the fish they consumed.[7] Thus fishing households were totally dependent on the cash they received from the sale of fish, and men had no access to cash except through their wives. Given that women alone possessed the skills of buying and selling, given that they had first access to cash, and given that they alone knew the whole picture concerning the income of the household, women exercised a very real power which men lacked.[8] In Ambakandawila they were viewed and saw themselves as the managers of households and thus responsible for all the expenditures of the household. Women negotiated most of the loans within the village whilst also dealing with the Chilaw pawnshops and the boutiques which gave credit. Even when it came to buying fishing gear, women often took the final decisions as they alone knew the economic position of the household. And in fishing, although men claimed the right to decide what types of fishing to engage in or what types of gear to use on any particular day, their wives could, and frequently did, assert their wishes if they disagreed with their husbands. They could, for example, refuse to give their husbands cash for engine fuel or, even more effectively, refuse the cash for arrack and let it be known that they would not meet any of their husbands' debts in the illegal arrack taverns around the village.[9]

It is not unusual for women in Sri Lanka to be petty traders. Many of the traders in the *polas* (periodic markets) are women. So too are many street traders. Furthermore, it appears that it is common for women to be considered the managers of the household budget (e.g., Alexander 1982). But it is rare for women to have quite the same degree of control over financial matters as they did in Ambakandawila. The result of women's control over the cash incomes of households in Ambakandawila was a certain dissonance between the ideology of male supremacy common throughout Sri Lanka and the actualities of power within the household. In Sri Lanka generally,

The male, particularly the father–husband, is associated with dominance and authority in the family, and the wife with subservience and submissiveness . . . Women are considered physically and mentally weak . . . and are supposed to engage in domestic activities . . . whilst the father is the provider, one who supplies the household with food and other amenities by his superior physical and mental abilities (Obeyesekere 1963: 236).[10]

I do not want to overstress the power of men in Ambakandawila for the picture is of course much more complicated,[11] but women did have a power and freedom *vis-à-vis* men in Ambakandawila which they lacked elsewhere in Sri Lanka. Women were less conscious of etiquette and status than were women elsewhere in the country and they took a certain delight in shocking their husbands by their behaviour, especially their language. Most wives in Ambakandawila drank arrack openly whilst many smoked cigars and small pipes, activities unthinkable for women elsewhere in Sri Lanka but for which the fisherwomen were well known. According to Obeyesekere, a woman in the interior of the island who took up such habits would be 'the victim of ridicule, vituperation or assault' (Obeyesekere 1963: 340) because such behaviour would involve women usurping some of the symbols of male dominance.

One concomitant of this dissonance between the pan-Sinhalese ideal of male dominance and the local fact of female control over money was, on the part of older men at least, a rather peculiar attitude towards cash. To many fishermen in Ambakandawila cash was in some ways considered to be 'dirty'. By this I do not mean to imply that cash was 'polluted' in the sense that women are polluted during menstruation or in the sense that faecal material or blood is dirty.[12] Rather, when men were asked about cash they tended to dismiss it as being somehow 'unclean', the term *apirissidu* sometimes being used. More often, if older men were asked about money they would dismiss the topic by spitting out, *chi* – a term of approbation used of filth in general. Thus many men would never carry money unless they had to. If they went to Chilaw they would carry just the required amount of cash or try to obtain goods on credit or get their wives to buy what they wanted. Admittedly these were extreme cases but it was very common for men to deny any knowledge of the proceeds from a day's fishing, to claim ignorance of how much money there was in the house, and to have little idea of the credit and debt position of the household. Most men even had to ask their wives how much their fishing gear had cost. The whole business of cash, particularly as it entered the household, as well as the financial management of the household, was viewed as being something particularly associated with women. As far as men were concerned, productive activity was catching fish. Selling the fish was simply a subsidiary female job, part of being a wife. 'True men' did not bother themselves with such matters, and especially with the money which entered the household from the sale of fish. Rather like aristocrats faced with a rising bourgeoisie, men in Ambakandawila would indignantly deny any knowledge of the market and money. Furthermore, to be a miser, to hoard money, was viewed as the depth of moral depravity.

Not surprisingly, women had a rather different view on the matter and found the men's attitude somewhat ludicrous. To the women, men appeared feckless and rather stupid when it came to handling cash. They were like children who could not be trusted where money was concerned, and wives were careful to control their husbands' access to it. Where possible, men had to be excluded from using money for they would just lose it, spend it on drink or be at the wrong end of any bargain. When men went to fishing camps without their wives the latter would try to insist that they, and not the men, negotiated the fish prices with the fish merchants before the men left. To the women the men were primarily the providers of the raw material which they then used to obtain the income of the household, and they contrasted what they saw as the brute strength required of fishing with the skill, guile and wit of the women in the market place. I have even heard women refer to their husbands as *ape kulikarayo* ('our labourers') – although not to their faces.

Linked to this male devaluation of cash and its association with women was the common view among men, particularly older men, that money somehow upset the normal and correct order of life. Thus a favourite jibe was to claim that a family's name was not truly inherited but had been 'bought with money'. More generally, money was seen as upsetting the correct order of caste relations. This is not the place to go into the subject of caste in Ambakandawila but two points should be made. First, caste in Ambakandawila depended on patrifiliation, the caste of the mother being totally unimportant. Secondly, caste was in various contexts related to names given by the kings, to the proper order of social relations which existed in the 'days of the kings', or was seen as a natural entity related to blood. This would all seem to suggest a conceptual association of men with order and tradition, with things as they should be; whilst women were associated with money and the disorder that money introduces into social life.[13] Thus disputes in the village and the partition of households were seen by men as being the result of women quarrelling over money. Furthermore, not only was money seen as upsetting the correct order of social relations in general but also as threatening the correct relations between male and female. All that men could do was to put the blame on cash and avoid it.

In a sense it could, I suppose, be argued that the men's attitude towards cash represented a rejection of the market economy; a rejection of the impersonal and amoral nature of commodity exchange in which the arbitrators of personal fortune are the fickle factors of demand and supply.[14] It seems to me that their attitude towards cash was at least in part a matter of what it did for female power and the threat women's control over cash posed to male authority. Furthermore, as I shall show later, even if there was an element of an 'anti-market mentality' in male attitudes towards cash, the situation was much more ambivalent than a simple rejection of commodity production and exchange *per se*. But before we can return to this topic we must first look at the nature of consumption.

The nature of consumption

One of the features of commodity production, production for the market, which has been noted by a number of writers on the subject, is its individuating effect. Harriet Friedman, writing about simple commodity production, has argued that, 'The process of commoditisation ultimately implies the individual status of each household. It becomes an enterprise whose relations to outsiders progressively takes the form of buying, selling and competition' (Friedman 1980: 163).

Whilst Friedman writes in a Marxist tradition, parallel sentiments can be found in de Tocqueville's classic writings on democracy in America written when commodity production and exchange were becoming dominant in America. Thus he writes that Americans, 'Owe nothing to any man, they expect nothing from any man; they acquire the habit of always considering themselves as standing alone, and they are apt to imagine that their whole destiny is in their own hands' (Tocqueville 1956: 194).

Such comments as de Tocqueville's and Friedman's are particularly apposite for Ambakandawila. Given the particular organisation of exchange in Chilaw market, and given the technology of production in fishing, each household becomes an autonomous economic unit. Commodity production in this case has generated a variety of household particularism; and in a culture in which status has been and still is associated with the ownership and consumption of goods, this particularism and inter-household competition is expressed through material symbols. Yet at the same time, and as Dumont reminds us, individualism is also associated with equality or at least the equivalence of social units. This in turn is linked to the second aspect of commodity production and exchange: that it can generate social identities in terms of the position of social categories in relation to the market. All fishing households in Ambakandawila share a common position in terms of their market position and in terms of their occupational role as fishermen in Sinhalese society. Thus there is a certain Janus-like quality about commodity production as exemplified by the Ambakandawila case. On the one hand it has created a particularistic and individualistic social universe in which each social unit is in competition with the other. Yet at the same time, such individualism implies a sort of equality, the equivalence of each unit whether it be the person or, as in this case, the household, and this equivalence creates the basis for a common class identity. The result in the context of Ambakandawila is that we find two contrasting moralities at work, one stressing competition, atomism and individualism: the other stressing balance, equivalence and solidarity. Let me begin with the second.

As I have indicated earlier, each household generally encapsulated the productive possibilities of the fishing economy of Ambakandawila and co-operation in production was rare. Yet there were certain points when co-operation became necessary or advantageous. The first of these was when the *theppans* were beached. They then had to be dragged up beyond high watermark, and for this four to six men were required depending on the size of the *theppan*. Only rarely did households have such labour resources, and at this point men from different households had to co-operate. Yet this co-operation was on the basis of a strict balance on a daily basis. If A helped to pull up B's *theppan* then B had to pull up A's, and such equivalences were strictly enforced. Thus the last *theppan* to come to the shore each morning was often in trouble, and people who made a habit of being late were in real difficulties. The debt had to be paid off immediately.

Secondly, at various points in the developmental cycle of households, imbalances occurred between labour and gear in the household. In such situations two or more households might co-operate in what was known as *havula rassaava* (partnership work). This again involved a strict balance. The catch was either divided equally between the two households and sold separately or the wives from both households went together to market to sell the fish. Only rarely was the joint catch sold by one woman and this reflected very close friendship between them. Furthermore, *havula rassaava* almost always meant mixed crews, men of different households fishing on the same *theppan* to ensure that there was no transfer of the catch at sea to other *theppans*. A variation on *havula rassaava* was the joint purchase of gear. This only involved relatively large investments, for instance, when engines were first introduced. Here the gear was generally jointly used and the costs always shared equally.

Yet all these cases of co-operation between households were short lived. *Havula rassaava* never lasted more than a few months and the longest I have known a piece of gear be jointly owned is about a year. Most of these cases of co-operation dissolved in argument and recriminations because the ideal of a strict balance, of strict equality, was in practice almost impossible to maintain. There was continual friction as to who was in charge, and it was also impossible for the partners to provide exactly the same amount of gear.[15]

The forms of co-operative labour exchange were premised on the ideal of equality and equivalence between fishing households in Ambakanda-wila. So too was the business of loans within the village. Like all small-scale producers these fishermen were highly dependent on various forms of credit. Much of it was obtained from outside the village: from pawnshops or boutiques or from traders' advances in the fishing camps. All these forms of credit involved the payment, open or otherwise, of interest. There was also credit which could be obtained from the government through the fishing societies. Here, despite vigorous efforts by the government, this often amounted to free gifts to fishing households, there being little in the way of a moral imperative to repay these loans. In contrast, loans within the village were generally interest free, and took two forms. The first, known as *siitus*, was the sort of rotating credit institution familiar throughout South and Southeast Asia in which the participants in the association made a weekly or monthly contribution and took the whole fund contributed in rotation (see Geertz 1962, Ardener 1964). The second involved interest-free loans on call between individual households. Both were arranged by women. Within Amba-kandawila the only interest-bearing loans I know of were made by fishing households to non-fishing households. In general the principle was that if A lent to B then A had the right to recall that loan whenever required. Furthermore, A could in the future demand a loan from B. Again the principle was one of equal exchange between autonomous units.

Now, although I have stressed the 'equality of individualism' in this summary of labour exchange and loans in Ambakandawila, what the people themselves stressed was something else. They contrasted the *balance* of relations within the village with the *imbalance* of relations between the fishing households on the one hand and non-fishers in Chilaw or elsewhere on the other. For people in Ambakandawila, the strict balancing of labour exchanges and the lack of any payment of interest on loans was represented in terms of the notion that they were all fishing households and as such owed equivalent aid to one another. Such behaviour was part of an ideology of equality and a common identity, an identity which was denied if wages were paid for labour or interest charged on loans. Thus in the very few cases of mortgages in Ambakandawila in which interest was paid, what was at stake was the marginality of the borrower to the fishing community as a whole.

The most obvious way in which such an identity was expressed, however, was not through exchange but through certain types of consumption and through a shared 'life-style'. In Ambakandawila there was a category of expenditure known as *ge viyadam*, (household expenses). This incorporated the day-to-day necessities of life, things like food, drink, basic household chattels and so on. Women considered a day's income good or bad in so far as it covered these basic requirements of the household. What was remarkable about *ge viyadam* in Ambakandawila was that despite large variations in income between households and equally great variations in the daily, weekly and seasonal incomes of households, household expenses on a *per capita* basis were remarkably constant throughout the village and there were no marked differences between the daily consumption pattern of fishing households within Ambakandawila. Furthermore, this level of consumption was seen as a moral imperative. Households which spent more than the norm were criticised as profligate, wasteful, or as trying to be 'above themselves': of putting on airs and graces. Households which spent under the norm were criticised as being over-mean and stingy. This in turn linked up with a general 'style of life' throughout the fishing households of Ambakandawila. No matter what their income or how much property they owned fishing households led much the same life as each other. And again, this uniformity of style was deliberately sought after. To live differently was essentially to say that one wasn't really a fisherman but was trying to be something else.[16]

Fishing households saw themselves as sharing a common and distinct life-style in contrast to traders, teachers, farmers or whoever. Part of this life-style was the attitude towards intra-village loans and labour exchanges which have to be seen in the same terms as 'household consumption': in terms of a common identity as fishing people which in part was generated by their common position in relation to the market.

Yet at the same time the market generated exactly the opposite tendency: a somewhat agonistic and frenetic competition which again was expressed through goods, which took the form of bouts of conspicuous consumption and conspicuous investment in consumer durables, and was just as much part of 'fishing culture' as was the constancy of *ge viyadam*. Furthermore, whilst women handled the day-to-day consumption needs of the household as well as managing money in general, and whilst women were the conduit through which the ideology of the marketplace was transmitted into the village, in this area of competitive expenditure men were much more actively involved. And to paraphrase Veblen, if the 'domestic life' of fishing families in Ambakandawila was 'relatively shabby', such competition was 'overt' and 'carried out before the eyes of observers' (Veblen 1924:112).

In the late sixties and early seventies, fishing households in Ambakandawila were relatively well off by Sri Lankan standards. In 1970, after allowance was made for the expenses of fishing, only the poorest (and most feckless) of fishing families earned less than teachers or minor government servants, and many earned much more. From the early sixties onwards, the relative economic position of small-scale fishermen in Sri Lanka rose steadily, partly as the result of the upward trend in fish prices, and partly due to the increased catches from the new equipment. Some of this increased income went to pay for the new equipment, but the rest was spent on the purchase and consumption of 'consumer goods' and took on a highly competitive nature. One of the major areas of competition was concerned with ceremonial, such things as first communions, confirmations, and church feasts, but the most important was marriage. Here again the whole object was differentiation through consumption.

Marriage in Ambakandawila is a somewhat complex matter which raises a number of intertwined issues. From one point of view it involved a basic asymmetry, the wife-givers being inferior to the wife-receivers, an asymmetry expressed in the kinship terminology and in certain of the rituals surrounding marriage (Stirrat 1977). But at the same time it was also about equality, of 'like marrying like', and the sentiments of the alliance created between the two households was a very frequent theme in the drunken speeches after weddings. Thus household A gave the bride, household B gave the groom, and through the marriage household C was created which acted as the link between A and B. In line with such an ideology the scale of celebrations on both sides were the subject of long negotiations in advance which were ostensibly designed to ensure equality. If household A was planning to give an extra ring to the bride, then household B would give an extra ring to the groom, and so on. In this context equality was what was stressed.

The same sort of principle was also at work for more distant kin and friends. All who came to the wedding feasts were supposed to make small financial contributions, and there was a general idea that this amount should rise from year to year with the rising wealth of the fishermen. Closer kin, especially the households of the siblings of the bride's and groom's parents, were meant to pay more. This too should rise. Thus if A gave X at B's child's wedding, then B should give X plus an increment at A's child's wedding, and so on. Here again marriage was presented in terms of an egalitarian ideology in which autonomous households maintained some sort of balance. Yet, at the same time, marriage celebrations and negotiations were the scene of some of the most extreme examples of competition between households.

First of all, it was pure nonsense on the part of the speech-makers at these weddings to talk about marriage creating an alliance between households in Ambakandawila since the natal households of bride and groom had no obligations to each other once the wedding was over.[17] Rather, what marriage did was to create a new household, a new autonomous unit which immediately became involved in competitive relations with others. Marriage split the sibling group. A married sibling had no major obligations to his or her unmarried siblings, and a couple's primary duties were to each other and their children. Furthermore, siblings were crucial in that they provided the reference points in the struggle for standing within the fishing community, for all siblings started off in much the same position, and thus success or failure could be best measured in relation to one's siblings.

Secondly, for all but the poorest households, dowry was paid along with the bride. This usually but not always took the form of pre-mortem inheritance and often involved large sums of cash. Again we might note the association of women with money but in this case men did not avoid money: indeed, one of the major areas for dispute was over dowry and all young men hoped to marry girls with good dowries. But this was not a matter of two households haggling over the size of the dowry. Rather, the bride's family knew how much they wanted to give and then they tried to attract the most prestigious husband for their daughter. And this prestige depended upon the economic standing of the groom's natal household. Here, the dowry was primarily a measure of, on the one hand, what the bride's family could pay, and on the other, a recognition of a certain level of standing, claimed by the groom's family. Thus those involved frequently lied over the size of the dowry. But it must be noted that the dowry did not go to the groom's natal household. Dowry was not part of a system of exchange but rather it should be seen as a matter of consumption.[18]

Thirdly, if marriages and the scale of marriage expenditures were part of a claim by both bride's and groom's households to a certain superior standing *vis-à-vis* other fishing households, marriage was also a stage for competition between bride's and groom's households. Earlier I mentioned how prior to the marriage, negotiations took place between households as to the size of the celebrations and any gifts that might be made to the bride and groom. In practice however it was very common for one side or both to try to outdo the other on the day of the wedding itself. The bride's party might be twice as large as expected when it turned up at the groom's house; the groom's mother might suddenly present the bride with an unexpected gold chain and so on. All these little extras were designed to shame the other party; to claim and prove superiority. And there was absolutely nothing that the shamed party could do for there was no chance of reciprocation; no opportunity for balanced reciprocity.

Finally, even the gifts from kin, supposedly gifts to help defray the costs of the celebrations, were also open to what might be called abuse. Ideally, if A gave to B then B should reciprocate. More successful households always had a few poor and possibly embarrassing relations, and one way of dealing with them, of shedding them, was to give such a large contribution that there was no possibiity of the recipient repaying. In sum, marriages could be very nasty affairs. Not surprisingly an enormous amount of time, energy, money and tension was expended on them.

If ceremonial expenditure was one area of competition, the second was over consumer durables such as houses, furniture, jewelry, clothes and radios, and by the mid-seventies large and complex stereo equipment and higher dowries. By the 1970s the major demand for furniture and houses in Chilaw town came from the neighbouring fishing villages whilst the jewelry, cloth and radio shops also depended on the fishing communities, even though fishing households were a minority in the area. What was important about all these commodities was not simply their practical utility but rather their role in the competition for social standing within the fishing community, the competition taking the form of conspicuous display. Let me give some examples:

1   *Houses*. By the early seventies around 35 per cent of all fishing houses in Ambakandawila were built of brick and tile, a proportion rising to over 50 per cent by the mid-seventies. What was striking about these houses was their style and decoration: very gaudy and very loud, and that their owners always compared them to other houses in Ambakandawila or other near-by villages. Thus A's house would have one more room than B's, and the reason it had one extra room would be simply to have one more room. Or C's house would have a car port not because they had a car, or were likely to have a car – nor was a car likely to come to a house on top of a sand dune half a mile from the road – but because no one else in the village had a car port. One of the best examples of this sort of behaviour was a house with an overhead water tank when the nearest

piped water was three miles away and the owner had no intention of installing a pump. Again the point was that no one else had a water tank.

2 *Furniture*. Just as houses were built and designed in terms of what others had or had not, so too was furniture. Thus households would vie with each other in terms of the number, style and price of chairs, but they would normally be stacked up in a heap in a locked room and only brought out on very special occasions.

3 *Electrical equipment*. By the mid-seventies, a number of houses owned large and expensive 'two-in-ones', and by the end of the seventies a few owned televisions. Yet these were never used. There was no electricity and no one expected it to come to the village.

The point about all these objects was simply to own them and for them to be displayed. The aim was to arouse jealousy in others. Through owning such objects social standing could be claimed over those who did *not* own them. The prestige of these objects derived from their association with the Sinhalese middle class, yet these objects were never used in the way the middle class used them. Any Ambakandawila family who sat around a table on chairs to eat their evening meal would have been ridiculed. The point was display. The aim was to claim separateness, autonomy and superiority in relation to other households, but this competition was constrained within the style of life of the fishing communities who remained 'unembourgeoisified'.

Let me try to draw together this description of what people do with money and goods. Broadly speaking, within Ambakandawila there were two types of transaction (or non-transaction) between households. The first was a series of exchanges which implied equality and reciprocality. Thus labour was exchanged between households on the basis of balanced reciprocity. Credit was organised either in terms of rotating credit institutions or through household-to-household loans which were free of interest. These forms of exchange were in turn related to the idea that fishing households shared a common style of life which took the form of homogeneous patterns of consumption and 'ways of behaving'. All fishing households shared something in common: they were all dependent on fishing and shared a common position in relation to the market. Thus compared with non-fishing Sinhalese villages there was little talk about 'the village' in Ambakandawila. Rather the stress lay on being fishers, on being members of a common community which stretched beyond the village and which shared a common position *vis-à-vis* the market and other sectors of Sinhalese society. As part of that commonality they also shared a common life-style which marked them off as distinct from other sections of Sinhalese society. On the one hand this involved ideas of balance and equality. Yet on the other it involved a series of transactions or rather expenditures which were to do with competition. These took the form of heavy and competitive expenditures on durable goods and on displays of conspicuous consumption. Here the competitive logic of the market place received social expression, and the aim was to gain a superior standing in relation to other households. The two styles of consumption effectively demonstrated the ambiguity of commodity exchange: on the one hand it creates collective identities, all sharing a common position in relation to the market, and on the other it creates isolation, particularism and competition between what are so often seen as the 'natural units' of society.

In both cases, exchange cannot be divorced from consumption. And although men might have had a peculiar attitude towards cash, expecially as it entered the household from the market, they were very interested in what they could do with this cash, and both men and women were equally active in the search for standing through the possession and consumption of commodities. If this was a community in an advanced capitalist economy one might start talking about the 'consumer society' where, to paraphrase Marcuse, the people recognise themselves through their commodities. This in a sense is just as true of Ambakandawila, for despite men's talk about money destroying the 'true order' of caste, they judged others in terms of goods, of what people have and of what they consume. When it came down to it, wealth was what counted, and even the most 'traditional' of men would at times admit this.

What I am suggesting is that there were two 'spheres of consumption' in Ambakandawila each involving different sets of moral ideas about relationships between people. The first 'sphere', *ge viyadam*, was concerned with the reproduction of the household and the identity of fishing households as fishing people: in a sense as a 'class'. In this sphere what was important in relations between households was 'balance' (I hesitate to use the term 'reciprocity'). The second 'sphere' of consumption was concerned with competition, in particular competition between households. Both of these patterns of consumption were part of the search for social identity. In the end they were part of what it meant to be a member of a fishing community in this part of Sri Lanka.

Yet such patterns of consumption were more than just *markers* of status, 'a symbolic manifestation of the individual's position in society: social status, class membership and so on' (Preteceille and Terrail 1985: 20). Rather, such consumption behaviour was part of 'cultural struggle'. The pattern of expenditure on consumer durables for instance was not just a matter of 'keeping up with the Fernandos' but was in a very real sense part of a symbolic struggle with the Sinhalese middle classes. And again to quote Preteceille and Terrail, 'Consumption is certainly not an innocent affair' (1985: 69). Rather, it involves the active and systematic manipulation of signs. Thus to return to houses, the models for the houses built in Ambakandawila were the houses of the middle class. The car ports without cars, the water tanks without water, were all part of an attempt to claim at least material equality with the middle class and at the same time undermine the materialistic pretensions of that class. The material symbols of another social class, the Sinhalese bourgeoisie, were usurped, wrenched out of context, and given new meanings. Things such as car ports, water tanks and television sets which were becoming integral to the life style of the Sinhalese middle class were here taken out of that context and given a new significance both in relation to other members of the fishing community and to members of the middle class. And the middle classes were not unaware of this challenge. For them the message was quite clear: that either the fishing community was becoming too rich or that they were becoming too poor. A continual refrain on the part of teachers, clerks and others was that they were underpaid precisely because the 'lower orders' could afford such commodities, and that therefore the markers of status were being devalued.

Conclusions

The picture I have drawn of Ambakandawila fishing households obviously gives rise to a number of questions, the most immediate being the nature of the conditions under which such a system of petty commodity production is reproduced or destroyed. If one follows Marx, for instance, commodity production and exchange should give rise to the inevitable demise of autonomous producers. In the particular context of Ambakandawila the problem can I think be phrased very simply: why are the large differentials in income and wealth between fishing households not transformed into more durable class relations in which the direct producers lose control over the means of production and the product of their labours? To put it differently, and in terms that the Sinhalese middle class (and western aid agencies) would understand, why do people in Ambakandawila 'waste' their money on such bouts of conspicuous consumption rather than investing in 'productive' assets?

First of all, it has to be said that Ambakandawila was in many ways a very odd Sri Lankan fishing village. Here, every fishing household owned its own gear, but in Sri Lanka as a whole this is only the case for under 35 per cent of fishing households (de Silva 1964). This, it seems to me, was partly due to the type of gear used in Ambakandawila. Rich households could have invested in extra equipment and attempted to employ labour to work it, but the problem was a matter of finding suitable workers. Entry into *theppan* fishing was relatively easy: the threshold in terms of the cost of the simplest possible gear was very low, and thus any competent fisherman could start fishing on his own and earn more than he could as a crewman. Furthermore, the fragmented nature of *theppan* fishing with its very small production units made the task of any would-be capitalist in organising his venture very difficult. Thus both outside capitalists and rich Ambakandawila fishermen shied away from such investments.

If one looks at other types of fishing in Sri Lanka the picture is very different. Thus, besides *theppans*, large five-man outrigger canoes and beach seines requiring crews of up to fifty men are also used in the Sri Lankan fisheries. In both cases, the impact of commodity production and exchange has been in general to encourage a polarisation between owners and workers. One example is Paul Alexander's study of beach seine fishing in southern Sri Lanka; nets which were entirely owned by net-pullers seventy-five years ago are now owned by one or two men (Alexander 1982). From being communities in which everyone owned a share in the means of production they have now become highly polarised villages split between a small elite of owners and a mass of propertyless labourers.

Alternatively, the rising wealth of fishing families in recent years in Ambakandawila could have been channelled into education for the young. Such a process is common enough in South Asia in general and Sri Lanka in particular. One example is provided by Bavinck's study of a fishing community in northern Sri Lanka (Bavinck 1984). Here, new fishing technologies came earlier than in Ambakandawila, and the wealthier fishing families educated their offspring and moved out of fishing. But by the sixties, as far as Ambakandawila was concerned, levels of unemployment amongst the 'educated youth', coupled with the relatively low incomes of the middle classes made such avenues to social mobility unattractive.

A third possibility is that the wealthy of Ambakandawila could have used their resources to gain control over the process of exchange, a much more interesting possibility in the present context. A very general feature of the fishing industry in Sri Lanka is the advance system. Traders make advances to fishermen and in return gain the right to buy all the fish caught. The price they give may be fixed or it may vary with fluctuations in the free market, but no matter how the prices are fixed, they are always slightly lower than those prevailing in the open market. As far as the fishermen are concerned, advances are in part a substitute for interest-bearing loans from other sources.

Ambakandawila people only became involved in this system in temporary fishing camps. At certain times of the year up to 60 per cent of all fishermen would move to these camps, receive advances from traders which 'tied' them to these traders, and give these traders all the fish they caught in the season, accounts being settled at its end. These trading relationships were temporary and only lasted for a season at a time, but in other *theppan* fishing communities on the west coast, such advance systems could be found in the villages themselves and lasted indefinitely, fishermen being in perpetual debt to traders. These traders were either from outside the area, or were fishermen who had used their otherwise transient wealth to gain control over other fishermen, take the latter's fish, and thus start up a part-time trading venture which in some cases took over from fishing. Again, Ambakandawila was unusual in that such developments had not taken place, and this was directly related to the existence of Chilaw market.

Ambakandawila was one of four or five *theppan* fishing villages on an isthmus separated from the mainland by a lagoon. The only route from the isthmus to the mainland was by a bridge in Chilaw at the narrowest point of the lagoon, and whoever controlled the bridge effectively controlled access to and from the villages on the isthmus. Right beside this bridge was Chilaw market. Founded in the early nineteenth century by the Church, since the 1890s it has been run by the Town or Urban Council in Chilaw who sold the rights to collect dues in the market to a series of renters on an annual basis. In the early seventies the renter was a character called Alphonsu who through the market controlled all the fish trade in the Chilaw area.

Alphonsu's income derived from a series of charges he made on transactions in the market and on fish transported across the bridge. The more numerous the transactions in the market and the higher the prices, the greater his income, and thus through force and the threat of force he prevented any other traders from moving into his area or the growth of independent marketing centres on the isthmus. All fish had to be brought to his market: all traders wanting to buy fish had to come to his market. Thus any attempt to set up an advance system as existed elsewhere was doomed to failure.

Historically it seems that Chilaw market is one of the last of a whole series of such markets in this area. Until the last twenty-five years two institutions were particularly interested in the income-generating possibilities of such market places. From the late nineteenth century local authorities had the right to set up such markets and levy dues on all such transactions in their area although today, except in the larger towns, such rights have fallen into disuse. More important was the Church. All the fishermen in this area were and are Roman Catholic, and after the abolition of the government fish tax in the 1830s, the Church took over the tax in the form of a tithe, the *renda*. From the middle of the nineteenth century the Church was active in setting up centralised auction points and markets simply because if sales were centralised the *renda* was much more easy to collect. But since independence in 1948 and more markedly since the late 1950s, the power of the Church has seriously declined (see Stirrat 1984), and it has been unable to keep control over the markets. The result was that traders began to by-pass the markets and went to the beach, buying the fish as it comes to the shore. Furthermore, it was at this time that traders began to give advances to the fishermen because now there were no authorities to maintain the impersonal market. In their wake rich fishermen began to realise the possibilities of advances and in turn became traders with the result that villages south of Ambakandawila began to experience a differentiation into tied fishermen, a kind of 'disguised proletariat', and traders whose power is based not on control over the means of production but over the mode of exchange. What is striking here is the ideology surrounding advances. Like intra-village loans in Ambakandawila advances are interest free and thus can be fitted into a system which stresses the equality of the participants. Thus relations between traders and the advance-receiving fishermen become personalised ties which the relationships between buyers and sellers in Chilaw market can never become. They become represented as 'reciprocal' ties, the traders giving the advances and the fishermen in return giving the fish, 'alienable things' being exchanged through a relationship presented as one of 'reciprocal dependence'. Such a development is unthinkable in the context of Chilaw market which is seen as being impersonal and where all are seen as autonomous individuals.

Finally, let me return to the topic of the first part of this chapter, the role of women and their relationship to money. There I argued that through their role as fish sellers women acted as the conduit through which the ideology of the market place entered the village, and that through their control over cash women gained a certain power in relation to men which was reflected in men's antipathy towards money. As must be clear, the women's control over money depended upon the existence of markets such as that in Chilaw. Given that selling fish was only one of women's roles, part of a whole series of 'wifely duties' broadly defined in terms of the household, women were never able to develop a truly autonomous trading role. In Chilaw market, the only women who were full-time traders rather than fishermen's wives were widows, and even they never became very important as independent traders.

With the movement of selling from the market place to the beach in other parts of the northwest coast, the role of women has changed. No more is there any necessity for them to take fish to the market. Instead, traders come to the beach and deal directly with men. Furthermore, as the Church lost its power and as the people of the fishing villages were brought into greater contact with main stream Sinhalese culture, so increased pressure was brought upon women to retire from fish selling into the home by 'do-gooders' interested in 'civilising' the fisherfolk.[19] In areas to the south of Ambakandawila only the older women still sell fish, and that mainly on a door-to-door retail basis. Instead, men sell the fish and have few worries about the 'dirtiness' of money. Indeed, it is not dirty any more because the women, partly through choice, have given up what was an embarrassing threat to male authority. Today, Ambakandawila girls want to marry into fishing communities where they do not have to sell the fish and it is becoming more and more difficult for outside women to be persuaded to marry into Ambakandawila.

However, there is also another factor that has to be mentioned. This shift in the sexual division of labour over the last decade or so has taken place at a time when the incomes of fishing families have been rising rapidly. Rather than being one of the poorest groups in Sinhalese society, fishing families are now relatively rich. The market economy rather than being the source of their impoverishment is the source of their wealth. It could therefore be argued that the older men's refusal to interest themselves in the workings of the market was primarily a matter of rejecting what the market economy did to the fishermen in the past. Thus I have to conclude with a question mark. On the one hand it can be argued, as I have in this paper, that because of the particular nature of commodity exchange in Ambakandawila, women control money which leads to a male antipathy to money and what it does for female power. On the other hand it could also be argued that the market and commodity exchange was the means through which fishing families were subjugated, and that by associating women with the market, men were effectively isolating themselves from the deleterious effects of commoditisation.

Notes

The fieldwork on which this chapter is based was carried out at various times between 1969 and 1980 and in the main was funded by the SSRC (now ESRC) to whom I express my thanks. I would also like to thank J. Parry and E. Nissan for their comments on earlier versions of this paper and J. Perkins for his advice.

1 The most poetic version of this dichotomy I have come across is in Nelson's book on usury (*The Idea of Usury*) which is subtitled, *From tribal brotherhood to universal otherhood* (Nelson 1949).

2 See Hart (1982) for a theoretical discussion of the nature of the 'commodity' and 'commodity production'.

3 Sahlins (1976) and Douglas and Isherwood (1979) are noticeable exceptions in anthropology. Elsewhere, Baudrillard (1981) and Preteceille and Terrail (1985) approach consumption in a neo-Marxist framework, whilst historians such as Bayly (1983: 57–63), McKendrick, Brewer and Plumb (1982) and Williams (1982) all make important contributions to the sociological understanding of consumption.

4 For other aspects of the fishing economy of Ambakandawila, see Stirrat 1974, 1975, 1989, n.d.

5 In a sense it could be argued that full time fishing is a result of the existence of a market economy. In Sri Lanka as well as other areas as disparate as Scotland and Africa, prior to the market economy it appears that fishermen were always also engaged in other productive activities.

6 After 1970 small fibreglass boats began to replace *theppans* in Ambakanda-wila. On the effects of technical innovation in Sri Lankan fisheries see Alexander 1975, Stirrat n.d.

7 The reason they bought so much fish is that they got bored eating the varieties they caught.

8 The situation is worth comparing with that in other fishing communities of the world. In Scotland during the late nineteenth and early twentieth centuries, women sold the fish and controlled the finances of the household (Thompson, Wailey and Lumnis 1983: 234–5). In Ghana, women sell their husbands' fish. Here they appear to have more autonomous power because of the matrilineal kinship system, but at the same time men can use other women as fish sellers if unhappy with their wives' performances (see Vercruijsse 1983, 1984).

9 For an example of an argument that men's control over women is predicated on male control over cash see Maher 1981.

10 At a different level, a similar hierarchical representation of the roles of male and female is apparent in a panegyric of Mrs Bandaranaike, the first and only female prime minister of Sri Lanka. This prophecies that, 'Very soon public management [i.e. government], like home management, should become a female occupation leaving us males the leisure and freedom to indulge in the speculations of science, poetry and philosophy wherein lies our spiritual emancipation'. (Mukerji 1960: ii)

11 Thus one reason that women never became full time traders is that their role as fish sellers was seen as an extension of their domestic duties. To move into full time trading would have been to move out of the 'domestic domain'. This contrasts with the situation in Ghana where a few women have become medium-size traders. Unlike in Ghana, it is not possible for an Ambakanda-wila man to use a non-kinsman to market his fish (cf. note 8).

12 'Purity' and 'pollution' remain major problems in Sri Lankan ethnography. Here is not the place to enter this quagmire.

13 On caste in Ambakandawila, see Stirrat 1982.

14 See the approach adopted by Taussig (1980) in his discussion of commoditi-sation in Latin America. However, his argument seems to me of limited relevance in the Sri Lankan context. What is striking in Sri Lanka is how easily accommodation has been reached with market exchange.

15 As far as the people of Ambakandawila were concerned, another reason for avoiding co-operation in production is that it was thought to involve a 'loss' as part of the proceeds from fishing had to be given up to another household.

16 Thus even the children of fishing families who had become teachers or clerks or whatever were teased over their airs and graces if they tried to assert their status through their life-styles. See Dennis, Henriques and Slaughter 1969 for a comparable case from industrial England.

17 Yalman (1967) has a lot to answer for in presenting a highly misleading but very influential picture of marriage in Sinhalese Sri Lanka as being a matter of 'alliance'.

18 'Dowry' in Ambakandawila could either involve 'pre-mortem inheritance' or it could take the form of 'groom-price'.
19 For a comparable case from Scotland, see Thompson, Wailey and Lumnis 1983: 236.

References

Alexander, P. 1975. 'Innovation in a cultural vacuum: the mechanization of Sri Lankan fisheries', *Human organisation*, 34: 333–4.
1982. *Sri Lankan fishermen*, Canberra, ANU.
Ardener, S. 1964. 'The comparative analysis of rotating credit institutions', *JRAI*, 94: 201–29.
Baudrillard, J. 1981. *For a critique of the political economy of the sign*, St Louis, Telos Press.
Bavinck, M. 1984. *Small fry. The economy of petty fishermen in northern Sri Lanka*, Amsterdam: Free University press.
Bayly, C. 1983. *Rulers, townsmen and bazaars*, Cambridge: Cambridge University Press.
de Silva, G. N. 1964. 'Socio-economic survey of fisher families 1958–59', *Bulletin of the Fisheries Research Station* (Colombo), 17: 1–44.
Dennis, N., Henriques, F. and Slaughter, C. 1969. *Coal is our life*, London, Tavistock Press.
Douglas, M. and Isherwood, B. 1979. *The world of goods*, London, Allen Lane.
Friedman, H. 1980. 'Concepts for the analysis of agrarian formations', *Journal of Peasant Studies*, 7: 158–84.
Geertz, C. 1962. 'The rotating credit association: a "middle rung" in development', *Economic Development and Cultural Change*, 10: 241–63.
Gregory, C. A. 1982. *Gifts and commodities*, London, Academic Press.
Hart, K. 1982. 'On Commoditisation', in E. N. Goody, ed., *From craft to industry*, Cambridge: Cambridge University Press.
McKendrick, N., Brewer, J. and Plumb, J. H. 1982. *The birth of a consumer society*, London, Europa Publications.
MacCormack, G. 1976. 'Reciprocity', *Man* (n.s.), 11: 89–103.
Maher, V. 1981. 'Work, consumption and authority within the household: a Moroccan case', in K. Young, C. Wolkowitz and R. McCullagh, eds, *Of marriage and the market*, London, CSE Books.
Mukerji, K. P. 1960. *Madame Prime Minister Sirimavo Bandaranaike*, Colombo, Gunasena.
Nelson, B. 1949. *The idea of usury*, Princeton: Princeton University Press.
Obeyesekere, G. 1963. 'Pregnancy cravings (Dola Duka) in relation to social structure and personality in a Sinhalese Village', *American Anthropologist*, 65: 323–42.
Preteceille, E. and Terrail, J. P. 1985. *Capitalism, consumption and needs*, Oxford, Blackwell.
Sahlins, M. 1976. *Culture and practical reason*, Chicago, University of Chicago Press.

Stirrat, R. L. 1974. 'Fish to market: traders in rural Sri Lanka', *South Asian Review*, 7: 189–208.

1975. 'The social organisation of production in a Sinhalese fishing village', *Modern Ceylon Studies*, 6: 140–62.

1977. 'Dravidian and non-Dravidian kinship terminologies in Sri Lanka', *Contributions to Indian Sociology*, 11: 271–93.

1982. 'Caste Conundrums', in D. McGilvray, ed., *Caste ideology and interaction*, Cambridge: Cambridge University Press.

1984. 'The riots and the Roman Catholic Church in historical perspective', in J. Manor, ed., *Sri Lanka in change and crisis*, London, Croom Helm.

1989. *On the beach*, Delhi, Hindustan.

n.d. 'Some implications of technical innovations in small scale fishing over the last two decades'. Paper presented at the Ceylon Studies Seminar Conference on the Post War Economic Development of Sri Lanka, Peradeniya, 1980.

Taussig, M. 1980. *The devil and commodity fetishism in South America*, Chapel Hill, University of North Carolina Press.

Thompson, P., Wailey, T. and Lumnis, T. 1983. *Living the fishing*, London, Routledge and Kegan Paul.

Tocqueville, A. de, 1956. (1835) *Democracy in America* (edited and abridged by R. D. Heffner), New York, New American Library.

Veblen, T. 1924. *The theory of the leisure class*, London, George Allen and Unwin.

Vercruijsse, E. 1983. 'Fishmongers, big dealers and fishermen: co-operation and conflict between the sexes in Ghanaian canoe fishing', in C. Oppong, ed., *Female and male in West Africa*, London, George Allen and Unwin.

1984. *The penetration of capitalism*, London, Zed Press.

Williams, R. H. 1982. *Dream worlds. Mass consumption in late nineteenth-century France*, Berkeley, University of California Press.

Yalman, N. 1967. *Under the bo tree*, Berkeley, University of California Press.

5

Cooking money: gender and the symbolic transformation of means of exchange in a Malay fishing community

JANET CARSTEN

Many writers have commented on what they conceive to be an apparent antipathy of Malays for money, commercial relations and even labour. This conception which has its roots in the colonial era[1] has led to a long debate centering on the nature or causes of a supposed 'economic retardation' among Malays and refutations of this charge.[2] While I do not wish to enter into the detail of this debate here, it is significant that much of it has centred around a perceived contrast between the Malay values and those of Chinese traders and middlemen with whom the former are in intense contact. (See, for example, Mahathir 1970, Freedman 1960.) The question of why it is that Chinese traders have managed to be highly successful in precisely the spheres which the Malays are conceived as having difficulty in penetrating has thus pushed the discussion towards a consideration of ethnic differences between Malays and Chinese.

There is an evident contrast between the kinship morality of the Malays and the business ethics of the Chinese. This has been documented by Lim (1981) for a Malay fishing village in Brunei. Lim argues that the moral emphasis of Malay fishermen is on mutual help based on kinship, while those of the Chinese traders centre on commercial relations and the profit motive. The Chinese, who are external to the moral community of the Malays, are thus ideally placed to play the commercial role which is antipathetical to the Malays themselves.

While this argument goes a long way towards explaining the widely observed importance of Chinese middlemen in Malay fishing communities (see Firth 1966, Lim 1981), it still leaves a number of questions unresolved with regard to the symbolic significance of money for Malays. In particular, the different relationship of men and women to money remains problematic. In a Malay fishing village on Pulau Langkawi from where the material presented in this chapter is drawn, as elsewhere in Malaysia and Brunei, men hand over their earnings to their wives who either exclusively manage or dominate in the economic running of the

117

household (see Rosemary Firth 1966: 27; Djamour 1959: 42; Lim 1981). We thus have a situation where men are the producers of money but it is women who almost exclusively handle it.

This brings us to a number of questions. Firstly, how is it possible to explain the fact that women are so closely involved in the handling of money, and men, having earned it, seem only too anxious to get rid of it. Secondly, following from this, it would seem that by giving money to women, men are relinquishing control and dominance to women, although this dominance is highly circumscribed, and does not, for example, extend to the political sphere. To what extent then is control over money linked to a dominance of women, and if it is, why are men willing to pass control to women in this way? And, further, we are led to consider the symbolic significance of money itself. For, if commercial relations are somehow antithetical to Malay kinship morality, how does giving money to women resolve the problem created by this antipathy. In the concluding section of this chapter an attempt will be made to answer these questions and to draw out the relationship between gender, money and ideas about the moral community.

In order to achieve this it is necessary first to trace out the uses of money – exchange, saving and consumption – in one particular community and to look at the processes of labour in which women and men engage. It will be argued that the household division of labour, practices of consumption, saving and inheritance all reveal a strong resistance to division within the house. Men earn money and fish outside the house in relations of exchange. These relations are conceived as being antithetical to the house and consanguineal kinship. The opposition between the unity of the house and the division represented by economic exchange between houses is played out in terms of gender symbolism. In its use money is mediated by women in and of the household. Just as they cook fish, women transform money from a means of exchange to a consumption good so that it ceases to threaten and actually sustains the household.

The island of Langkawi is situated off the west coast of Malaysia and administratively forms part of the state of Kedah. The village, on the south-west coast of the island, has a population of about 3,000 divided among several named hamlets. The main economic activity of the male inhabitants is fishing, although rice cultivation forms an important agricultural base. It may be helpful to briefly describe the household and its composition in Langkawi.

Perhaps the most important principle embodied by the household is that of unity and resistance to division. Household unity is expressed in a number of ways. It is reflected in the spatial arrangements of the house. In particular, the house never has more than one hearth, *dapur*.

However many couples reside together in one house, they always cook and eat together. And this commensality is a prime focus of what it means to be of one household. There is no gradual spatial separation of young couples before the establishment of a new household.

Another reflection of household unity is the close bond that should exist between siblings. Disputes between adult siblings are always highly threatening and are particularly disruptive when they occur. Appropriately enough, such disputes are particularly likely to arise over the division of household property – inheritance – and generally have far-reaching consequences for those involved. It is in order to safeguard the harmony of these relations that married siblings never co-reside. Members of a single household may be vertically disposed over two, three or four generations, or may consist of a single generation only, but there are no laterally extended households. This proscription is explicitly an attempt to avoid any conflict of interests that may arise between siblings through their obligations to their own nuclear families. That harmony between brothers and sisters should be so carefully safeguarded relates to the fact that siblings more than all other categories of kin represent household unity (as well as wider kinship relations and those with co-villagers). For it is the sibling group that has its origins in one house.

The importance of unity between siblings is reflected in a number of other ways. Marriages of a group of brothers and sisters should ideally take place in the order of their birth and this is particularly important between sisters. The in-marrying spouse who destroys the harmony within a group of siblings by marrying on whose older brother or sister is still unwed is said to 'step over the threshold', *lankah bendul*, in other words to violate the integrity of the house, and incurs a ritual fine. The close ties between sisters is apparent in their warm and affectionate relations as adults. Because of this close emotional bond, the mother's sister is regarded as a particularly appropriate foster mother for a child whose own mother has died or moved away.

Across the generations too, the tie between female consanguines is of major significance. Mothers and daughters tend to have close, intense relations, and daughters prefer to reside with their mothers than with mothers-in-law after marriage. Similarly, in old age, widows prefer to live with their married dauthers than sons. If the house represents unity, then this unity is created and upheld above all by female consanguines.

Marriage is the ideal and the norm for all adults. There are no bachelors or spinsters in the village and divorce or widowhood are generally followed by remarriage, even in old age. After marriage residence is rather mobile, villagers lay great emphasis on its uncertainty and unpredictability, and explicitly deny the existence of rules governing post-marital residence. This can be connected with a more general unwillingness to accord prior rights over a young couple to either the wife's or the husband's kin. However, a general pattern of residence may be discerned: initially a couple commute between the two parental households, spending periods of varying length in each; this is followed by a period of uxorilocality lasting until the couple have one or two children. After this a new household is often established in either the husband's or the wife's natal compound. This is often done prior to the marriage of a younger sibling to avoid the necessity of co-residence.

Most households in the village have about four or five members. Adult men and women do not live alone, nor do married couples before the birth of at least one child. The single person household is sterile, unproductive and asocial. Although households embody both the consanguineal and the affinal principle, the latter tends to be subsumed to the former. As is revealed by the frequency of divorce, the marital bond is potentially more fragile than those of consanguinity. Nor are new households established until this consanguineal principle has been asserted through the birth of children. It is through marriage and the birth of children that new sibling groups come into being and new households are established, households which embody the principle of consanguineal unity and indivision, and which are dominated by a core of related women.

Division of labour between household members

The two fundamental principles which govern the division of labour within the household are sex and age. The most clear division is that women do not go fishing and men do not generally engage in household labour. Agricultural labour is, to some extent, shared between the sexes. However, women predominate in all but the heaviest tasks. Age governs the extent to which the two sexes engage in their respective spheres of labour activity, both by imposing physical limitations and through the operation of an age-based hierarchy within the household.

Household labour

All household labour is performed by women. Men do not engage in the major tasks of household work which are shared between women of the same household. The sharing is not an equitable division but operates according to the principle of age hierarchy whereby older women do less work and only the more prestigious kinds.

Young girls are expected to help with household labour from an early age, although the amount they are expected to do gradually increases with age. During school years they perform tasks rather intermittently and generally only after some nagging from their elders. In contrast, young boys are not expected to help with these kinds of labour. Once she has left school a young girl, *anak dara*, is expected to apply herself to housework with great diligence. Her work is supervised by her mother and general conduct will be noted by visitors to the household.

It is not infrequent to find *anak dara* in their late teens or early twenties who perform the major part of all the household work while their mothers criticise and supervise their efforts, taking only a minimum role in the labour themselves. When there is more than one young female household member, they will share the main tasks of household labour between them. The division will not be formalised and will vary, depending on the age and capacity of the women concerned; but the more menial household tasks will generally be performed by the younger women. As a woman grows older, she will gradually resign household work to her adult daughters unless she is the only adult female in the household.

We can see, then, three main principles of organisation of household labour. The first is that it is shared between women of one house. All women, unless incapacitated by age or illness, participate in the labour of the household of which they are members. However, in the case of older women who co-reside with younger, the labour tends to be occasional and rather symbolic. The second principle, then, is that of an age-based hierarchy operating between women of one house. This is strongly expressed between generations and is also present, although in a weaker form, within generations – that is, between sisters or sisters and sisters-in-law. Thirdly, it is important to emphasise that household labour is performed separately by women of different households. Cooperative work does not take place in this sphere, although in exceptional circumstances, for example, illness or childbirth, neighbours from the same compound or close kin may give their assistance.

Agricultural labour

While household labour is exclusively female, and is shared only by women of one house, agricultural labour is undertaken by both women and men, and its organisation is often the subject of a variety of rather complex cooperative labour arrangements. There are two main spheres of agricultural labour: the wet rice fields and vegetable gardens. I shall discuss here only the more important of these: rice cultivation. However, the same broad principles apply to work in the vegetable gardens.

Rice labour

The different tasks of rice cultivation, associated with different phases in the crop's growth, are generally performed by either men or women but not by both together. However, the division of labour is flexible enough for it not to be unusual to see exceptions to this rule. The organisation and most of the labour itself are dominated by women, particularly by those in middle age who are no longer tied to the house by young children. Indeed, this division of labour between younger and older women is one of the marks of the dominance of the latter within the house. Work in the rice fields, *kerja bendang*, is generally preferred to housework, *kerja rumah*. Although older women sometimes claim that their daughters remain at home because they enjoy housework, this is usually strenuously denied in private by young women themselves.

The fact that rice production is predominantly female is partly a concomitant of men's involvement in fishing. In this respect women see a difference between themselves as the wives of fishermen, and women in mainland communities who are perceived as being more confined within the home. Women's dominance in the sphere of rice cultivation is not merely of practical significance. The centrality of rice in South-east Asian cultures is well documented. For Malays, not only is rice the basic staple and the most important constituent of all meals (in fact 'cooked rice' in Malay means food), it also plays a role in almost every ritual and, in the recent past, padi was itself the subject of a major set of rituals. The vital role of women in the cultivation of this economically crucial crop with its rich symbolic load provides us with one clue to the authority of women in Langkawi, and this authority in fact begins to rise at precisely the age when women are most active in the organisation of rice labour.

The rice seed is sown in nurseries by women. The work is generally done individually; however, women who are not planting a large area frequently use the same nursery. A charge may be levied but when those concerned are close kin and neighbours, as is usually the case, this is generally not paid.

Clearing and ploughing the padi fields is men's work and today is done with the aid of Japanese mini tractors, which are hired along with the labourers to use them. Once the land has been cleared, ploughed, fertilised and flooded, all tasks performed by men, it is ready for the seedlings. Preparation of the padi fields, then, the only phase of rice cultivation undertaken exclusively by men, has been almost completely commercialised, utilising hired labour and machinery.

Transplanting the seedlings from the nurseries to the padi fields is exclusively female labour. The work is occasionally done individually but generally women prefer to work in groups. After transplanting, rice plots must be kept free of weeds and the water levels checked. This mainte-nance is performed by men or women individually. The final stage of the rice cycle is the harvesting. While reaping is done exclusively by women, threshing is undertaken mainly, but not exclusively, by men.

Harvesting and threshing small plots are sometimes done by members of a single household working together, but in general larger labour groups consisting of up to twenty-five people, many of them from different households, are preferred. Harvesting, even more than transplanting, is a time of cooperative labour. The atmosphere during such work sessions is festive: the midday meal and break are minor informal celebrations where news and stories are exchanged. Children may be present, food is plentiful and good, it is eaten with particular relish; behaviour is highly informal and women and men tease each other and act without the constraint that is normal within the house. Women may dress up in each other's clothes, exchange jokes which are often heavy with sexual innuendo with each other and with men, and they laugh freely. It is no wonder, then, that women say they prefer to work in groups, that it is faster, pleasanter and less lonely, that way.

People in Langkawi distinguish several different ways of recruiting the collective labour that is used in transplanting and harvesting, and it is significant that both of these labour processes are dominated by women. Of these different categories one of the most widely used is *gotong pinjam* (literally, 'borrowed cooperation'). This is unpaid help given to kin, neighbours and friends on a single occasion, for example, one day of harvesting, for which no short-term reciprocation is required. In practice, labour reciprocation, though not precisely calculated, is often made within one planting and harvesting season. Those who are called upon to help are usually close consanguines, neighbours or affines. Often these categories overlap, and, in general, those involved are those with whom ego is closely involved and with whom exchanges of visits, food and services are frequent. There is often a noticeably high proportion of affinal kin in such groups.

A second important category of cooperative labour is *berderau*. Under this system a team of women (usually between two and thirty) work together for one season of planting and harvesting. They all transplant or harvest each member's crop in turn, exchanging labour on an equal basis on each person's land in rotation. Reciprocation always occurs therefore in the short term, and is rather precisely calculated. The composition of these groups does not present a great contrast with those of *gotong pinjam*. Once again close consanguines and affines are well represented. In the larger groups unrelated neighbours or more distant relatives are included, categories that would not normally be found in *gotong pinjam* groups.

Villagers say that in the past the *berderau* system was used more extensively than today and it does appear that the role of wage labour is increasing. As we have seen, it is particularly prevalent in the preparation of the fields for planting, the only exclusively male task of the rice cycle. Where hired labour is used for transplanting and harvesting, i.e., female tasks, it is often used together with the unpaid or partly paid labour of close kin.

Between reciprocated labour exchange and wage labour there is thus a further category of cooperation known as *upah pinjam* (literally, 'borrowed wages') whereby a proportion of the going wage rate is paid usually to distant kin or affines. Generally, those recruited in this way live outside the immediate neighbourhood of those who are paying them and are not involved in the intense exchange relationships that are characteristic between neighbours of one compound or between close kin or affines.

Although *upah pinjam* is strictly speaking wage labour, it in fact occupies an intermediate space between relations which are so close as to be quite incompatible with financial reimbursement for labour and those which are distant enough to tolerate a pure commercial content. Such intermediate relations are typically with distant consanguines and affines. In other words, they are with co-villagers. Wages paid for rice production are thus always qualified by kinship and community ties. Labour recruitment through *upah pinjam* and other arrangements which have a commercial element but are yet not fully commercialised and which rely heavily on the moral content of such ties show this very clearly.

Cultivation is almost entirely for household consumption. Female dominated rice production then involves household members, their closest consanguines and affines and co-members of the community in subsistence production which is for the household as an individual unit. While some aspects of production are partially commercialised, in particular, those in which men predominate, the degree of commercialisation is limited by the moral precepts of kinship and community. In all these aspects rice cultivation provides an almost complete contrast to fishing.

Fishing

I will summarise the basic principles concerning ownership of boats, division of earnings and recruitment to fishing crews in order to be able to sketch a comparison between male and female cooperation.

First and most important, women do not go fishing.[3] Menstruating women may bring misfortune to a fishing trip through their presence on the boat or by touching the nets. The effect of this belief is to exclude all women from marine fishing trips.

Men begin to fish after leaving school when the normal practice is to engage in migrant work on the mainland. Most young men leave the village and work on the big fishing trawlers that operate from the mainland Kedah coast. This phase of productivity is a prelude to marriage and the assumption of full adult status in the village. The young men's earnings which are crucial to this process are sometimes remitted to the parents and are defrayed against the expenses of marriage. It is significant that the greater part of this money is normally spent on rebuilding or extending a parental house at the time of a marriage.

After marriage, men reside and work in the village. It is a husband's duty to remain with his wife. Men fish in local waters in small boats, most but not all of which have inboard engines. Some of the fish caught are sold and consumed locally but the majority are bought by Chinese middlemen, *towkays*, and exported to Penang and Singapore. Fishing is thus highly commercialised and is not a subsistence occupation.

Most fishing crews consist of between two to four men, aged between early twenties and late forties – the most productive years for fishermen. The majority of fishing boats in the village are owned individually by single owner-users. Joint ownership is rare but a significant minority of boats are owned by the government fishing development agency which puts up the money, which the fisherman then repays in monthly instalments, eventually becoming the owner himself. The third type of boat ownership involves those owned by Chinese middlemen who usually take 50 percent of the earnings of the boat or buy the catch at half price. The rest is divided between the crew.

The heavy investment necessary to buy boats and nets is generally financed by loans – either from the government or from Chinese *towkays*. Thus, the category of single owner–users includes many fishermen who are repaying loans to Chinese *towkays*. In these cases the fisherman repays the loan gradually. Payments are made with fish rather than money, and the amounts vary with the catch. From the fisherman's point of view, a more flexible open arrangement with a Chinese *towkay* may seem more attractive than a government loan with scheduled repayments, especially as the former loan is 'interest free' in contrast to the latter.

Fishermen who are repaying loans to Chinese *towkays* are involved in a long-term contractual relationship. They sell all their catch to the *towkay* at a fixed price which is usually 5 to 10 per cent less than the market price. The fisherman is described as being *terikat*, 'tied', 'bound', to the *towkay* who in return distributes various 'favours'. He may agree to defer a repayment during a poor fishing period, use his connections to negotiate a good price on new equipment, give further loans for repairs to the boat or engine, or may loan his own boat when that of the fisherman has broken down. It is clear that such 'favours' in fact serve to perpetuate the relationship until the fisherman is bound in a web of debts and obligations, and this fact is clearly perceived by the fishermen themselves. The relationship between *towkay* and fisherman may even be passed from father to son. When a young man begins to fish on his own, the most likely person to look to for a loan to finance new capital will be the *towkay* of his father with whom there is already an established relationship.[4]

The distribution of earnings between crew members, the captain, and the boat owner if different from the latter, varies according to the kind of fishing and the particular crew.[5] However, in all cases one basic principle applies: apart from each person's earnings, a separate share is calculated for the boat, this is the *syir bot* which accrues to the boat owner. From it he pays for fuel, the cost of maintenance of the boat and, in many cases, repayments on loans. As much as possible of the boat share is saved separately against future expenses on fishing equipment. It is not used for general household expenses.

The usual practice is for the earnings to be divided in half. One half is the boat share and the other is divided equally between crew members, including the captain. Apart from their cash earnings, fishermen also divide up a small proportion of the day's catch between them. In contrast to their money earnings, however, the shares of fish are precisely calculated so that each member of the crew, including the captain, takes an exactly equal portion of the catch home with them.

While participants state that the particular division of cash is fixed for each fishing crew and type of operation, it is in fact subject to substantial variation depending on the size of the catch. Almost all the owners reduce the boat share when the catch is small. In the majority of cases I was told that if the earnings were very low – as often happens – they would be equally divided so that on these occasions the income of the owner was the same as that of the other crew members. Periods of successful fishing would maximise income differences between the two categories of fishermen, while periods of low productivity would be associated with greater equality of income.[6] Reductions in the boat share are particularly likely to occur when (a) the captain is also the owner and (b) when he and the crew members are closely related, generally through kin ties. The tendency to reduce the boat share reveals very clearly the tension involved in engaging in purely commercial relations with Malay co-villagers, especially when they are close kin.

Informants comment that in recruiting fishing crews there is a clear preference for non-kin. The relationship between crew members is temporary, flexible and mobile; there is a rather rapid turnover in the personnel of fishing crews, with people frequently participating for a matter of months or even weeks. This mobility coupled with the highly commercial nature of the relationship is ill-adapted to the kind of behaviour ideally associated with close kin – relations which are built above all on a notion of permanence and reciprocity.

The overriding commercial nature of the relationship is underlined not only by the precise calculation of earnings and the temporary nature of crews, but even in the way that fishermen eat together on the boat. Or rather, in the way that they do not eat together, for instead, each fisherman brings his own individual portion of rice and takes his meal separately and without sharing. Eating rice together is a potent symbol of household and kin unity which does not occur on a fishing boat. Fishermen, it seems, are neither of one house nor even of one boat. After a successful day's fishing the captain may treat the crew in the coffee shop but this food consists of drinks and snacks, not a full rice meal. It is neither eaten in the boat nor in the house and, most important, it is bought. If it is paid for by the captain, *tuan bot*, this further underlines the hierarchy of the relationship. It is worth contrasting these commensal patterns with those already described for cooperative work parties in rice production. In the latter case, when kin and neighbours work together, they eat a full rice meal together in the most festive and informal atmosphere. The meal is indeed the climax of the occasion.

Fishermen frequently spoke of the dangers which might result from having kinsmen as crew members: any disputes arising from the commercial activity of fishing would have severe repercussions on harmonious relations between kin. The manner in which this subject was discussed was reminiscent of the way fears were expressed on the subject of marriages between kin. In the latter case the potential for disputes between the married couple having a wider significance for relations between kin was seen as an important factor working against kin endogamy. In much the same way it seems that a highly commercialised relationship is unsuitable amongst kinsmen – there is simply too great a risk of disputes arising and disrupting the community.

The low proportion of kin in fishing crews, which is also documented for Malays in other areas,[7] relates to another aspect of relations between crew members which makes them problematic for some categories of close kin. The relationship between the *tuan bot* and his crew is a highly hierarchical one. Not only does the *tuan* receive an income which is at times substantially higher than that of his crew, but his behaviour during fishing trips clearly reveals his superior status. The *tuan bot* continually gives orders to the crew and supervises the work of its members. He is responsible for the route the boat takes, the timing of the casting of the nets and for all other aspects of the labour process as well as the division of the earnings at the end of the day. He is in many ways in the position of boss.

The strongly egalitarian nature of social relations in Langkawi, and the attempt to cast all relations as far as possible in a non-hierarchical mode is very marked. This is particularly true of relations within the same generation where this is a narrow age difference and there is no overriding difference of status.

Where kin ties are recorded within the fishing crew the most frequent are those between father and son or between brothers. The former relation is always a hierarchical one, while the latter tends to take this form when there is a large age difference between the brothers. In other words, although fishing together is best done with those who are completely unrelated, the activity *is* compatible with one form of kin relation: that between kin who already have a clearly hierarchical relationship – father and son or older and young brother. It is highly problematic in a relation of amicable equality such as that between first cousins, and it is notable that cousins are rarely found together in fishing crews.

As in other spheres, we see that the avoidance of disputes, especially between affines, is one of the most important factors in determining recruitment to fishing crews. Relations within the crew are preferably with those with whom a dispute would be least disruptive – non-kin, or with categories of close kin where there is a relatively great ability to avoid such disputes because of an 'inbuilt' tolerance of hierarchy and where the closeness itself inhibits the possibility of relations breaking.

Not only do crews preferably consist of non-kin, but many of the above characteristics of fishing are categorically in opposition to ideals of behaviour between kin. In a community united by a web of consanguineal and affinal ties and in which there is, moreover, a concern to conduct relations on an egalitarian basis, fishing is in many senses 'anti-community' as well as 'anti-kinship'. It is therefore perhaps unsurprising that there has been traditionally a tendency to enter relationships in this sphere with the Chinese who remain outside the social and moral community of the Malays.

Finally, it is possible to draw out the contrast between fishing and rice cultivation. We have seen that the former, carried out exclusively by men, is conducted on an entirely different basis from the latter which is female-dominated. Whereas rice is grown almost entirely as a subsistence crop for the household, fishing is the most important means of acquiring cash; it is a highly commercialised activity. While rice production involves cooperation with close consanguineal and affinal kin as well as more distant relatives and co-villagers, fishing is carried out either individually or, ideally, with unrelated men. Cooperation between women in rice production for cash, when undertaken, typically involves equal sharing of earnings, whereas we have seen that income from fishing is highly differentiated and the labour process itself is one in which orders are given and taken.

If fishing can be seen as in some way 'anti-household' and 'anti-community' and this is symbolised by the non-commensal relations of men of one boat, rice cultivation, by contrast, can be seen as precisely embodying many household and community values. And this is neatly summed up by the fact that cooperative labour groups always eat a full rice meal, *makan nasi*, together – indeed this is the high point of the working day. We can now begin to understand why it is that women are completely excluded from fishing – an activity which embodies a negation of all the values with which they are most closely associated. Perhaps even more significantly, we can also see why it is that men are *not* explicitly excluded from rice production, why they *must* be included in this activity. For the contrast between male economic relations and those which underlie predominantly female cooperation in rice cultivation is not only interesting in itself, but is highly significant when we consider the notion of community and its basis in social relations. It is out of the kind of cooperation which women engage in that at least one notion of community can be seen to derive. And yet, as we shall see, the fact that this notion is a 'female' one is often problematic. Men's inclusion or reintegration into this notion of community is always finally necessary.

Income

Without going into the details of household income here, it is clear from the division of labour between household members that almost all cash income is earned by men – in their youth as migrant workers and later through local fishing. Women's ability to earn money is extremely limited: small amounts may be earned through the sale of home-made cakes and snacks, from collecting bivalves from the rocks along the sea shore and from the sale of eggs, fruit and vegetables. However, such produce tends to be consumed at home rather than sold for profit. Cash income from these sources is both limited in amount and occasional. As supplements to the diet these contributions are highly valued. More so than any other is the basic staple and most ideologically significant crop, rice. Almost no households in the village produce a big enough rice surplus to sell but perhaps one third manage to achieve self-sufficiency. In this way women's labour provides a major contribution to household income and provides perhaps one clue to the basis for their domestic authority.

It is important to emphasise here that women neither engage in the processing nor the marketing of fish. Nor, indeed, do women in the village engage in trade in any major way, as they do elsewhere in Malaysia.[8] Most of the sundry shops in the village (and the main town of the island) are Chinese owned and run. In fact it is notable that, even when selling such items as home-made snacks, women tend to use men or children of the household as intermediaries. In this way the material presented here provides a direct contrast to that of Stirrat for a Sri Lankan fishing village (see chapter 4) where women and the market are closely associated. I will return to this point in the conclusion.

Household budgeting: expenditure and saving

Although it is men who provide most of the household's cash income, it is women who have the major role in running the household finances. At the end of the day, when men return from fishing, they turn over their day's earnings to their wives, keeping only a small amount of 'coffee money', *duit kopi*, for themselves. As well as the money that men hand over to their wives, they also give them the fish which they have brought home. The fish will be cooked by women in the kitchen and eaten later in the day.

Although I knew of cases of husbands who were known to keep money back from their wives, in general these cases were exceptions. When a fisherman returns home after a day's work his wife will ask him how much he has earned and expects to be given the day's earnings. Men are expected to ask their wives for money when they need it and, just as the husband who keeps money back from his wife is frowned upon, so is the wife who does not give money to her husband when he asks for it. Both forms of behaviour occur but are likely to cause disputes. Income earned by either a husband or a wife is regarded as belonging to the couple jointly and equally. Husbands and wives do not maintain separate funds or save separately. Cash handed over by a husband to the wife is thus administered by her but belongs to both of them.

While spending patterns may vary from household to household, certain principles clearly emerge. The most obvious point is that household budgeting operates on a daily basis. Almost all necessities are bought in small quantities every one or two days and these take up the major part of a household's income. All regular items of household expenditure are administered by women. It is they who thus have control over the day to day running of the household economy and this in fact means the greater part of decisions over expenses. Although women control the way money is spent, they often send children or men of the household to do the actual buying in a manner which is reminiscent of their reluctance to engage in direct sale for cash.

Major decisions over expenditure are usually arrived at after joint discussion by wife and husband (or the main income earner of the household). While in some households men may take a more active role in decision making, I know of no case in which a woman was totally passive in the running of household affairs. They may share important decision making with a husband or father but they never completely resign their control over the household economy. Women's authority continues to rise with age long after men's has begun to decline. This means that in old age a wife's control of the household economy is at its peak, while her husband, by contrast, no longer active in fishing, is in a state of almost childlike economic dependency in which he must ask his wife for pocket money if he wishes to visit the coffee shop.

When more than one adult couple reside together, decision making and accounting can become more complex since it is the married couple that is the basic economic unit of the household. We have seen that the earnings of husband and wife are regarded as joint property, *benda syarikat*. As long as the co-resident couples continue to be economically self-sufficient they always maintain their own funds and save separately. This also applies to unmarried young men, who, as we saw, are substantial income earners. These young men, however, although they spend more freely than married men, nevertheless do not save money on their own behalves. Instead, they give their surplus to their mothers or sisters for saving.

Once a couple has ceased to be self-sufficient, the economic separation within the household will no longer be maintained. For example, in one household, consisting of a married couple of which the husband no longer went out fishing and their married daughter, almost all expenses were met by the young son-in-law's earnings as a fisherman. The household operated out of one fund, all earnings were pooled. In contrast, another household I knew well was maintaining three separate funds, that of the parents (still self-sufficient), a married son and his wife and an unmarried son. All three economic units saved separately and the household also kept three totally separate savings pools for the running expenses of three fishing boats.

So far we have seen that cash enters the household economy mainly through the individual efforts of men; once there it becomes part of the joint property of a married couple. The married couple is the smallest unit which can make up a household. As long as couples living together in one house continue to be economically self-sufficient they could potentially form a viable household unit by themselves. The maintenance of separate savings can be seen, then, as a way of avoiding a potential conflict of interests within the house and of facilitating separation of resident couples should disputes occur.

The separation and division represented by highly individuated earnings and, for households with more than one conjugal unit, only partially unified household funds, is negated in the way money is spent. We have already seen that the notional centre of the house is the single undivided *dapur*, kitchen, hearth, stove. It is highly significant that while couples may save separately from each other, the precise division of everyday household expenses, which are actually called *belanja dapur*, literally 'kitchen expenses', is explicitly left uncalculated. Thus, although I was able to obtain detailed accounts of household expenditure with great ease, it was extremely difficult to get accurate information on how much money had been spent by individual household members and on what.

Women in all these households would say the division of daily expenses was not calculated, 'whoever has money goes to buy'. 'Whoever has money spends.'[9]

In this way the individuation represented by money earned through fishing is negated by the interposition of women. We have seen how fishing is in many ways opposed to the principles which the house represents. When money enters the house it is first transferred from men to women, and, secondly, it is de-individualised, becoming the property of the married couple. Thirdly, this de-individualisation is pushed further in the way that money is spent by women on household expenses, *belanja dapu*. Division within the household is deliberately played down; there is one *dapur* to the house and its running expenses are, at least in theory, met by all adult household members collectively. 'Whoever has money spends', in other words, individual ability to pay is unmarked, differentiation between household members and between couples is minimised. Earnings may be tainted by ideas opposed to kinship, by commercial and individualistic values, but in their passage through the house, the central symbol of kin unity, and through the hands of women, they become imbued with the ideals of kinship and thus 'socialised'. The negative, anti-social power of money is thus neutralised through the action of women associated with the house.

If spending and consumption seem to be as far as possible undifferentiated within the house, saving is not necessarily confined within one house. There is one form of saving which in fact involves cooperation between houses. As we shall see, it is in fact aimed less at the accumulation of money and more at a kind of generalised consumption focusing on the house, and especially on the very heart of the house, the *dapur*, and which involves many houses in a kind of chain of generalised consumption.

As we have seen, married couples save jointly: one household may have more than one post office savings account for each couple's personal savings as well as for the running expenses of any fishing boat owned by household members. Apart from these accounts and cash kept in the house, there is another method of saving which operates according to different principles. This is the rotating saving society, *kut*.[10] This institution is dominated by women and is a further example of women's power to negate the 'anti-kinship' and 'anti-social' aspects of money. In this case, however, the 'socialisation' of money goes further for it involves not just the single household but neighbours, kin and affines – the wider community.

The *kut* is a mode of saving which usually involves about ten to twenty women, organised by one woman known as the *kepala kut* – head of the *kut*. Each member of the society contributes a fixed sum of money which is usually collected weekly by the *kepala kut*. Each week one member of the *kut* receives the total amount of money collected from all members. Often a small sum is deducted from this and kept as a commission by the *kepala*. The order in which the different members receive the total sum is fixed by drawing lots or by mutual agreement at the beginning of the *kut*'s existence.

The *kut* may be terminated after each member has received the total collection once – or it may begin again. There are cases of *kut* which endure for many months in this way although some terminate after only one cycle. Some *kut* are a means of collecting cash but in the majority of cases money is raised for a specific purpose, such as buying crockery, cooking pots or other household articles, each member receiving the same article in rotation.

Although the amounts involved in each contribution are usually small, many women are members of several associations. This means that the total amounts of money paid to *kut* per month can be quite significant. It also means that even if the membership of different *kut* overlap, each woman's participation in several involves her in relations with a wide circle of other women. In terms of the total amounts of money and the numbers of people involved, these associations are, then, highly significant in the community.

It is important to stress that these organisations are run by and for women. They either raise cash for the purpose of buying household articles or these articles are directly acquired. However, these goods are not just associated with the household in general, they are often closely associated with cooking and eating and with the *dapur* (for example, cooking pots, crockery, trays, glasses).

When women were asked about how members of the *kut* were recruited, they always mentioned the importance of being able to trust, *caya*, other members of the *kut*. The persons involved must be reasonable and reliable, capable of committing themselves to giving a fixed sum every week over a period of several months. Equally, the members must trust the *kepala* to administer the *kut* honestly and responsibly.

Kepala kut prefer to recruit *orang dekat*, literally 'close people', as members. This means neighbours and relatives; geographic closeness is partly a matter of convenience, since it makes the collection of contributions easier. But as one *kepala* emphasised when discussing this, *orang dekat jadi adik-beradik juga*, 'neighbours too become (are like) kin'. In other words, the closeness of relations with others is based as much on locality as on kinship. It is in fact the overlapping and cross-cutting of the categories of neighbour and kin that is at the heart of the intense exchanges between people of one neighbourhood.[11]

Analysing the kin relations between the *kepala kut* and other *kut* members, as well as any kin ties between the members themselves, I found that out of 170 women involved in 11 *kut*, only 16 were unrelated to any other *kut* member. In other words, the mutual trust between members of a *kut* has its basis above all in kinship; the large majority of members are kin either of the *kepala* or of other members. The most frequent kinship links in these associations are those between first cousins, between aunts and nieces, mother and daughter and between sisters. In other words, *kut* members tend to be united by close consanguineal lines. There is a relatively low proportion of affinal connections between *kut* members which can be related to qualitative aspects of relationships between female affines. Briefly, these relationships are often tense and strained and women tend to prefer to cooperate with their consanguines rather than with affines in many contexts of their daily life.

If we recall the principles of recruitment to fishing crews discussed above, the difference between male and female association for economic purposes becomes even more clear. We saw earlier how there is a preference for non-kin in fishing crews and that nearly two-thirds of all fishermen are in fact unrelated to other members of their crew. The principles of recruitment to those two forms of cooperation offer a very clear contrast in this respect. In the one case non-kin are ideal members of a temporary, commercial, hierarchically-based association and this is explicitly to avoid the possibility of disputes with kin; in the other it is kin who can be trusted and relied upon in a relationship which, although economic, has a strong social and moral content.

If the categories of kin which regularly occur in the two forms of organisation are compared we find a further contrast. In fishing groups, the prevalence of the father/son tie was linked to the relation of dominance which the *tuan bot* has with the crew members and the fact that this is difficult to accommodate to more egalitarian kin relations. Between the *kepala kut* and members, however, it is ties between first cousins and between aunt and niece which are more frequent than any other. The more egalitarian kin relations dominate in an association whose hierarchical content, even between *kepala* and ordinary members, is minimal. The *kut* is an association of equals in which the head is, essentially, an organiser without significant power, and the benefits are reaped by all members in rotation. The commission levied by the head is either non-existent or minimal. Significantly, then, it is precisely the categories of kin that are totally absent in fishing crews that are the most frequently represented in the *kut*.

While both forms of association show fewer affinal connections than consanguineal ones, and this has been related to the tension involved in the former, it appears that there are a higher proportion of affinal relations between *kepala kut* and members than within fishing crews. This can be linked to the previous point – that it is more easy to maintain these kind of fragile or tense relations within an egalitarian context than in a hierarchical one. Whereas such relations might be directly threatened by the kind of cooperation involved in fishing, they may actually be strengthened by that of the rotating saving society.

The *kut*, then, is another example of how women's economic cooperation is embedded in relations of kinship and in this respect is very different from its male counterpart. Once again, money is removed from the context in which it is earned by men, an individualistic and commercial one, and circulates through the activity of women in associations which have their basis in kinship and locality and which involve the participants in economic exchange which is firmly based on the morality of kinship and community. Once again 'individual male money' becomes 'shared-female-kin-money'.[12]

We have also seen that although the *kut* and institutions like it tend to be characterised by the actors themselves and by anthropologists as saving or credit associations (see Ardener 1964: 217), in Langkawi they are in fact focused on consumption of household articles, in particular, articles associated with the *dapur*. But, significantly, this consumption is shared between houses rather than involving one individual household. Houses or hearths are linked together in a chain of equal and shared consumption of the same articles. And, in this way, there is an avoidance of an association between the house and the accumulation of money, i.e., of values which somehow negate the house. In other words, just as in budgeting and day-to-day expenditure there is an attempt to avoid the divisive and individuating effects of money, this is also present in the way money is saved, which, in the last analysis, is here only a deferred and generalised form of consumption involving many houses.

Conclusion

I have argued that there is an opposition between male and female labour. Whereas women share labour between them within the house and cooperate extensively in labour groups in the cultivation of rice on an equal basis, men form fishing groups that, ideally, are not based on the household or kinship links and in which relations are hierarchical, short term and commercialised. Further, while women's labour is almost exclusively within the subsistence sphere, it is fishing which is the main cash earning activity in the village. Men bring money into the house where it is handed over to women who control the day-to-day running of household expenses. Expenditure and saving are unmarked and de-individualised as far as possible within the house. Women save in associations of kin and neighbours which once again operate on an egalitarian basis. In this way women create an association of households, a community, through the circulation of money for the purpose of the household, in other words, of domestic consumption.

We can begin to see that men and women have a very different relationship to money respectively. In the introduction to this paper reference was made to Lim's account of a Malay fishing village in Brunei, where women seem to occupy a very similar position to that of women in Langkawi, controlling daily household expenditure. Lim argues that the commercial relations of fishing are opposed to the values of reciprocity and equality and the kinship morality of the Malay community. Money itself is 'hot' and in some sense anti-social (Lim 1981: 203). Thus far our arguments are essentially the same. Lim, however, goes on to state that 'The men also see their village as a community of men, as most village affairs in reality are the men's concern. Women in general are isolated and removed from the central stage and often banished to the kitchen' (ibid.: 204).

As far as men are concerned, he argues, women are outsiders to the Malay community. In this capacity the polluting and anti-social qualities of money can be banished to the world of women. In contrast, I would suggest that women, being central to the Malay house, Malay kinship, and the Malay community, have the ability to purify money, to socialise it and invest it with the values and morality with which they themselves are most closely associated. Divided male money becomes united kin money through the interposition of women in the house.

How can we reconcile these two perspectives? From one point of view they can be seen perhaps as reflections of the gender of the individual field worker, or more significantly, of his or her informants. For one aspect of this issue is that through working in a society which is to a large degree sex-segregated, Lim has elicited a 'men's view', while the model I have outlined can be glossed as a 'women's view'. This however, only raises the more fundamental question of the place of women in the Malay kinship system and community, and, further, the very notion of community begins to be revealed as problematic.

We have seen that economic activities take different forms for men and women respectively. Women associate with others of the same household, with kin and neighbours; they emphasise hierarchy in their relations with close kin across the generations, but equality on a wider cooperative basis. Above all, they avoid purely commercial relations and it is important to remember that women in Langkawi do not usually trade. Men on the other hand, tend not to engage economically with their close kin but form more commercialised exchange relations in the wider community, particularly evident in fishing groups and in their relations with the Chinese.

Rather than seeing Malay women as outsiders to their own community, it is possible to see that there is a basis for more than one notion of community. On the one hand, there is the model of community based on exchange relations, for example through fishing crews, in the coffee shop or in marital exchanges. This model stresses differentiation, competition and alliance; it is potentially divisive and liable to disruption. This is the model which underlies the male political community, men's relations in the coffee shop, the fishing economy and the predominantly male Muslim community centred on the mosque. It is also present, although in a more problematic and ambivalent way, in the manner in which men and women exchange brides and grooms in marriage.

The second model is one based on the household. This unit is dominated by a group of consanguineally related women. Men are, to a great extent, marginal to it. In all contexts what is stressed within the house is unity and indivision. This appears clearly in the down-playing of individual ownership of property within the house, and in the enormous problems caused by inheritance, resulting both in an avoidance of discussion of the topic and in a tendency to defer inheritance until long after a particular death has occurred. Division within the house, demarcation and differentiation are avoided because they are antithetical to the principles on which the house is founded. In terms of kinship relations this is expressed in the close ties between female consanguines and in the great emphasis placed on close and harmonious ties between a group of siblings who have their origin in one house.

At the core of the house there is, as we have seen, the single, undivided *dapur* where the full rice meal is cooked by women and eaten by co-resident household members. Thus, the *dapur* and commensality are at the centre of what it means to be of one house. This model of community, then, is that of a collection of similar households, dominated by women, united internally by close consanguineal ties which receive expression in commensality.

These two models of community are not isolated from each other. Men participate as household members in the 'female-household' model. Finally, men are also part of the female community and this is clear in the way work parties for rice cultivation operate and also in the context of communal feasts. Thus money earned by men and associated with inequality and competition becomes problematic for them. Just as fish are given to women to be cooked in the *dapur*, so money, the equivalent of fish, can be transformed by being handed over to women in the house for 'cooking' and then consumed. The *dapur* is not just the place where raw fish is cooked by women and eaten by the household, it is the site of a many-faceted act of transformation, or 'cooking', performed by women, on fish, on money, and even on themselves, as in the well known Malay rituals that follow childbirth, where women are actually heated over a fire or hearth.[13] The *dapur* is the centre of the house and the central location of these transformations.

Women, then, purify or socialise money, endowing it with the values of kinship morality, by cooking it in the *dapur*. By so doing they transform the one kind of community, based on differentiation, exchange and alliance, and primarily male, into the other, based on the notion of a collection of similar female-dominated houses.

We can now understand that the symbolism of money is not just that of a means of exchange (although it is that too, at least for men) but more importantly, it is that of a consumption good. Women's close association with money is founded on consumption. In spending money for the house women reproduce the household. Further, in organising the *kut*, women actually create a community of households, a female community, by linking houses together in a chain of *dapur*-centred consumption.

There is thus both a female and a male meaning for money, just as there is a predominantly male and a predominantly female model of community. And this female version of money can itself help in understanding the notion of the female community. We can also see why it is that women in Langkawi avoid trading while yet associating themselves so closely with money. For money as a symbol of exchange is particularly male, and only as a symbol of consumption is it associated with women. In order to be able to transform the one into the other, women must isolate themselves from the former.

The contrast with the Sri Lankan case mentioned above (Stirrat, chapter 4) now becomes clear. There women are the channel through which the ideology of the market enters the village. Women's close association with the market and the further association that is made between money and pollution enables men to isolate themselves from the competitive and disruptive effects of commoditisation in the community. In Langkawi, as we have seen, although women are closely associated with money, it is precisely from money as a means of exchange that women isolate themselves. Thus it is women who transform and overcome the competitive and disruptive relations of the market.

While it is possible to build up a series of oppositions between

women	and	men
cooperation		individualism, competition,
kinship, the house,		commerce, achieved
ascribed relations		relations
unity		division

which seems to culminate with that of community/anti-community, these oppositions are not as straightforward as they perhaps appear; the final one does not lead to a resolution of the problem of the nature of the

Malay community, but instead must lead to a closer examination of the concept of community itself. For the world of men, achieved relations, commerce and competition is not in any straightforward way antithetical to the community, it is itself in fact an aspect of this notion. Nor can it be satisfactory to exclude one half of the population – men or women – from 'the community'. Rather we can see that there is a basis for more than one notion of community, corresponding to three terrains of labour which were examined at the beginning of this paper.

Firstly, there is the household and the unity of consanguineally related women within it, who perform household labour together. Secondly, on a wider basis, there is the unity of female kin, neighbours and affines of different households who are mobilised in agricultural labour and in saving associations. Finally, there is male cooperation in fishing: achieved, anti-kin, commercial, competitive. These three spheres of labour can be seen as the building blocks of community in its different aspects. However, these aspects are not isolated from each other, or they are only partially so. Finally, as was clear in the operation of work parties of rice cultivation, men, at least, are reintegrated into the 'female community'.

In handing money over to women, men avoid the divisive dangers of a community as a group of potential rivals, engaged in complex, tense and competitive exchange relations. By cooking fish or money in the *dapur*, women transform this kind of community into one based on the idea of a family meal dominated by consanguineally related women, a collection of like households.

Notes

The fieldwork on which this paper is based was conducted on the island of Langkawi, Malaysia between October 1980 and April 1982. It was funded by the SSRC (now ESRC). Additional funds were provided by the Central Research Fund of the University of London. I should like to thank Maurice Bloch, Lady Rosemary and Sir Raymond Firth, Akis Papataxiarchis and Jonathan Parry for their comments on earlier drafts.

1 See Swettenham 1955: 134; Clifford 1927: 19, cited in Lim 1981:23.
2 See Firth 1950; 1966: 82, 96; Parkinson 1967; Wilder 1968; Senu Abdul Rahman 1971; Mahathir 1970; Alatas 1977.
3 This is also true elsewhere in Malaysia, see Raymond Firth (1966: 105).
4 See Raymond Firth's references to the *daganang* system for a similar description (1966: 60–2, 377–84.)
5 See Raymond Firth (1966: 235–57, 318–29) on the complexities of the distribution of earnings among east coast fishermen and the difficulties of acquiring such data. I did not conduct detailed research into this area. The following information is therefore only a rough guide to the principles involved.

6 Scarlett Epstein (1967: 241ff) has described a similar correlation between agricultural yields and rewards in rural South India.

7 See, for example, Firth (1966: 105) for the non-kin based composition of fishing crews on the east coast; and Fraser (1966: 34–5) for Malays in southern Thailand.

8 See Strange's (1980) description of women's involvement in the processing of fish, and hawking in Trengganu as well as that of Rosemary Firth (1966) and Raymond Firth (1966).

9 In contrast Rosemary Firth (1966: 17) notes that it is 'quite easy for different groups to live under the same roof, and conduct quite separate cooking and budgeting activities'. However, her own data (pp. 17–21) make clear the diversity of procedure over separate budgeting with certain resources being pooled. She continues, 'The eating of meals on all ordinary occasions is not the social affair it is with us, and food is frequently eaten in solitude.' In Langkawi I would argue that separate saving and budgeting do occur but only to a limited extent within the household. And it is precisely in cooking and eating that the division is negated.

10 This is short for *kutipan*, a 'collection', 'subscription', or *kutipan duit* from *duit*, 'money'. See Ardener (1964) for a comparative survey of such institutions.

11 Jay (1969: 418) also notes that in rural Java the core membership of credit associations are based on the neighbourhood. As in Langkawi, they are also organised by women. However, in contrast to Java (Geertz 1962) and Minahasa (Lundstrom-Burghoorn 1981), where members of such organisations hold regular meetings which constitute elaborate social occasions, in Langkawi such meetings are not held and frequently children are sent round to collect the contributions.

12 Similar, Jay (1969: 419) has shown that the concept of mutual aid in these organisations is derived from that which pertains to close kin and neighbours.

13 Space does not allow an analysis of these rituals here. Briefly, I argue elsewhere (Carsten 1987) that these rites, which focus on the production of children in marriage, can be seen as a transformation or cooking of affinity into consanguinity.

References

Alatas, S. H. 1977. *The myth of the lazy native*, London: Frank Cass.

Ardener, Shirley 1964. 'The comparative study of rotating credit associations', *JRAI*, 94 (2): 201–29.

Carsten, J. F. 1987. 'Women, kinship and community in a Malay fishing village on Pulau Langkawi, Malaysia, PhD thesis, University of London.

Clifford, Hugh 1927. *In court and kampong*, London: Grant Richards.

Djamour, J. 1959. *Malay kinship and marriage in Singapore*, London School of Economics Monographs on Social Anthropology No. 21, London: Athlone Press.

Epstein, Scarlett 1967. 'Productive efficiency and customary systems of rewards in rural South India', in *Themes in Economic Anthropology*, ed., Raymond Firth, London: Tavistock.

Firth, Raymond 1950. 'The peasantry of South East Asia', *International Affairs*, 26: 503–14.

1966. (2nd edn.), *Malay fishermen: their peasant economy*, London: Routledge and Kegan Paul.

Firth, Rosemary 1966. 2nd edn. *Housekeeping among Malay peasants*, London School of Economics Monographs of Social Anthropology No. 7, London: Athlone Press.

Fraser, T. M. 1966. *Fishermen of South Thailand*, New York: Holt, Rienhardt and Winston.

Freedman, M. 1960. 'The growth of a plural society in Malaya', *Pacific Affairs*, 23 (2): 158–68.

Geertz, C. 1962. 'The rotating credit association: a "middle rung" in development', *Economic Development and Cultural Change*, 10: 241–63.

Jay, Robert R. 1969. *Javanese villagers: social relations in rural Modjokuto*, Cambridge, Mass.: MIT Press.

Lim, J. S. 1981. 'The interrelationship of technology, economy and social organization in a fishing village in Brunei, M.Phil. thesis, University of London.

Lundstrom-Burghoorn, W. 1981. *Minahasa civilization: a tradition of change*, Gothenburg Studies in Social Anthropology No. 2, University of Gothenburg.

Mahathir, Mohamad 1970. *The Malay dilemma*, Singapore.

Parkinson, Brian K. 1967. 'Non-economic factors in the economic retardation of the rural Malays', *Modern Asian Studies* 1 (1): 31–46.

Senu Abdul Rahman 1971. *Revolusi mental*, Kuala Lumpur: UMNO.

Strange, H. 1980. 'Some changing socio-economic roles of rural Malay women', in *Asian women in transition*, eds. Sylvia Chipp and Julia Green, pp. 123–51, University Park, Pa.: Pennsylvania University Press.

Swettenham, F. A. 1955. *British Malaya*, London: Allen and Unwin.

Wilder, W. D. 1968. 'Islam, other factors and Malay backwardness: comments on an argument', *Modern Asian Studies*, 3 (2): 155–64.

6

Drinking cash: the purification of money through ceremonial exchange in Fiji

C. TOREN

Many times during the eighteen months of my fieldwork in the village of Sawaieke on the island of Gau, Central Fiji, I listened to one or other of my hosts champion *na i vakarau ni bula vakaviti*, 'the Fijian way of life' which he or she contrasted with *na i vakarau ni bula vakailavo se vakavavalagi*, 'a way of life in the manner of money or in the European way'. Virtually all Fijian villagers remark on this contrast to visiting Europeans and they do so in an entirely predictable way. The speech below is that of the elderly man who, in the early months of my fieldwork, gave me lessons in Fijian:

The Fijian way of life is good eh? Nothing is paid for. If you want to eat there are many kinds of food available – taro, cassava, chestnuts, yams, green vegetables, pawpaw, pineapples. The food's not paid for, it is just given. You are hungry? Yes. Fine. Come and eat, come and eat here. Come here and eat fish. You want to drink? Fine, come and drink *yaqona* here. Should a guest come here we look after him. If he wants something it is given to him at once. It is not paid for. No, not at all. This is the Fijian way, the chiefly way, the way according to kinship. Kinship and life in the manner of kinship are good things – there are never any problems. No, not at all. But it is different with you Europeans. Everything is paid for. You all live alone, each family by itself. Not one of your kin is nearby. They are perhaps far away. With us kinship is the most important thing of all, for you it is not.

This succinct statement of an enduring ideal contrasts 'giving' with 'payment'. What is 'given' is food and *yaqona* (*piper methysticum* or 'kava') and the 'giving' is made identical with Fijian tradition. So 'the way according to kinship' and 'the chiefly way' are made antithetical to 'the European way' by which kinship is not valued and everything is paid for. The Fijian way is conceived of as highly moral and ordered, the European way as amoral and without order – an association of strangers. Here, by implication, an assertion of the overriding value of money results in the alienation of one's kin.

However, this ideal contrast does not reflect empirical reality; it

142

ignores the practical organisation of contemporary village life in Fiji and denies historical change. The Fijian village economy is a mixed cash and subsistence economy. Villagers today want a secondary education for their children, a western style house, furniture, radios and so on. In addition every family needs money to buy a variety of commodities in standard use and to meet their obligations in respect of village funds. The money for these wants is obtained, for the most part, from the sale of cash crops. Moreover, villagers have to engage in monetary transactions with each other – buying and selling, paying for food and other items and even sometimes for labour. *Yaqona* is an important commodity and *yaqona*-drinking too has taken on a modern form – one that reflects profound historical change rather than an unalterable tradition. Nevertheless, villagers are able, with justice, to assert their ideals as reality, even in the face of these apparent contradictions. How they manage to do so is the subject of this chapter.

The gift and the status quo

My teacher's speech does not suggest that there is anything wrong, in itself, with money. Rather, it is money as symbolic of a commodity exchange that is seen as antithetical to the Fijian way. Villagers make a sharp distinction between an ideal commodity exchange, which assumes the independence (and thus a notional equality) of transactors, and an ideal gift exchange, which assumes a relation between them. This distinction is *not* an empirical one; rather it depends on the construction that may be placed on any given transaction. This construction should not challenge the high moral value attached to the recognition of proper social relations 'in the manner of the land'. In other words, the notion of 'the gift' is essential for the maintenance of a status quo that is supposed to depend upon a set of part-ascribed, part-achieved traditional statuses that everyone recognises and accepts.

In the traditional status quo in the chiefly village of Sawaieke the chiefs of ranked clans (*yavusa*) hold sway over their own clan and, to a lesser extent, over villages that are traditionally subject to it.[1] These chiefs are the focus of exchange processes in the kinship/gift economy. Thus one can, to a great extent, map differential status onto differential access to various forms of labour and produce.[2] Clan ranking is ambiguous in that, while everyone believes the clans and the lineages (*mataqali*) within them to be ranked in accordance with their traditional tasks *vakavanua* ('in the manner of the land'), people differ as to the precise order of this ranking according to their view of the place of their own clan within it.[3]

The rank of one's clan is important for one's personal status within the community and interacts with two other equally dominant principles:

seniority and gender.[4] These latter principles structure hierarchical kinship relations within the domestic group.[5] The term for kin, *veiwekani*, subsumes affines and friends as well as consanguines; ideally all Fijians are kin to one another. With the exception of the relation between cross-cousins *all* kinship relations are hierarchical. The equality of cross-cousins poses an implicit threat to the assertion of hierarchy as identical with social order. However, this threat is effectively de-fused by the fact that, when two cross-cousins marry (and by definition all marriages are between cross-cousins) the equality between them gives way to the axiomatic hierarchy of husband over wife. In effect this means that kinship hierarchy is able to 'contain' the equality of cross-cousins by subordinating it to the hierarchy of the domestic group. Thus hierarchy is dominant in 'the way according to kinship' which is itself synonymous with 'the Fijian way'.[6]

This traditional organisation is maintained in the face of both governmental aid programmes to encourage village development and individual as well as cooperative businesses, and of people's own desires for manufactured items – desires that in the fulfilling bring people of necessity into the monetary economy and thus into market relations with one another.

The process by which an apparently traditional status quo is maintained in spite of radical changes in village politico-economy during the past 150 years is in essence an uncomplicated one. Fundamentally it consists in a constant reiteration of a clear *conceptual* distinction between commodity exchange and gift exchange, while simultaneously allowing for the incorporation of money and commercial products into gift exchanges. Money is the primary symbol of commodity exchange, *yaqona* the primary symbol of gift exchange among the community of kin; their meaning as antithetical symbols is examined below.[7]

The ideal distinction between 'gift' and 'commodity'

For Fijians the moral value of money changes according to the construction they place on transactions in which it is included. Money has a neutral moral value in explicit commodity exchanges because such exchanges are considered irrelevant to the creation, fulfilment or maintenance of social bonds. It is good in a gift exchange because, like any other gift, it marks the continuing obligations between kin. Money becomes problematic only when its exchange threatens to confuse the ideal distinction between commodity and gift and thus to call into question existing social relations. In other words, monetary transactions must not be allowed to confuse the social relations of the market with social relations 'in the manner of the land'.

In any exchange that is understood to come within the ambit of the 'traditional', one cannot simply pay for a service rendered as if service and payment described the sum total of the social situation. This became apparent to me very early on in my fieldwork in that people absolutely refused to state a monetary value for their services. This was so even when it was clear that they expected payment and had a definite idea of how much that payment should be, but in all cases where I was clearly obliged to make payment, I also had to decide on its amount. I was living with a family – how much was I to pay them for food and rent? I had to decide this for myself because our relationship could not be defined impersonally in terms of landlord and tenant (i.e., as a 'market' relationship). Rather, it was defined at the outset as 'traditional' in that I was accepted into their family: it was they who ceremonially presented a *tabua* (whalestooth) to the chiefs on my behalf and thus publicly affirmed my incorporation into their lineage and into the community. As a quasi-family member then, I was expected to contribute according to my status and my means and not merely to pay a fixed weekly sum for food and shelter.

My teacher, the elderly man mentioned above, refused to be paid daily or weekly for the lessons he gave me, but this did not mean that he refused money. Rather, what was required of me was that I hand over the money at irregular intervals in such a way that it looked like a gift that reciprocated his own gift – that of teaching me. I would hand over the money saying, 'This is just a small thing by way of thanking you for all your help to me' and then would ensue an exchange of thanks in which each of us tried to outdo the other. This minor ritual effectively asserted that our relationship was not entirely encompassed by saying that I paid him money to teach me; it was not an impersonal payment calculated against his labour. Instead, he was helping me and I was showing my appreciation.

In other words, what we would see as commodity transactions are made to take the form of 'gift'. So a woman who pays others to make mats for her invites them to her house, presides over the *yaqona* bowl and compliments them on their work. When she pays over the money, it is a reciprocal gesture in acknowledgement of their labour. This transaction does not preclude the possibility, on another occasion, of the *same* services being performed by and for the *same* people as part of a gift exchange that does *not* involve money. The transactors are explicitly recognised as kin and the exchange is seen as an expression of the continuing obligations obtaining between them. As we shall see below, 'traditional' forms of exchange vary according to the relative status of the parties involved.

There are many occasions, large and small, when exchange takes place. The big occasions include all major events in the life cycle, as well as occasions that require some material acknowledgement of gratitude or pleasure as when a group of people visit one of their senior kin in the same or a different village who has recently recovered from a serious illness. Money may be incorporated into all of these exchanges – usually in the form of store-bought goods. Large-scale formal exchanges take place too on grand fund-raising occasions where, for instance, the object might be to raise enough money to build a new church. Then all those one-time villagers who now live in Suva, Levuka, Sigatoka and other towns and who, on a day to day basis, might be said to live their lives 'in the manner of money' are invited *en masse* to the village during the Christmas/New Year holiday season. They are expected to give large sums of money and are looked after, feasted, and sent on their way with many mats, whalesteeth and such-like items derived from the subsistence economy, when the days of celebration are over.

One who refuses to take part in such a *soli* or 'giving' is failing to publicly avow a link with the village. In any public fund-raising the amount given by each person or family is noted down and read out to those assembled and any derelictions are noticed and become the subject of criticism. This is true for all money gifts – from the weekly contributions every Sunday in church to those made to school or village. Any large donation is always a public affair: one should be seen to give and those of highest status to give the most. The idea of an anonymous donation is absurd in Fiji where all instances of giving mark the fulfilment of a recognised obligation to one's kin and incur obligations from the receivers. If the giving is generous it can increase one's status in the community and guarantee one's ability to mobilise a large labour force on occasions that require it, e.g., when one builds a new house or marries a child.

One who is covetous (*dau kocokoco*) may attempt to manipulate the conceptual separation between commodity exchange and gift exchange by pretending that it means that money is irrelevant in the village economy. He or she uses the rhetoric whereby in the village 'nothing is paid for' and pretends that the economy is entirely a subsistence one. This is not tolerated for it is not only a clear failure to fulfil one's obligations, but an insult to the intelligence as well. Thus I once heard a woman criticise the behaviour of her elder sister from Suva who, on a visit to the village, exploited her younger sibling's labour and food resources without making any return:

She thinks I'm crazy. She comes here, brings her children here: 'Oh village life is good, I'm tired of the town.' Yes, it's good for her. She's sharp. She doesn't bring a thing with her: no flour, no food for her children to eat. No money. She says she's sick, she can't work. Only I can. Her children want to eat, they cry out.

Only I am doing the cooking. When I ask her for money to go and buy flour there is no cash. But I know she has plenty of money. Her husband is a good man, always gives her money. She thinks I'm stupid. Enough of cooking and washing. I'm not crazy. I refuse.

Despite the overwhelming importance of 'the gift', certain common transactions are constructed as explicit commodity exchanges. However, such exchanges are in effect relegated to a context symbolically 'outside' the village. Thus, cooperative stores tend to be located on the boundaries of villages and one who sells tomatoes or fish (a relatively rare event since most locally produced foods are not sold) does so at the roadside – not so much because people are passing, but rather because this is the only appropriate place for explicit commodity exchanges.

Money is neutral in what is constructed as an explicit commodity exchange because the kin relation between transactors is ideally seen as irrelevant. While certain commodity exchanges (e.g., payment for mat-making) are routinely *transformed* into gift exchanges, it is nevertheless considered immoral to *confuse* the two types of transaction. Thus the behaviour of those who try to exploit a close kin tie with a store manager is frowned on and said to be 'shameful'; it is considered 'out of place'. This is apparently because it attempts to make kin relations relevant to an exchange which, by definition, assumes the independence of transactors. The ideal commodity transaction does not 'carry forward'. If one runs up too large a debt in the village store, credit is simply cut off and the debt published. Such transactions do not disrupt social bonds even though the creditor's debt to the village cooperative is a debt to the village itself. The fact that the store depends for its success on a recognition of obligation to one's kin at large is not acknowledged, because exchanges there are not considered to be 'in the manner of the land'. Being unable to clear one's debt to the store may place one in a somewhat onerous position, but the matter is not particularly a subject for criticism as is failure to contribute to the funds for the church or the village school – these being considered to be 'traditional' obligations.

It should be apparent from the above that, from the analyst's point of view, the distinction between gift exchange and commodity exchange is often artificial. One can easily view the exchange of labour for money as an intrusion of the market economy and as part of 'the way in the manner of money' or, conversely, see the cooperative store as dependent upon notions of traditional obligations and 'the Fijian way'. However, villagers construct an ideal separation between commodity and gift exchange that allows them to behave as if the distinction between the two 'ways' is unambiguous.

Within the village, people tend to privilege gift exchange over commodity exchange – most exchanges are constructed as 'gift'. This is essential if the gift is to retain its power as a constitutive element in hierarchical kin relations. It is the possible ultimate triumph of market relations that makes payment potentially undermining: if 'the European way' were in force, then all social relations would be determined by the market where transactors are presumed to be independent and equal, everything is paid for and one's kin are 'far away'. So it is the market relationship that is resisted by ceremonial exchange which invariably divests money of any moral neutrality and places it firmly within the context of 'tradition'.

I use the term ceremonial exchange very broadly here to cover all exchanges that are accompanied – as it were compulsorily – by ritual formulae, be they of the order of the small but effusive exchange of thanks and self-denigration that regularly accompanied my handing over any money to my teacher, or of the ritual speeches of the imposing *solevu* on the occasion of an arranged marriage or a big fund-raising drive. The construction of the symbolic opposition between market relations and traditional relations, between ideal societies 'in the manner of money' and 'in the manner of kinship', and the substitution of the highly valued morality of gift exchange for the neutral morality of commodity exchange, is nowhere more clearly seen than in the way in which *yaqona* and money are allowed to move against each other. As will be seen below, notions about *yaqona* and the behaviour appropriate to its use are crucial for the construction of the 'traditional' side of the symbolic contrast between 'the Fijian way' and 'the European way'.

Yaqona as gift and tribute

The *yaqona* ceremony and the *sevusevu* – or presentation of the roots of the plant – are the central rituals of Fijian social life. The centrality of *yaqona*-drinking is such that the arrangement of persons in relation to one another as they sit on the mat around the *tanoa* (the large bowl in which the ground root is infused in water and from which it is served) provides an image of a hierarchical society ordered according to an interaction between principles of rank, seniority and gender.

No matter how informal the occasion, persons of the highest status sit in a semi-circle 'above' the *tanoa* – which is so designed that one side may be designated that which 'faces the chiefs' – while those of lower status sit 'below' it, facing the chiefs. The seating position that is called 'above' is defined by its being the place of chiefs, the position 'below' by its being the place of women. This mode of drinking *yaqona* is understood to be *vakavanua* (traditional), and eminently Fijian, in spite of the fact that people are aware that historically, women and young men were not permitted to drink *yaqona* at all. Women were actually excluded from *yaqona*-drinking groups, while young men were allowed only to prepare and serve the drink to older men, that is, to those classified as *turaga*. This term refers specifically to chiefs but is also used to cover all married men. The image of an ordered and stratified society exemplified in people's positions relative to one another around the *tanoa* is one that is encountered virtually every day in the village of Sawaieke.

Yaqona is prepared by squeezing the pounded root through water to produce a pleasant and slightly astringent brew; on formal occasions the very gestures of the man preparing the drink are highly ritualised and orchestrated by a traditional chant given out by the men. Once the drink is prepared it is served in bowls of polished half-coconut shells one after another to the assembled people according to their position in the social hierarchy, with the highest-status person present being served first. *Yaqona* is drunk on *all* social occasions ranging from half-a-dozen men getting together for an afternoon or evening of chat around the *tanoa*, through occasions requiring community labour as when a house is built or pandanus stretched to make mats, at all ceremonies attendant upon life-cycle events, as well as during the grand and lengthy ceremonial mounted to install a chief or to welcome a high chief.

When a chief is installed it is the presentation to him within the appropriate ritual context of the chiefly bowl of *yaqona* under the aegis of the chief of that clan that is said to be able to 'make the chief', that actually gives him the 'real power', that is, the spiritual power that confirms and entrenches the political power inherent in the position when he was only designated high chief but had not yet been properly installed. Once he has drunk the chiefly *yaqona* his every command must be fulfilled on pain of his mystical power causing illness to those who fail to do their duty; a high chief does not will this punishment, it simply occurs because *sa tu vei ira na sau*, the command (or prohibition) is his, i.e., has become as it were intrinsic to him and mystically effective so that his will is simply asserted since no dereliction of duty can be concealed from one who now has the powers of a god.

The *sevusevu*, the ceremony that precedes or accompanies the drinking of *yaqona*, involves the presentation of a bundle of *yaqona* roots, or, on grander occasions, an entire uprooted *yaqona* plant six feet or more in length. Essentially the *sevusevu* is a form of tribute to chiefs that, once presented and accepted, confers on those who present it the freedom of the place where they are and entails obligations of hospitality etc. from those who accept it. Thus, one always takes a *sevusevu* when going to another village or, within one's own village, when one wishes to join a group of people who are already drinking. Similarly, if one wishes to ask someone a favour – the use of land or the right to name a child perhaps, or to beg forgiveness for a fault committed – raising one's hand against one's father or one's wife for example, then one asks a senior man to present *yaqona* on one's behalf with a speech that asks the favour or begs forgiveness, and in the acceptance and the subsequent drinking the favour is granted or the fault buried. It should be apparent from this that the *sevusevu*, while always performed, may consist on informal occasions of a few ritual phrases of acceptance, this being a highly attenuated form of the full ceremony where speeches are made by both givers and receivers.

The drinking of *yaqona* being, for Fijian villagers, an act that both expresses and in part constitutes a particular and ritually defined social order, it follows that to accuse someone of drinking *yaqona* alone is to accuse that person of witchcraft. Only one who is intent upon evil magic would prepare and drink *yaqona* alone behind closed doors. By pouring out the first bowl as a libation to one's original ancestor god or *kalou vu* and drinking the second bowl oneself, one summons the gods to one's aid and is tested by having to select one of one's nearest kin as first victim to the god's death-dealing power. That person having died one is then able, in subsequent lonely *yaqona* rituals, to ask for aid in acquiring riches, sexual magnetism of an utterly irresistible kind, or whatever else it is that one wants. In pouring out the first bowl as a libation to the god and drinking the second, one places oneself in a position analogous to that of a chief's *matanivanua* ('executive', lit. 'the face of the land'), who is traditionally the mouthpiece of the chief in transmitting his orders to the people and has his ear for the asking of favours – a position that traditionally entailed real political and economic power.[8]

Yaqona is a necessary and essential form of gift and/or tribute. However, the conceptual separation between gift exchange and commodity exchange and the importance of *yaqona* ritual has not interfered with the incorporation of *yaqona* into the market economy. Rather it is the source of its status as a valuable commodity. In the last ten to twelve years or so *yaqona* has become an important cash crop.

Nevertheless, the two statuses of *yaqona* as gift/tribute on the one hand and commodity on the other are generally kept as far apart from one another as possible. In *sevusevu* one gives *yaqona* as if its status as commodity was irrelevant. No social occasion can take place without *yaqona*; moreover the obligatory nature of the *sevusevu*, together with the central importance of *yaqona*-drinking itself in constructing the 'traditional' social order, is such that any reference to the high monetary value of the root – a comparatively recent occurrence – would probably be seen as an explicit attack on traditional values.

This is not because Fijians view references to the cost of things as ill-bred but rather because a man is expected to fulfil his obligations to kin and community and these include an adequate production of *yaqona* to meet all day-to-day drinking and ceremonial requirements. He is offering, when he presents *yaqona*, the literal fruits of his labour and any reference to the sale price of *yaqona* would be redundant. It is interesting, by contrast, to note that if *yaqona* is not available in the village store and one has no ready supply of one's own one can, on joining a group that is drinking, *sevusevu* by presenting tobacco, cigarettes, sweets or chewing gum. In this case – and especially if the amount given is large – someone almost always calculates out loud the amount spent and praises the buyer's generosity.

Its status as commodity does not mean that one cannot *kerekere yaqona* (lit. ask for *yaqona*). *Kerekere* is crucial in 'the way according to kinship' and when discussed as such the generosity it entails is usually contrasted to the profit motive in 'the European way'. *Kerekere* is a traditional means of getting hold of something one needs by simply asking for it with varying degrees of formality depending upon what the thing is and what is one's relationship to the owner. Conventionally, the owner should if at all possible, accede to the request. Not to do so is to incur disapproval. However, if the owner is unable, because of personal need, to do so then no grudge should be borne by the one who asks. People *kerekere* anything from a little salt or a single cigarette to significant sums of money, e.g., $40 to make the return trip on the plane to Suva. One should not expect to be repaid, though sometimes the thing asked for – a spade or a cooking pot for instance – is borrowed and returned rather than kept. People say explicitly of *kerekere* that there is both an obligation to give and an obligation for the receiver to accede to some future *kerekere* on the part of the giver, that is to say a *kerekere* of a similar kind, but that this may not occur until a considerable time has passed.

Despite its being 'in the manner of the land', Fijians complain quite readily about actual instances of *kerekere* and often refuse a request if they can do so without being seen to be mean, i.e., they say they do not have any *yaqona* or salt or money etc. There is therefore a certain tension about *kerekere* that is apparent sometimes when one sees the process itself, but which never appears when people are waxing eloquent about 'true kinship' and the harmonious nature of Fijian village life.

'Yaqona' and money as material symbols

The symbolic contrast between an ideally moral society 'in the Fijian way' and an ideally amoral society 'in the European way' is, as we have seen, constructed around ideas of kinship, order, generosity etc. and operated by two material symbols: *yaqona* being the positive material symbol and money the negative material symbol. At the level of the symbolic construct the opposition looks like this:

yaqona	money
Fijian	European
gift/tribute	commodity
insiders	outsiders
kinship	no kinship
morality	amorality
order	lack of order
community	independence
hierarchy	equality
generosity	profit motive
traditional	new

However, neither side of this opposition corresponds to an empirical reality.[9]

Yaqona is an important commodity and money is in routine use in the village. Its immediate source is market transactions with other Fijians and with Indians, rather than with Europeans. The notion of 'the European way' is a legacy of British colonisation; however, in the current political situation in an independent Fiji, it also implicitly refers to the way of life of the large indigenous Indian community. Indians are often said both 'to have no kinship' and to be entirely conversant with 'the path of business'.[10] Moreover, the European way is in some respects regarded as entirely moral; the British queen – whose picture hangs in a place of honour in most Fijian houses – is also queen of Fiji and the highest of high chiefs. In accordance with this, Fijians often assert that the stratified order of the British aristocracy is 'the same' as their own.

Thus the village is not a closed world, nor is its economy separate from the wider monetary economy. Kinship, morality and order are not confined to 'the Fijian way' and neither is amorality excluded from it. Indeed, the ideal construct of 'the Fijian way' is not as unambiguous as it appears here, even to those who represent it in terms of the contrast described above. So my teacher, who usually made ancestral practice the precedent for everything 'in the manner of the land', also referred to the pre-colonial era as 'the time of the devils' and to Christianity as 'the light'. These very common expressions suggest that Fijians view their past as amoral, if not immoral, especially with respect to polygamy, witchcraft and cannibalism, which are said to be 'ancestral practices in the manner of the land'.[11]

Perhaps most important however is that what is understood to be most 'traditional' – and I am speaking here of ritual behaviour and particularly of yaqona-drinking – is in fact in continuous process of transformation.

Not only has the conduct of *yaqona*-drinking itself changed in that women and young men are routinely included, but *yaqona*-drinking appears to be in the process of becoming ever more central to the image of the hierarchically ordered society.

In the past chiefs had real political and economic power, including the power of life and death over their subjects. This power was dependent on the mystical power or *mana* bestowed on any given chief by the *kalou vu* or 'ancestor god' who was the original 'owner' of the land. The chief himself was not thought to be a direct descendant of this ancestral 'owner', but his own *mana* as one of a line of chiefs was greatly enhanced by virtue of his installation as high chief by those who were considered to be the jural 'owners' of the land.[12] Today, in Sawaieke district, a paramount chief must still depend for his *mana* on proper installation in office by those who are said to be the original owners of the chiefly village of Sawaieke. However, people say that the *mana* of a paramount chief is not what it was and attribute this to their commitment to Christianity. The ancestors are still said to exist, but their power is diminished because 'no one attends on them anymore'. Moreover, in the past the relative status of *yavusa* (clan) and *mataqali* (lineage) was linked to their traditional obligations (as warriors, priests, fishermen, carpentei etc.) to chiefs. Not only have several of these categories of tradiuonal obligation disappeared but those which are observed are a matter of ritual performance only once or twice a year. In addition, today all adults have voting rights – in the weekly meetings of the village council as well as in general elections. So, according to law, all adults are jural equals and matters concerning all should be subject to democratic processes. In the district of Sawaieke the authority that remains to contemporary chiefs and elders is constructed in ritual and largely dependent upon their pre-eminence there.

It is in this context that *yaqona*-drinking has become of central importance; indeed there is said to have been a marked increase in frequency of drinking as well as in inclusiveness of persons involved. *Yaqona*-drinking is today the prime ritual manifestation of the 'traditional' order, where chiefs and elders are paid tribute and are seen to be 'above' others who are seated in their due order 'below' them. Here the imagery of *yaqona*-drinking stresses a hierarchy that depends on political, economic and spiritual inequalities that differ in kind from those that obtained in the recent historical past and at the same time effectively denies that irreversible changes have occurred. Thus 'the way in the manner of the land' is not a mere 'leftover' from an earlier era, but is itself being continuously constructed and transformed.[13]

This contemporary construction of 'tradition' is, as we have seen, taking place over against the concurrent construction of an image of 'the

European way'. The experience of the past 150 years, of colonialism, of independence, of insertion into a world-wide capitalist economy, has been drawn on to produce an ideal contrast between 'the gift' as the essence of the Fijian way and 'the commodity' as its antithesis. *Yaqona*-drinking being a crucial form of ceremonial exchange where *yaqona* is at once tribute and gift, it would seem necessary that here *yaqona* and money should be ķept entirely separate from one another. In general this is so. However, there is one context in which money and *yaqona* are brought together in ceremonial exchange. This is when people gather for *gunu sede*, ('drinking cash').

'Drinking cash'

Gunu sede as opposed to ordinary, everyday *gunu yaqona* (*yaqona*-drinking) is the name given to those occasions where money is raised by buying and drinking *yaqona* together with other members of the community. This is the *only* context inside the village in which money is exchanged for a bowl of ready-prepared *yaqona*.[14]

From late March or so to early August in 1982 villagers in Sawaieke – and in other Gau villages – met once a week to *gunu sede* in order to raise enough money to send all members of the local rugby and basketball teams to Suva for the annual inter-island games. The organisation of the affair never varied. The date and time would be announced in the weekly village meeting and sometimes the village chief (an elected administrator, not a traditional chief) would remind villagers on the evening before by calling out the details as he made a round of the village during the hour of the evening meal. A certain sum was always stipulated as *yavu* – 'foundation' or 'base' – usually 50c for men and young men and 30c for women and young women, this being decided upon by all those present at the weekly village meeting.

On the evening in question one made one's way to the village hall along with a small group of one's peers, entered, sat down on the mat'in a position appropriate to one's sex and status in the community relative to those already present, passed one's *yavu* across to the village treasurer, who noted the sum down against one's name in a big book and then set oneself to join in the fun, using the small store of cash one had brought in addition to one's *yavu* to promote good feeling and lots of enjoyment. *Gunu sede* is often uproarious, full of high good humour and ridiculous jokes all derived from the way one spends one's money in buying drinks for other people but *never* for oneself.[15] Several young men walk around among the assembled people holding containers in which to receive the money. They act as criers, retailing one's wishes as to who is to benefit from one's contribution and the hall resounds with announcements like this: '10c given that the mother of Pita may drink, paid for by grandfather Taniela', '20c given that those young men may drink who are looking after the *yaqona*; paid for by Jone', '40c that the gentlemen sitting "above" may drink; paid for by Adi Varanisese', '5c that Sosi may drink; paid for by Seru', and frequently those who have been pledged will call out in response, asking the crier to come to them: 'Here' (offering some money) 'another one for him' (or her, or whomever the donor might be.)

One can, by judicious pledging of drinks set up a mock flirtation that amuses everyone, e.g., a young man and a much older married woman who are cross-cousins might exchange drink after drink in this way; or several girls might get together and one after another pledge drinks in fast succession to one shy and as yet unmarried man in order to tease him by bringing him reluctantly into the social limelight and forcing him to drink great quantities of *yaqona*. Similarly a competitive exchange can take place where a woman for instance, having pledged a bowl to a male cross-cousin who refuses it by paying to have it given back to her, then adds a further increment to the money given so that she may herself refuse to drink and have the bowl sent back again to him. The competition goes on, each adding 10c or so to the money they have pledged each time they continue to refuse to drink. One of them is bound to accept the bowl in the end – *yaqona* can never be returned to the *tanoa*. Once the sum has risen to $1 or $1.50, or even more if both parties are really flush, one of them signifies surrender by, perhaps, slapping a hand down on the mat in a highly exaggerated version of the clapping of cupped hands that always precedes one's acceptance of a bowl of *yaqona*. So a single bowl may wind up fetching $2 to $3 since each party is bound to pay out to the crier the final sum that he or she has named. There is much joking and plotting and giggling and loud laughter, with spontaneous clapping and expressions of thanks from all the onlookers when someone brings off a particularly good joke, or at the culmination of competitive payment to force the acceptance of a single bowl.

After three hours or so, everyone having spent the money they brought, the last few cents remaining to people are collected and *gunu sede* comes to an end. The names of all who contributed their *yavu* are read out together with the sum given, and the money collected from the drinking is totalled and read out. Any expenses incurred, e.g., the cost of buying the *yaqona* root from the village store, are set against the sum total raised and the final total is announced and everyone claps and thanks each other for coming, for drinking and for spending money and the evening of fun is over.

What is interesting sociologically about *gunu sede* is the way that it is acknowledged in the naming to be very different from *gunu yaqona* – one is 'drinking cash' not 'drinking *yaqona*' – and at the same time explicitly allied to it, made analogous to that central ritual of Fijian social life that, on any occasion, offers an image of an ordered and stratified society in which the participant both finds his or her own place and is confirmed in it. It will be recalled that to drink *yaqona* alone would be to lay oneself open to an accusation of witchcraft; drinking alone cannot be countenanced because the act of drinking *yaqona* is above all a *social* act. It follows from the centrality of the *yaqona* ceremony for the symbolising of social relations that, in the village, one can never, under any circumstances, buy oneself a bowl of *yaqona*. To buy oneself a bowl of the ready-prepared brew would be to threaten the powerful symbolism of *yaqona*-drinking with the ideal neutrality of the commodity transaction. Any act that effectively asserts neutral relations cannot be allowed to impinge on a context that demands acknowledgement of specific ranked kin relations, for it would undermine the very notion of social order. By 'drinking cash' rather than 'drinking *yaqona*', money and the exchange of money is made identical with *yaqona* and the exchange of *yaqona*. Money is not allowed to escape the kinship nexus. *Gunu sede* is an historically recent phenomenon, but it is seen as part of 'the Fijian way' and so comes within the ambit of 'tradition'.[16] In this context, to buy a bowl for oneself would constitute a symbolic severing of one's social ties in a self-referential act that denies connection to kin and community.

In *gunu sede* virtually all drinks are bought for affines and potential affines, i.e., they are bought for cross-cousins. This behaviour is inherent in the situation since it is only with one's cross-cousins that, both within and across sex, one has complete freedom of behaviour in social relations. All other relatives have to be accorded varying degrees of respect and avoidance, with avoidance being strongest between true and classificatory *veiganeni* (brothers and sisters) and true and classificatory *veivugoni* (children-in-law and parents-in-law, i.e., mother's brother, father's sister). Drinks *are* bought for persons classified as members of other kinship categories, but only within sex, i.e., a woman for her 'sister' and a man for his 'brother', and only rarely by comparison with buying for cross-cousins. Thus in *gunu sede* exchanges of money are made to express the bonds between affines. So money is seen to be susceptible of the same kind of treatment as any other object of exchange between them.

It might possibly be said that money is implicitly incorporated into the exchange relations between affines that are enshrined in the *vasu* relation that obtains between a person and his or her mother's brother's lineage, mother's brother being a matrilateral 'father-in-law'.[17] The junior relative or *vasu* is said to be able to take anything from the mother's brother's lineage without asking for it and without comment being made or ill-feeling aroused. When I asked if money was included here I was told that yes, it was but, as one informant remarked, 'money is not usually visible; it is usually hidden away'. The important thing to note here is that the *vasu* can *take* from mother's brother's lineage but cannot, because of the avoidance rule, directly *ask* things of his or her mother's brother. In any case, given the high degree of village exogamy, the *vasu* relation often obtains between ego and a lineage in another village, so the visibility of money in exchange between affines and potential affines could be said to be a matter of some importance. That is to say, it is not perhaps immediately apparent that money can be an exchange object as such and should be used in accordance with the conventions that govern the exchange of other objects between affines.

I concentrate here on exchange of money between affines since its circulation within the group of one's close kin is taken for granted in that one routinely benefits from money available in the domestic group or in the *tokatoka* (the smallest kinship unit beyond the domestic group) in the form of day-to-day requirements such as store-bought food etc. Again, one's obligations to the community, to one's kin at large, incorporate the giving of money in donations to the church, to community building projects and so on. Indeed a recognition of the necessity for this kind of giving – where there is no direct exchange – is made in *gunu sede* in the form of the *yavu* (base) of 30c or 50c. This term is the same as that used for the earth foundation of a house, the height of which traditionally signified the rank of the house owners, and is the root of *yavusa*, meaning 'clan'.[18] Thus the *yavu* in *gunu sede* has strong associations with very basic notions of hierarchy and kinship and the obligations that kinship entails. The giving of the *yavu* entitles one to join the group that is *gunu sede*, i.e., it is made partly analogous to a *sevusevu*. However, whether one actually drinks or not is, for those 'below' the *tanoa* (whose status is below that of chief or elder), a matter of whether drinks are bought for one. No direct return is made on the *yavu* and so, like all other donations of this kind, it must be placed within an apparently 'traditional' context where giving is obligatory and entails long-term and perhaps intangible returns.

In *gunu sede* money, cash, is made into an object in itself. One drinks money. That money is not literally drunk but is in fact amassed for a community purpose is not however obscured by the way *gunu sede* is organised. In 'drinking cash' a twofold recognition is made of the peculiarities of money. Firstly, that it is a store of value, has a use value and an exchange value that will translate directly from one context to another, from the kinship context of personal relations into the market context of impersonal relations; so the money raised in *gunu sede* buys tickets on the boat and covers the expenses of young people and their chaperones in Suva. Secondly, that because of these qualities money has to be recognised as a viable object of gift exchange and forced into the nexus of direct exchanges between kin and, more particularly, between affines. Villagers are obliged to use money. So, to confine it to the sphere from which it originated – where brief and limited transactions take place between persons whose kin relation to one another is ideally irrelevant and money is quintessentially private property – would be to undermine kinship relations and the balance of obligations that is fundamental to the gift economy. This means that money has to be symbolically 'laundered' in ceremonial exchange and it is this purification that is achieved in *gunu sede*.

Gift, commodity and affinity

The continuous process of construction of 'the Fijian way' is clear in *gunu sede*. The context is defined as traditional but is at the same time made to contain and to symbolically resolve a number of ambiguities that are inherent in the contrast between 'the Fijian way' and 'the European way', but which are not acknowledged when people are speaking about it.

In *gunu sede* money is made into an object in itself and is exchanged for money through the medium of *yaqona*. Thus, while a twofold recognition is being made of the properties of money, it is also being made of the properties of *yaqona*. *Yaqona* is allowed to move against cash in ritual exchange and in effect this implies recognition of its status as a source of considerable sums in a market context. At the same time it is a valuable ceremonial object that as gift/tribute acknowledges the bonds between kin according to their relative positions in the traditional status quo. So, in *gunu sede* any status one has acquired as a result of holding relatively large amounts of cash is *apparently* outweighed by the ascribed status given by one's seating position relative to all other persons present. This apparent dominance of traditional hierarchy arises from the fact that virtually all buying is done by and for those who call each other cross-cousin and they are allowed to joke, to compete and effectively to challenge hierarchy under the circumstances of day-to-day *yaqona*-drinking as well as in *gunu sede*.

The point is that the relation between cross-cousins is a relation between equals, whatever the respective position of each party in the hierarchy given by the three-way interaction between rank, seniority and gender. Thus the cross-cousin relationship cuts across hierarchy in the sense that, for instance, a young man may joke boisterously with a woman thirty years his senior or compete in buying drinks with a chief who sits 'above' the *tanoa*, provided he is cross-cousin to each of them. In this way the cross-cousin relationship is made to 'carry' and to symbolically undermine any status that may be attached to control of a large sum of cash. Moreover, in *gunu sede* traditional chiefs (*turaga ni vanua* or *na malo*), who are sitting 'above' the *tanoa*, are served with bowls of *yaqona* at regular intervals whether or not anyone has pledged drinks for them. The image of the ordered and stratified society, in which each person knows his place and chiefs have properties and privileges that set them apart from others, is maintained. In *gunu sede* money and monetary transactions with their potential for disruption are explicitly subordinated to kinship relations, which subsume the relation between cross-cousins (i.e., between affines), within an existing status quo.

In fact, affinity is the 'hidden' third term that mediates between the contrast posed between kinship relations and market relations, between 'the Fijian way' and 'the European way'.[19] The behaviour appropriate between cross-cousins partakes of both sides of the contrast in that it is at once contained within the notion of 'kinship' but at the same time implicitly threatens the hierarchy of kinship relations with the lack of order implicit in the joking, competitiveness and occasional hostility that is traditionally allowed between them. Again, one's cross-cousins are at once 'insiders' because they are kin and 'outsiders' because they are the only category of kin who are marriageable and because marriage is exogamous to the *mataqali* (lineage) and often to the village or to the island. Indeed, one may not be able to trace any actual kin relation to the person one marries from another island so one's affines may in effect become kin by virtue of the marriage, since by definition any married couple are cross-cousins to one another.[20]

Note that the *vasu* relation between ego and mother's brother lineage referred to above mediates between the extreme of equality (and potential anarchy) that is allowed in the behaviour between cross-cousins and the varying degrees of respect and avoidance that govern relations between ego and all other kin. The *vasu* can traditionally take anything from mother's brother's lineage i.e., from the father of the matrilateral cross-cousins, but the *vasu*'s rights do not preclude the utmost respect and avoidance of the senior relative nor absolute obedience to his orders.[21]

Here it becomes evident that the symbolic contrast between 'the Fijian way' and 'the European way' is perhaps not so closely allied to the gift/commodity distinction as it is made to appear. The point is that the construction of hierarchy in the traditional status quo has historically demanded a struggle to overcome the egalitarian relations between cross-cousins. Their equality is based in exchange relations of balanced reciprocity – a symbolic antithesis to 'tribute'. This struggle goes on to this day; it is inherent in 'the way in the manner of the land'.

Explicit commodity exchanges are seen as morally neutral, provided they are kept in their place, 'outside'. They are potentially evil only in so far as they might threaten or confuse traditional relations – hierarchical *or* equal – both of which are seen as unquestionably morally correct and good in their proper conduct within their proper limits. Just as gift exchange is not allowed to be confused with commodity exchange, so hierarchical relations exemplified by those of chief and commoner are not allowed to confuse, or be confused by, equal relations between affines. Cross-cousins may joke outrageously and treat each other to bowls of *yaqona* but they do this under the auspices of chiefs and do not violate the conventions that govern hierarchical seating arrangements around the *tanoa* or the privileges due to chiefs.

Conclusion

Three different types of social relations have emerged from the above analysis. First, market relations, in which the transactors are conceptually 'independent' and 'equal' (because the kin relation between them is ideally irrelevant), engaged in a short-term transaction that neither confirms, denies nor creates a bond between them. Second, hierarchical relations, exemplified by chief and commoner where *yaqona* is given 'raw' as tribute to be disposed of by a chief, who re-distributes it as drink that can only be accepted; this is the model for all prestations to chiefs and for their re-distribution. Third, relations between equals, exemplified by cross-cousins where all exchanges are equally reciprocated and where this equality is seen both as essential for 'a good time' and as a challenge to the hierarchy that 'contains' it.

The ethnography has revealed that the symbolic contrast between money and *yaqona*, the commodity and the gift, 'the European way' and 'the Fijian way' cannot be entirely explained in terms of a reaction against colonialism and insertion into a world-wide capitalist economy. Rather, both sides of the contrast have their historical roots in the egalitarian and hierarchical relations that together constitute 'the way according to kinship'. This is *not* to say that the symbolism of commodity and gift was always inherent in Fijian economic processes but rather that the contemporary contrast is in part a transformation of a continuing struggle to contain the notion of balanced reciprocity within that of tribute to chiefs and thus to make affinity subordinate to hierarchical kinship.

So in *gunu sede* the relation between cross-cousins is made to mediate between the positive and the negative poles of an opposition that is operated by the material symbols given by *yaqona* and money. In the process money is divested of moral neutrality, purified of any potentially threatening associations with the market and, by being made an object of ceremonial exchange, is seen to be amenable to incorporation into what is understood to be the traditional politico-economy, such that 'the Fijian way' is seen to emerge intact from a confrontation with 'the European way' or 'the way in the manner of money'.

Notes

Thanks are due to Maurice Bloch, Peter Gow, Jonathan Parry and Maria Phylactou for their constructive comments on an earlier draft of this paper.

1 I translate *yavusa* as 'clan' and *mataqali* as 'lineage' to distinguish higher and lower levels of integration; the terms are often used in this sense, though *mataqali* may refer to either level. Within *mataqali*, *tokatoka* are ranked against each other on the model of elder brother and younger brother.

2 Chiefs are able to give more because they get more and in giving more they are seen to deserve their status. However, chiefs are not necessarily any better off than others: they cannot easily accumulate because they should, ideally, redistribute all they receive. This is not to say that an economic advantage over others may not be manipulated so as to achieve higher status than one might otherwise have obtained.

3 In Sawaieke, it is at *yavusa* level that traditional obligations to chiefs are stressed. In the central government model of the Fijian village the *yavusa* is said to be co-terminous with the village, but in Sawaieke there are five *yavusa*. In general I agree with France (1969) and Clammer (1973) on the distortions produced by the colonial administration's standardisation of what had been different principles of land tenure; however it is *not* clear that the apparently unusual situation in Sawaieke is a direct product of the Lands Commissions' investigations. Oral history/myth attributes the large number of *yavusa* to an amalgamation of what were once separate villages, the remains of which are still to be seen.

4 For an analysis of the nature of the interaction between rank, seniority and gender and its construction in ritual, see Toren (1988).

5 Eating together on a routine basis defines the domestic group; food exchange is also a defining marker for groups at a higher level of integration. Thus Hocart (1952: 22) defines *mataqali* (lineage) as 'an assessment unit for feasts'; note too that in Lau the *tokatoka* (sub-lineages) are called *bati ni lovo*, 'sides of the oven'.

6 Kinship terminology is Dravidian; both the terminology and marriage preferences in the district of Sawaieke largely accord with descriptions given by Nayacakalou (1955) for Tokatoka, Tailevu, by Sahlins (1962: 147ff) for Moala, and by Hocart (1929: 33–42), Thompson (1940: 53–65) and Phelps Hooper (1982: 20–3) for Lau.

7 Note that the giving of food is also important for the construction of 'the way according to kinship', but *yaqona* is the primary ritual object of gift and tribute and so I concentrate my analysis upon it.

8 For a more extensive analysis of *yaqona* ritual see Sahlins (1982), also Toren (1988).

9 For eastern Lau, Knapman & Walter (1977/80) make a sharp empirical distinction between 'the way of the land' and 'the path of money' that presumably corresponds to an indigenous ideal construction of the contrast between the two ways. Note that the status of *yaqona* as commodity has not, in Sawaieke, introduced the 'decline in custom and the rise of cash' that they describe with respect to the cash cropping of copra in Mavana (see p. 207). They also maintain that: 'Ceremonial has become largely divorced from the hard realities of the new economic life and diminished in social and cultural importance.' This is not the case in Sawaieke even though, like Mavana, it is unquestionably involved in the monetary economy.

10 Note that Indians are routinely distinguished from Fijians and that the latter refer to themselves as *i taukei* (owners) when making the distinction between them. There is no Indian community in Gau; the majority of the Indian population is concentrated on the two largest islands, Viti Levu and Vanua Levu. Thus, Sawaieke villagers are able to view Indians as 'outsiders' in the strict sense of the term.

11 On the whole I prefer to use the term amoral, simply because practices such as polygamy, witchcraft and cannibalism are often said to have occurred because the ancestors 'did not know the light'.

12 See Walter (1978/9).

13 In this respect I have to disagree with McNaught, who views 'Fijian culture' as having been 'lost' as a result of the impact of colonialism and a monetary economy. See McNaught (1982).

14 I am told that *yaqona*-drinking stalls are run by Indians in the markets of large towns and that a generation ago *yaqona* saloons were common in Suva, the capital of Fiji, and that here bowls of *yaqona* are paid for. Apparently one or two of these saloons still exist but unfortunately I have never visited one. Neither market stall nor saloon existed on the island of Gau during the period of my fieldwork, nor did I ever hear that they had ever existed there.

15 I understand that buying for oneself alone *may* occur in the stalls or saloons mentioned in note 14 above but am unable to say whether this is in fact done. It is probable however that this context mediates between 'traditional' and 'market' contexts in that I suspect that men in groups would pay for others' drinks as well as for their own, much as one 'buys a round' in a pub. This is emphatically *not* the case in *gunu sede*.

16 I am unable to discover when *gunu sede* began, but am told by various informants that this method of money-raising was already common over forty years ago. One informant also said that a similar practice obtained with respect to raising money from dances, until this was banned by church authorities who considered it more than unseemly. Apparently one paid for someone else to dance with a particular person. Note that only cross-cousins would have been able to dance with one another.

17 The *vasu* relationship is formally established at any time from infancy onwards by the ceremony of *kau mata ni gone* (lit. carrying the face of the child) when the child or adolescent is taken by his father's kin to be presented to his mother's kin. See Phelps Hooper (1982: 199–218) for a detailed account of this ceremony. See also Hocart (1915 and 1929: 40).

18 The *yavu* as named house sites within the village are distinguished from *yavu tabu* (sacred *yavu*) on clan and lineage gardening land and old village sites and associated with the ancestor gods (*kalou vu*); this association apparently being derived from the fact that traditionally the dead were buried in the *yavu* of the house.

19 The importance of affinity as the 'hidden' third term that mediates between 'the Fijian way' and 'the European way' is amply borne out by the earlier practice of selling dances, mentioned in note 16 above.

20 In Sawaieke there is said to have formerly been a prohibition on marriage between immediate cross-cousins, but today this is not the case; rather, if one can call someone cross-cousin, that person is marriageable. For a somewhat different case, see Walter (1975).

21 Today the *vasu* does not often avail him or herself of the privileges that are said to be his due. Most persons with whom I discussed this matter said either that they had never done so or related what seemed to be considered a 'daring' incident of their youth. Only once did I myself see an instance of the *vasu* seizing property from his mother's brother.

References

Clammer, J. R. 1973. 'Colonialism and the perception of tradition in Fiji', in T. Asad, ed., *Anthropology and the colonial encounter*, London: Ithaca Press.

France, P. 1969. *The charter of the land*, Melbourne: Oxford University Press.

Hocart, A. M. 1915. 'Chieftainship and the sister's son in the Pacific', *American Anthropologist*, 17: 631–46.

1929. *Lau Islands, Fiji*, Honolulu: Bernice P. Bishop Museum Bulletin 62.

1952. *The Northern States of Fiji*, Occasional Publication No. 11, London: Royal Anthropological Institute.

Knapman, B. and M. A. H. B. Walter 1979/80.' 'The way of the land and the path of money: the generation of economic inequality in Eastern Fiji', *Journal of Developing Areas*, 14: 201–22.

MacNaught, T. J. 1982. 'We are no longer Fijians', *Pacific Studies*, 1–2: 15–24.

Nayacakalou, R. R. 1955. 'The Fijian system of kinship and marriage', *Journal of the Polynesian Society*, 64: 44–56.

Phelps Hooper, S. 1983. 'A study of valuables in the chiefdom of Lau, Fiji, PhD thesis, University of Cambridge.

Sahlins, M. 1962. *Moala: culture and nature on a Fijian island*, Ann Arbor: University of Michigan Press.

1982. 'Raw women, cooked men and other "great things" of the Fiji islands', in P. Brown and D. Tuzin, eds., *The ethnography of cannibalism*, Special Publication, Society for Psychological Anthropology.

Thompson, L. M. 1940. *Southern Lau, Fiji: an ethnography*, Honolulu: Bernice P. Bishop Museum.

Toren, C. 1988. 'The chief sits above and the ladies sit below: children's perceptions of gender and hierarchy in Fiji', in G. Jahoda and I. M. Lewis, eds., *Acquiring culture: Cross-cultural studies of childhood*, London: Routledge.

Walter, M. A. H. B. 1975. 'Kinship and marriage in Mualevu: a Dravidian variant in Fiji?', *Ethnology*, 14: 181–95.

—— 1978/79. 'An examination of hierarchical notions in Fijian society: a test case for the applicability of the term "chief"', *Oceania*, 49: 7.

7

The symbolism of money in Imerina

MAURICE BLOCH

One of the more disturbing moments of my field work occurred at the very end of my first period with the Merina of central Madagascar. As I was about to leave, the head of the family in which I had become partly integrated, presented to me a significant sum of money in Malagasy bank notes. These were intended to help me on my journey and perhaps also to be used when I arrived back in England. The cause of my embarrassment, I told myself at the time, was the difficulty I felt in receiving money from people who were clearly much poorer than myself. Another element was perhaps the recurrent sense of guilt of fieldworkers who feel that they are putting a relationship of mutual moral obligation to quite another purpose. This is made all the worse by the suspicion that the fieldworker benefits from this in a way which does not include the other party in the relationship.

However, as I think back over this episode, which was to repeat itself on my subsequent visits, I am not sure that my worries were not really of a different nature. The moral problem of the fieldwork relationship I had partly resolved at the time, by having made what I was doing as clear as I could. The problem of taking from people who were poorer than me was also an unsatisfactory explanation. First of all I am not sure that it was literally true in this particular case. Secondly, I had accepted rice and livestock from the same people with nothing like the same unease. That the money was equivalent to these gifts in kind was very clearly, and very sensibly, stated by the elder who had given me the money. He had pointed out that I could not easily take live pigs or geese with me 'over the water', i.e. to Europe, and so, as was common on such occasions, he had substituted cash. The cause of my embarrassment was therefore the money itself, handed to me without even a decontaminating envelope, and the origin of the unease came from the way I had been brought up to regard money. The source of the problem lay in my natal rather than in Malagasy culture. In Europe there is a general feeling that morally

165

binding relations, especially kinship relations, should be kept apart as far as possible from money transactions. It was this separation which appeared to have been breached by the elder's action.

Of course there is variation over this in European culture. For example, in England it is normal for parents to give their children pocket money on a near wage basis, while in France such a transaction still causes deep unease, but overall the barrier between relationships where money can be allowed to come to the fore and those where it cannot is common to both France and England, and contrasts with the Merina attitude.[1] This is perhaps nowhere better illustrated than in sexual and marital relations. In Europe the linking of monetary exchange and sexual or familial exchange is seen as either typically immoral or as a source of humour and dissonance. By contrast, in Madagascar the need to keep the two areas separate is not present. The right thing for a man to do is to give his lover a present of money or goods after sexual intercourse. This applies not only to pre-marital or extra-marital sex, but also to marital relations, though on a less regular basis. This does not mean that these types of sexuality merge with prostitution, which also exists among the Merina but which takes a completely different form and is defined by the casualness of the relationship rather than by the kind of objects exchanged. The point is that, for the Merina at least, the transfer of money in cash is not a sign defining the type of relationship involved as it is in Europe.

The moral neutrality of money in rural Imerina is made evident again and again. For example, at any feast, marriage, secondary funeral, etc., there is always someone at the entrance receiving monetary contributions from the guests. These are carefully noted down in a book and then read out aloud in the middle of the proceedings without the least embarrassment, which such a practice would surely cause in most of Europe or North America.

Similarly, in Imerina any traditional gift can be made either in kind or in money without the substitution having much significance. If cash is used the money gift is called by the name of the thing it replaces, even if what is replaced is quite specific and charged with meaning. For example, at a marriage the groom's family is expected to hand over a part of a sheep, this gift being loaded with complex symbolical associations (Bloch 1978). In fact a small sum of cash is actually given, the substitution being symbolically irrelevant. Hence the money gift when I was in the field.

There are many other practices which reveal the Merina's and other Malagasy's relaxed attitude to money. Among these is the fact that a popular name for girls is *Vola*, a word which means money. As a name it is an equivalent of such other names as *Soa* (beautiful), *Lalao* (playful).[2] Finally, among non-Merina groups, such as the neighbouring Zafimaniry, it is common to pin on the clothes of particularly pleasing dancers at religious rituals paper currency which becomes a kind of decoration.

For the rural Merina the use of money in a transaction does not give that transaction a special meaning, nor are there contexts where the presence of currency is objectionable.[3] An ironical implication of this finding is that it seems to reverse one of the most commonly accepted theories in economic anthropology concerning money. This characterises primitive economies, in contrast to evolved market economies, as having 'spheres of exchange' (Bohannan and Dalton 1962: 3–7) where not everything is exchangeable for everything else, since different goods and services have incompatible moral value. According to this theory only when the general purpose money of industrialised society is introduced do the barriers to exchange between different types of goods and services disappear (Bohannan 1954). This is because 'general purpose money' is, according to this theory, morally neutral and it therefore makes all goods and services potentially convertible (Dalton 1965). What the Merina example seems to highlight however is exactly the opposite. It is in European culture that money is far from morally neutral and its moral charge hinders conversion from one sphere of activity to another. By contrast, for the rural Merina, who live in an economic setting much less dominated by the market, money is much more neutral and facilitates all kinds of exchanges. While for the latter it might be accurate to say that money is 'what money does', this is completely misleading for the former.

It is thus clear that if the Merina attitude to money strikes us, as it did me when I was given money on my journey back to England, as needing elucidation it is because the symbolism of money is powerful, not in Merina culture, but in European culture. The questions we are tempted to ask are dictated by our own tradition which on close examination is revealed to be more 'exotic' than that of many of the people whom anthropologists study. This means that in order to understand our understanding of the Merina, we first need an anthropological analysis of the assumptions which have been formed by our history and which we have assimilated. This of course is true for any anthropological enterprise but such a self-analysis is rarely seriously attempted. In the area of economic anthropology, above all, the need for such historical self-ethnography is central because money is such a powerful Western symbol. As we shall see, the absence of a simultaneous analysis of our own concepts with that of the people we study has seriously misled anthropological analyses of money in Madagascar and in other non-Western societies.[4]

Mauss, Marx *et al.*, on the symbolism of money

A study of the history of the symbolism of money in European society is a daunting enterprise but fortunately we do have excellent guides (e.g., Simmel 1978 *et al*). I want to consider two such guides here, because they have not only tried to explain our views about money but also because they have strongly influenced the anthropological study of money. These two writers are Mauss and Marx.

Mauss's essay on the gift is perhaps one of the most fundamental yet most misunderstood texts in anthropology. The misunderstanding comes from the fact that it has been homogenised in anthropological theory in general, and in economic anthropology in particular, together with totally incompatible ideas. This point has been made most clearly by a recent careful reading of Mauss's famous essay on the gift by J. Parry, which genuinely reconstructs the original intentions of the author (Parry 1986). Parry points out how first and foremost *The Gift* is an evolutionary study of transactions. For Mauss the earliest stage of prestations were what he calls 'total prestations', involving groups and clans in massive reciprocal exchanges. These total prestations between groups actually defined these groups in the way structural anthropology has taught us to view exchange as constructing subjects. These total prestations are little discussed in the essay. Rather, Mauss chooses to focus on a later stage characterised by gift exchange. Gift exchange differs from total prestations in that it may occur between individuals. As a result, unlike total prestations, gift exchange can take on a competitive form such as the potlatch. For Mauss, as Parry emphasises, it is the combination of *interest and moral obligation* which characterises gift exchange and which he contrasts with the modern industrial world of the *laissez-faire* economists, which Mauss saw as an unfortunate later third stage. This third stage, as Parry shows us, is characterised by the attempt to separate moral obligation and economic interest. In the modern world, according to its apologists, there is, on the one hand, the world of money, which pretends it has nothing to do with social obligation, and another separate antithetical world, the world of charity where those who have benefited from commerce salve their consciences by 'free gifts' to inferiors, an act which they see as in no way caused by an obligation on their part but merely as due to the internal prompting of their consciences. Against this view of transactions Mauss argues that in the modern world it is wrong to see either commerce or giving as not implying social obligations and so he repudiates the symbolical contrast between charity and commerce. Particularly revealing on this point is Mauss's insistence, which appeared wrongheaded to many commentators (Malinowski 1922, Firth 1967) that the famous ceremonial objects exchanged in the Trobriand Kula should be considered in some ways as money. The reason why he rejects Malinowski's contrast between these and money is that such a contrast implies the sharp distinction between monetary commerce, seen as totally impersonal, and gift exchange seen as being marked by total economic disinterest. Since Mauss is saying that this antithesis does not exist in primitive economies, it follows that there can be no such sharp analytical divide between cash and the objects of gift exchange. (See Strathern 1985 for a discussion of this point.)

Mauss's theory, revealed in Parry's analysis, proves quite suitable for dealing with the apparent contrast between the rural Merina and European society since it is the latter which, according to Mauss, would want to draw a sharp barrier between money and moral relationships and not the former. This is indeed the case.

If Mauss's original ideas fit with the Merina case, however, this is not so for the way Mauss's ideas have generally been received in anthropology where, again as Parry shows so well, they have been merged with much older ideas which were crystallised in the work of Malinowski, Polanyi and after them Bohannan, Dalton and Sahlins. This 'received wisdom' in anthropology contrasts commercial exchange and gifts, as Mauss had done, but introduces the modification that such primitive gift exchanges as the *kula* lack any economic motivation, and are purely a matter of establishing social relations (Sahlins 1972: 185–91). Furthermore, unlike Mauss who saw commerce and pure gifts as mutually defining each other by antithesis, and therefore as being necessarily complementary, the received wisdom of anthropology sees 'pure gifts' as being antecedent to market exchange even though pure gifts are seen as surviving in an attenuated form in modern society (Davis 1973).

This view of the evolution of transactions is seen as correlated with the presence or absence of 'general purpose money'. In societies where only gift exchange prevails, there is no money, but with the coming of commerce money makes its appearance. As a result the introduction of money comes to signify almost automatically an assault on a disinterested autarchic society dominated by pure morality. This assault is not just an empirical fact for the economic anthropologist but is in many cases also supposedly seen in this way by the people concerned. According to such a theory a peasant society such as the Merina would be one which until recently was free of money but which had just been penetrated by it. Simultaneously the Merina would be aware of this assault and would feel an instinctive revulsion against money. This sequence of events is what has been imputed in a number of cases often creating a kind of unexamined pseudo-history for primitive and peasant societies which, as we shall see for the Merina and as is shown in other cases in this book, is quite erroneous.

Before examining further the pseudo-history created by the received wisdom of economic anthropology it is necessary to note that unlike many other tenets of the sub-discipline, this theory of exchange and money has not been challenged by the recent re-introduction of Marxist ideas into the debate; if anything it has been strengthened. The reason for this is that one element of Marxist theory is the product of the same tradition of thought which produced the ideas of such writers as Malinowski, Polanyi, etc., a tradition which goes back to Aristotle. In this Marxist view money is equated with capitalist encroachment into societies regulated by pre-capitalist modes of production.[5] For these writers, as for Marx in some places, money of itself is seen as an acid attacking the very fabric of kinship-based moral society, an acid operating through the impersonal relationships it introduces. Again, a consciousness of this process is attributed to the actors, and is said to take the form of a revolutionary opposition to money as such. This is exactly what Taussig does in a book discussed in other places in this volume, and it is also what Gerard Althabe does in a study of another part of Madagascar (Althabe 1969). Following the lines just indicated, Althabe reaches conclusions which appear to contradict directly what I outlined above for the Merina, when I argued that for the Malagasy money had totally different meanings to those which it has in our society.

The problem with such approaches are many. Firstly, it is assumed that money represents for the actors what it is imputed to represent by the anthropologists, and furthermore that the actors have foreknowledge of what will happen to them. Secondly, it is assumed that it will inevitably be money as such which will be used as a symbol to refer to the new relations of production. Thirdly, and perhaps most importantly, such an analysis inevitably leads to an oversimple contrast between a pre-monetary state of affairs and a post-monetary state of affairs where the former is nothing more than an antithesis to a nightmarish view of commerce. This is roughly what writers such as Polanyi (1971) and Sahlins (1972) would also have us do; but if we had read Mauss more carefully, as Parry urges us to do, we would not have made this mistake since he points out that the image of commerce and its opposite are mutually self-defining and therefore contemporary.

However, if Mauss would have helped us to predict the differences between European and Merina concepts of money and exchange better than the classical economic anthropologists his work would not, I believe, have enabled us to go much further than this. Mauss it turns out is particularly interesting about our own bifurcation between commerce and charity but his analysis of societies where no such bifurcation has occurred is not very illuminating, and does not advance our understanding of Merina attitudes to money and exchange. The reason is, first of all, the old one that these societies cannot be lumped together simply because they contrast with what are seen to be 'modern societies'. These systems must be understood for themselves and as such will be revealed to vary tremendously. The examples of non-bifurcated systems of exchange Mauss instances, the Trobriands, the North-west Coast Amerindians, Hindu India of the Dharmaśastra texts, and the Maori vary much more fundamentally among themselves than he believes and in any case are far from a representative sample of primitive or archaic societies. The reason for this is that the very nature of his study, focused as it is on prestations, make him privilege those societies which give great symbolical weight to exchange. For example, these systems just do not correspond to anything which exists today or, as far as we can know, has ever existed in rural Imerina.

Yet clearly we must understand the nature of exchange and the symbolism of money in non-commercial societies in ways which are more than just saying that in these societies it is *different* from what it is in industrialised societies. This is so even if our interest lies in seeing the effect of the introduction of capitalism in a pre-capitalist system, since the way in which this introduction will be visualised by the actors will be in terms of what these actors have known before. Much more useful than the work of Mauss, however, are certain ideas from Marx which as we shall see are fundamentally different from those of the writers examined above. I am not referring to Marx's ideas about economic evolution, which as we saw are as misleading as those of such writers as Polanyi and Sahlins, and for the same reasons, but rather to certain of his ideas about the symbolism of exchange, ideas which are dealt with in his discussion of fetishism and are found throughout *Capital*.

Marx's idea of fetishism is ultimately Voltairean (see the *Dictionnaire Philosophique*) via a number of intermediaries. For Voltaire and Diderot, fetishism was the worship of sticks and stones which were believed to have active power. Marx develops the concept further with the Hegelian idea of alienation in which subject and object are inverted so that Man creates things which he believes create him. Marx's discussion of fetishism, however, can only be understood as part of his discussion of capitalism, seen as a mode of production in which the fact that human production and reproduction are the result of human activity is negated, so that it seems that production and reproduction are the product of a mysterious force called capital. Within that system, commodities or money which are inanimate substances, and exchange which is a non-productive activity, appear to give forth life, as in the Voltairian view of fetishes, where sticks and stones were worshipped because they were mistakenly believed to bring forth children, crops, wealth. In this way Marx showed that what had been represented by economists as merely technical devices were in fact ideological transformers which hid the true source of productivity and attributed productivity to things and activities which were not productive in themselves. This identification of the ideological and symbolical process at the heart of capitalism was merely the first step. In order to understand fetishes they had to be placed within a much wider symbolical and political context, and so Marx carried out a symbolical analysis of capitalism which forms a major part of his study.

This symbolical analysis is quite different from what we would find in the tradition of economic anthropology which saw an evolution from gift exchange to commodity and money exchange as merely a technical change in the mechanisms of exchange, precisely the approach which Mauss attacked. It is also different from Mauss' own analysis but for a different reason. Mauss, like Marx, saw the need for symbolical analysis; but unlike Marx he failed to appreciate that it is necessary to understand the nature and meaning of money and commodities, not simply in terms of the transactions in which they occurred, but in terms of the total politico-social system of production and reproduction. This totalising approach applied both to the study of exchange as part of the mode of production, and as part of a symbolical system, is the strength of Marx, while to my mind the poverty of a work such as that of Mauss is that it focuses on exchange without discussing the variable place and importance of exchange in equally developed different total politico-economic social systems. What Marx does, and what Mauss fails to do, is to see that the ideological stress on the image of exchange rather than on the image of production within the total system is itself variable. As a result Mauss' analysis starts too late. Although he is careful to distinguish the different meanings of transactions in different societies he does not ask the prior questions: in what societies are transactions symbolically prominent and what role is given to exchange as a whole in relation to other similar symbols such as female production? As a result, he produces a classification of types of exchanges which to me is of relatively little significance since we do not know if we are comparing like with like.

For example, it can be argued that in certain New Guinea societies exchange becomes symbolical production (Josephides 1985: 207–9), while in other societies it is the work of the ancestors (Bloch 1975) that takes on this role. In other words, the equivalent of the symbolism of transactions in one total system may be the symbolism of mystical production in another total system and it is then misleading to compare transactions in the one with transactions in the other. With the notion of fetishism Marx puts in question the place of transactions and of its adjuncts, for example money, when he argues that in capitalism exchange is a false representation of production.

Marx's contribution, which we can see in his discussion of capitalism, is almost the opposite of the isolation of exchange. When discussing capitalist commodity exchange he tells us that if we only take exchange into account we reach an absurd conclusion – that in capitalist ideology it looks as if exchange could replace production since commodities like money are made to appear to 'grow' of their own accord in the capitalist market. In order to avoid this absurdity Marx tells us we must understand the underpinning of this illusion, we must put exchange and the ideology of exchange in the wider context of production and reproduction to see what it is all about. This is the subject matter of *Capital*.

It is of course not possible to review here the whole of this often discussed theory and I shall simply limit myself to trying briefly to outline the steps Marx takes to place the symbolism of exchange in a wider context. The first step in Marx's theory is to show why we must understand the capitalist representation of labour. Capitalism, Marx argues, is based on a fundamental symbolical division between the private and domestic and the public and economic; and on the appearance that the two are ruled by totally different moralities. Here we are very close to Mauss. The next step involves Marx in showing the economic and political significance of this division. The part of the person which is involved in the economic process is represented as though it was a thing which can therefore be bought and sold in the economic world as though it were a commodity like any other commodity. The worker, represented as a private domestic actor, is obliged to sell himself, represented as a commodity, because he cannot produce as himself as a result of his lack of access to the means of production. This representation of an aspect of the person as though it were a commodity makes it possible for exchange to appear to be production because 'exchange' is nothing more than the manipulation of productive activity. Once this bizarre construction is in place the economic world can then be made to appear to be purely a matter of economic transaction and exchange of things or commodities whether these be labour or raw materials or land or produced goods, etc. All these things can then be shifted around by capitalists irrespective of social consequence so that – hey presto – production seems to occur without human participation. It can then appear 'only right' that manipulators of exchange should reap the richest rewards since it has been made to appear that it is they who are the real producers of wealth. It is also 'inevitable' that economics, the study of the creation of wealth, should concentrate on exchange.

Marx not only shows us the logic of all this, but also the logical premise for such a crazy picture: the illusion that people are double (private citizens and workers), and that their potential for production – their creativity – is divisible between a private productivity and domestic labour on the one hand, and on the other the quite separate world of the economy. This 'quite other world' of the economy can then appear to reproduce through a non-human agency – by the fetishes. The result of such production can then appear as alien to the actors who have been defined as productive individuals only in the domestic sphere in terms of love, sex and the family where they seem not to participate in 'production'.

What Marx shows is that the ideology of capitalism makes it appear as though exchange had replaced production, but that in fact what we consider as exchange is actually a way of talking about the general productive process. As such it is misleading to allow our analysis to follow this ideological lead and to separate exchange from the total mode of production as the economists have done, and also as Mauss unwittingly does.

The full irony of pretending that exchange is a form of production is revealed in the symbolism of money. Money in Marx's phrase, repeated many times, 'becomes pregnant' (a phrase borrowed significantly from Goethe's Mephisto) (Marx: 1959, vol. 3: 343). Marx's point explains well why we are taught a horror of bringing money into moral and kinship relations. It is because the fetishism of money and the illusion that the market produces on its own is made possible by the fundamental symbolical division of people in the capitalist market. If this division is challenged, as Marx challenges it, the whole ideological edifice of capitalism would collapse, so the two sides must be kept apart at all costs; hence the opposition money/love and the equation money=sterility discussed by a number of writers.

Marx, unlike Mauss, Polanyi, etc., proposes therefore that we carry out a total analysis of the symbolism of production within which we must place both exchange and the ideology of exchange. I shall try to follow him for the Merina in order to understand Merina ideas of money of which we already have had a glimpse. We must follow Marx in attempting an overall symbolical construction of the representation of the mode of production by Merina peasants, both in order to place Merina concepts of money within an explanatory context, and also to try to understand the historical potential of such a construction. In other words we need to begin to do for the Merina what Marx did for capitalism and in the process we shall see that one of his tools, the notion of fetishism, also turns out to be of value in this case.

The Merina and the symbolism of exchange

I have so far given only a very preliminary picture of rural Merina concepts of money. It is now necessary to consider more data.

Even if, by and large, it is true that the Merina are little disquieted by the moral implications of money as such, there are two important facts which seem to contradict this general assertion. The first concerns wage labour, the other concerns the sale of ancestral lands.

The Merina make a sharp distinction between unpaid work, carried out within the broad idiom of kinship obligations, and paid work carried out for strangers. The two are described by totally different words, *miasa* and *mikarama*. The former is seen as a morally *good* activity, part of ancestral duty, an aspect of obedience to elders and therefore to ancestors. The latter, working for a wage, is seen as an *ambiguous* activity which may often be downright immoral. For a long time, I thought, because of my native culture, that this was because of the money association of working for a wage. This however is off the point, something which was made very clear to me by an older informant, who, when discussing his son who was then working as a labourer on the road for the government, said: 'It is good that he has money, when I was young I was the only one who had no trousers . . . but he works every day even on Tuesday (a day banned by the ancestors) and so when Razafin- drazaka invites me I cannot say "Yes, elder, we thank you" [We shall all come], and I work without all my children and grandchildren . . . He is "lazy", "*kamo*".' *Kamo* is a word normally translated as 'lazy', but it really means not performing one's ancestral obligations. In other words, what I was being told was not that wage-labouring is bad in itself but that it is bad when, and only when, it competes with kinship obligations. In order to understand the distinction between paid work and other work it is misleading to focus on the European symbol of money. Rather one must focus on the Merina symbol of kinship obedience.

The same picture emerges when we look at the prohibition on selling ancestral lands. Again my understanding of this prohibition had tended to be that it was a way of keeping this sphere out of contact with commercial transactions. In other words I had interpreted it in terms of the European system, where money cannot be involved in the field of kinship and morality. It is interesting that such an interpretation seems to fit at first. But on fuller examination of the evidence I realised that this congruence was off the point because of two exceptions to the rule which contradict the simple view that money cannot be brought into contact with the things of the ancestors. The first is that there is no objection to selling land for money to close relatives who are presumed to share the same tomb with you. The second is that there is no objection, indeed it is a duty, to sell land in order to carry out the only truly obligatory secondary funeral, that is the bringing back of a corpse which has been buried elsewhere into the family tomb (Bloch 1971: 163–4).

These two exceptions clarify the significance of the prohibition of selling ancestral land. It is not, as I had misleadingly assumed, a horror of commercial morality and money. This is shown by the fact that commercial transactions among co-descendants are irrelevant as they do not involve dispersal of the ancestral substance, and the sale of land loses its negative aspect if it is encompassed within that supreme moral act: regrouping the corpses of the ancestors.

We are therefore brought back to a fundamental methodological point. Although money is important for the rural Merina it is not *an organising concept* for them. This means that it is possible to make observations about the use of money and attitudes to money among the Merina but these observations will not lead us to understand the rationale underlying their production. Rather we must look at those symbols, kinship and tombs, which *do organise* Merina concepts, and understand *their* nature in order to account for the practices and beliefs concerning money in Imerina. In other words, we should carry out the kind of analysis which Marx did for money for the central symbols of the Merina, which are not money, in order to understand Merina views of money. Indeed the same point applies to exchange generally, and here – for reasons already given – we part company with Mauss. Since exchange does not have the same central symbolical place for the Merina as it has in Europe (or for that matter in Melanesia), we cannot understand the rationale of Merina concepts of exchange by concentrating on exchange. We must, as with money, turn to those concepts which *do* organise Merina symbolism, and which deal with continuity and reproduction. These take the material form of ancestral tombs. However this does not mean that we cannot retain some of the content of Marx's analysis, for although the Merina do not make money into a fetish, they do make their tombs into symbols which share some of the characteristics of money in capitalist modes of production. Prominently among these is the characteristic which Marx stressed as encapsulating money fetishism in capitalism, that it is ideologically 'pregnant'. This applies in a modified form to the Merina notion of the tomb.

In order to understand this, we need to understand the Merina notion of blessing. This is the transferral of the creative power of the ancestors to descendants through the practice of blowing on water. For the Merina, the ancestors in the tomb are the source of the moral creativity of the living, and so in blessing the elders go to the tomb to ask for children, wealth, health – in other words creativity – and they pass this on to the junior generation through the mystical process of blessing. Indeed this blessing is the explanation for the prohibition on the dispersal of ancestral substance and for the need to regroup because it is this substance which enables the living to produce and reproduce. It is the tomb, and the dead which it contains, which is therefore life-giving in

Merina ideology, while the creative acts of people, whether biological reproduction or labour, are made to appear as only possible because of this fetishised power (Bloch 1975, 1986).

The parallel to capital and money as understood in the work of Marx is therefore the tomb and the bodies of the dead for the Merina. These, like capital, symbolically appropriate the creativity of people and labour and attribute it to a fetish. In both cases, the symbolical construction has devalued the creative power of people and has attributed it to an inanimate substance; commodities and money in the case of capitalism, tombs and human remains, in the case of the Merina.

The parallel goes further. We saw how the attribution of creativity to money and capital required the segregation of money from the processes of birth and kinship so that the duality of people as being involved in two distinct types of creativity as workers and individuals could be maintained. Similarly, the attribution of creativity to the tomb and the human remains in it, requires the segregation of fetishised creativity from the creativity which results from biological reproduction and the strength of labour. This antipathy also leads to a division of the person not along the cleavage of domestic individual versus worker, but along the line, ancestral being/animal being (Bloch 1986).

For the Merina, as a person goes through life he or she increasingly receives the blessings of the ancestors so that ultimately he or she becomes entirely an ancestor, that is, a moral person. However, there is another element to the body than its developing ancestral side. This other side is associated with the biological aspect of life, with sexuality, strength and enjoyment. This animal side is amoral and therefore potentially immoral if it is not gradually harnessed by the ancestral. However, it is also necessary for human beings so that they may reproduce not only mystically but also naturally.[6] This animal side thus involves a creativity in people which contrasts with the mystical creativity of the tomb and the ancestors, and which therefore has to be kept separated from anything to do with the tomb and its authority. This duality of creativity is acted out in Merina ritual in a number of ways (see Bloch 1982, 1986), and in avoidances which immediately remind us of the antipathy between money and the domestic domain.

The fundamental principle of the morality of Merina transactions could therefore be represented as the need to maintain the tomb and to regroup the undivided ancestral substance in it so that the fetishised fertility of the descendants may be maintained by the avoidance of dispersal of this substance. The concern for maintenance and regrouping lies at the heart of such activities as returning corpses to the family tomb and endogamous marriage which ensure not only the non-dispersal of people but also of ancestral land through inheritance. It also explains the value of such activity as working for kinsmen and presenting gifts to elders and seniors since this is all part of receiving the blessing of the ancestors by obeying them and those who are more ancestral than oneself, that is the elders.

This fundamental principle of maintenance of ancestral substance has at first sight nothing to do with transactions in non-ancestral substance; indeed it could be right to say that transactions not concerned with ancestral substance are by definition morally neutral since the ancestral equals the moral. These non-ancestral goods are called *harena* (Bloch 1984). *Harena* and ancestral resources mutually define each other by antithesis. While ancestral resources are not individually owned but are only temporarily held in trust by individuals during their lifetime, and therefore cannot be alienated, *harena* are individual property which must be alienated before death. While ancestral resources are austere and moral, *harena* is to be enjoyed sensually: finally, while *harena* is linked to action, movement, strength and sensuality, ancestral substances imply stillness and mystical reproduction. While the typical ancestral resources are rice lands and tombs, the most typical *harena* are cattle, cloth, jewellery and in the past, slaves and money. The contrast between the ancestral part of the self and the animal part of the self which we have just noted is therefore also found in the contrast between ancestral things and *harena*.

The symbolism of money for the Merina can only be understood as part of this fundamental opposition between ancestral resources and *harena*, since money is one of the many kinds of *harena*. All are clearly desirable but morally irrelevant. Blessings, for example, wish on the person blessed that he will get a lot of *harena*. Similarly the Merina are unnervingly enthusiastic and unembarrassed by activities which lead to obtaining *harena*. They are quite obsessive traders. Any opportunity to buy and sell is embraced even though it might bring very little profit. Roads to markets are lined by tens, sometimes hundreds, of tiny traders selling rice cakes or chopped up sugar cane in the hope of tiny profit. I find in my notes rather annoyed comments about walking through a village with a young man I knew well, which says that it was rather like walking through a showroom before an auction. The potential price of everything and every animal was discussed, even though there was not the slightest reason to believe they were up for sale. In a sense, for the Merina, everything is up for sale all the time and they are certainly unworried by this commercialism and continual handling of money.

There is even quite a romance about trade, something which is present in many non-capitalist economies. Ellis's description of this in the early nineteenth century would still be appropriate today.

The occupation in which the people especially delight, is traffic carried on by hawking different things about for sale. Some go down to the coast, and obtain articles of British manufacture from the merchants. Others purchase articles manufactured by their own countrymen, in the hope of realising some profit by selling them. Perhaps no class of men gain less than these hawkers, certainly none endure greater hardships; yet none are so devoted to their employment, and so unwilling to exchange it for another. The native songs often describe the mpivarotra, hawkers, sitting patiently all day at the market, or travelling from house to house until the sun sets upon their path, yet unwilling to cook a meal of rice until their hearts have been encouraged by obtaining some profit on their goods (Ellis 1838, vol. 1: 322).

The Merina are not worried about wanting to obtain *harena* whether in money or in any other form. There is no reason why they should since *harena* are, as such, of no concern to the ancestors. Yet it is not really so simple since there are two aspects of these types of transactions in *harena* which 'in the end' link up with the fetish of the tomb and the remains of the ancestors in it and which are therefore morally charged. One of these aspects I shall call the problem of individualisation, and the other the problem of degradation. To understand both of these it is necessary to further extend our understanding of Merina ideas concerning tombs and ancestors.

One of the fundamental concepts of Merina descent is that the group in the tomb is an undifferentiated group. It contains people who have been literally 'reduced' to their ancestral substance, which is therefore identical with that of the other corpses and from which it cannot be separated (Bloch 1971: 70). Individuation is a thing of this life which in the end must be relinquished if the descent group is to endure through the passing on of blessing from the tomb.

Individuation is therefore anti-descent. Now there is clearly a sense in which the acquiring of *harena* is a matter of individuation. This however does not make it bad, because in this life, before being dried as a corpse in the tomb, individuation is still quite acceptable and even, as we saw, desirable. The problem occurs when this individuation and personal enjoyment of the living somehow threatens to become permanent and thereby stop the undifferentiated return to the fetish life-giving tomb. That this is not a problem dreamt up by me can be shown by a number of rules which express this notion very concretely. First there is a rule that one should have distributed all one's *harena* before death. Secondly, there is the prohibition on the planting of trees. Although most economic activity is welcomed by the Merina, planting fruit trees is forbidden for the explicit reason that these endure longer than the individual's life. (Banana trees which do not outlive people are allowed.) This type of *harena*, unlike other *harena* which is theoretically distributed before death, would therefore compete with descent in an absolute way. It would render something of the individual permanent and stop the re-unification with the undifferentiated dead in the stone tombs which is the only legitimate continuity. *Harena* are therefore fine for this life, but they should not eternalise a source of creativity which would compete with the tomb. In the end one *must* be reduced to impersonal descent substance in the tomb and be nothing else.

The other way in which *harena* and ancestry affect each other is less direct and is linked with the Merina notion of degradation embodied in the Merina concept of *tsiny*. This has been discussed in a theological thesis by Pastor Andriamanjato (1957). The notion of *tsiny* is, at its most general, the idea that the very fact of being alive and acting inevitably implies that one is failing the ancestors. More specifically, it implies that one is causing the *dispersal* of the ancestral substance. One does this by any form of movement which can be construed as moving away from the land and the ancestors, and is typified by something which nearly all Merina do, leaving one's ancestral village, that is leaving the village where one's tomb is. This is a typical activity of traders and of women; the latter because they are often involved in virilocal marriage which implies the dispersal of their ancestral substance, and potentially that of their children as well as of the lands which they and their children may inherit. Indeed, all movement is antithetical to the cold, dry, eternal stillness of the ancestors in the tomb. This is especially true of the supreme movement of birth and death, which offers a challenge to the creating fetish of the tomb in which the difference between birth and death has been abolished. One could go as far as to say that being alive is in itself a potential problem for Merina ideology. The Merina believe that all their actions, by their very nature as actions, incur *tsiny* since they all lead to dispersal. This is so of such activities as trade or other activities including those which lead to obtaining money, but it is not more so of such activities. In this light it is possible to see *harena* not any more as neutral but as positively negative.

However, the possession of *harena* money, can become in certain circumstances positively morally good. To understand why, it is essential to see that the idea of degradation implied in the concept of *tsiny* is not absolute. The degradation of *tsiny* can be and should be reversed by performing rituals of re-grouping which repair the dispersal of *tsiny* and which therefore lead to blessing. This is how *harena* can become morally good. This is because *harena* can be used to cancel out *tsiny* by replacing what has been dispersed through lines. The second connection of *harena* to ancestry is therefore positive.

For example, the expenditure of wealth for keeping up the ancestral tomb and for secondary funerals is excellent. Nobody need be bothered about money used for these purposes. It is the use of wealth for the removal of *tsiny* by compensation. For the Merina one could say that since the tomb is eternal its decay must be caused by the *tsiny* of the living and so repair is not recreation but restoration. This becomes clear when we note that the greatest obligation to make monetary contributions falls on those descendants of the ancestors who, by their actions, have caused the greatest dispersal of ancestral substances: the sons-in-law who have taken their wives to live with them away from their parents and their parents' tombs. It might be surprising to Africanists or South Asianists to see wife-takers as errant children of their wives' parents, but that is exactly how the Merina view them. The Merina marriage ritual is a ritual of affiliation of the son-in-law to his wife's parents and ancestors. However in most circumstances this 'son' takes himself away, as well as his 'sister-wife' and his children. He therefore must atone for this terrible dispersion by a massive contribution to his wife's group's tomb and secondary funerals so that its substance can be regrouped and the blessing which its continued existence implies be maintained (Bloch 1974, 1978). There are no greater transfers of property than those 'reimbursements' to the ancestors of one's wife for the dispersion that one has caused. This, however, need not always be limited to dispersion caused by the removal of women. In the case of uxorilocal marriage, sons who have left can obliterate, or at least limit the disgrace of their action by very similar massive contributions to the ancestral activities centred on their own parents' tomb.

These large restitutions at rituals carried out to remove *tsiny* are only extreme manifestations of what is going on all the time on a smaller scale. Every time a person asks for a blessing from an elder he is expected at the same time to make a gift to the elder which nearly always takes the form of money. It would, however, be wrong to assume that the Merina visualise this as a repayment for the blessing. Such an idea would indeed be shocking since the blessing comes from God and the ancestors. For the Merina the gift to the elder is part of the general atonement for dispersal, and in the same way as the elder is an intermediary between the ancestors and his descendants when he gives blessing, he is also such an intermediary when he receives money in atonement for *tsiny*. Indeed all gifts and help in the form of labour to elders are seen in this light, and this is why, as we saw in the example given above, it is wrong to work for *harena* for oneself to such an extent that one cannot obey elders and in this way atone for *tsiny*; to do this is to eternalise the dispersal of ancestral resources.

Because there is *tsiny*, the fruit of transactions must in the end be returned to atone for dispersal. This is so not only for affinity but also *in the end* for all exchange. Trade, exchange, money, are desirable because (1) they are enjoyable in this life and (2) potentially they are good if used to restore the waste one has caused by the nasty habit of being alive.

Our understanding of Merina ideas about money is therefore entirely dependent on its place in a wider framework of significance which accords money as such a minor symbolical role. First, we must understand that money is a special type of *harena*, then we must understand the subtle antithesis between ancestral resources and *harena*, which is governed by the fetish of the tomb with the ancestral remains which it contains.

Such an analysis has, however, not just static structural significance, it also explains aspects of the historical response of the Merina to changing economic circumstances, since whatever their causes, these circumstances could only be interpreted and dealt with by the Merina within the framework of ideas obtained from the past. An attempt to show this process is briefly attempted in the next section.

The Merina symbolism of money and exchange in historical perspective

Only the very briefest outline of the historical interpretation of money in Imerina can be attempted here. A fuller study would require as background an analysis of the economic history of the region which is only beginning. We do, however, possess a number of relevant facts from previous studies and some clear patterns emerge.

Some form of currency has been found in Madagascar from as far back as the tenth or eleventh century. By the seventeenth century at least there are numerous indications that foreign currency was found throughout Madagascar, and that though this currency was very scarce and used in probably only a few transactions many people must have known how to use this currency in exchange. Our earliest clear indiction of the use of money in Imerina dates from the late eighteenth century and comes from the diaries of a trader–adventurer–spy called Nicolas Mayeur, who visited what was to become Imerina in 1777 and subsequently. He has a lot to say about trade and money as might be expected. The image he gives concerning money seems at first contradictory but is repeated in all our sources: on the one hand, he talks of the use of money in markets where the stuff is considered in a highly uninhibited way; and on the other, of the use of money for royal tribute or taxation where it is treated with great reverence and is referred to by the term *harena* which might be preliminarily translated as *holiness*. Here is his description of Merina markets for 1777 in my translation:

There is a public market established by the present king in each province on different days of the week. Saturday is the day for the capital . . . The listing of the objects for sale at these fairs will make clear the nature and the products of the country, and the kinds of industry of its people. Apart from the various types of livestock to which I have already referred the following articles are to be found, silk cocoons, raw silk, spun and dyed silk, sarongs and 'langoutis' of the three types I described, sarongs made of raphia cloth obtained from leaves from the east coast, iron ore, pig iron, iron made into spades, axes, knives of all kinds, irons for slaves, spears, chick peas, white and red beans, sweet potatoes, bananas . . . beef sold cut up as it would be in our butchers' shops. A little beef can be obtained even for a 120th of a dollar if one cannot afford more.

Then Mayeur described the international nature of the markets and the presence of so-called Arabs, probably Muslim Indians, selling cloth from Gujerat and above all, the presence of slave traders from the coast. He then describes the money changers in the corner of the market, commenting:

These people do not have currency marked by the insignia of their rulers. Any coins, so long as they are of silver and are of the right weight will do. They may use non-monetised silver but prefer it monetised . . . The money is weighed in very accurate scales of their making. The weights are full unhusked rice grains. According to them the Spanish dollar weighs 720 rice grains (Mayeur 1913).

He then goes on to describe how it is cut down to tiny fractions to obtain lower denominations, all checked according to weight.

We seem to be dealing with a monetised economy already in the latter half of the eighteenth century when not only are the Merina well acquainted with currency but it is fair to assume that this had been the case for a long time. Certain qualifications however need to be made. First of all, Merina markets were quite clearly, in Bohannan's and Dalton's terms, 'peripheral markets' since most production was not commercialised (Bohannan and Dalton 1962). Secondly, we also know from Mayeur that there was a great shortage of silver coins and of other foreign commodities which led to periods when the whole marketing economy simply did not work. However, there was money and everybody knew about it. This money was foreign silver coins which were cut up, divided and weighed to obtain smaller denominations. These coins were mainly Maria Theresa Thalers, but a whole variety of different silver coins were also used. Although present since very early times, it is clear that the amount of money must have dramatically increased fairly shortly before Mayeur's arrival; indeed both his coming and the increase in the amount of currency have the same cause, the great growth in trade that took place in the eighteenth century. This was mainly due to the slave trade directed first to Mauritius and Reunion. Such trade had been going on in the coastal areas of Madagascar, but for reasons which are not clear, around 1770 the Merina managed to capture much of this trade and to become major suppliers of slaves. In return for these slaves, they obtained weapons, which enabled them to conquer their neighbours, and silver, which in the end, made its appearance in the markets drawing a variety of traders usually described as Arabs, but who seem for the most part to have been Muslim Gujeratis trading principally in cloth.

The political significance of this trade and of the possibility offered by money as a source of potential power not controlled by political authority, is very evident at this period. The famous Merina King Andrianampoinimerina, the memory of whose speeches form a large part of Merina history, offers a good example of the significance of this. What is coming out from recent research (Ayachre 1976: 178ff), is that this great traditional hero was in fact a successful slave trader who was able to organise a revolt against the local ruler and that from then on he began the successful conquest of his neighbours. The problem however was that what had been possible for him was also possible for others. In other words all accumulators of money were potential political threats. Partly for this reason and partly for others the Merina rulers were desperate to acquire money themselves and to somehow control its flow. Money in Madagascar, as elsewhere, meant power; the ability to control others either through commerce or through coercion. Trade was a continual horizontal cross-current of power to what might be called the vertical attempts at control from rulers. It is not too fanciful to see the flow of trade in eighteenth- and nineteenth-century Merina as a horizontal irrigation of power which concentrated at certain nodal points, while royal power was the attempt to pump off this loosely flowing power in order to reduce the possibility of challenge and to strengthen the government.

The obvious way of doing this was the issuing of money by the political authority and the banning of what may be called international commodity money. The Merina made several attempts at this (Molet 1970) but it proved quite beyond both their technological and administrative competence. In any case, the rulers just did not have enough silver. Andrianampoinimerina made some headway towards regulating the currency by the very strict regulations he introduced to control the activities of money changers and the ways in which they cut up and handled coins.

The other way of controlling monetary flow was by taxation in money. We know a lot about Merina taxation but the general policy seems to have been roughly 'if it moves, tax it'! There were a totally bewildering number of taxes. For example, during the annual feast of the royal bath no less than six different taxes could be collected. The list is endless: there was a tax for each spade; for each harvest; for the first breaking of the soil; for first fruits; for adoption; for circumcision (again six different ones); etc., etc. However, it is probable that most of this taxation was never collected in money, but was substituted for, by goods or labour, and often was not collected at all. Very significantly Mayeur comments:

The tribute which the king receives should be paid fairly regularly; however in order not to get on the wrong side of his subjects, the king only demands them when foreigners come to the kingdom, because he then uses them to pay for the goods which they bring (Mayeur 1913).

The reason however must have also been that since these strangers were slave traders, who paid largely in silver, that was the time when money was available.

Now if all this is fairly straightforward in economic and political terms, there is an aspect of money transactions which is emphasised in all our sources and which is surprising. Unlike the matter-of-fact transactions Mayeur describes for the marketplaces, he also makes it clear that the giving and receiving of taxes was a very different matter. It was a 'holy' activity and indeed the money so transferred was called 'holiness' (Berg 1985).

The actual word is *hasina*, a word which I have discussed in an earlier publication (Bloch 1977). It is extremely difficult to render its meaning exactly. It is the power of the ancestors at its purest. It is the essence of differential *hasina* which explains the differential ranks of Merina society and the prominence of rulers. At its very heart however there is an interesting ambiguity in the concept, which I have tried to highlight by calling the two sides *hasina* mark I and *hasina* mark II. *Hasina* mark I is the innate *hasina* which resides in the purity and sanctity of ancestors and rulers, and *hasina* mark II is the gift to those who possess *hasina* mark I: that is, the coins of taxation represented as a constituent part of this two-way flow which constitutes the transfer of sanctity. To understand this rather strange way of seeing taxation it is essential to place it within the wider context of the representation of Merina monarchy.

By means of great royal rituals such as the annual royal bath, or the circumcision ceremony, the Merina kingdom was made to appear as one big descent group of which the king was an elder and the subjects his descendants. This idea implied that the kingdom was organised around the idea of blessing since this is what should regulate the relation between generations. The rituals were occasions when the king, acting as an elder, transferred the life-giving power of the ancestors to the subjects, acting as his children. In other words the meaning of taxation was encompassed within the overall framework of descent discussed in the previous section (Berg n.d.).

As we saw, for the blessing of the ancestors to be successful the substance of the ancestors must not be dispersed, but since it is inevitably dispersed through *tsiny*, this unavoidable dispersion has to be counterbalanced by restoration, by means of the *harena* one has obtained in life so that it can be used to replace those ancestral resources one has dispersed. This is the logic which underlies the payments a son-in-law must make to his wife's family rituals and the reason why one must obey the elders and work for them. Since the whole kingdom was like one descent group within which blessing was dispensed from the ancestors by the intermediary of the king acting as elder, it followed that the subjects should atone for *tsiny* by restoring that ancestral substance which they had dispersed. That is, they should use their *harena* for ancestral purposes, in this case by giving them to the king, the intermediary of the ancestors.

Taxation given to the sovereign was therefore not neutral money but holy *hasina* since it was restoring the ancestors. We find here the pattern already discussed. While transactions in *harena* are normally neutral, they can become positive when *harena* is used to atone for *tsiny*.

Money as taxation was therefore, rather surprisingly to our mind, holy in contrast to its normal moral neutrality. This difference between neutral instrumental money and 'holy' money received some material elaboration in the distinction which seems to have been drawn in the nineteenth century between the uses of the pure uncut coins (*tsy vaky*=uncut), and the more ordinary neutral cut money. This contrast between cut and uncut coins, however, should not be taken too far. We know that most taxes were in fact collected as cut money but were spoken of as if they were uncut following the same principle of unproblematic substitution which I discussed at the beginning of this chapter.

As we see, if we are to understand the interpretation that was put on politico-economic development in the eighteenth and nineteenth century by the Merina, it is not enough to see events in extra-cultural terms but we must also understand how these events were interpreted in terms of pre-existing patterns. How else could we make sense of the contrast between cut and uncut coins and of the 'holiness' of taxation?

This, however, does not mean that politico-economic events did not bring about changes in the symbolism of money but these need to be understood in terms of pre-existing structures. A recent study by S. Ellis illustrates this point (Ellis 1985). In *The Rising of the Red Shawls* he discusses the moral climate of the Merina at the end of the nineteenth century. This was a period when various people in Antananarivo, the capital, began to establish a society which was attempting to break away from the moral obligations which traditionally bound people and to replace it by an impersonal financial order on a European model. This was a complex system of debts of a form introduced through French and British influence which brought about a new order of subjugation of ordinary Merina to a few plutocrats in the capital. The result of this state of affairs seems to have been the development of a symbolism of money not unlike that of modern Europe. This took the form of an attack on the symbol of money as such by those who were opposed to the plutocrats as well as to European influence and to Christianity. This attack and the rhetoric concerning money it employed is reminiscent of some millenarian movements in Europe (Ellis 1985: 154). Yet it seems to me that we should be wary of such similarity. What those opposed to the plutocrats were complaining about was the unacceptability of legitimising subjugation through the force of *harena* rather than through the symbolism of descent. As such, their response was well within the repertory of Merina symbolism. The use of money as a negative symbol did not mean that the kind of avoidance that we have in our own society was present. Of this there is no evidence.

However, even this negative symbolism of money did not persist, at least in rural Imerina. I found no trace of it in my fieldwork in the 1960s and 1970s. The reason is probably that the situation described by Ellis for the late nineteenth century was soon replaced by colonial rule and that the opposition to exploitation could then focus on other symbols, especially the conflict between whites and Malagasy.

The traditional symbolic logic of the Merina did however continue to affect the way they symbolised money in the twentieth century but this was in an unexpected way. In 1895, the French invaded Madagascar and replaced the old silver currency with French money. Indeed it looks as if this replacement may have begun to occur earlier, perhaps as a result of the fact that silver lost its fixed exchange value to gold towards the end of the nineteenth century. In any case the old silver dollars ceased to be used as currency. They were preciously kept, not any more as money, but as heirlooms, that is as things of the ancestors to be kept and not dispersed. In this way silver coins joined the ancestral land and the bones of the dead as ancestral resources and their use reflects this removal from the sphere of *harena*. These old coins are often put in the water that is used in blessings together with other 'ancestral' items. The ordinary money in use has, however, retained its moral neutrality. The distinction between the symbolical use of ancestral coin and actual currency is a development of the division which we saw developing in the nineteenth century between uncut coins, which began to become ancestral, and cut coins which were neutral *harena*. Indeed the ancestral coins are always qualified today as *tsy vaky* even though the cut coins have not survived.

Once again, events in the politico-economic field have brought about changes, but these are transformations of previously existing systems of meaning not direct importations from other systems. Even though we seem to recognise similarities between the Merina and the European symbolical system, these are misleading unless we try, as I have attempted in this chapter, to reintegrate these significances within the wider symbolical system.

The meanings attributed to money, in a case such as this, cannot therefore be understood simply by Dalton's phrase 'money is what money does'. In a sense this point has become fairly standard in anthropology since Mauss, but even he directly correlated the symbolism of money to the types of prevailing prestations and ultimately correlates these with the nature of the economy itself. Bohannan's insistence on the moral aspects of transactions might have helped, but again the close correlation between the meanings of money and the types of exchange postulated cannot be substantiated. Rather we need a much more fundamental approach which not only challenges our assumption that we can understand the symbolism of money *ab initio* but also one which questions the place of exchange in the ideological system with which inevitably the symbolism of money is linked. The Merina, as we saw, define transactions together with the domestic, in opposition to the unchanging ancestral which is seen as mystically creating. They therefore push exchange and the things exchanged as well as money outside the sphere of the moral. In Western ideology, as Marx showed, money and trade are seen as a mysterious creative force which contrasts with the domestic. As a result we find Merina tombs to be the analytical equivalent of Western commerce.

Notes

1 There is a lot of variation in European attitudes.
2 There is a problem here in that the word *vola* also means silver and so it might be argued that the girls are being called silver. Even if that was so the association with currency would inevitably be present.
3 Among the nearby Zafimaniry there are certain contexts where money is forbidden.
4 Polanyi in several places half begins the attempt only to fall back immediately on an analysis of the functions of money in market economies. He seems to believe that these functions of money are sufficient to understand its meanings (Polanyi 1944 and 1957).
5 Of course Marx in many cases is careful to distinguish between capitalism and other types of market dominated systems; but in many places he does not, and a similar unexamined merging is found in much more recent Marxist literature.
6 In some of my earlier writings, e.g. 1984, I may have given the impression that this animal side is seen as simply negative. This is because in rituals, especially in funerary rituals which are not concerned with the continuation of earthly life, it is often acted out in this way. This, however, is misleading: the vital side is not so much immoral as amoral and therefore in need of control by the ancestral side (Bloch 1985).

References

Althabe, G. 1969. *Oppression et libération dans l'imaginaire*, Paris: Maspero.

Andriamanjato, R. 1957. *Le Tsiny et le Tody dans le pensée Malgache*, Paris: Présence Africaine.

Ayache, S. 1976. *Raombana l'historien (1809–1855)*. *Introduction à l'édition critique de son oeuvre*, Fianarantsoa: Ambozontany.

Berg, G. 1985. 'The sacred musket: tactics, technology and power in eighteenth century Madagascar', *Comparative Studies in Society and History*, vol. 27.

n.d. 'Perceptions of technology in Imerina 1780–1825'.

Bloch, M. 1971. *Placing the dead: tombs, ancestral villages and kinship organisation among the Merina of Madagascar*, London: Seminar Press.

1974. 'Madagascar seen from Roti' in *Bijdragen tot de Taal-Land-en Volkenkunde*, vol. 130.

1975. 'Property and the end of affinity', in M. Bloch, ed., *Marxist analyses and social anthropology*, A.S.A. studies, London: Malaby Press.

1977. 'The disconnection between rank and power as a process: an outline of the development of kingdoms in central Madagascar', in J. Friedman and M. Rowlands, eds., *The evolution of social systems*, London: Duckworth.

1978. 'Marriage among equals: an analysis of Merina marriage rituals', *Man* (n.s.), 13: 21–33.

1982. 'Death, women and power', in M. Bloch and J. Parry, eds., *Death and the regeneration of life*, Cambridge: Cambridge University Press.

1984. 'Almost eating the ancestors', *Man* (n.s.), 20.

1986. *From blessing to violence: history and ideology in the circumcision ritual of the Merina of Madagascar*, Cambridge: Cambridge University Press.

Bohannan, P. 1959. 'The impact of money on an African subsistence economy', *The Journal of Economic History*, 19 (4).

Bohannan, P. and Dalton, G., eds., 1962. *Markets in Africa*, Evanston: Northwestern University Press.

Dalton, G. 1965. 'Primitive money', *American Anthropologist*, 67.

Davis, J. 1973. 'Forms and norms: the economy of social relations', *Man* (n.s.), vol. 18.

Ellis, S. 1985. *The rising of the red shawls: a revolt in Madagascar 1896–1899*, African Studies Series 43, Cambridge: Cambridge University Press.

Ellis, W. 1838. *History of Madagascar* (2 vols.), London: Fisher.

Firth, R. 1967. 'Themes in economic anthropology: a general comment', in R. Firth, ed., *Themes in economic anthropology*, A.S.A. Monograph No. 6, London: Tavistock.

Josephides, L. 1985. *The production of inequality: gender and exchange among the Kewa*, London: Tavistock.

Malinowski, B. 1922. *Argonauts of the Western Pacific*, London: Routledge and Kegan Paul.

Marx, K. 1959. *Capital: a critique of political economy*, vol. 3, London: Lawrence and Wishart.

Mauss, M. 1923–4. 'Essai sur le don: forme et raison de l'échange dans les sociétés archaïques', *l'Année Sociologique*, 2nd series, vol. 1.

Mayeur, N. 1913. 'Voyage dans le sud et dans l'intérieur des terres et plus particulièrement au pays d'Ancove', reprinted in *Bulletin de l'Académie Malgache*, 12.

Molet, L. 1970. 'Les Monnaies à Madagascar', Cahiers Wilfred Pareto, no. 21.

Parry, J. 1986. 'The gift, the Indian gift, and the "Indian gift"', *Man*, 21 (3).

Polanyi, K. 1971. *Primitive, archaic and modern economies: essays of Karl Polanyi*, ed. G. Dalton, Boston: Beacon Press.

Sahlins, M. 1972. *Stone age economies*, Chicago: Aldine.

Simmel, G. 1978. *The philosophy of money*, London: Routledge and Kegan Paul.

Strathern, M. 1985. 'Kinship and economy: constitutive orders of a provisional kind', *American Ethnologist*, 12.

8

Resistance to the present by the past: mediums and money in Zimbabwe

DAVID LAN

The most characteristic form of religious experience among the Shona people of Zimbabwe is spirit possession. A variety of forms of possession exist. The most important and the most widely described is possession by the spirits of the chiefs of the past. These spirits, known as *mhondoro* or lion spirits, have featured in a number of books and articles and they are the leading figures of this chapter as well.[1]

One reason for the notoriety of the *mhondoro* is the part played by their mediums in organising resistance to the Rhodesian state. Many *mhondoro* mediums took a key role in the rebellion that broke out in the years immediately following the arrival of the British pioneer column in 1890. A large number were active on the side of the nationalist guerrillas during the civil war between 1972 and 1979 culminating in the achievement of majority rule in 1980. In another publication I have analysed and assessed the contribution to this achievement made by recent mediums in an area known as Dande (Lan 1985). In this chapter I describe an aspect of the rebellious nature of these mediums which is especially puzzling and intriguing.

This relates to the ritual practice of the mediums as it was in the years before Independence. By means of a set of ritual prohibitions, mediums expressed their belief that certain commercially produced commodities available on the open market were extremely dangerous to them. However, money itself, without which these markets could not operate, was not thought of as dangerous in the same way. This is not to say that money was regarded as symbolically neutral but, whereas it was believed for example that if a medium drank a bottle of Coca Cola he would die, mediums regularly handled cash without any fear at all.

I should make clear straight away precisely who it is that is capable of handling money without danger. Is it the medium or the spirit that possesses him? The question might seem absurd. How can a spirit – a being without form, without hands – be said to handle money? But a very

191

clear distinction is drawn between the money that belongs to the medium and the money of the spirit itself. In fact, though neither medium nor spirit may have contact with the commodities I have mentioned as well as a range of other objects, neither need have any fear of money. The point of this observation will be clearer if I say a little more about these royal spirits, the *mhondoro*, and the society in which they, through their mediums, play a part.

Chiefs, ancestors and the land

Dande is a small section of the Zambezi Valley in the extreme north of Zimbabwe on the Mozambiquan and Zambian borders. Within Dande live four more or less distinct language groups. I deal here only with the Korekore and the Tande who between them comprise roughly three-quarters of the total population. Their most important crops are maize and sorghum. The most significant factor affecting the economy of the region is the uncertainty of the rains which, almost invariably, fail one year in three. The bulk of cultivation is along river banks but in the most serious droughts even the largest rivers run dry.

Because of the poor rain and dry soils, the intense heat and the presence of tsetse fly which sooner or later puts paid to any cattle that enter the Valley, little more than a bare subsistence is achieved by the majority of the farmers. However, I estimate that perhaps one quarter of the population will, in a good year, produce a small surplus of grain for sale. In addition, perhaps 10 per cent of farmers grow cash crops, especially cotton. Not more than a handful of households derive profits of any remarkable size from sale to the markets. By far the most important source of cash is migrant labour. The last available figure is from 1961 when 72 per cent of the men of Dande spent at least part of the year working in mines or on plantations out of the Valley.[2]

Apart from a few scattered shops owned and controlled from outside the valley and the sale of surplus vegetables between households, there are no markets operating within Dande itself. Grain surpluses must be transported up the mountain side to the nearest town where all purchases of clothes, furniture and other household goods are made.

In the course of military operations carried out during the recent war, government forces destroyed almost all the property of most of the people of Dande, their houses and all their contents. In the years that followed, various commodities began to appear once again: mass-produced clothes, some items of furniture, metal pots, bicycles, radios, the odd sewing machine. Despite this, there remains a marked difference between the levels of affluence of the people of Dande and those who live on the plateau above them.

In the past, the most significant political affiliation of the people of Dande was to a chief, either the chief of the territory in which they lived or, if they were members of a royal lineage, to the chief who was head of that lineage. A chieftaincy consists of two elements: a bounded territory and a chiefly lineage. Both are believed to derive from the senior ancestor of the chieftaincy who is thought to have founded the royal lineage and to have conquered or been the first occupant of the chief's territory. This has two important consequences. The first is that the territory of the chieftaincy is thought of as the property of the royal ancestors. It cannot be bought or sold. No one may live on or cultivate it except the descendants of the ancestor unless the ancestor has given specific permission for them to do so. The members of the royal lineage make up on average about one-third of the inhabitants of a chieftaincy. The remaining two-thirds are people who have been awarded this right and descendants of such people.

The second consequence is that each royal lineage possesses a genealogy of up to fifteen generations linking the present chief to his most distant ancestor. Non-royal lineages have genealogies which are not related to those of the royals and are no more than three or four generations deep. The ancestors named on the royal genealogy are the *mhondoro* who, as the original conquerors and owners of the territory, are believed to control the fertility of the earth and to bring the rain. In addition, they are in control of all the ritual aspects of agricultural production. They announce the start of the ploughing and sowing seasons, they provide medicines to control pests and, in return for these services, they receive an offering of the first crops at each harvest.

The most idiosyncratic feature of Dande chieftaincies is that they are divided into what have been called 'spirit provinces'.[3] These vary in size from a few to a hundred square miles. Each is thought to be under the protection of one of the ancestors that appears on the royal genealogy. At the same time, all of the provinces together are under the protection of the most senior (i.e., most distant in time) of the *mhondoro*, or royal lion spirits.

From time to time, each *mhondoro* will possess a medium who, once initiated, takes up residence within the province controlled by his spirit, acting as a channel of communication between the living inhabitants of the province and the long dead ancestor. In addition to controlling the supply of rain, the *mhondoro* are also capable of curing the sick, of providing medicines to protect crops against attack by insects and other pests, and may be consulted by anyone who requires advice about events of the future or the past. When each of the spirit provinces is occupied by a medium possessed by a *mhondoro* it is as if the entire history of the royal lineage has returned to life and is available to protect and advise their followers once again.

In sum then, the *mhondoro* seem to provide legitimacy and authority to two separate institutions: chiefs and *mhondoro* mediums. Chiefs draw their authority from the claim to *descent* from these ancestors, the original conquerors of the territory they now rule. The spirit mediums, on the other hand, draw their authority from the claim to *possession* by the *mhondoro*, the chiefs of the past.

According to local theory, a chief and the mediums of his ancestors should work closely together; chiefs ruling, mediums advising and teaching. The chief's duty is to hold court, to judge crimes and restore order to the social world. The duty of the mediums is to maintain the balance and hence the fertility of the natural world, curing the sick and bringing the rain. In practice however this division of authorities may become a battleground with chiefs and mediums claiming precedence and superiority over one another, disputing the legitimacy of the authority of the other partner in the relationship.

Medium and spirit[4]

Apart from the *mhondoro* there are a range of other spirits that take mediums as well. Just as the ancestors of the royal lineages are believed to take care of the territory over which the chiefs rule, so ancestors of commoner lineages look after their immediate descendants. The main difference between the minor forms of mediumship and the mediums of the *mhondoro* is that the minor mediums only fulfil a distinctive role when they are actually in a state of possession. At all other times they are regarded as more or less ordinary people. By contrast, the *mhondoro* medium is a full time professional. One of the ways in which this is indicated is that these mediums observe certain prohibitions on their day to day behaviour. These remain in force throughout the medium's professional life. Unless he is discredited, a relatively rare occurrence, this continues until his death.

The first and most obvious of these prohibitions is that against wearing ordinary clothes. The medium's costume is unique consisting of some lengths of black or sky-blue cloth, sandals, strings of black and white beads worn round the neck and a wide-brimmed straw or fur hat. This outfit seems to be based on the dress of chiefs from the seventeenth century onwards. A second set of prohibitions controls the life of the medium in a far more profound manner. These demand that the medium avoid having any part in or contact with the activities surrounding the birth and death of other people. They must avoid all contact with the making and unmaking of human life.

It is believed that if a medium comes into contact with a pregnant or menstruating woman, if he attends a funeral or sees a dead body he will die. I have suggested elsewhere that these avoidances point to the nature of the authority the *mhondoro* spirit commands.[5] It is an authority above and beyond human, mundane experience. It is the authority of the dead who have the power to return to life, to inhabit the body of a human medium, to participate once again in human affairs but now as omniscient and omnipotent. This quality of the *mhondoro*, that their life is self-sufficient and never-ending, is powerfully expressed by the mediums' fear and avoidance of the colour red which stands (in their own words) for human blood, the blood of death and of menstruation, which signifies the temporary nature of life as humans experience it. The working out of this symbolism leads to the belief that if a medium sees the colour red he will die.

It is important to grasp the conceptual fusion of spirit and medium that habitually occurs. Though it is the *mhondoro* that is put in danger by human blood, it is the medium that must keep away from funerals or pregnant women and this is true whether or not he is actually possessed by the spirit at the time. Similarly, modern commercially produced commodities are harmful to the medium himself no matter in what state of consciousness he happens to be. This fusion is so complete that the medium is commonly referred to and even addressed by the name of his spirit.

However, in other contexts the disjunction between medium and spirit is rigorously insisted on. One of these contexts is the accumulation by mediums and by spirits of wealth either in the form of goods or of money.

For each of the services that the *mhondoro* perform for their followers a payment must be made. This may take the form of a length of cloth or a lump of tobacco but more typically it is made in the form of cash. There can be no doubt that this money is thought of as a payment to the spirit rather than to his medium. In many cases it will be placed in a dish held by the medium while in a state of trance. Alternatively it may be given to an official known as a *mutapi*, the keeper of the spirit's shrine.

The key point is that this money may be used only to the advantage of the spirit and his followers. It may be used by the medium only to the extent that it provides him with a home at the shrine and ritual clothes to wear. If it comes to be believed that a medium is making use of money paid to the spirit to accumulate unusually great wealth or a large number of wives, this may lead to a suspicion that the medium is not genuine, that his claims to possession by the *mhondoro* are cynical and fraudulent.

The disjunction between medium and *mhondoro* is crucial to the institution of mediumship as the Shona practise it. The process by which an individual becomes a medium is long and complex. The aspect that matters here is the belief that a medium must be the totally passive recipient and executor of a spirit's will. When a medium is possessed he is believed to abandon his own personality, his consciousness, his volition totally. No word the *mhondoro* speaks, no action he performs, should bear any relation to the life or experience of the medium. It is only if his followers can believe in his capacity to obliterate his own personality and thus allow the spirit to speak out with no distortion or interception that his authenticity as a medium will be accepted. As the one essential characteristic of the *mhondoro* is his altruism, if a medium grows rich through the practice of mediumship this implies that the will of the medium rather than that of the spirit has prevailed. On the other hand, the medium may earn money in his own right by selling surplus agricultural produce or handicrafts such as woven baskets or hats.

The crucial point is this: it is a characteristic of *mhondoro* mediums that they express the nature of the spirit that possesses them by abstaining from the use of or contact with certain objects and processes. Fear and hence avoidance of human blood, birth and death expresses the nature of the *mhondoro* as distinct from and opposed to the experience of human life. Mediums also avoid the products of modern capitalist society. Money, on the other hand, is not dangerous to mediums or *mhondoro*. Indeed so intensely is the money of the *mhondoro* thought of as being his own that if a medium makes use of it the authenticity of his possession may be called into question.

The avoidance of modern commodities is very fully worked out. Apart from their wearing of non-Western clothes, mediums may not consume tinned or otherwise processed foods or drinks or even enter the shops where these are sold. They may not use Western medicines or smoke cigarettes. They may not ride in motorcars or buses, use telephones or have their photograph taken. However, commodities that were part of trade cycles before British colonialism such as cloth and beads they may wear without danger. In fact the wearing of these identifies them as chosen men and women, as valued religious specialists. The difficulty then is to explain why modern commodities are dangerous, whereas money, historically the agent of commoditisation, is not. To do this requires a brisk survey of the ninety years of colonial rule in Zimbabwe.

Mediums and chiefs

To start with, here is a description of a *mhondoro* medium taken from a journal kept by the explorer David Livingstone in the year 1861, that is thirty years before the arrival of Cecil Rhodes' pioneer column, the heralds of colonialism, in Mashonaland:

A man came to see us who stated that he was the Pandora [i.e., the *mhondoro*] of the place. [I] asked him to change himself into a lion then, that we might see and believe. [He] said that it was only the heart that changed, that he pointed out witches to be killed, that he told when rains would come . . . [he] said he made offerings of beer by pouring it out on the ground. . . . He smelt gun powder from one loading his gun, and went to one side, trembling very successfully . . . He is the presider over their superstitions and gives them medicines to kill game. (Livingstone 1956)

A Portuguese state official, Albino Manuel Pacheco, who travelled up the Zambezi in 1861 notes in his extremely valuable ethnography of the Dande region of the time that the *mhondoro* medium he met with was 'barred from seeing arms and weapons of war and also anything that is red' (Pacheco 1883). It would seem therefore that the major functions of the *mhondoro* mediums and the way the *mhondoro* are conceptualised has not changed for 120 years and that many of the restrictions observable today were in force before the colonial period. However, one group of restrictions were not recorded by either of these writers. These relate to the avoidance of commodities produced outside Dande.

I have mentioned that the most important problem presented by the environment to the local agriculture was frequent periods of drought. Grain is edible after one year at the most but droughts often continue for two or three years in succession. The effects of drought might have been alleviated had a means of storing grain been found so that the abundance of a good year might provide for the thin years that followed. But no such means was discovered. A solution to this dilemma was trade. The temporary wealth provided by one year's harvest was converted into permanent wealth which might, when the need arose, be converted back into grain. The environment provided highly commercial trade goods: ivory and gold. By trading these to Portuguese merchants the people of Dande involved themselves intimately and directly with the international cycles of trade which underlay the development of European capitalism in its earliest years. The gold and ivory of northern Zimbabwe, traded with the Portuguese for cloth and beads from India, were exchanged by these Portuguese in the Far East for commodities desired in Europe. Cloth and beads, as well as being important items of trade, were also stores of value. Others were produced in Dande itself including locally woven cloth, salt and iron goods, the most important of which were hoes.[6]

My point is this: at this period *mhondoro* mediums made no attempt to avoid commodities obtained by exchange on the market. In fact, the contrary was true, for among the items worn by the mediums to identify their profession were two of the most significant of the manufactured goods available at the time. The standard gift to a *mhondoro* medium even today is a length of cloth – blue, black or white – and in the past they were also presented with hoes. A relic of this practice is that today any gift made to a *mhondoro* medium is referred to as a *badza*, the Shona word for hoe.

I turn now very briefly to three effects of the coming of British colonialism and the creation of the state of Rhodesia: the widespread loss of land, the imposition of taxation and the new status acquired by the chiefs. It is important to remember that the 'pioneer column' arrived in what became Rhodesia in the 1890s and that the effect of this was felt in the north as late as the first decade of this century. The imposition of the authority of the new state over the Shona took place very quickly, very abruptly and with great violence. It was part of the experience of the fathers and the grandfathers of people alive today.

The hope of the pioneers was that they would find gold. As this hope faded they turned their attention to the land, taking control of vast expanses of cultivable terrain, allocating to the displaced indigenes ever smaller and less fertile reserves. In the early years the settlers had traded with the Shona for grain. The local economy has expanded to accommo-date the new demand. As we shall see, this recently uncovered capacity of the nineteenth century Shona economy is of very great importance. However, as the whites became farmers so legislation was passed to favour their production at the expense of the Shona cultivators. The process of converting tribesmen into a peasantry had begun.[7]

The conversion of this peasantry into a proletariat began with the imposition of a tax on all adult men. This tax was payable only in cash. This law had the intention and the effect of forcing the villagers out of their homes onto the white-owned plantations and mines (and later factories) to earn the cash to pay their taxes. The annexation of land and the imposition of tax were more than the previously welcoming Shona would tolerate. The rebellion which broke out in 1896 had nearly put paid to the Rhodesian state before it had established itself. But it failed, and one consequence of this failure was that many of the chiefs who had championed the resistance were removed from power.

Large numbers of chieftaincies were remodelled or abolished by the state so that the administration of the indigenous population might be the more easily accomplished. The chiefs who remained were integrated into the structures of the state as the lowest level of government admini-strators and made responsible for the extraction of tax, the recruitment of gangs for forced labour and the implementation of extremely unpopu-lar agricultural legislation. Chiefs who refused to cooperate were deposed and new ones installed. In return for their loyalty and cooper-ation, these chiefs received a salary from the state.

I suggested earlier that both chiefs and spirit mediums represent the authority of the ancestors but that they obtain their legitimacy in different ways, the chief as the ancestors' representative, ruling and judging on their behalf, the medium as their voice, allowing them to participate directly in the lives of their descendants. Now, however, the legitimacy of the chiefs was provided by the state. Gradually their authority as representatives of the ancestors diminished. The state had set itself up, with what degree of consciousness it is not easy to be sure, in opposition to the ancestors. This was powerfully demonstrated by the substitution of officers of the state, the Native Commissioners, for spirit mediums in a key political ritual.

The Shona practise an adelphic system of succession. As a result, each time that a chief dies there are a number of candidates in a position to advance a claim. In the past these claims were judged by spirit mediums speaking in trance. To be legitimate a chief must be both a member of a royal lineage as well as the chosen candidate of a spirit medium. However, after the establishment of the Rhodesian state, the chiefs were selected by Native Commissioners whose choice of an individual willing to implement government policy was frequently at odds with the candidate considered legitimate by the medium. The Native Commissioner had the power to force his decision through but not the authority to procure for his candidate the backing of the ancestors. Though these chiefs might rule with the authority of the state, in the eyes of the people their legitimacy was doubtful. Battle between ancestors and the state had been joined with many (though by no means all) of the chiefs conscripted, however unhappily, into the ranks of the state.

Furthermore, the authority to administer law in all but the most trivial cases was taken out of the hands of the chiefs and placed in those of the Native Commissioners. In cases of murder or theft, the courts of the state would hear argument and make judgement. On the other hand, cases involving witches, the implacable enemies of the ancestors and the most threatening and dangerous of criminals, which in the past had been heard by the chief were not heard by the state courts. But nor were they allowed to be heard by anyone else. The law did not acknowledge the existence of witches and forbade the making of an accusation of witchcraft on pain of arrest. By seeming to protect witches, the state had once again declared itself to be opposed to the ancestors.

I have described the varied consequences of this 'delegitimisation' of the chiefs in detail elsewhere.[8] What matters here is that, from the peasants' point of view, as the authority of the chiefs declined so that of the spirit mediums increased. Both chief and medium exemplify the authority of the ancestors, the chief through the idiom of descent, the medium through that of possession. As one representative of the *mhondoro* became ever more bound up with the new colonial regime so the other began to express opposition towards it. As the chiefs became tax collectors, organisers of forced labour and enforcers of the colonial law so the mediums began to express by their behaviour a vision of the world as it had existed before the Whites came to the country.

It is in these terms that the refusal of mediums to make use of or even to come into contact with the products of White society fall into place. The journals of Livingstone and Pacheco contain many passages describing the readiness of the nineteenth-century *mhondoro* mediums who lived along the banks of the Zambezi to receive them and offer them hospitality. Among present day mediums in Dande it is considered extremely dangerous either to see whites or to be seen by them. When I asked why this was so I was told that the ancestors had lived at a time long before the whites had come. They did not like to see Whites or any of the objects they brought with them in their land.

It is especially striking that this refusal is believed to be a characteristic of the *mhondoro* even when their mediums are not present. For example, sacred pools of water believed to be under the protection of the *mhondoro* are found all over Dande. It is believed that they will run dry if mass-produced metal mugs rather than traditional gourds are used to draw their waters. Similarly, no samples of crops grown exclusively for the market are offered to the ancestors as thanksgiving at the first harvest of each year and so on.

And yet, despite the fact that the commodities produced outside the spheres of production over which the *mhondoro* have control are categorised as dangerous, and despite the fact that the mediums expressed their opposition to the state by renouncing it and all its works, money was never included within this category and continued to be used by mediums and to be acceptable to the *mhondoro*.

It would be convenient were it the case that money had been used by traders in Dande for so long before the British pioneer column arrived that it was not associated with the Rhodesian state. Portuguese traders had established markets in Dande as early as the sixteenth century. Muslim African traders had carried goods from Dande to India two centuries before that. But in fact the currency used by the Portuguese was cloth. Modern coinage was introduced for the first time by the British at the end of the nineteenth century.[9] Another source of explanation must be looked for. Let us consider very briefly four cycles of exchange which have in the past taken place within Dande society and that may be regarded as 'traditional' to it.

Cycles of exchange[10]

The first cycle of exchange is that between people and their ancestors. In this exchange a quantity of beer is poured on the earth at the start of almost any ceremonial occasion while the ancestors are asked to provide their blessings. In the offerings to royal ancestors, the exchange element is more explicit than in those made to non-royal lineage ancestors. Beer is prepared by combining water and grain. The *mhondoro*, as it were, recycle this beer separating it into its two constituent elements and returning them as rain and healthy maize and sorghum plants.

The second cycle of exchange is the reciprocity that occurs within the lineage. Members of a lineage can expect as of right that their fellow lineage members will feed them and share their wealth with them either within the household, when visiting other households or in time of serious need. This reciprocity may be extended to include fellow clan members. Although no previous meeting may have occurred between them, clan members should be shared with as though they were kin. To refuse to exchange and share in this way is to invite severe criticism which, at its most extreme, may culminate in an accusation of witchcraft.

A third exchange takes place between lineages at marriage. The classic sub-Sahara marital exchange of wives for cattle is impossible here as there are no cattle within Dande. Instead, the majority of men provide labour for their fathers-in-law, living uxorilocally for an agreed period of years. Marriage within the clan is regarded as incest, so this form of exchange can be seen to operate between clans as well as between lineages.

The fourth and last exchange is between the chief and his followers. On certain days of each lunar month, the followers of a chief were obliged to perform labour on his fields. One way of thinking about this cycle is as a return made by followers to their chief in exchange for their use of the land which is the inalienable possession of his royal ancestors. However, the grain that results from this labour could be returned to those who had produced it by one of two routes. Either it was made available to individuals whose harvests had failed, or it might be distributed more widely at a time of drought. In addition, it formed the raw material for the beer brewed for the annual rituals at which the royal ancestors were requested to provide rain. This cycle therefore consists of labour in exchange for economic security either in direct exchange for access to land or grain, or in indirect exchange for rain.

Fertility and exchange

Each year beer is offered to the royal ancestors in exchange for rain. But what if the rains fail? In this case, the cause of the failure is explained by the chief on the grounds that someone has committed one of three major crimes: incest, murder, or witchcraft. The rain can only be restored once the criminal has been apprehended and judged by the chief and after reparation has been made to the *mhondoro* in whose province the crime took place.

The first of these crimes, incest, is quite clearly an act opposed to the third of the cycles I have described, exchange of women between lineages and clans. It is slightly less straightforward that murder is an act opposed to the second of these cycles, reciprocity within lineage and clan. To cut a long story very short, the kind of murder referred to in this context is murder by witchcraft and witches are, in the first instance, found within one's own lineage or, in a broader perspective, within the clan. It is believed to be impossible for a person of clan X to harm a member of clan Y by witchcraft unless a member of clan X can be found who is willing to collaborate in the attack on his clansman. It should be clear therefore that these two cycles of exchange are endorsed and demanded by the *mhondoro*. It is also clear that all four cycles are interlinked: (1) Men give labour to the chief who (2) uses the grain that results to make beer for ancestors and – provided that (3) there is reciprocity within the lineage and (4) reciprocity of women between lineages and clans – the rains will come.

In sum then, to perform the exchanges I have described brings the blessings of the ancestors: fertility, rain, continuity, increase. To disrupt any one of these exchanges can cause the offender to be accused of causing the community as a whole to suffer from infertility, drought, cessation and death.

Exchange and money

Let us look now at the way in which the introduction of money and industrially produced commodities affected the four cycles of exchange. Within the sphere of exchange between members of a lineage or clan, money is a most acceptable item. It is more common for gifts to take the form of food or other objects but money can be given as a present without the need for 'decontamination'.[11] For example, small sums of money may be given by neighbours and kinsmen to the holders of rituals or any other celebratory event, the sum offered being announced to the assembled crowd, the givers receiving cheers and praise for their generosity.

The most immediate effect of the substitution of cash for labour in exchange for wives, is inflation of brideprice. As the growing labour market allows young men to escape from the control of elders by earning their brideprice away from the village, so elders raise the amount of cash required in an attempt to exert their authority over their sons-in-law for the longest period possible while extracting the maximum payment from them. This process has been described exhaustively by numerous writers. The only point we need hold onto is that within this exchange the introduction of money poses a threat to the authority of the elders of whom the *mhondoro* mediums are the most authoritative.

Of the remaining exchanges, that between people and their ancestors has suffered a profound alteration; that between the chief and his followers has ceased to operate altogether. The principal cause is the salaries which the chiefs received from the state and which were, in the majority of cases, used exclusively to their own advantage. The 'traditional' exchange relationships were transformed into three separate cycles: the state exchanged money with the chiefs for their loyalty; adult men offered their labour to the market in exchange for cash; and thirdly and most significantly, adult men began to contribute the grain necessary for the annual ancestral ceremonies individually or from each household and no longer through the chief.

Mediums, money and resistance

Given the large-scale disruption money and capitalist markets seem to have caused to the cycles of exchange protected by the *mhondoro*, and given the practice of categorising as abhorrent to the long dead chiefs whatever the mediums perceive as damaging to the well-being of their present day followers, one might have predicted with confidence that money would be imbued with precisely the same sense of danger that characterises modern commodities. And yet, once again, it is not.

However, as I hinted at the start of this chapter, this does not mean that money is regarded as morally totally neutral. Cash paid or given either to mediums or to the officers of their shrines is recategorised and to some extent withdrawn from ordinary circulation. Like all other gifts to an ancestor it is referred to as a hoe (*badza*). In this way, money, the new store of wealth, is 'traditionalised'. Its disruptive powers are disguised by forcing it into a system of tribute which is sanctified by the past and under the control of the mediums. This money may not be used to benefit any individual, even the medium of the spirit to whom it was paid, but only to benefit the whole of the community that makes use of the *mhondoro*'s shrine.

But this 'traditionalising' of money simply poses the old problem in a new form. The question it raises is: why is it money that is treated in this way? After all, this process of recategorisation could as easily and logically be used to incorporate bottles of Coca Cola within the category of *badza*. And yet this is not done. On the other hand, the cloth and beads that modern mediums dress in are commercially produced commodities and these *are* recategorised as *badza* when they are presented to a medium.[12] The choice of objects to exclude or to recategorise seems to be arbitrary. Do any rules at all apply?

I think that the overall answer to this question is no. And there are one or two suggestive factors that go some way to explain why money escapes the net of the 'dangerous' in which the commodities it has helped call into being get caught.

The introduction of money at the end of the nineteenth century provided the indigenous economy with an element it conspicuously lacked, a convenient store of value. The forced introduction of sterling into the village economy by taxation coincided with the collapse of the long-established international trade in cloth, beads, gold and ivory. The influence of Portuguese traders had been fought off by the British. Within decades the local production of cloth, hoes and salt declined under competition from cheaper commercially produced substitutes. In the parts of the country where cattle flourished, these provided an alternative store of value. But in tsetse-ridden Dande the introduction of money permitted hope of survival through periods of drought and disaster. This point was made with particular force during the recent war when all that was left to the people of Dande was, quite literally, the money in their pockets.

And there is yet another aspect of the use of money which may contribute to the failure to categorise it as hostile to the ancestors. This aspect leads us back to the post-colonial cycles of exchange.

From the point of view of the people of Dande an exchange on the White controlled markets has always been an unequal exchange. When the men of Rhodesia were forced by the imposition of a tax in money to take employment on the plantations and mines, the subsistence economy in the Reserves was encouraged to continue at a level sufficiently high to provide for the wives and the young children left behind, in other words for the next generation of labourers, but not high enough to support the whole household or to pay tax. This meant that wages paid to blacks in industrial and agricultural employment could be kept extremely low. This exploitation was quite clearly perceived by the people of Dande, by their mediums and by their ancestors. A frequent refrain of my discussions about the reasons for resistance to the state by people in Dande was that if a white man does job A he earns X, whereas if a black man puts in the same labour he earns a tiny fragment of X. If you exchange your labour on the market you simply never receive a fair price.

That this perception was not a recent one is demonstrated by the message sent in the 1930s from the priests of the Mwari shrine in the southwest of Zimbabwe, quoted in an article by R. P. Werbner. Though this shrine is very distant from Dande, it has famously supported resistance to colonialism. By the very explicitness of the statement made the similarities to Dande can be seen.

Nyusa (messengers) brought the instructions that (black people) were not to sell grain to white people except for salt, and then as little grain as possible, as Mwari (the local deity/ancestor) desired them to obtain their salt at Brak (sic., brackish) places or by burning salt grasses, as they did before the white people came. Should they barter grain for salt, they were to cover their baskets so that Mwari could not see it. (They) were told through (messengers) that Mwari would send a great wind and that all the white people would leave the country in the night. On their departure, Mwari would introduce other white men who would charge 1 shilling tax only, and sell goods at a quarter of their present price. (Werbner 1977)

The message is clear. It is not Whites or their money that the ancestors are opposed to but Whites who tax their descendants and followers so heavily. It is not commodities as such that they object to but commodities that are sold at so grossly inflated a price. As the recent historiography of Zimbabwe has shown, when the first British settlers arrived and began their search for gold, the Shona were happy to supply them with agricultural produce and the early years were a time of successful and profitable trade. It seems likely that it was only when the white settlers began to take over the fertile land by force and to use the law to turn the terms of trade against the indigenous cultivators that the categorization of the newly available commodities as dangerous began to occur.

Let me pull the strands of my argument together. Firstly, spirit mediums cannot display wealth without raising suspicions about the authenticity of their calling, the main feature of which is the altruism of their possessing spirit. As chiefs became more and more closely identified with the state and lost their legitimacy as representatives of the ancestors, so the *mhondoro* mediums took over many of the responsibilities which they had held in the past. Analytically, the focus of traditional authority had shifted from chief and spirit medium to spirit medium alone but in local conception what had happened was a shift from the chiefs of the present to the chiefs of the past. And these long dead chiefs took a firm stance in opposition to the source of the legitimacy of these de-ancestralised chiefs, the Rhodesian state. The two most typical means by which the people of Dande came into contact with the state was either by infringing the law or by seeking employment which, under the laws of the state, ensured that in exchange for their labour they would always receive an inadequate reward. One means of demonstrating their opposition to the state which the ancestors adopted through their mediums was to refuse to make use of any of the commodities which could be obtained only in exchange for cash.[13]

Secondly, despite the destructive effect of money on cycles of exchange within Dande which had been protected and endorsed by the mediums, money was not included within the category 'dangerous'. Indeed, it was recategorised as 'hoes' and thus made safe for both mediums and *mhondoro* to handle. The only modern commodities which received the same treatment were beads and cloth which had been the currency at the time of the more equal and controllable trade relations that had prevailed between the people of Dande and the Portuguese.

Notes

1 The principal works on Shona spirit mediums are Garbett (1966) and (1969), Fry (1976) and Ranger (1979) and (1982). Throughout this essay I refer to *mhondoro* mediums as male. The majority of them are, though a few female mediums are also found in Dande.

2 Quoted in Garbett (1966).

3 The phrase was coined by Kingsley Garbett. See e.g., Garbett (1966).

4 The basis of my argument in this chapter is historical. I suggest that the mediums' refusal to participate with Europeans in commodity exchange is a consequence of and a reaction to the Shona's loss of autonomy over their own production and exchange. This raises certain technical difficulties. For a full explanation I would need to describe a moral, ritual and political system before, during and in resistance to colonialism. This is clearly beyond the scope of this chapter. The bulk of the material presented here was collected between 1980 and 1982, beginning some eight months after the end of hostilities. The description of the politico-moral system before and during colonialism as given here is as it was described to me by villagers, including mediums and chiefs, and represents a more or less coherent view of how, ideally, they consider that their system *ought to have* functioned in the past. It was the attempt to reestablish this system of moral order, believed to be under serious threat, that provoked the response of the mediums with whom I am concerned here.

5 See Lan (1985), chapter 5.

6 This section is based largely on Beach (1977).

7 This paragraph and those following are based on Palmer (1977).

8 See Lan (1985), chapter 8.

9 See Beach (1977).

10 With these cycles, as with the politico-moral system, problems of periodisation arise. I am concerned with the changes that occurred to these cycles as a resistance to colonialism; but colonialism does not penetrate to the most accessible and the most remote areas at the same speed or to the same degree. Indeed it is the variations of the speed and degree of penetration that

constitutes the remote as remote in the first place. Nor does it reach all levels of the society to the same effect, nor do all those affected choose to resist with the same resilience or improvisatory skill. Some of what I describe as pre-colonial is practised today, some not. It is by a comparison of the cycles of exchange that have accommodated to colonialism with those that have not, and again with those that remained impervious to it, that one approach to explaining the symbolic expression that commodities, money and market exchange have achieved can be made.

11 The phrase is Maurice Bloch's.

12 One medium living some miles to the east of Dande is said to have refused to wear cloth woven in mills inside Rhodesia and insisted that his cloth came from Mozambique thus keeping the old 'pure' trade routes alive.

13 Not every *mhondoro* medium was opposed to the state. A small number were persuaded to lend their support to the security forces during the war. These mediums were immediately recognisable due to their willingness to make use of commercially produced commodities – metal mugs instead of gourds, black wind-breakers instead of cloths and so on. One, perhaps the most deeply compromised, wore a pair of prescription spectacles obtained for him by the local District Commissioner.

References

Beach, D. N. 1977. 'The Shona Economy: Branches of Production', in R. H. Parsons, ed., *The roots of rural poverty in South Central Africa*, London: Heinemann Educational Books.

1979. '"Chimurenga", the Shona rising of 1896–7', in *Journal of African History*, 20: 3.

Beach, D. N. and H. Naronha 1980. 'The Shona and the Portuguese 1575–1980, Typescript: Dept. of History, University of Zimbabwe.

Fry, P. 1976. *Spirits of protest: spirit mediums and the articulation of consensus among the Zezuru of Southern Rhodesia*, Cambridge: Cambridge University Press.

Garbett, G. K. 1966. 'Religious aspects of political succession among the Valley Korekore', in R. Brown and E. Stokes, eds., *The history of the Central African Peoples*, Manchester: Manchester University Press.

1969. 'Spirit mediums as mediators in Korekore society', in J. Beattie and J. Middleton, eds., *Spirit mediumship and society in Africa*, London: Routledge & Kegan Paul.

Lan, D. 1985. *Guns and rain: guerrillas and spirit mediums in Zimbabwe*, London: James Currey.

Livingstone, D. 1956. *The Zambezi expedition of David Livingstone*, vols. 1 and 2, Openheimer Series no. 9, London: Chatto and Windus.

Pacheco, A. 1883. 'Uma viagem de tete a Zumbo', in D. N. Beach and H. Naronha, eds., *The Shona and the Portuguese, 1575–1980*, Typescript: Dept. of History, University of Zimbabwe, 1980.

Palmer, R. 1977. *Land and racial domination in Rhodesia*, London: Heinemann Educational Books.

Ranger, T. O. 1979. *Revolt in Southern Rhodesia 1896–7*, London: Heinemann Educational Books.

    1982. 'The death of Chaminuka: spirit mediums, nationalism and the guerrilla war in Zimbabwe', *African Affairs*, June.

Werbner, R. P. 1977. 'Continuity and policy in Southern Africa's High God Cult' in R. P. Werbner, ed., *Regional Cults*, ASA 17, London: Academic Press.

9

Precious metals in the Andean moral economy

M. J. SALLNOW

Of the rich variety of resources which the diversified ecology of the Andes has yielded to its human inhabitants down the centuries, precious metals have for long been the most highly prized. In pre-Inka and Inka times gold and silver, fashioned into exquisite ornaments, woven into cloth and encasing entire buildings, gilded and encoded the power of local chiefs, ethnic lords and state elites. The conquistadors' lust for gold and silver, in its turn, fired the Spanish conquest of the Inka empire. In the colonial era the mining of Andean precious metals, chiefly silver, was the armature around which the entire Spanish imperial economy revolved. Thanks to a common cultural fixation in both the Old World and the New on gold and silver as the supreme forms of value, the gift-symbols of political power in native Andean society were transmuted after the Spanish conquest into the global commodity-currencies of mercantile capitalism.

Today, gold and silver no longer perform such prominent political or economic functions in Andean society. Since the late nineteenth century, industrial mining in the region has been directed primarily at the extraction of base metals, chiefly tin, lead, iron, zinc and copper. Precious metals are still mined on a small scale, however, not just industrially but also by individuals, for whom gold promises a rapid route to riches. But for many of these private prospectors, gold is by no means an unencumbered commodity. One frequently encounters notions associated with its extraction and circulation that at first sight read as a kind of negative complement to the vaunted status that gold enjoys as the supercurrency of capitalism. Typically, these notions cast goldmining as an illicit, amoral and ritually dangerous activity, in which the successful prospector may well pay for his new-found wealth with his life.

I shall attempt in this chapter to make sense of this constellation of beliefs that so often attends the mining of precious metals, and under certain circumstances that of base metals as well. My starting point is the collection of ideas surrounding subterranean gold and its extraction that I encountered among the people of Qamawara, a peasant community in the department of Cusco in the southern highlands of Peru. The following discussion embraces beliefs about mining and precious metals to be found elsewhere in the Andean ethnography, and also the mining and gifting of gold and silver in pre-Columbian times. I shall argue that, quite apart from the value which capitalism has vested upon them, precious metals continue to occupy a distinct niche within the Andean cultural schema, and that only by uncovering the logic of this schema can we understand the mystical dangers of gaining access to such a coveted resource.

Gold and the apus in Qamawara[1]

The farmsteads of Qamawara, together with those of its neighbouring community of Oqoruro, are scattered across a broad swathe of partially irrigated mountainside in the Cordillera Vilcanota, some 25 kilometres east of Cusco city, at an altitude of about 4,000 metres. There are no roads to the area, nor services of any kind. The community falls within the administrative ambit of the valley village of San Salvador, capital of the district of the same name, and is registered as a *comunidad campesina* (peasant community), a legal status that affords a degree of protection to communal resources but which renders the community liable to a national government bureaucracy. The people are Quechua speakers, some of whom have acquired competence in Spanish through military conscription or urban migration, and they practise a mixture of agriculture and animal husbandry geared mainly to subsistence.

The territory of the community extends upwards from the irrigated, intensively farmed plots yielding barley, quinoa, pulses and a variety of tubers, through the seasonal fields slashed out of the mountainside that produce bitter tubers for processing into *ch'uñu* (freeze-dried potato), to the high pastures where sheep, llamas and alpacas are grazed. Rights to cultivation and pasturage are held by member households, and along with chattels are inherited bilaterally.

Production is realised, however, not at the level of the household but through informal inter-household networks, with labour being shared between kin, ritual kin, neighbours and friends ostensibly according to the standard Andean forms of non-market collaboration. Thus, cooperation is represented as *yanapay* (generalised assistance); *ayni* (short-term reciprocity); or *mink'a*, which can connote long-term reciprocity, festive labour or payment in kind. These neat normative categories are frequently blurred in practice, and amount to variant expressions of the same ideological commitment to mutual sustenance through the sharing of labour. This is made explicit in the food-sharing that accompanies all inter-household cooperation, the person to whom the assistance accrues being obliged to provide lunch and coca and sometimes regaling his workers with supper as well. Subsistence labour and its transformed product, cooked food, in effect constitute a single sphere of exchange, and the social relations within which they circulate acquire an axiomatic, moral character.

Survival is thought to depend, however, less on social relations than on supernatural ones. In common with peasants throughout the central Andes, the people of the locality vest mountain peaks and certain other features of the natural landscape with the role of spiritual guardian and protector. The mountain spirits, known in this region as *apus* – the term means lord or chief – are the divine tutelars of those who dwell in their shadows, and it is from them that the fertility of the land flows. They are ranked in power and importance according to the relative altitudes of their abodes, with local *apus* subordinate to those of the highest mountains of the region. Local *apus* are loosely associated with the distant ancestors of the people; they are also frequently likened to *misti* patrons and political authorities in San Salvador, to whose secular power the Qamawarans are subject.[2] *Apus*, being territorially specific, are the complements of a more general earth-force known as the Pachamama, a concept that is alleged to have a pan-Andean distribution (Mariscotti de Görlitz 1978).

The fertility which the *apus* and the Pachamama bestow on the soil and the protection they extend to humans and livestock are conditional, given only in return for periodic offerings. Today these consist of food and drink, typically offered by groups of close kin in the course of the annual rites of increase for the various categories of livestock. In the past, however, llamas were regularly sacrificed, as they are today in other areas (see e.g. Bastien 1978). In the past, too, the community used to participate in an annual encounter, the *tinkuy*, in the high puna, in which coalitions of communities would engage in a day-long pitched battle, the objects being to kill members of the opposing side and to abduct their women. The last such battle was fought in the 1940s, but similar events still take place today elsewhere in the Andes (Gorbak, Lischetti and Muñoz 1962). Deaths in these battles were construed as sacrifices to the *apus*, and as being especially effective in enhancing the fertility of the soil. The red-coloured earth at the place where the fighters were customarily buried is said to have been dyed with their blood; significantly this earth is used to make the dye for staining the coats of sheep and llamas at their respective rites of increase, the connection being explicitly stated. There is, then, a sense in which food offerings to the *apus* are direct surrogates for llamas, and llamas for human beings.

The craggy peaks that dominate the community on all sides are not only the dwelling places of the *apus*, but are also popularly believed to contain gold in abundance. Some mountains are thought to be more richly endowed than others. The richest of them all, Pachatusan – the tallest mountain in the immediate vicinity – was in fact mined intensively by both the Inkas and the Spanish, though the workings have long since been abandoned. The interior of the mountain is said to be a veritable honeycomb of shafts and galleries, with many seams of gold as yet untapped. In addition, there are numerous placer sites on Pachatusan and elsewhere which it was claimed had yielded large pieces of ore in the recent past. Everyone I spoke to on the subject was knowledgeable concerning the appearance of metal in the ore, the techniques of panning, and the approximate price of gold on the black market in the port of Callao. It seemed to be everyone's private dream to win a fortune with gold.

The whole business of goldmining, however, was hedged about with secrecy and fraught with danger. When I first became aware of this, I attributed the secrecy to an entirely rational desire to keep the profits of prospecting for oneself, and the belief in danger to be an equally rational recognition of the very real risks entailed in penetrating ancient underground galleries. One of my first informants on the matter, a man from San Salvador who considered himself to be a mestizo, confided in me that he regularly went 'working' in the abandoned mines of Pachatusan. It soon became apparent, however, that such rationalist explanations were inadequate.

Prospecting for gold was referred to as *el oculto* (the occult). People would drop their voices to a whisper when discussing it with me, and would immediately change the subject if someone else came within earshot. Indeed, I never heard the subject being discussed conversationally between the people themselves, eager though they were to raise it privately with me. I was told that a person always went searching for gold at night, either alone or in the company of a single close kinsman or trusted friend. Certain prohibitions had to be scrupulously observed. One could not smoke cigarettes, nor talk about God, nor even bear a cross on one's person, else the metal would disappear and the expedition would be fruitless. The ore had to be removed from the ground with a silver spoon. But this was the moment of greatest danger, for the gold was guarded by demons (Quechua *supay*, Spanish *diablo*), who might attack a prospector and sap him of his life-force. If this happened, death would inevitably follow within a few days.

These demons were, of course, the *apus* in a malignant guise, threatening death to anyone who secretly extracted gold from their domains. It is worth noting that, in contrast to the people of San Salvador

who on the whole were somewhat sceptical of these beliefs, no Qamawaran I spoke to ever claimed actually to have ventured into the disused
mines of Pachatusan. Placer mining was dangerous enough; to enter the
underground domain of an *apu*, and the most powerful in the locality at
that, would have been suicidal.

For those willing to take the risk, however, even placer mining
promised rich rewards. The largest find that came to my notice was of a
nugget the size of a man's hand unearthed by someone in Oqoruro,
which he was hoping to sell for 15,000 *soles*, about £150 – this at a time
when the rate for wage labour in the area was about 30 *soles* a day. I
suspect that stories of such finds were rather more common than the finds
themselves. I only once saw a piece of ore, unearthed by one of the sons
of my Qamawaran host and offered to me for 800 *soles*, which I was
assured was less than half the black market price in Callao.

In fact, it was initially assumed by most people that I was keenly
interested in mineral prospecting – indeed, that it was the reason I was
there. I was suspected of carrying a metal detector and other apparatus
for extracting and purifying the gold in my rucksack, and I lost count of
the number of individuals who tried furtively to enlist my aid, promising
to lead me to the placer deposits in return for a share of the proceeds. My
denials met only with knowing smiles; even emptying the entire contents
of my rucksack on the ground failed to dislodge their suspicions. So as
not to encourage the rumours I never did go gold prospecting, and
consequently lack detailed data on how it was carried out. Gradually, the
innuendo and conspiratorial offers of assistance abated, though they
never disappeared entirely.

To sum up: gold prospecting in Qamawara promises an individual
instant riches and must be pursued in secret, either alone, or with a
trusted confidant, or indeed with an outsider. But a prospector must run
the gauntlet of the *apus*, normally the guardians of the common weal but
who threaten death to those who try to appropriate their subterranean
treasure. How might we interpret this twin association of goldmining
with clandestineness on the one hand and mystical danger on the other?

Mining ideologies: a comparative perspective

We can begin to answer this question by considering an extreme case of
the phenomenon which in Qamawaran cosmology is only sketchily
represented, a case in which the beliefs associated with the spiritual
owners and protectors of metals are elaborated into a fullblown cult. I
refer to the fulltime waged tin miners of Oruro, Bolivia, described by
June Nash, on whose ethnography I now draw (Nash 1979).

The interior of Oruro's tin mines is presided over by a spirit known as

Tío (Uncle) or Supay (Devil). Tío is the *apu* of the mountain above the mine, otherwise known as Wari (Huari), transformed into a spirit superficially akin to the Christian Satan. Nash stresses, however, that Tío is not hated as a malignant devil, and that this term distorts the concept of the force as a potentially benevolent source of riches. All the wealth issuing from the mine is the bounty of Tío. Constant caution is demanded on the part of the miners to avoid offending him and thereby making the veins of tin disappear. Once having entered his domain one must not utter the names of Christian deities or saints, nor bear any Christian symbols. In return for the protection of the miners and for the mineral that is extracted from the mountain, Tío demands sacrifices before his sculptured likenesses deep inside the mine – coca and cigarettes daily, llamas at fiestas. Occasionally, though, Tío demands the ultimate sacrifice, that of a miner himself (Nash 1979: 7, 123, 137–8, 316).

Different facets of Tío's character come to the fore in different historical periods, depending ultimately on the way in which labour is organised and recompensed. When the mines were privately owned, miners were paid according to the amount of actual tin which they brought to the surface. This encouraged miners to compete with one another for access to the richest seams. In those days, it is said, miners commonly forged explicit contracts with Tío to increase their output. Such contracts were always secret and were always with single individuals; they would guarantee the miner enormous wealth but would ultimately cost him his life – sometimes his physical annihilation in the bowels of the mine. Following nationalisation in 1952, the wage structure was altered. Miners were now paid on the basis of the amount of crude ore that they extracted, rather than the amount of the purified metal, and this mitigated competition between them. Tío now came to be seen less as a generator of riches and more as a protector against accidents, less as an abetter of individual gratification and more as an ally of the workforce as a whole. This perception was reinforced following the military takeover of the mines in 1965, when the Tío cult was expressly forbidden; it now came to symbolise directly the miner's resistance to brutal army repression (Nash 1979: 190–2, 317–18).

That the cases of Qamawara and Oruro represent two poles – albeit randomly selected – of a continuum of ideological and ritual elaboration with regard to mining is illustrated by Platt's documentation of an intermediate instance, that of the peasant miners of Ayllu Macha, Norte de Potosí, Bolivia (Platt 1983). Here, the people are agropastoralists who occasionally work for wages at a small mine near by. As Platt shows, the cult dedicated to the spirit of this mine stands midway between the beliefs of casual peasant prospectors and ore thieves in a malevolent spirit protector of the metal, and the fully developed cult of Tío in Oruro, where images of the rampant god are scattered through all the principal galleries and where sacrifices of coca and cigarettes are part of the daily routine.

Ideologies of mining vary, then, according to whether the miners are peasants engaged in casual prospecting, part-time peasant miners, or full-time miners. In their fundamentals, all pertain to the same symbolic universe as those ideologies that mediate agropastoral production. There is no radical disjunction between the cults of nature spirits in the respective domains of agropastoral and mineral production, as Harris in this volume (chapter 10) makes abundantly clear. Indeed, across the central Andean region as a whole, there tends rather to be a division of labour between those spirits that preside over agriculture on the one hand, and those that preside over mining *and* pastoralism on the other, though the two roles are invariably overlapping and not mutually exclusive (Martínez 1980). Nature spirits are typically regarded as the founts of fertility, wellbeing and material wealth in all its forms.

But nature spirits are at the same time unpredictable and capricious in their treatment of mortals, and must be continually appeased through sacrifice. If they can preserve or improve a person's wellbeing or material standing, they can equally bring sudden misfortune, sickness or death. There is a wide variety of circumstances, apart from mining, under which they will claim a human life or be offered one by their devotees – from the chance killing of a fighter in a *tinkuy*, where death benefits all, to the poignant example from Matapuquio (Apurímac), in which a man was afflicted with sickness by an *apu* because of an insult uttered against the spirit of his dead mother, and whose daughter successfully implored the *apu* through a shaman to spare him and to take her infant son instead (Skar 1982: 22–3).

Only with regard to mining as a productive pursuit, however, does death at the hands of the nature spirits become a *permanent occupational hazard*. Neither agriculture nor pastoralism entails such a heightened and continual exposure to supernatural danger. Extracting metal from the ground is necessarily to court death in recompense. The risk may be slight, in which case the prospector might simply take a chance; under certain circumstances it becomes more acute, with ritual propitiations rising to a frenzied pitch; and finally it can become a certainty, with the miner deliberately trading mineral riches for his life. In mining, as compared to agropastoralism, surrogate sacrifices begin to lose their efficacy, and the nature spirits increasingly demand the real thing.

One possible explanation of this bloodlust of the nature spirits with regard to mining would fasten on the cultural perception of the physical processes involved. The penetration of the surface of the earth and the withdrawal of its substance, it could be argued, disturb the spirits' very abode, nature itself, thus unleashing their ire. Indeed, major earthworks seem to provoke the same reaction. The people of Moya (Huancavelica) claimed that a human sacrifice, usually of a hapless traveller, took place in the region whenever the nature spirits, here known as *wamanis*, were disarranged due to road building, railway construction, tunnelling or whatever; if this were not done, the *wamani* would claim lives himself (Favre 1967: 131–2). Similar sacrifices – always live interments – are said to take place elsewhere in the central Andes prior to the erection of church towers, bridges and the like (Ortiz 1980: 85).

Such an explanation in terms of the cultural mechanics of the activity clearly has some force as far as underground mining is concerned. It does not, however, account very convincingly for the analogous beliefs associated with our original example of placer mining, which takes place above ground and which arguably violates the soil rather less than, say, ploughing does. There is also the question of variation in the intensity of the cult, what Platt calls the emotional climate of the activity, between part-time and full-time miners, both of whom penetrate and derange the spirits' underground domain to a similar degree. One is therefore led to examine the social as well as the cultural conditions under which mining takes place, and the political and economic parameters of the engagement of individuals in the mining enterprise.

Michael Taussig, in an inventive re-analysis of June Nash's ethnography, addresses these issues directly (Taussig 1980).[3] His thesis rests on what he perceives as a contrast, indeed a polarity, between peasant agriculture and capitalist mining, a contrast personified by the relatively benign nature spirits – Pachamama and the mountain gods – that preside over the former, and the malevolent, or at best ambivalent, Tío that controls the Oruro mines. His explanation of this purported contrast runs as follows.

The peasant, he claims, retains a measure of control over the means of production: he is as yet unalienated from his land, his labour and the fruits of his labour. Peasant production accordingly takes place in terms of a harmonious system of gift exchanges between the peasant community on the one hand and the mountain spirits and Pachamama on the other. The tin miner, in contrast, is obliged to work for a wage; in doing so he is alienated from his own labour and from the product of his labour, which is transformed into a commodity and sold on the international capitalist market. Gift exchanges with Tío, the spirit owner of the mine, still mediate the extraction of ore, but the metal then passes out of the sphere of reciprocity into that of market exchange, and the miner is compensated in cash. The miner therefore stands at the interface between two worlds, pre-capitalist and capitalist; from his privileged vantage-point betwixt and between he can yet perceive the evil of the latter, founded upon the unnatural proletarianisation of labour and the commoditisation of its products, but he expresses this evil in the idiom of the former, in the fetishism of the devil owner of the mines (Taussig 1980: 207–28).

Tío, then, owes his peculiarly diabolic characteristics ultimately to the fact that mining labour is waged and that the mineral, as the embodiment of that labour, is sold as a commodity. Clearly, the contrast that has been set up here between capitalist mining and peasant agriculture is over-drawn. Ever since the Spanish conquest, Andean peasants have habitu-ally entered both product and labour markets, and are no strangers to capitalist relations of production and exchange. Qamawarans, for example, regularly market a proportion of their subsistence crops, wool and livestock to middlemen and itinerant traders, and some families produce a cash crop, barley, for the brewery in Cusco, which provides seed and fertiliser under contract. Involvement in labour markets takes several forms: seasonal work on the maize haciendas (now mostly cooperatives) farther down the Vilcanota valley; indentured labour on the fruit, tea and coffee plantations in the *montaña*, the subtropical zone on the eastern flanks of the Andes; and long-term employment in the urban industrial and service sectors in Cusco and Lima. In all these activi-ties save the last, the products of the bounty of the nature spirits enter the capitalist market either through direct sale or through the mediation of wage labour; yet in none was there any detectable ideological reaction analogous to that provoked by mining. Commoditisation, then, cannot provide an explanation for the particular features of mining ideology.

What, though, of proletarianisation? Here, Taussig's thesis does suggest a lead. The degree of elaboration of mining ideology would indeed appear to vary with the degree of alienation from an actual or ideal grouping dedicated to production through mutual aid and suste-nance, that is, with the degree of disengagement from a moral collecti-vity, in favour of private, individual benefit. The Qamawaran in pursuit of gold temporarily alienates himself from his network of moral cooper-ators, prospecting in secret at night, either alone or accompanied only by a close kinsman or – appropriately enough – an alien. That personal aggra-ndisement is a key factor here is also illustrated by Harris's remarks in this volume that a Bolivian Laymi can gain access to subterranean treasure only by renouncing all personal greed and ambition, or alter-natively by making a human sacrifice. Full-time miners, for their part, are permanently compromised, torn between the individualistic pursuit of wealth and livelihood from mining and the ideal of Andean production as a collective, mutualistic enterprise. A miner can choose to resolve this tension by a secret pact with Tío, giving him untrammelled personal enrichment for the price of his life.

To correlate mining beliefs with an amoral commitment to private gain is only to shift the problem. Why should private gain arising from mining be so pernicious, while the pursuit of personal wealth in other spheres – though such wealth is also bestowed by the nature spirits – ordinarily present no such danger? To answer this, we must examine the cosmological significance of the mineral product itself. In Qamawara, this is gold; in Oruro, it is ostensibly a base metal, tin. In the Inka, colonial and early republican periods, however, the Oruro mines produced silver, being exploited for tin only since the latter half of the nineteenth century; the ore which is mined today is in fact a complex of tin, copper, lead, silver and gold. It was in the colonial period, the period of silver production, that the cult of Tío established itself and took shape (Nash 1979: 22–4, 90). We may hypothesise, then, that it is in the cultural conceptualisation of precious metals, rather than in that of mining *per se*, that the answer lies.

Precious metals, power and the state

The gold and silver over which nature spirits preside symbolise not so much their wealth as their power. The *wamanis* recognised by the community of Chuschi (Ayacucho), for example, have underground palaces sumptuously furnished with gold and silver. As in Qamawara, the hierarchy of *wamanis* is likened to the structure of local government: they occupy positions such as *alcalde* (mayor), *regidores* (councillors) and *alguaciles* (constables), and carry staffs of office of gold and silver accordingly. The articulation of the local *wamani* hierarchy with their regional counterparts lying further afield keys in directly with the structure of the state: the three most powerful *wamanis* in southern Peru are likened to the three cities of Ayacucho, Ica and Lima, while the most important *wamani* of Chuschi communicates directly with the President of the republic (Isbell 1978: 59, 151).

In many areas, subterranean gold and silver are said to be the tribute which maintains the hierarchy of nature spirits and their vassalage to the state. A particularly coherent account is provided by the people of San Miguel (Ayacucho). Here, too, the *wamanis* are thought to be ultimately subordinate to the President of Peru, to whom they appeal directly in the event of disputes among themselves. Their subterranean treasure of precious metals is said to derive directly from the offerings of food, alcohol, coca and occasionally livestock which they receive from the peasants in return for their fertility and tutelage. The *wamanis* are sometimes said to appear in the form of socially superior mestizos, often policemen, in order to enforce the oblations due to them. Some people alleged that the spirits had underground machines to transmute the offerings into gold and silver. The *wamanis* do not, however, retain these riches for themselves. Each year in the month of August, when throughout the central Andes the earth is believed to be open and alive, the mountains open their doors, load their treasure on to their vicuñas and viscachas which they have changed into burros and mules for the purpose, and send it across the hills to their own chiefs. These in turn surrender it to the two most powerful mountain spirits of the region, who finally hand it over to the government of the republic (Earls 1969: 69–70). Thus gold and silver, the byproducts of the transactions between peasants and the local spirit owners of nature, form the tribute which sustains the entire state edifice, mapped on to the landscape as a hierarchy of natural icons beneath the maximal authority of the President in Lima.

This representation, encountered elsewhere in the central Andes (cf. Morote Best 1956), in which gold and silver flow as tribute from local gods to the state, is strikingly inverted in a myth from Oruro (Nash 1979). According to this myth the Uru people, the original inhabitants of the area who dedicated themselves to fishing and farming, recognised the Sun as their pre-eminent deity. Wari, the spirit of the mountain above the mine, coveted the princess Ñusta, daughter of the Sun, but the Sun thwarted Wari's plans. In revenge Wari turned the people against their god by tempting them away from the true religion with the lure of gold and silver from the mountain. Desirous of riches, the people abandoned their work in the fields and rebelled against their traditional authorities, casting them out of the land. Drunkenness, theft and immorality ensued. But Ñusta later led the exiled chiefs and priests back to their homeland, and gradually the people reverted to their former, civilised ways. The Uru tongue gave way to Quechua, the language of the Inkas. This time Wari wreaked his vengeance by sending plagues of giant lizards and ants to devour the people, but thanks to the intervention of Ñusta they were all killed. Today, stone images of two of the giant lizards are marked by miraculous Christ shrines, while sand dunes said to represent the remains of the horde of ants are marked by a miraculous image of Santiago. Ñusta, for her part, is identified with a much revered Marian shrine known as the Virgin of the Mineshaft, situated at the sealed entrance to the oldest mine in the area, long since abandoned (Nash 1979: 18–19).

This myth obviously contains some Christian accretions. Allowing for these, however, we can see that it also exhibits many of the same elements encountered in the San Miguel material, but that it establishes an altogether different set of relations between them. Here, the local mountain spirit, instead of surrendering his subterranean gold and silver to his superiors as tribute, offers them in a fit of pique to the people, appealing to their basest motives of greed and avarice. As a result the subsistence foundation of society is undermined, morality degenerates and the local politico-religious hierarchy crumbles. Civilisation has been subverted by the unlicensed pursuit of mineral wealth. Order is restored only by the advent of the Inka empire and the re-imposition of the solar cult. The latter, of course, was proper to the Inkas; by crediting it to the Urus the myth represents Inka domination as a return to the *status quo ante*.

We now begin to detect the lineaments of a cultural logic, in which ideas about the extraction and circulation of precious metals are determinately joined to conceptions of morality on the one hand and superordination on the other. In one permutation, the local nature spirits channel gold and silver upwards to their lords, and in so doing preserve intact not merely the hierarchical state structure in its religious projection but also the moral fabric of the local agropastoral community. In the other permutation, the exchange system is short-circuited: gold and silver pass not upwards but downwards to the people, leading to political disintegration, moral decay and the collapse of food production. In the first case gold and silver support the political structure; in the second they subvert it.

These two accounts respectively refer, of course, to two historically distinct political formations, the Inka empire and the modern republican state. In Andean thought, however, the Inka era and the present, Hispanic one are commonly represented as constituting the same, continuous epoch. The Spanish conquest is here elided: it is the state structure itself, rather than its particular ethnic cast, which assumes primacy in the cultural chronology. The Inkas and Spanish together define an age of sunlight and civilised existence (cf. Urbano 1980: 121).

There is, though, an alternative representation, one which does register the Spanish conquest as a traumatic and epoch-making event and which measures the miseries of the present against the supposed ease and happiness of the Inka era. Here, the cultural logic of metals, morality and power is permuted yet again. The central character in this representation is Inkarrí (King Inka), a quasi-messianic figure variously associated with the Inka king Atawalpa and the eighteenth-century rebel leader Tupac Amaru, both of whom were executed by the Spanish. A myth from Puquío (Ayacucho), tells of how Inkarrí, son of the Sun, was decapitated by the Spaniards, but that on the point of death he ordered all the gold and silver in the realm to conceal itself. His head was taken to Cusco and buried, but a body is growing on to it; when it is fully reconstituted, the Day of Judgement will have arrived (Arguedas & Roel Pineda 1973: 223). In Ch'eqa Pupuja (Puno), it is alleged that a mountain near Cusco at one time consisted of pure gold, but that when the Spanish killed Inkarrí all the gold was turned to stone. In the golden age before Inkarrí's murder, even tiny fields yielded abundant crops without any effort, and there was much gold. Had Inkarrí not been killed, the people would have plenty of gold and everyone would be rich and powerful. Another informant says that the gold and silver will reappear at the last judgement (Flores Ochoa 1973: 317, 319, 335).

In such accounts, the logic undergoes a profound transformation. The extinction of Inka supremacy by what is now perceived as an alien power is matched by the instantaneous disappearance of all the underground gold and silver. Furthermore, in the millennial frame which the myths establish, the portrayal of the lost Inka world merges with the dream of what might have been and might yet be, a dream in which the logic is collapsed and irreconcilables are reconciled. Food all but produces itself, so the morality underpinning production is redundant; and gold and silver are available in abundance to all, so everyone is powerful – in effect, to anticipate our later discussion, divine. The ideology has been transformed into a utopia.

Gold in the pre-Hispanic central Andes

In these various depictions of gold and silver in mythoreligious discourse, contemporary Andean culture is adhering to a view of precious metals which long predates their roles in the market economy of the post-conquest Andes. The development of these ideas across the three millennia since Peruvian mining and metallurgy first made their appearance in the archaeological record reached its culmination in the last, the largest and the most complex of a succession of aboriginal states, that of the Inkas (cf. Lothrop 1967). Here, as in much else, the Inkas built upon local indigenous practices, expanding and transforming them to embrace an empire. In the central Andes gold and silver were not used for trading purposes as they were in the chiefdoms of Colombia further north (Bray 1978: 25–6); indeed, there is little evidence for trade as such in any commodities. Treasure was for display, to enhance the prestige of a ruler or a god. Under the solar dynasty of the Inkas, gold and silver, represented respectively as the sweat of the Sun and the tears of the Moon, became state monopolies dedicated to the glorification and controlled delegation of state power.

There was another contrast in the use of precious metals between the northern and central Andes, recently highlighted by Mary Helms (1981). Whereas in the Intermediate Area of Colombia and Lower Central America the predominant metallurgical technique was the casting of small ornaments by the lost-wax method, in Peru and southern Ecuador there was a bias, at least during the Inka period, towards hammering rather than casting, towards the use of sheet metal to construct three-dimensional objects both large and small – utensils, plants, life-size effigies of people and animals – and to sheath entire buildings and monuments in gold leaf. In other words, while Intermediate Area cultures favoured a metallurgy suited to the production of finely crafted items of personal adornment, Inka metalsmiths chose those techniques which best enabled them to create total golden environments, the most spectacular examples being the artificial gardens of the royal palaces and state temples – where everything, from the fountains to the ears of corn, was exquisitely fashioned in silver and gold (Helms 1981: 219–20).

Helms relates this contrast between what she calls 'personalistic' and 'architectural' metalworking styles to different types of political organisation. In the Intermediate Area small-scale chiefdoms were the rule. Here, elite status derived directly from kin status, and sculpted metal ornaments of varying degrees of refinement were worn to express gradations in personal rank, in the degree of golden and hence divine associations, within polities having no rigid class division between chiefs and commoners. The portability of the cast items also facilitated their exchange in the long-distance trade networks characteristic of the region. In the Inka state, by contrast, the nobility were distinguished qualitatively from commoners: the divine realm to which the Inka elite pertained was summoned up by the fabrication of an entire metallic world whose inner quality or essence was held to be manifested by its surface appearance – golden, celestial, apart. The architectural use of precious metals thus directly legitimised the inherent superiority of the elite of the Inka empire (Helms 1981).[4]

Insightful as Helms's hypothesis is as a set of broad contrasts, we should not forget that under the Inkas, too, gold and silver were used for items of personal adornment, not only by the nobility but also by the local ethnic lords or *kurakas* (though not by commoners); and that objects of precious metal, while they were not traded, were constantly exchanged as gifts and tribute. Of the leading Indian participants in a sixteenth-century Catholic festival in the archdiocese of Lima, for example, 'some came dressed in shirts of silver [thread], and others in shirts covered in silver plates, and the most important wore shirts of gold; and all of them helmets of silver, with a great quantity of feathers' (Gómez [1571] 1966: 243). Gifts of gold and silver were conferred by the king upon other royals, provincial administrators and *kurakas*. Thus, a son of the king Wayna Qhapaq was once favoured with a tunic embroidered with gold thread for having acquitted himself well in some administrative task (Murúa [1611] 1964: 171–2). Conversely, *kurakas*, the local ethnic lords, had to give gifts of gold and silver to the king: 'the *kurakas* never kissed his hands without presenting him with all the gold and silver and precious stones that their Indians could collect when they had no other work to do' (Garcilaso [1617] 1966, 1: 254). The king also made offerings of gold and silver to important provincial shrines, many of which predated the Inka empire and with which it was politic for the conquerors to maintain cordial relations.

The use of precious metals in Inka times would therefore seem to be an amalgam of the personalistic and the architectural modes, the latter having crystallised out of the former in the course of the formation of the Inka state and perhaps, in a cumulative process, of earlier states as well.[5] The principal loci of state power were thus transfigured into divine enclaves of gold and silver; all personal gifts and ornaments circulating in the empire could then be construed as fragments of this celestial world, deriving – like the prestige and rank which they signalled – from the Inka king himself. This polar quality of the gilt furnishings of the state is evidenced by the law that no gold which entered the imperial capital was ever allowed to leave, under pain of death (Moore 1958: 165). As regional polities were drawn into the ambit of the state, precious metals ceased to be merely the markers of personal rank and standing within independent chiefdoms and became the universal symbols of state power and vassalage.

Beyond the significance of different metallurgical techniques and styles, there lies a broader question to be asked not just of Andean societies but of all which make certain metals 'precious'. Why gold? The answer must, I think, be sought in its physical properties, which silver shares to a lesser degree. Gold endures. It does not decay, or corrode, or even tarnish. It is, in a sense, eternal. This, coupled with the practical consideration that it is relatively easy to work, makes it an ideal material objectification of permanence in the midst of human transitoriness. For Andean societies, and the Inkas especially, gold made power eternal.

Not surprisingly, during the brief ascendancy of the Inkas precious metals were amassed on a far greater scale than before. One of the earliest Spanish chroniclers estimated that during the last years of the empire annual production was in excess of 190 tons of gold and 635 tons of silver (Cieza de León [1554] 1973: 69). The scattered data on Inka mining, discussed briefly by Murra (1980) and Moore (1958) and more recently assembled by Berthelot (1986), provide us with a reasonably detailed picture of this important activity as it was operating at the time of the Spanish invasion.

Mainly on the basis of information from two areas of Qollasuyu, to the northeast and southeast of Lake Titicaca, Berthelot shows that there were two categories of mine: those pertaining exclusively to the state in the person of the Inka king, which exploited the richer seams by means of complex underground shafts and galleries, and those whose use was granted to local *kurakas*, consisting of scattered and isolated placer sites or rudimentary workings around the poorer seams.

The state mines, many of which operated all year round, drew on labour – both male and female – furnished under the idiom of *mit'a* (*corvée*), according to which a proportion of able-bodied adults in each community were obliged to work for specified periods on state enterprises. Care was taken to ensure that *corvée* obligations – there were many others besides mining – did not disrupt agropastoral production in the communities: a *corvée* worker's dependants were supported during his or her absence by the community at large. In one area the proportion of the tribute-paying population engaged in mining is reported to have amounted to no more than 1 per cent at any one time. It was the duty of the *kurakas* to mobilise the *mit'a* workers (Berthelot 1986: 71–3). An eye-witness account of a state mining complex still fully operational in 1533 observed that in the largest mine the men and women engaged in extracting the gold were from all over the region – twenty from one *kuraka*, fifty from another, thirty from another – and other workgroups of varying size depending upon the populations of the communities from which they were drawn (Sancho [1543] 1962: 94).

Not all mining labour, however, was part-time, collective, community-based *mit'a* labour. There are explicit references in two of the chronicles, those by Valera and Falcón, to the fact that *full-time* mining was a form of punishment and exile (Murra 1980: 108). According to Valera, crimes which warranted this sentence included the acceptance of a bribe or the robbery of a village by an inspector; *lèse-majesté* by a priest; and certain categories of incest and rape (Moore 1958: 166–70).

State mining operated according to a system of quotas set by Cusco, and was rigorously supervised and controlled by the officers and guards on the site. These functionaries were agents of the king; in some cases, indeed, they were Inka nobles, members of the ruling caste. In one mine, as fast as the ore was extracted it had to be passed to one of these officers, such that the workers had no idea of the total quantity of ore they had mined. At another, the entrances were patrolled by guards who controlled all the comings and goings of the miners. Each night the miners were obliged to pass before an officer of the king to hand over the day's takings. Any miner attempting to keep a piece of ore risked grave sanctions if discovered. The gold and silver was smelted on site and transported to the provincial capital or to Cusco (Berthelot 1986: 73–7).

The community mines in the areas covered by Berthelot's sources were exploited less intensively than the state mines; some were worked only in the dry season, when not only was agricultural labour at a minimum but also alluvial deposits were more accessible on the dry stream beds. Labour was mobilised from the local community or ethnic group. All the ore was surrendered to the *kuraka*; the sources are silent on the surveillance techniques employed, as they are on many other details of the community mines (Berthelot 1986: 77–80).

Each state mine had its spirit owner. Not only was the mountain above the mine an object of worship, but in the case of galleried workings there was also an underground shrine to the *mama* of the mine. The *mama* was a piece of ore selected for its singular appearance, often of exceptional size, but not figuratively modelled. Some of these *mamas* are said to have been ancient stones, and to have predated the Inka exploitation of the mines in question. *Mamas* were supplicated through sacrifice to give up their subterranean riches. Placer mines did not have *mamas* – they did not, of course, yield such agglomerations of ore – but one can assume that the local mountain spirits were appealed to in similar fashion (Berthelot 1986: 82–4).

Why, if gold and silver were royal monopolies, did the state exercise such strict control over its own mines, yet permit others to operate entirely outside its jurisdiction? The answer lies in the Andean pattern of gifting and counter-gifting to which the circulation of precious metals had to conform. It was from the community mines that the *kurakas* derived their stocks of precious metals with which to regale the king. None remained in their charge: 'the gold and silver which they extracted from the mines, . . . all was taken to Cusco without anything being left in the hands of the *kuraka*, because they were not able to have any part of it if it were not given by the Inka' (Santillán [1563] 1968: 116).

Inka mining, as noted, was a collaborative task. *Corvée* workers in the state mines, like those in other sectors of the economy, entered production not so much as individuals but as members of this or that community or ethnic group, and these prior allegiances determined the composition of workgroups underground, as Sancho's account makes clear. In the case of community mines, community-based workgroups were axiomatic. In other words, mining mobilised those same moral relationships that were founded upon mutual assistance and sustenance in agropastoral production of food and also of cloth (cf. Murra 1962). The Inkas were adept at extracting surplus from these moral solidarities, as Godelier (1977) has shown. Unlike food and cloth production, however, where in each case only a proportion of the yield was handed over to state and church, with the bulk being retained for subsistence, mining entailed the instant and total appropriation of the product by the *kuraka* or the officers of the king. All the precious metals extracted by the miners were immediately removed from their charge, to be eventually channelled through the social hierarchy as the medium through which imperial power and the articulation of local, regional and state elites were expressed.

The elaborate system of guards by which the state mines, at least, were protected and policed betrays a concern verging on paranoia lest the pre-eminent prestige good go astray. Now Berthelot rightly dismisses the chroniclers' ethnocentric interpretation that the guards were there to prevent 'theft' in the sense in which the Spanish understood the term (1986: 76); but this does not mean, as he later implies, that the guards were superfluous in that the workers would in any case have been unswervingly loyal to the state (1986: 85). Certainly it was not the case in the non-market economy of Tawantinsuyu that the embezzlement of precious metals would have made a person wealthy by conferring buying power, as they would subsequently with the incorporation of Andean society into the mercantile capitalist system. Rather the reverse: their unlicensed dissipation through the population at large would actually have rendered them valueless, since it was only through their circulation being so tightly controlled by the central authority and its local representatives that they could continue to serve as symbols of divinity, political power and vassalage. In a marketless economy, access to a prestige good must be strictly controlled; conversely, it is that very control which makes the good prestigious.

Flows of gold and silver, then, constituted a restricted, 'prestige' sphere of exchange, distinct from those twin spheres centred on the circulation of food and cloth. Commoners, though they mined the raw materials, were wholly excluded from participation. The mine police were present, in other words, to protect not so much state property as state privilege; and given the religious elaboration of political power and its divine, golden associations, individual appropriation of precious metals would have been not so much theft as sacrilege.

In terms of the ideological construct, the puncturing of state privilege in this way would have had further implications. The mining *corvée* was predicated, like the production of food and cloth, upon the moral solidarities of local groups. Misappropriation by a commoner of the pre-eminent prestige good could only have taken place outside this moral domain, detaching him from the collectivity and its tutelary deities on which he relied for subsistence. It would have been an act of hubris, at once sacrilegious, seditious and amoral.

It can now be seen that the extraction, control and circulation of precious metals in pre-Hispanic times was wholly congruent with the cultural logic that was earlier induced from contemporary mythoreligious discourse. According to this logic, state power, community morality and subsistence production, locked together in a single ideological *gestalt*, are symbolised by the controlled release and transmission of gold and silver to the state. Anarchy and its inevitable concomitants, moral breakdown and the abandonment of food production, are symbolised by the collapse of those controls, the dissemination of precious metals to the populace. The controls – whether exercised by human guards, as in the state mines of the Inkas, or by the *kurakas*, as was presumably the case in the community mines, or by the nature spirits coopted by the state, as in the animistic projection – are crucial. The cultural 'logic' is of course circular, a parallogism: for without the controls, gold and silver are worthless.

Or they were. Today gold is pure profit, disposed of for cash. Yet the combined forces of the nature spirits and the state continue to exert an inexorable control over peasant livelihood. The nature spirits are both the immediate sources of fertility and wellbeing, and also the religious counterparts of the local agents of the state. The modern state, for its part, is viewed as being continuous with the Inka one, both of them defining the same era. The collective pursuit of subsistence is doubly fetishised: survival is seen as flowing, not from the joint efforts of people engaged in the mutual satisfaction of their interests, but instead from a fantastic pantheon of vengeful gods behind which lies the power and privilege of the state. The winning of precious metals cannot easily be divorced from this nexus, for they are an integral part of the represen-tation: they pertain to the gods as substance and to the state as tribute, and to deflect them from this circuit, to derange the *apus* in the pursuit of precious metals for purely private ends, is to engage in an activity fundamentally at odds with their proper role in the fetishised Andean world, one which must hence be pursued wholly outside the context of normal social relations and which risks violent supernatural retribution. Thus a Qamawaran prospects in secret, at night, alone, or with a single confidant, or with an outsider, a moral stranger; and death is always a possibility. If this was so in the case of the placer mines surrounding the community, how much more dangerous was the spirit of the former Inka state mine of Pachatusan, whose ruined galleries no Qamawaran dared enter.

The mining of gold in Qamawara thus derives its ideological cast not from the fact that it is extracted as a gift and disposed of as a commodity – that is, from the imperfect articulation between the dictates of capitalism and the norms of Andean culture – but rather from within the culture itself. Now, of course, there is a strong material incentive to run the gauntlet of the *apus*. But as we saw, other peasant products besides gold are sold on the market, with no comparable connotations of mystical danger or ambivalence. The supernatural perils of goldmining are a consequence, not of the ultimate commoditisation of the product, but of the cultural logic in which it is initially embedded.

This same mystical danger, vastly amplified and distorted, pervades the lives of the tin miners of Oruro. Like the criminals whom the Inkas condemned to a life of permanent exile in the mines, they too are cut off permanently from the communal world of agropastoral subsistence; furthermore, they are forced to appropriate the wealth of an erstwhile silver mine in order to secure their own livelihoods. They have come to terms with the moral limbo they are obliged to inhabit by institutionalising Tío as a kind of malevolent benefactor who is at once bloodthirsty and bountiful. Like his counterpart Wari in the myth cited earlier, he abjures his commitment to the state and gives the miners the ore they crave, but exacts a heavy price. The greatest riches can only be gained by isolating oneself even from one's workmates and entering into a private and inevitably fatal relationship with this Andean Nemesis. Tío's character has of course varied according to historical circumstance, the danger he represents being at times accentuated, at others attenuated. Again, though, this danger does not derive from the passage of mineral wealth from gift to commodity, but from the conception of precious metals and their extraction which lies within the Andean cultural matrix itself. The perversion is complete: the workers literally 'eat the mines'. Nature's entrails now support not the life of the state, but life itself.

Finally, what of the injunctions – common to both the Qamawaran and the Oruro cases – against verbal or symbolic references to things Christian, lest the metal disappear? The theme of disappearing metals was also encountered in the Inkarrí myths, where gold and silver either buried themselves or turned to stone in the instant that Inkarrí was killed by the Spanish. Indeed, there is an historical foundation to such accounts. In order to evade the Spanish looters, large amounts of gold and silver were carried to isolated spots by porters, directed by Inka nobles; after burying the hoard the porters would be led far away and hanged, and the nobles would commit suicide (Pizarro [1571] 1965: 196). In the cultural representation of the Andean state – the Inka empire and its Hispanic successors – precious metals are conceptualised as either supporting or subverting the legitimate, established powers. The parallel representation of the Spanish conquest of the Inkas, on the other hand, views the intervention of the Spanish, their gods and their talismans as that of alien and usurping powers, presenting a challenge not from within the system but to the very system itself. In these critical moments the system responds, in effect, by closing down – the metal vanishes.

Notes

I acknowledge the helpful comments of the editors and of the members of the London University Intercollegiate Seminar on earlier drafts of this article.
1 The fieldwork on which this section is based was carried out in 1973–4, and was made possible by a Foreign Area Fellowship from the US Social Science Research Program supplemented by a grant from the Radcliffe-Brown Fund of

the Association of Social Anthropologists. I am grateful to both these bodies for this support.

2 Ethnic dualism portrays the village of San Salvador as *misti*, mestizo or Hispanicised, in contrast with the so-called *indígenas*, Indians, of the upland communities.

3 Taussig's re-analysis is in fact based on Nash's earlier articles (1970, 1972 and 1976) rather than on the full-length monograph (Nash 1979).

4 Helms acknowledges the ideas of Heather Lechtman, who has argued that the predilection throughout the Andes for depletion gilding using a gold-copper alloy (*tumbaga*), a process in which the gold in the body of the object is technically 'wasted', indicates a cultural precept that the appearance of an object be a direct manifestation of its inherent qualities (Lechtman 1975: 8–10; 1979: 31–3; 1984: 29–35).

5 In a similar vein, Rowe (1976) has argued that across the successive though discontinuous periods of statehood and quasi-statehood in the prehistoric Andes can be discerned a cumulative process of the harnessing of religion to centralised political control.

References

Arguedas, J. M. and Roel Pineda, J. 1973. 'Tres versiones del mito de Inkarrí', in *Ideología mesiánica del mundo andino*, J. M. Ossio, ed., pp. 217–24, Lima: Ignacio Prado Pastor.

Bastien, J. W. 1978. *Mountain of the condor: metaphor and ritual in an Andean ayllu*, St Paul: West Publishing Co.

Berthelot, J. 1986. 'The extraction of precious metals at the time of the Inkas', in *Anthropological history of Andean polities*, ed., J. Murra, N. Wachtel and J. Revel, pp. 68–88, Cambridge: Cambridge University Press.

Bray, W. 1978. *The gold of El Dorado*, London: Times Newspapers Ltd.

Cieza de León, P. de [1554] 1973. *El señorío de los Incas*, Lima: Editorial Universo.

Earls, J. 1969. 'The organization of power in Quechua mythology', *Journal of the Steward Anthropological Society*, 1: 63–82.

Favre, H. 1967. 'Tayta wamani: le culte des montagnes dans le centre sud des Andes peruviennes', in *Colloque d'études peruviennes*. Publications des annales de la Faculté des Lettres No. 61, pp. 121–40, Aix-en-Provence: Editions Phrys.

Flores Ochoa, J. 1973. 'Inkariy y Qollariy en una comunidad del altiplano', in *Ideología mesiánica del mundo andino*, J. M. Ossio, ed., pp. 301–36.

Garcilaso de la Vega, El Inca [1617] 1966. *Primera parte de los comentarios reales de los Incas* (trans. H. V. Livermore), Austin: University of Texas Press.

Godelier, M. 1977. 'The concept of a "social and economic formation": the Inca example', in *Perspectives in Marxist anthropology*, pp. 63–9, Cambridge University Press.

Gómez, J. [1571] 1966. Letter to Francisco de Borgia, in *Dioses y hombres de Huarochirí*, ed., J. M. Arguedas, pp. 241–4, Lima: Instituto de Estudios Peruanos.

Gorbak, C., Lischetti, M. and Muñoz, C. P. 1962. 'Batallas rituales del Chiaraje y del Toqto de la provincia de Kanas (Cuzco-Peru)', *Revista del Museo Nacional de Lima*, 31: 245–304.

Helms, M. W. 1981. 'Precious metals and politics: style and ideology in the Intermediate Area and Peru', *Journal of Latin American Lore*, 7 (2): 215–38.

Isbell, B. J. 1978. *To defend ourselves: ecology and ritual in an Andean village*, Austin: Institute of Latin American Studies, University of Texas.

Lechtman, H. 1975. 'Style in technology – some early thoughts', in *Material culture: styles, organization and dynamics of technology*, eds., H. Lechtman and R. S. Merill, pp. 3–20. St Paul: West Publishing Co.

1979. 'Issues in Andean metallurgy', in *Pre-Columbian metallurgy of South America*, ed., E. P. Benson, pp. 1–40. Washington, DC: Dumbarton Oaks Library and Collections.

1984. 'Andean value systems and the development of prehistoric metallurgy', *Technology and Culture*, 25 (1): 1–36.

Lothrop, S. K. 1938. *Inca treasure as depicted by Spanish historians*, Los Angeles: The Southwest Museum.

1967. 'Peruvian metallurgy', in *Peruvian archaeology: selected readings*, eds., J. H. Rowe and D. Menzel, pp. 258–63, Palo Alto: Peek Publications.

Mariscotti de Görlitz, A. M. 1978. *Pachamama Santa Tierra*, Berlin: Gebr. Mann Verlag.

Martínez, G. 1983. 'Los dioses de los cerros en los Andes', *Journal de la Société des Americanistes*, 69: 85–115.

Moore, S. F. 1958. *Power and property in Inca Peru*, New York: Columbia University Press.

Morote Best, E. 1956. 'Espiritus de montes', *Letras*, 56–7: 288–306.

Murra, J. V. 1962. 'Cloth and its functions in the Inca state', *American Anthropologist*, 64: 710–28.

1980. *The economic organization of the Inka state*, Research in Economic Anthropology Supplement No. 1, ed., G. Dalton, Greenwich, Connecticut: JAI Press.

Murúa, M. de [1611] 1964. *Historia general del Peru. Origen y descendencia de los Incas*, ed., M. Ballesteros-Gabrois. Madrid: Gonzalo Fernández de Orviedo.

Nash, J. 1970. 'Mitos y costumbres en las minas nacionalizadas de Bolivia', *Estudios Andinos*, 1 (3): 69–82.

1972. 'The devil in Bolivia's nationalized tin mines', *Science and Society*, 36 (2): 221–3.

1976. 'Basilia', in *Dos mujeres indígenas*, J. Nash and M. M. Rocca, pp. 1–130, Mexico: Instituto Indigenista Interamericano.,

1979. *We eat the mines and the mines eat us*, New York: Columbia University Press.

Ortíz, A. 1980. *Huarochirí, 400 años después*, Lima: Pontificia Universidad Católica del Perú.

Pizarro, P. [1571] 1965. *Relación del descubrimiento y conquista de los reinos del Perú*, Biblioteca de Autores Españoles, 168: 158–242, Madrid: Ediciones Atlas.

Platt, T. 1983. 'Conciencia andina y conciencia proletaria: qhuyaruna y aylluruna en el norte de Potosí', *Revista Latinoamericana de Historia Económica y Social*, 2: 47–73.

Rowe, J. 1976. 'Religión e imperio en el Perú antiguo', *Antropología Andina*, 1–2: 5–12'.

Sancho, P. [1543] 1962. *Relación de la conquista del Perú*, Madrid: José Porrua Turanzas.

Santillán, H. de [1563] 1968. *Relación del origen, descendencia, política y gobierno de los Incas*, Biblioteca de Autores Españoles, 209, 97–150, Madrid: Ediciones Atlas.

Skar, H. 1982. 'An Andean cosmology', Working papers of the Department of Social Anthropology, University of Gothenburg. Unpublished ms.

Urbano, H. O. 1980. 'Dios Yaya, Dios Churi y Dios Espiritu: modelos trinitarios y arqueología mental en los Andes', *Journal of Latin American Lore*, 6 (1): 111–27.

10

The earth and the state: the sources and meanings of money in Northern Potosí, Bolivia

OLIVIA HARRIS

The patron saint of the tin-mining centre of Llallagua is the Virgin of the Assumption. Her annual feast is celebrated on 15 August by extra-ordinary processions of dancers through the streets, which seem to defy the human condition by their hours of intense physical exertion and heavy drinking, in the hot sun at an altitude of some 12,000 ft.[1] In 1983, after two days watching the dancers, I met up with a group of Laymi men who were preparing to return home to their villages some eight hours' walk away.

It was eight o'clock in the morning and they were pouring libations in the spirit of the preceding festival, as well as to ask protection for the journey home. With my arrival more cheap rum (*alcool de caña*) was purchased and we began a new round of libations, starting in the proper way by drinking for God and his consort the moon, then for the mountains and for *pachamama*, the earth. Next, since it was her feast, we drank for the Virgin of the Assumption (*mamita asunta*) and the money that she brings to her worshippers. The morning wore on, the sun rose towards its zenith, we bought more rum and continued pouring libations, with greater and greater fervour, to all the divinities honoured by the local Andean population but especially to money and the sources of money. My drinking companions told me that *mamita asunta*'s 'husband' was Saint Michael, and that he is the *segunda mayor* of the mine (the term is that used in Northern Potosí for the highest-ranking indigenous authority). Saint Michael's is the other important feast-day in the mining district, celebrated in a spirit of both rivalry and complementarity in the nearby town of Uncia. He is also represented at the head of one of the dance troupes – the *diablada*, or devils' dance. We also poured libation after libation for the 'devils'. Thought to be the guardians and owners of the mine, they are frequently referred to in ritual language as *tio* and *tia*, the Spanish terms for uncle and aunt. They live underground in the mines, and also inhabit banks. They are distinguished from the Virgin

232

and Saint Michael – according to one man – because 'they do not have names'.

Talking about money leads on to other, more secret aspects. They contrast today's money with that of ancient times (*layra timpu qullqi*); this is 'Inka money' and has stamped on it the head of 'Hernando' with long loose hair (*ch'aska jirnantu p'iqimpi*). (Hernando is almost certainly the late eighteenth-century Spanish king Ferdinand VII, whose reign marked the end of effective Spanish hegemony over the Andean region.) Unlike present-day money, 'Inka money' is very good. And there is yet a third different sort of 'money', *chullpa qullqi* which is buried under ground.

The irony of this fervent pouring of libations became clear as the day wore on. My Laymi companions knew they should set off for home, and yet they stayed on, each of us in turn buying another round, in order to honour the local sources of money. The paradox of the situation was of course that in the name of ensuring continued access to money, and the overall reproduction of their society, they were drinking away cash which could, as I thought, be put to other uses.[2] Some Laymi would have agreed with me. One old man asked me a few days later if I knew where he could go to become a Protestant, since he had heard that they outlawed festive expenditure. He himself thoroughly disapproved of the waste of time, but more particularly of the squandering of money, in the long days devoted to pouring libations which celebrate every significant aspect of life. Some women, too, are cynical about the drinking bouts carried on in the name of religious devotion, but while they may dislike the drunkenness, and the violence that often ensues, they direct their complaints more against the squandering of money, since drunkenness is a virtually obligatory state in order to worship the divine beings of the Andean cosmos.

The incident conjures up the spectre of the so-called 'irrationality' of peasants. Why were these men not affected by the Protestant ethic? Why in a situation of scarcity were they spending their resources in such a non-utilitarian way? While we can readily understand that they should pray to the *contemporary* sources of money, talk of Inka coins and pre-Inka money is more mysterious.

Such questions are of course based on a naive European rationality. Those who study the workings of other economic systems would be unlikely to ask them in such a way, but the dilemma remains that while we know that not all people behave according to the same canons of economic rationality, we assume that money itself can be subject to scientific scrutiny, and its behaviour analysed in terms of universal laws. The significance of money today extends beyond the limits of any particular culture; it is an *international language*, which since the development of the modern world market has by definition transcended political boundaries.[3] It is ambiguous, created by the state, and yet not fully controlled by the state. It is a human invention but it evades our complete understanding.

Money in European discourse

If the objective behaviour of money eludes comprehension, its ambiguity is heightened by the multiple levels at which it operates as a signifier. Probably the primary signifying function of money in Europe – at least since the early modern period – is to refer to the value of what is exchanged (Polanyi 1977, ch. 9; Foucault 1970, ch. 6); thence it comes to signify not only exchange value but *exchange itself*. The fact that economic textbooks constantly reiterate that money has other functions apart from that of the means of exchange, only serves to reinforce this primary semantic identification.

The discursive functions of money are multiple, but two major currents can be identified, both of which have played an important role in how Andean history is represented. The first current is romantic and nostalgic, treating money as the sign of alienation, individualism and the breakdown of social and communal values. The second is based on liberal philosophy and by contrast sees in money the advent of rationality in social behaviour, and the sign of civilization, freeing human beings from the shackles of dependency.

The discourse of nostalgia

The first current is quite common in anthropological and historical writings on the Central Andes. The history of the Europeans' annexation of the region is hard to recount without invoking their lust for precious metals. Christopher Columbus had written eulogistically from Jamaica in 1503: 'Gold is a wonderful thing! Its owner is master of all he desires. Gold can even enable souls to enter Paradise.'[4] And the drawing of the first encounter between European and Inka by the Andean nobleman Waman Puma makes the point tersely; the 'Spaniard' Candia (he was in fact Greek) is depicted kneeling before the Inka Wayna Qapaq, who offers him a dish filled with pieces of gold, asking him *cay coritachu micunqui?* (is it this gold that you eat?). Candia replies *este oro comemos* (we eat this gold) (Waman Puma 1980: 369).

The incompatibility of Andean and European attitudes to precious metals found perhaps its most dramatic historical expression in the ransom of the last Inka, Atawallpa, who thinking that the Spanish would leave once they had enough treasure, offered a large room filled from floor to ceiling with precious metal in return for his freedom. When the ransom arrived, all the adornments and religious sacra were melted down to make room for more; within a few years, most of the extraordinary artistry of the Andean gold- and silversmiths was destroyed. 'Peru' became in European tongues synonymous with fabulous wealth; to this image was added that of Potosí, the 'rich mountain' whose veins of silver, located by the Spanish in 1545, fulfilled their most extravagant hope of the riches to be found in the new colonies. By the time Cervantes was writing *Don Quixote*, Potosí and silver had replaced gold as the symbols of quickly-made fortunes (Vilar 1976: 119).

Such images have been used to powerful effect by generations of writers on Andean history; indeed the inherent drama of this moment of European colonial expansion is not uncommonly enhanced by portraying the Inka world as a particularly noble one. Bartolomé de las Casas, the Dominican champion of the American peoples, set the tone in the 1550s:

That which led the Spaniards to these unsanctified impieties was the desire of Gold, to make themselves suddenly rich, for the obtaining of dignities and honours which were in no way fit for them. (1972: 4)

I am an eye-witness, and do affirm upon my knowledge that the inhabitants of Peru were a Nation very courteous, affable, and loving to the Spaniards . . . (ibid. p. 62)

John Phillips, the English translator of Las Casas at the height of anti-Spanish feeling in the mid seventeenth century writes of 'these sad Relations of the devout CASAUS [Las Casas], by reason of the cruel Slaughters and Butcheries of the Jesuitical Spaniards, perpetrated upon so many Millions of poor innocent Heathens, who having only the light of Nature, not knowing their Saviour Jesus Christ, were sacrificed to the Politick Interest and Avarice of the wicked Spaniards'.[5] Prescott, picking up the same theme in *The Conquest of Peru*, notes:

The mild and docile character of the Peruvians would have well fitted them to receive the teachings of Christianity, had the love of conversion, instead of gold, animated the breasts of the Conquerors. And a philosopher of later time . . . pronounces 'the moral man in Peru far superior to the European'. (1889: 82)

This tendency to idealise the pristine Andean world finds expression today in the view of Tawantinsuyu as a sacred, harmonious state in which exploitation was minimised through the reciprocal relationship uniting ruler and ruled. This is contrasted to the mercenary Europeans' desire for individual gain, and their desecration and sacking of holy places. The Andean appreciation of the artistic potential of gold and silver as material substances stands against the European obsession with specie.

The contrast can be further emphasised by the fact that the Inka economy was organised in such a way as to preclude the circulation of a generalised standard that we would recognise as money, and that trade and markets were probably entirely absent in the heartlands of the empire. This feature of Tawantinsuyu, little remarked upon by Spanish chroniclers at the time,[6] has been demonstrated by Murra's work (1972; 1979); since he drew attention to its significance for understanding the Andean economy, money and markets have been used by some as a key signifier of European domination, of the rupture with the Andean past.

The contrast between non-monetary and monetary economies is also built into the very structure of anthropology as a discipline, whose theories are so often articulated around a play of oppositions: primitive and civilised, traditional and modern, pre-capitalist and capitalist, non-literate and literate. Money and markets, their presence or absence, have provided a central axis along which historical reality has been divided into two polarised and contrasted fields. The appearance of money then becomes an index of inexorable transition ('monetisation') from a previous state, subsistence-oriented and based on use-values, to the economy that we know, based on exchange-value, dominated by money and the market. The appearance of Western money in an economy where circulation was previously organised on some other basis easily comes to imply a whole teleological sequence involving its destruction and replacement by a system in which the priority of collective interests and social ties has been replaced by accumulation for individual gain.

Such a contrast, particularly in the form of self-sufficiency versus exchange, has long historical antecedents in European thought. Aristotle in the *Politics* wrote of self-sufficiency as the perfect state (1962: 59); his ideas were fundamental to the development of Marx's political economy. For Marx, money develops as a corollary of exchange; exchange-value evolves between groups whose relation is one of 'reciprocal isolation and foreignness', conditions which 'do not exist for the members of a primitive community of natural origin, whether it takes the form of a patriarchal family, an ancient Indian commune, or an Inca state' (1976: 182). For Aristotle, then, there was a 'natural' (*oikonomike*) use of money; but there was also an 'unnatural' (*chrematistike*) use. The former is a means of satisfying wants; in the latter wealth-getting has become an end in itself. Marx reproduces this distinction: for him the merchant 'parasitically inserts himself' between the selling and the buying pro-ducers (ibid: 256), and he then builds the moral contrast into the general formula for capital that he opposes to simple reproduction.

It was on the basis of Aristotle's formulation that Thomist law and the medieval church banned usury. As Vilar notes, the booming Spanish economy of the sixteenth century led to intense debates on monetary issues: 'the confessor's handbook became a veritable economics text-book'. While usury and associated financial transactions were outlawed, a 'rationally justified profit', based on a 'just price' (i.e., the 'common price of the market place') was admitted (1976: 158). The idea of the *chrematistike*, the parasite who recognises no social and human responsibilities towards other members of the community, was of course immortalised in the person of Shylock, the archetypal covetous outsider. (Only this type of person, typically Jewish, was permitted by the church to practise usury.)

In principle, Marx maintains the distinction between the benign and the unacceptable uses of money, but in practice he blurs it. In his terminology, economies in which goods do not circulate by means of exchange are called 'natural'; this terminology relies on his fundamental distinction between use-value and exchange-value, and suggests by implication that there is something *unnatural* about exchange. (The unsatisfactoriness of this vocabulary is made evident by his use of the 'patriarchal family', the 'Indian commune' and the Inka state to illustrate what he means by the natural economy.) Moreover, although he devotes some consideration to the historical and theoretical problem of the development of exchange-value, at heart for him this concept assumes the existence of money as a generalised equivalent. On the other hand, in many passages it is clear that he is drawn to an image of money as destructive *in itself*; thus he cites approvingly Augier's apocalyptic pronouncement that money 'comes into the world with a congenital blood-stain on one cheek' (1976: 926). This suggests a slippage in his thinking; his stated position is that the source of outrage is *capital*, i.e., money-making in which the aim is profit and social and human responsibilities are ignored (echoing Aristotle's distinction). But lurking in his writing is an implicit critique of money itself, and thus, since his concept of exchange relies so heavily on *monetary* exchange, also a critique of *exchange*.[7]

This slippage is not at all unique to Marx. Its familiarity in western discourse is one of the reasons why money and its multifarious operations are so hard to analyse. Money is an objective historical phenomenon, but it also operates as a general signifier at many levels. It often stands for the profit motive as such – for the rule of purely 'economic' laws in contrast to the consideration of social needs. It is also closely associated with markets; in fact in many contexts money and the market are virtually synonymous.[8]

The slippage from the condemnation of usury/profit-making to that of money itself is mirrored in everyday English speech; for example, Mammon, meaning the devil of *covetousness* (*Shorter Oxford English Dictionary*) is frequently used to mean simply money. Similarly the original biblical statement that 'the love of money is the root of all evil' (Timothy I:6:10) is usually cited merely as 'money is the root of all evil'. In such elisions, money is treated as identical with some of the more baleful consequences of its generalised use. Whether it be Luther fulminating against the sale of indulgences, or Tawney dissecting the conscience of the Puritans, or the poetry of those early romantic opponents of the industrial system – Blake and Shelley – the theme of money haunts the European imagination.[9]

Since in its discursive effects money frequently signifies the interest of individuals as opposed to that of the community, it is easy to see how money comes to be the antithesis of the holy. The religious community has itself often been defined in opposition to money.[10] In anthropological writing on millennarian religions, the notion of the radical incompatibility of money and religion has been combined with the idea of money as the signifier of Western domination to argue that 'money seems to be the most *frequent* and *convenient* axis on which millennarian movements form' (Burridge 1969: 146). Since money is a potent symbol of the evils of capitalism, its abolition has often been proposed by socialist or anarchist projects. The Owenites in the 1820s and 1830s, the rural anarchists of Catalunya and Andalusia in the 1930s, Pol Pot's regime in Cambodia in the 1970s, all aimed to abolish money.[11]

The discourse of civilisation

The alternative tradition in the interpretation of money while attributing similar powers to it, sees these powers as positive rather than as destructive. It finds perhaps its fullest expression in liberalism as the political and economic doctrine that developed in nineteenth-century Europe with manufacturing capitalism itself, and emphasises the capacity of money to erode and destroy previous forms of social hierarchy. In this view, money is 'a radical leveller, it extinguishes all distinctions' (Marx 1976: 229). For liberal philosophy, the breaking down of feudal hierarchy (or for that matter of any hierarchy that does not arise out of the 'natural' mechanisms of free competition and market forces) is progressive. Money is the signifier of progress insofar as it dissolves bonds of personal dependency and 'frees' the individual to choose how he will earn his living, in accordance with the laws of the market.

In the Andean republics formed at the beginning of the nineteenth century, liberalism as a doctrine underlay repeated attempts to break up the *ayllus* (Indian communities) and, in particular, to dissolve the communal lands and replace them with a regime of individual private property (Sánchez-Albornóz, 1978; Platt 1982a). As Platt has shown, the resistance of the *ayllus* to such attempts was construed as demonstrating their irremediably savage state. According to the evocatively-named 'Law of Unchaining the Peasant Communities', enacted in 1874, individual titles were to be issued in order to create a market in land and thus draw the Indians into the sphere of the civilising influence of the market. Narciso de la Riva, a land inspector of the time, commented that the need to open up the Indians to exchange was 'very applicable in the case of our Indians, since while they do not entirely avoid exchange, they practise it in such minute quantities that they perceive none of its beneficial effects' (Platt 1982a: 98).

It is not clear, however, that low levels of Indian participation in the market were inevitable. While the public discourse of the liberals was castigating the *ayllus* for 'refusing' to engage in commerce, some evidence suggests that local landowners and mestizo intermediaries were in practice actively *depriving* Indians of access to markets (Rivera 1984: ch. 2).

According to the terms of liberal discourse, money does not merely embody the beneficial effect of destroying unnatural constraints on its own operations: it represents rationality itself. This is evidenced, for example, in the writings of Simmel, for whom money corresponds to the intellect rather than the emotions (1978: 173). The tradition is alive to this day in the language of development and underdevelopment, when those who fail to, or refuse to participate fully in the market, or who use their profits for religious expenditure rather than accumulation and investment, are deemed irrational.

Andean participation in colonial markets

Given the strength of the liberal vision, it comes as something of a surprise to discover that the early decades of European colonial rule witnessed the rapid, massive and above all successful intervention of Andean peoples in the expanding market economy. As we have noted, the Inka state was organised in such a way as to preclude the circulation of money as a generalised equivalent and to minimise the existence of markets (although to term it, as Marx does, a 'natural' economy, in the sense of one without *exchange*, illustrates the poverty of simple dualist models as approximations of economic reality). But it is mistaken to accept the common deduction that Andean peoples of the early colonial period only engaged in commercial activity under pressure, or that they resisted money. A series of recent articles has provided conclusive evidence to the contrary. Assadourian detailed the Indian control of mining and marketing in the boom city of Potosí in the early, so-called *wayra* period of silver production (1979); while Rivera (1978), Choque

(1978) and Murra (1978) chronicled the substantial trading activities of different Andean lords and the wealth that they controlled. More recently, Bakewell's work has reaffirmed the significance of 'free' Indian labour in Potosí before the organisation of the mita (1985).

Cieza de León had written of the city of Potosí in the 1550s: 'business was on such a scale that between Indians alone without the participation of the Christians each day in times of prosperity in the mines twenty-five or thirty thousand gold pesos were sold, and sometimes more than forty thousand' (Corónica, p. 375, cited in Assadourian 1979).

This view of the commercial success of the Indians was echoed in more general terms by the *oidor* Juan Matienzo, using a familiar simile in his description of the inhabitants of Collao (present-day Bolivia): 'These people are very rich in livestock of this land, and are great merchants and traders. They seem like Jews in their trading and dealing . . .' (1567 [1967]: 275, cited in Assadourian 1982: 183)

Circulation in the Laymi economy today

Both the romantic and liberal currents can be found in contemporary writings on the Andes. Lest it be thought by implication that Andean peasants are immune to such attitudes, let me quote two opinions commonly voiced by peasants of my acquaintance, which illustrate the contradictory values assigned to money as a signifier. I have heard it said that miners in the tin-mining towns are nicer and less abusive when they have little money; this seems to indicate a 'romantic' position that sees money and solidarity as antithetical and money itself as a corrupting influence. A different opinion contrasts this and echoes the liberal position by equating money with civilisation: Indians often observe that those who live in the highlands (i.e., nearer the mining towns) are more civilised than valley dwellers, since they understand better how to use money. By a similar logic men in general are said to be 'more civilised' than women since they have more experience in handling money.

However, these views by no means exhaust the signifying functions of money in Andean culture. In order to be able to examine these functions let us first outline the ways in which money circulates in Northern Potosí today.

For some four centuries, tribute paid to the state in the money form shaped the economic life of the Andean *ayllus*. In this century the dependence of the Bolivian state on this source of revenue has declined, and since the Agrarian Reform Law of 1953, which abolished the previous tributary system, there has been an ambiguous situation as regards the fiscal obligations of the independent Indian communities. With the inability of the state to institute a new system of rural taxation, the *ayllus* have continued to pay tax voluntarily according to the size of their land.

These days the amounts are symbolic and are no longer a burden on household income. However, the payment of the tribute retains its significance, both politically and symbolically, for the *ayllus* of Northern Potosí today. They are proud of their regular delivery, and see it as an essential means of regulating and reproducing their relationship with the state, and hence of maintaining the existing tenure system.[12] As we shall see, the twin processes of tribute payment and mining economy have structured the meaning of money in this region. The Andean *ayllus* produced the money in a literal sense for centuries, and provided the fiscal basis for the state. Thus while the money introduced by the Europeans was used for exchange, and retains this function today, it has never in my view come to dominate the meanings which money has in Andean concepts. The usurer and the miser, key figures in the European mythology of money, whose characteristics derive from its exchange function, seem strikingly absent in Andean folklore.

Moreover, the Andean economy has long been structured by a particular form of circulation that derives from the intense differentiation of the tropical mountain environment. The Inka administration elaborated this system to the point where markets and specialised traders were not found at all in the heartlands of the state. However, the local organisation of the 'vertical economy', by which each political or ethnic unit was distributed across a discontinuous territory, both existed before the time of Inka hegemony and persisted after its destruction. In this system, each unit had access to a wide range of ecozones whose different products circulated primarily within the group, transported by the producers or consumers themselves, and not by outsider intermediaries (Murra 1972; Flores 1978; Masuda *et al* 1985). Today in spite of the pressure by the Bolivian state on collective *ayllu* control of land, a reduced version of this system still operates in Northern Potosí (Platt 1982b; Harris 1982a).

The consequences of these forms of circulation is that there is little mystery for the consumers about where things come from, or about how they are produced. The typical indigenous traders of the Central and Southern Andes were not intermediaries, but people who travelled in order to obtain consumption goods from elsewhere for themselves and their kin. Bertonio, compiler of the first Aymara dictionary (1612) is explicit: he contrasts 'our sort of trader' (*mercader a nuestro modo*) to the 'Indian style of trader' (*mercader a modo de indios*) whom he defines as 'he who travels to other areas to acquire food'.[13] I suspect that this enduring economic system has significantly affected the way money is represented in the Central Andes, since the fetishistic quality of money derives in good measure from the way it appears to produce wealth, and thus the power to acquire everything, in and of itself.

Circulation in Northern Potosí today is largely structured by the *ayllus* or ethnic units. The basic characteristic of the 'ethnic economy' is that the rates and forms of circulation, of both goods and labour, are different between members of a single *ayllu* than they are with members of other *ayllus*, or with townspeople (Harris 1982a). This has consequences for the distribution of labour, and of the distinctive produce of the various eco-zones within the dispersed *ayllu* territory. In many cases circulation within the *ayllu* cannot be called 'exchange' at all; in others, exchange is carried out using rates which do not involve calculations based on money as a standard of value, but derive from the volume of the item exchanged, or its particular material quality. Nonetheless, it would be false to suggest that the ethnic economy is a 'natural' economy, or a 'use-value' economy, protected from the money form that mediates exchanges with outsiders. Quite the reverse: many exchanges with outsiders whether of labour or products specifically *avoid* the use of money, while exchanges between *ayllu* members not uncommonly do involve money.

Cash enters the Laymi economy mainly through the sale of a species of potato (*papa imilla*) particularly favoured by urban consumers. Laymi distinguish those potato fields that are planted 'for food' (*maq'ataki*) from those that are planted 'for money' (*qullqitaki*). However, the 'cash crop' potato is also appreciated and consumed by Laymi households, so that when the harvest is poor it can be held back, or withdrawn for domestic use. For example, the 1983 drought led to a second disastrous harvest in succession, and townswomen in order to obtain their *papa imilla* had to woo their peasant providers with invitations to come and eat with them. The townspeople, schooled in the logic of the market, complained that the Indians were deliberately speculating – holding back the sale of potatoes out of sheer malice until the price had risen;[14] whereas, in the main, Indians were holding back their potatoes for seed and domestic consumption.

When money enters the Laymi economy, it may circulate internally in the form of payments, debts and small gifts between *ayllu* members, and above all for the highland potato producers to acquire maize and other temperate products from their kin living at lower altitudes. However, the two major uses of money these days are for external purchases – on the one hand, livestock (bulls, mules, donkeys and to a lesser extent llamas) and, on the other, festive expenditure. Payments for mass to be said are today not a big expense unlike in the past; nonetheless festive expenditure is the single most important stimulus for entering the market whether to sell produce or labour. Coca leaf, the basis of all ritual, is generally acquired for cash; and crude rum and cigarettes are also important ingredients of ritual. Festive expenditure is a regular outgoing for everybody, and when a household takes its turn to sponsor a community feast the costs have to be budgeted for in advance and spread over several years. Compared with these expenses, purchases of food for household consumption or of clothing are small-scale.

However, neither of the major forms of expenditure are simple individual purchases. This is perhaps obvious in the case of festive expenses whose purpose is to acquire the necessary materials to communicate with the divine sources of power and so to reproduce the *ayllu*. Livestock purchases are at first sight more individually oriented. Animals are usually owned by individuals or by households, and the number of livestock owned is the basis for classifying differences of wealth among Laymi themselves, as it is for many Andean societies. (This fact was assimilated in the sixteenth century by the *oidor* Matienzo, as his statement quoted above indicates.) But as we shall see, livestock are not simply an individual investment, but are harnessed to the reproduction of the *ayllu* as a whole.

In short, there are exchanges which involve money, and exchanges which don't. Is there then a systematic difference between monetary transactions and barter? Or between those with whom one barters and those for whom money acts as a medium of exchange? It seems not; barter can be part of an extended circuit involving money at some point, one in which profits are carefully calculated by at least one partner; it can also be the exchange of use-values at rates which are not based on monetary price. Only the context will determine which it is, and this context includes both the social relationship of those exchanging and, more importantly, where the transaction takes place. In the remote valleys, far from the roads, Laymi will only exchange maize for money with members of the *ayllu*, and then usually only with close kin. Anyone else wanting their maize has to offer a direct use-value in exchange. This may well be something previously purchased for money (coca leaf, rum, sandals etc.) or it may be something the outsiders themselves have produced, such as *ch'uñu*, cloth or clay pots. If townspeople come out to the rural areas in search of potatoes and maize they must exchange by barter; if *ayllu* members go to the town they prefer to sell for money. The logic is clear: when markets are far away, money is mainly avoided in the *ayllu* economy since there are few uses to which it can be put. The little money that is needed in the remote valleys is accepted almost as a favour from close kin who find it more convenient than carrying huge loads of produce to exchange. Nonetheless prices are a constant topic of conversation. Whether exchanges are carried out with or without the medium of money, rates of exchange appear to be uniform, monitored by discussion and little affected by the personal relationships of those completing any particular transactions.[15] There are no products which are exclusively exchanged for cash; conversely, all items that are obtained with cash may also be acquired without it. As we shall see, however, there are certain uses to which money or products cannot be put when they are acquired as gifts.

Distance from markets is fundamental in determining whether cash is used in a transaction, but it is not the only factor. As noted, women are thought to be less civilised than men because they do not understand money. Rural men use money more than women (unlike the urban situation) since while women are not prohibited from travelling or from trading, the inflexibility of their domestic and herding commitments allows them less mobility than men. Besides, women as housewives are responsible for the household budget, and are therefore often cautious about making conversions into cash because of the excessive fluidity of money. Conversions are acceptable if they are made with a particular purchase in view to complete the circuit rapidly. This makes sense not only as a guard against inflation, but also because money can too easily be converted into alcohol and thence drunkenness by men. Even when women do not explicitly complain about alcohol consumption, many of them resist conversions into money for this reason.

The process of circulation cannot, in spite of these provisos, be divided into a monetised and a non-monetised sphere. The economy is not completely open, but the points of restriction or closure do not coincide with the boundary between the presence of money and its absence. The fact is that money as such is neutral; the flow of cash in the *ayllu* economy is limited for practical rather than for cultural or ideological reasons.

Two examples help to illustrate this neutrality. The first is linguistic. In Aymara there is no exclusive term for transactions involving money. For economic exchanges the same root is used whether money is the medium of exchange or not: *alasiña*, or the Spanish-derived *kampiaña*. The nature of the exchange is signalled by specifying – where relevant – what was given to effect the purchase; thus *qullqiru alasta* means 'I acquired for money', *ch'uqiru alasta* means 'I acquired for potatoes.'

The distinction between purchase and sale, derived from the monetary economy, is predictably slight in Aymara. Bertonio's entry makes the point: 'Alatha; to buy, and to sell, depending on the construction, with Ro it means to sell, with na it is to buy' (1612: II, 9). In contemporary Aymara the difference between selling and buying is signalled by adding the suffix '-ja-', which designates the separation of a part from the whole (Clearman England 1974: 153).

The second example concerns the ceremonial gifts known as *arkhu* which are made to cross-sex siblings who sponsor a community feast; they are usually in the form of cloth or clothing, but sometimes also money, which should ideally be spent on buying livestock. The worst thing one can do with *arkhu* money is to spend it on petty luxuries for personal consumption such as bread, sweets, oranges. *Arkhu* are reciprocal prestations, based on the principle of *ayni*, which reward those who take their turn to feast their neighbours and their divine guardians. Converting *arkhu* into livestock contributes to long-term recycling; gratification through individual consumption is potentially incompatible with this aim. It is not only money gifts whose use is restricted in this way. Gifts of cloth are also surrounded by the same taboos; they may be converted into money, but again only for the purpose of purchasing livestock. Any other use would be wrong. One woman who wove a cloth (*awayu*) for her brother when he celebrated a feast was so outraged when he sold it to buy a pair of boots that she refused to speak to him for some time, and has never woven for him since.

Arkhu money then, is restricted in its use not because money is profane in itself (it is after all offered as a ceremonial gift); but it should only be used to acquire livestock, fundamental to the prosperity of the *ayllu*, and not for petty *personal* consumption.

In general, money does not only facilitate and accelerate the circulation of commodities, it also crucially serves as a means to command labour. However in the Laymi context this function is of secondary importance. Within the *ayllu* labour is rarely recruited by day-wages (*jornales*), but rather by the non-monetary institutions of *mink'a* or *ayni*.

Most men, however wealthy they are, work occasionally in the nearby mining centres for extra cash for personal or domestic consumption, usually as porters or building labourers, but remarkably few work in mining itself. Laymi who leave the *ayllu* for longer periods of wage labour go usually to Llica on the Chilean frontier, where in addition to earning some cash they are paid in livestock (llamas and donkeys) and quinoa (the protein-rich Andean cereal); or they go to the tropical Chapare region to the north-east where in addition to money they earn coca leaf, and other tropical products such as rice. The usual reason for such migration is either to acquire livestock or, more generally, to obtain produce and money for festive expenditure. It is thus harnessed to the reproduction of *ayllu* prosperity.[16]

In general it is misleading to talk of attitudes to money or its behaviour without taking fiscal and monetary history into account. From the early days, Peruvian coinage was subject to debasement and low confidence (McLeod 1984: 375). The writings of Assadourian (1982), Tandeter and Wachtel (1983) and Platt (1986) have begun to chart for different periods the fluctuations of the monetary system in Alto Peru/Bolivia and their consequences for the functioning of the internal market. While in recent decades Bolivian currency was among the most stable in Latin America, it collapsed in 1984 and by 1985 inflation was the highest in the world, at a vertiginous 8,163.4 per cent per annum (LAB 1987). Various writers have argued that economic crises cause a return to barter (recently Humphrey 1985, Orlove 1986). Whether this has happened in Northern Potosí, I am not able to determine; however it does seem probable that the rural economy of the region is less monetised today than at certain periods in the past.[17]

While high inflation probably causes changes in economic behaviour and shows up the limitations of money as a store of value, it may equally demystify its role as an independent cause or agent of historical trans-formation. Certainly in Northern Potosí today there is little evidence that the peasants and miners see money itself as either the symbol, or as directly the cause, of their problems.

Circulation and fertility

Money is not seen *per se* as threatening by Laymi, and is not singled out by them as a signifier of the alien and destructive. Outside traders may be generous or they may be mean, but they are not treated categorically as a burden on the *ayllu* economy. When Laymi complain that they are being 'robbed' of their livelihood, it is not prices and trading that they refer to, but *extra-economic* forms of coercion. For example, sometimes in the mining centres they are intimidated into surrendering their potatoes at well below the going rate, or even for nothing. In 1974, the authorities in Uncia requisitioned peasant produce in order to cope with a severe shortage of food in town. One Laymi man was put in jail for protesting at this injustice.

I realise in retrospect that I automatically assumed that the relationship between the peasants and urban traders was a hostile one, and was con-stantly looking for empirical evidence to support this view. I can recall several conversations with Laymi householders in which I questioned their acceptance of what seemed to me to be exorbitant profits made at their expense by local traders. However, they were often aware of the inequality of particular transactions, and would justify them by the con-venience of the traders coming out to the countryside, thus saving them an arduous journey. For them profits made in this way are not 'robbery' in the sense that extra-economic coercion is. One woman trader described as 'bad' by most people did indeed wrest a living from the *ayllu* Indians by charging high prices or selling for credit to be repaid in kind at harvest-time. However, it was not these activities that people were alluding to when they called her bad. Rather, they meant that she was mean in not offering food and hospitality (*no sabe invitar*). Other traders who com-bined profit-making with generosity were described as good (*k'acha*).

One of the constant complaints against me by Laymi friends is my refusal to enter into any kind of trading relationship with them. They tell me I could finance my air trips to Bolivia by trading: and that I am behaving in a positively anti-social way by not bringing with me for sale the special products of 'Inkiltira', for example, local varieties of potato, or clothing. Everyone wants to buy the old training shoes that I wear, and when I protest that I need them for myself, they reply that I should have thought to bring a whole sackful with me – preferably second-hand since they agree they would be unable to afford the price of new ones. They would pay me in potato which I could then sell in town. These arguments silence me. The inconvenience, and the customs duties for importing such things could be explained, but there is a more fundamental problem; I find unpalatable in itself the idea of entering into trade relationships with the people whose tolerance and generosity I am already abusing by my constant questions. I give them gifts, and hope to retain as a result people's goodwill; but I make a clear distinction in my mind between this and commerce. This self-ethnography perhaps reveals something about the conceptual boundaries between 'gift' and 'commerce' which I as an English person take to Bolivia, and also the degree to which these are not shared by my Andean hosts. Travel is always associated by them with the desire to acquire something not available locally. When people go off on a journey, they are asked: 'What will you bring back?' It is assumed that what is brought back will be distributed in one way or another.

Laymi consider that people who travel deserve to compensate their expenditure and effort by making a profit. Profit is explained as deriving from the costs of transport and travel, that is, the costs of circulation itself. However, profit is objectively visible of course only when a circuit of exchange begins and ends with the money form; money is unique in that it alone both initiates and completes a circuit of exchange. A Laymi producer does not exchange part of the potato crop for something else in order to exchange that for a greater quantity of identical potatoes. In principle it would be possible to calculate an increment in value even when exchanges are made by barter, by mentally converting what is exchanged to their monetary equivalents. However Laymi do not make such calculations. As a result it is only when a particular circuit begins and ends with the money form that a profit is visible. Indians, too, engage in petty trading. For example, a man buys a stock of earrings in town; on his return home he sells them to the women and obtains more money than his original outlay. Or a household buys rum in bulk to sell by the shot during feasts. In such contexts, money is said to 'give birth' (*wawachi*). People who make money to give birth in this way are thought to perform a valuable social service. Money, when it returns in the form of profit, is thus fertile in some way, though its fertility is realised not through the process of planting and maturation, but through exchange.[18]

The concept of debt too has close associations with fertility, not through the metaphor of giving birth, but through that of manure. In the Aymara spoken by the *ayllus* of Northern Potosí, the word for debt is in fact the very same as that for manure (*wanu*), whose Spanish rendering, *guano*, has become synonymous with the nitrate-rich deposits of bird droppings along the Pacific coast in what is today northern Chile and southern Peru. I do not think this association is a mere homonym, since a similar conclusion can be drawn from the glosses given in Bertonio's 1612 *Vocabulario*. 'Debt' and 'loan' are both given in Aymara as *manu*. The Spanish *logro*, which can mean both profit and interest, is also translated by Bertonio as *manusitha*, with *mirani chasitha* as an alternative gloss. This second root, *mira*, means not only profit or interest (sp. *logro*) but also increase (*multiplico*). *Mira marmi*, for example, means a fertile woman, and *miracatha* is translated as 'the multiplication of money producing a profit'. Furthermore a synonym for *miracatha* is *hamacatha*, whose root, *hama*, means manure.[19]

Laymi believe that it is good to have both credit and debt relationships. In the metaphorical association of debt and credit with manure we can detect a vision of circulation itself – or rather delayed circulation – as a fertilising force.

Seen from an economic perspective, money is of course not part of the subsistence base of the peasants of Northern Potosí in the same way as the products of agriculture and herding, even though it may grow 'like potatoes' in the entrails of the mines. (It is probably not a coincidence that the sale of potatoes is the main source of cash in the Laymi economy.) However, the Laymi notion that profits are a form of 'giving birth' and that they arise from the time and effort expended in travel and transport suggests that for them circulation and production are part of a single process, and that we should be wary of separating them. Of course, monetary transactions with outsiders to the *ayllu* inevitably mean that some of the wealth created within the *ayllu* flows out of it – the 'unequal exchange' postulate. This flow is I believe both recognised and tolerated by *ayllu* members. There is no sense in which the *ayllu* is a self-contained unit; rather it is embedded in wider circuits of reproduction. Moreover the primary uses to which money is put – the purchase of ritual materials and the acquisition of livestock – counteract outward flow since they are productive and 'reproductive'.[20] Livestock constitute a long-term investment; ritual offerings harness the protection and fertilising powers of the sacred beings worshipped by Andean peoples. In Laymi thought the metaphor used to represent libation, sacrifice and other ritual offerings is not exchange; rather it is feeding. Humans must feed the sacred beings so that they will in turn provide food for human society. As we have already noted, a bad person is one who is stingy with offers of food and a good person one who gives generously.[21]

It is not just because of its function in the reproductive process of the *ayllu* that money is associated with fertility and with the sacred beings who ensure fertility. In order to explore this connection further let us return to the libations for the Virgin of the Assumption in the Llallagua festival and the link between money and religious worship.

The sources of wealth

What is the connection between the ascended Mother of God and money? As good Catholics, the inhabitants of the mining towns celebrate the feast of their patron with devotion. In the mining centre of Oruro, the patron is known as the Virgin of the Mineshaft, whose annual feast is celebrated at Carnival (Nash 1979: 128–34); in both Oruro and Llallagua religious devotion is expressed particularly by dancing in a troupe at the Virgin's feast in three successive years. To sponsor one of the troupes is a great financial outlay, and the sponsors walk at the head of the dancers bearing its banner and burning incense. In front of them come cars and lorries which they have decorated with silver objects and utensils. The dancers too make a major financial commitment, since they must buy or hire their costume, and rehearse once a week for several months and more intensively as the festival approaches. During the celebration the dancers perform for hours on end, leaping, cavorting and sometimes somersaulting through the streets under the midday sun, weighed down by elaborate costumes, in front of a large, admiring and critical audience. The most renowned of the dance troupes is the *diablada* (the devil dance), whose performers wear full masks with long fangs and bulbous eyes, topped by four horns and lizards. Their red satin cloaks are decorated with snakes. Led by a figure impersonating Saint Michael, and accompanied by several female devils (*china supay*, formerly acted by men in exaggerated and provocative female clothing, but nowadays by women) the *diablada* is one of the most dramatic and the most prestigious of all the dance troupes.

These devils who so proudly take over the streets are identified as *supay* or *tio*. This figure is the presiding deity of the mines from which the town survives and prospers. He owns the veins of mineral, and gives sometimes abundantly, sometimes sparingly, as well as on occasion killing those who work to extract the ore.[22] Each mine or sector of the mine has its own image of the horned *tio*, phallus erect, mouth gaping, to which the miners make regular offerings. They chew coca leaf and offer cigarettes every day; once or twice a week they pour libations and once or twice a year make a sacrifice. The feast most explicitly dedicated to the devils of the mines is the beginning of the month of August, known as the 'month of the devils'. At this season, which is the dead of winter, all the minerals buried underground rise to the surface, and hidden treasure is revealed. It is said that to possess the treasure one must make a human sacrifice to the devils.

Devils are primarily masculine, and the guardian of the veins of ore is uninhibitedly so, sitting in the mineshaft with penis erect. However they also have female consorts, who appear in a number of guises. In the *diablada* they are the *china supay*, as exaggeratedly sexual as is the *tio* himself. They are sometimes also known as *awicha*, in which form they intercede with the *tio* for the safety of the miners. In Laymi ritual libations the female consort of the *tio* is usually referred to as the *tia* (aunt). This figure is ambiguous: sometimes they say *tia* is the Virgin of the Assumption and is 'like the moon' (*phaxsïma*). *Phaxsïma* is the common ritual term for money, silver like the moon. The identification of the 'aunt' then, makes an association between the devils who own the mineral, the metal that becomes money, and the Virgin who is the Christian patron of the mine.

The relationship between explicitly Christian figures (saints and advocations of the Virgin), and the devils is expressed in terms of contrasted 'spheres' which Laymi call 'God's sphere' (*tyusa parti*) and the 'devils' sphere' (*saxra parti*). However, while these spheres are symbolically contrasted in many contexts, they sometimes merge. The feast of the Virgin of the Assumption in Llallagua is emphatically Christian and I never heard it said that it was a feast of the devils, yet the Virgin is linked directly to the devil of the mine by being addressed as *tia*. It is hardly accidental, moreover, that the patron selected for the urban population of the mining area has her feast midway through the 'month of the devils'.[23] The same duality is evident in Nash's description of the worship of the Virgin of the Mineshaft alongside the cult of the devils at Carnival in the mining city of Oruro. In both cases potential ambiguity is overtly neutralised by having the devil dancers remove their masks on the second day, when the mass for the Virgin is celebrated.

In the Christian calendar, Carnival heralds the beginning of Lent, but in this region it is known as the 'feast of devils' and, at least in the countryside, is particularly a celebration of the fertility of flocks and fields (Harris 1982b). The deity associated with the fertility of the crops is *pachamama*, identified both with the fields themselves and with the power that makes them fruitful. Pachamama is normally represented as female; and is often said to be the wife of the *tio* who presides over the mines. Indeed, in Laymi libations for the *tio* and the *tia*, '*tia*' usually means the *pachamama*, except during the feast of the Virgin of the Assumption.

Pachamama in Laymi religious classification belongs primarily to the domain of the devils (although there is ambiguity, as the association with the Virgin indicates). Today in Northern Potosí, and elsewhere in the Aymara world, the concept of 'devil' (known variously as *yawlu*, *saxra*, *supay*, *wak'a*) includes a whole spectrum of sacred beings: the mountains, the dead, powerful untamed places such as gullies and waterfalls, and shrines where the lightning has struck and killed an animal or human being, as well as the *tio* and the *pachamama* (Harris and Bouysse 1987). The defining character of these devils is not so much evil or malice, as abundance, chaos and hunger. Humans enter into and maintain a relationship with them by offering them food, whether a full sacrifice of blood (*wilani*) or merely coca leaf, cigarettes and libations. In return the devils may give unprecedented fortune, or adequate prosperity, or they may not. They may 'eat' their worshippers, making them ill or even die, if their own hunger – manifested by the ever-gaping mouth of the *tio* in the underground corridors of the mines – is not assuaged. The devils are the source both of fertility and of wealth, and of sickness, misfortune, death. They are unpredictable and very powerful, a bit like wild animals, to which they are likened and whose 'owners' they are.[24]

Professional miners, even those who have received secondary education, talk of the need to make regular offerings to the devils. A local attorney who used to be a miner told me that he had long ago realised that the *tio* was a mere superstition; almost in the same breath he related how his house used to be full to the rafters with food and stores, but that after he stopped observing the devil's cult, his luck had turned.[25] Among peasants similar stories are told, although usually less dramatic. In the hamlet I know best there is one man who is strikingly well-off. The cycnical observer might note that he farms large parcels of good land. His neighbours say that *in addition* to his good land, he has a special relationship with the *pachamama* whom he feeds liberally each year. The suggestion that such special relationships with the devils are a result of the distortion of the 'natural economy' resulting from proletarianisation therefore seems implausible.[26]

Devils are not associated exclusively with mining, nor with wage labour. On the contrary, Andean classification does not assign mining and agriculture to two separate categories as the Western observer tends to do (the former belonging to the industrial, profit-oriented world and the latter to the subsistence-oriented, traditional sphere); it links mining, agriculture and livestock-rearing together. The union between the primarily agricultural *pachamama* and the *tio* of the mines makes this explicit. Moreover, there are striking similarities between the rituals performed for the fertility of the mines, and those for the *pachamama* and other guardians of the fertility of fields and flocks, such as the mountains. As Platt has described, there is an overall continuity of ritual practice between the huge state-owned mines and the rural cultivators, which is made evident in the rituals of small mines scattered throughout the region, which are brought into production when the price of minerals on the world market reaches a certain level, or during the slack season (1983).

It is widely believed that mineral grows in the mines like potatoes (this belief is not unique to the Andes). Particularly striking lumps of ore are today called *llallawa*, just as are strangely-shaped potatoes, or double cobs of maize.[27] The same association was noted in the sixteenth century by the 'extirpator of idolatry', Cristobal de Albornóz, with reference to the concept *mama*:

There is another type of sacred object, which they revere and serve with great care; this is the first fruits which they gather from some field which was not sown. They select the most beautiful of the yield and keep it, and make others in its likeness from different stones or gold or silver, such as a cob of maize or a potato and they call them mamaçara and mamapapa; and the same for the other crops and in the same manner for all the minerals of gold or silver or mercury which were discovered in remote times. (1967: 18)

Laymi peasants today rarely work in the large mines, and only work in smaller mining enterprises close to their own land and communities. Nonetheless, even those who have never worked as miners express a collective pride in the strength of 'their' mines. Not only the small mines within their own territory, but also the huge tin-mines round Llallagua continue to yield their mineral harvest in part thanks to the efficacy of their own rituals. They compare Llallagua with the Potosí mine, which is now nearly exhausted. 'Our mine is stronger' they say. 'We have allowed it to rest and recuperate its fertility and that is why it continues to produce. The Potosí mine was never allowed to lie fallow, and that is why the mineral no longer grows there.'

This has always been an important mining region. One of the Inkas' sources of gold lies on the edge of Laymi territory in Amayapampa, and there were also mines in operation in the local pre-Inka kingdoms (W. Espinoza 1969; 1981). The silver mine of Potosí lies not far to the south in the territory of the former Qharaqhara kingdom. Throughout the period of Spanish colonial hegemony Laymi tribute-payers, together with other ethnic groups of the region, were a major source of the obligatory *mita* labour for the Potosí mine (Tandeter 1982). The silver boom of the 1860s and 1870s brought new prosperity to the region: of the major silver mines, Huanchaca lay to the south of Potosí, and nearby in Macha territory was the equally important Aullagas (Mitre 1981). All these mines are known about and talked of in Laymi oral tradition. And as the nineteenth century ended and the silver demand declined, the mining economy was salvaged by the rising price of tin on the world metal markets. The mining operation round Llallagua constitutes one of the largest tin mines in the world, and made its owner and entrepreneur Simón Patiño, who started life penniless and ill-educated, one of the richest men in the world.

When rural Laymi pour libations for the local mines, it is important that they are celebrating and entreating fertility not just for themselves, but for the whole universe of which they form part. The libations are for all the sources of wealth in whose circuits they are implicitly or explicitly involved, whether they personally have direct links with them or not. Prosperity, it seems, is not a competitive state, a 'limited good'. Rather the prosperity of all is desired, hence the libations for the mines, where few if any of them work, and for the boom lowland city of Santa Cruz, as well as for more local sources of their subsistence. This I think is one of the reasons why there is little structured antagonism to traders from the towns, or to the profits of the urban shopkeepers and chicha sellers. The generosity of the 'devils' can benefit all.

However, it is not only mining that is associated with natural fertility, but also the money itself. Even in the mining centres the cult of the devils is not exclusive to miners. In Llallagua and Uncia the *diablada* is danced also by traders and shopkeepers; they say that this is because the miners cannot afford the financial strain of the elaborate costume. In Oruro the development of the *diablada* dance at the end of the nineteenth century was initiated by the traders, not by the miners themselves (Nock and Armstrong 1985). All these towns owe their prosperity to the wealth produced in the mines, and the commercial sector – i.e., those who have profited most directly from that wealth – is also assiduous in its attentions to the devils.

In Laymi libations the identification of money with fertility is explicit. Offerings to the most important deities are followed by libations for the three forms of abundance, addressed by their ritual names: *phaqhara*, *llallawa*, *phaxsïma*. *Phaqhara* means literally 'flowers' and in ritual is used to refer to the increase of the flocks and to livestock in general. *Llallawa*, the name of strange-shaped tubers or maize cobs, stands for an abundant harvest, while *phaxsïma* ('like the moon') means money. The three concepts are so closely linked that on one occasion I heard a libation offered for 'the three' (*kinsataki*) and was told that it meant the triad of *phaqhara*, *llallawa* and *phaxsïma*. The same trinity is repeated in a different form by pouring libations not only for money, livestock and crops but also for their containers; the 'strong and enduring corral' (*chukhi uyu*), and the 'strong and enduring storage bin' (*chukhi pirwa*) and the 'strong and enduring purse' (*chukhi bolsa*).[28] Far from being treated as antithetical to the sources of fertility on which the economy is based (agriculture and livestock raising), money is closely identified with them. Placed in a wider setting, the ritual priority given to money and metals in the month of August forms part of a ritual cycle in which all sources of wellbeing and increase are honoured.

Hardly surprisingly, a close association between mining and money is made in this region; it was of course the silver of the Potosí mine that shifted the emphasis from gold to silver in the European monetary system (Vilar 1976; McLeod 1984). In both French and Castilian to this day the same term – *argent* and *plata* respectively – denotes both the precious metal and money in general. The same is true for Aymara and Quechua *qullqi*, which means both silver and money. The process of conversion of raw metal into money can have held little mystery in the Andes since the establishment of the mint beside the silver mountain in the early days of mining in Potosí.[29] Minting carried on in Potosí, with various interruptions, until the middle of this century (Benavides 1972). Today Laymi are still quite clear how money is made: 'It is in the bank. The metal goes to the United States and the money is made in a factory.'

What then are Laymi addressing when they pour libations for *phaxsïma*? They aim to ensure the fertility of the mines which not only produce money in the sense of minerals, but are also the source of markets, of urban consumers cut off from the process of food-production, and of monetary wealth. Also, the libations aim to ensure enough currency to buy the things they require, in particular to reproduce the wealth of the *ayllu*. But the meaning of *phaxsïma* is also more precise and more arcane than this.

The raw and the minted

Money comes from the same sources that ensure the potato and maize harvest, and the reproduction of the flocks. By offering food, humans enter into communication with this source – the shadowy domain of the devils or *saxra*. But while money comes from the earth and the sphere of the *saxra*, it also paradoxically originates from the state, in that it is the state which creates and guarantees its function as a means of circulation. The state apparatus and the authorities whose job it is to secure the functioning of social order belong not to the devils' sphere but to that of God. The devils' sphere is a source of abundance, and of misfortune; above all it is chaotic and unpredictable. God's sphere in contrast establishes and maintains order, morality and 'good government' (Bouysse and Harris 1987).

It is through religion that each society establishes cosmic order and articulates its meanings, with reference both to nature and to the law. We have already noted that Judaeo-Christian traditions are unusual in treating money as alien to, and potentially destructive of the religious community. By contrast the meaning given to money in Andean thought goes to the heart of religious understanding. Money is of course used by Indians for economic exchanges; it is also, as we have noted, seen in different contexts as destructive of social bonds or as a symbol of civilisation. But in Andean discourse the 'romantic' and 'liberal' attitudes to money are muted; it relates primarily to the core value of prosperity and its reproduction on the one hand, and the state on the other. Money is generated by natural fertility, in the same way as all aspects of wealth and abundance, but at the same time it is created by the state, as is evident from the very appearance of coins and bank-notes. It derives, then, both from nature and from the law, and since these two sources are antithetical to each other, money itself has a dual, ambivalent character.[30]

This duality is evident in ritual practices, for example, in the distinct offerings made to the devils on the one hand, and to God and the saints on the other. In the case of the devils, they are fed not with coins but with raw metal, for example, fragments of gold and silver leaf and sometimes other minerals too, or gold and silver paper. In Laymi offerings the raw mineral was represented by pieces of gold and silver paper a few centimetres square known as 'gold book' (*quri libru*) and tiny strips of multicoloured cellophane also called 'gold' (*quri limphi*). In other areas, offerings include gold and silver leaf, or galena ore and iron pyrites representing gold and silver, or 'crude' gold and silver scraped off larger lumps of metal (Tschopik 1951: 231; Isbell 1978: 157). Conversely, raw minerals are not offered to the saints, but worked metal sometimes is. For example, on patronal saints' days in the mining districts, silver plate is used to decorate the ceremonial arches and the motor vehicles that accompany the procession.

However, there are uses of money in rituals which do not at first sight fit this scheme of interpretation. For example, coins are part of the ritual gear of the Laymi shaman (the *wayuri*, known in other regions as *paqu* or *ch'amakani*). Not only does he keep a coin with his other instruments, but also those who employ his services to communicate with the devils have to give him a coin which is known as 'silla'. It would be reasonable to assume that the 'silla' is some sort of payment for services rendered, particularly because in a different context gravediggers are also given coins known as 'silla'. However this explanation cannot account for the coins kept by shamans in their bags of sacred instruments, nor does it throw any light on the name 'silla' itself, seemingly of Spanish origin. A description by the Peruvian folklorist José Lira of a séance in southern Peru sheds light on the term. Before the shaman begins, he asks his client for a coin which is known as a *sellada* (1950: 38). This Spanish word means 'stamped, sealed, franked, hallmarked' and is an obvious allusion to the way the coin is *minted*, with the symbols of the state stamped upon it.

Why then do the shaman and the gravediggers have special need of minted coins to fulfil their functions? The beginnings of an answer can be made by piecing together fragmentary indications.

Tschopik, writing of the Titicaca region, offers one explanation. A typical séance round Chucuito started with the shaman telling all those present to place the coins on top of the stone *mesa* (table) to enable him 'to see and think more clearly'. These coins are called 'eyes' (*nairanca* in Tschopik's orthography). Eyes, like coins, have multiple meanings in Andean cultures. In Laymi thought there is a close connection between eyes and mirrors; mirrors are said to 'have good eyes' (*sum layraniw*) or are actually called eyes. Thus a simple round mirror is *sillp'a layra* (thin eye), while one divided into different sections is *phatu layra* (thick eye). In addition, there are ways in which mirrors are directly associated with coins. It is known that the mirrors used by the Inkas and their predecessors were usually small and round, made occasionally of silver and frequently of pyrite, which has a silver sheen (Muelle 1940); and today's Laymi believe that neither mirrors nor coins should be taken on fishing expeditions since they will cause the fish to disappear. As Tristan Platt has shown, mirrors in Andean culture represent duality, and duality as expressed in the Quechua concept of *yanantin* is the state of wholeness that typifies social order. This, it would seem, is why Macha say that mirrors are 'the enemies of the soul of the dead', and are able to prevent a person from dying prematurely if they are posted at the entrance to the graveyard.[31]

This quality of mirrors that helps to keep death at bay helps to shed light on yet another ritual use of coins. When Laymi prepare a mortuary bundle for a dead person to take on their long journey they include not only food and personal effects but also a coin. However the coin in this instance is not whole but deliberately broken or defaced. When I asked what these coins were for, people would tell me impatiently that they were for the dead to buy a house in the world they were going to. This seems unsatisfactory in that it fails to explain why the coin should be defaced. However, a comparison with the 'silla' coins is illuminating. The name 'silla' emphasises the qualities that make the coin what it is: its 'mintedness'. By contrast the coins given to the dead explicitly have their identity as coins defaced. Coins, as we have already noted, are able to 'see' like mirrors, like eyes; they belong to ordered human society; stamped on them is the image of the state. The defacing of this image parallels the changed essence of the dead person. The living form part of ordered society, illuminated by the divine light of the sun; the dead, in contrast, form part of the shadowy world of the devils (Harris 1982b). A complete coin, like a complete mirror, would be antithetical to the condition of death.[32] Thus it seems that the need for coins by shamans and gravediggers is the need to protect themselves and separate themselves from the dangerous powers of the devils, and the souls of the dead. 'Silla' coins here have a comparable function to mirrors as reported by Platt for the Macha; and the ethnohistorical record indicates a similar connection between God's sphere and mirrors. Muelle quotes the myth of Inka Yuupanki who was helped to victory in battle by the sun who appeared to help him and gave him a mirror (1940: 7).

A further ritual use of coins by Laymi today reinforces their association with 'God's sphere' in contrast to the sphere of the devils. At a critical moment in 1973, several valley communities were racked by two disasters: the rains were two months late, and a virulent fever broke out, killing ten people in the course of only two weeks. As the crisis worsened, people began to agree that the individual misfortunes could no longer be interpreted singly, but were a punishment (*kastiku*) visited by God upon the whole community. In order to expel the destructive power, all households contributed to a collective rite known as the 'money offering' (*qullqi arkhu*). This offering included various 'cool' (*phirisku*) medicines: *molle* twigs, rice, coal, rosemary, and also silver coins. It was carried from house to house to expel the 'heat' and the following day at dawn it was removed from the community and deposited far down the mountainside near the river where it would be out of harm's way. The offering was made in order to 'ask pardon' (*pirun mayt'asiña*) from God, and as on all the occasions when people ask pardon collectively from God it was accompanied by a troupe of men playing bamboo pipes (*suqusu*) with two young girls (*mit'ani*) at their head waving white banners.

This troupe, known like the music they play as *wayli* (cf Spanish *baile*, dance), represents perhaps in its most concentrated form the communication of human beings with God; it is they who attend the feasts of saints celebrated in the different colonial parishes. The *suqusu* pipes should never be played during the rainy season for fear of offending the souls of the dead who are present in human society (Harris 1982b); this indicates that their sound is not a possible means of communicating with the sphere of devils, of which the dead form part. Given that the 'money offering' ritual is enacted by this troupe of *suqusu* players who thereby implore God for pardon, we have here a further indication of the way that coins are associated not with the devils' sphere but with God, and are here used as a means of deflecting his righteous anger against his worshippers through the beseeching and granting of pardon. It should not be forgotten, moreover, that for nearly 400 years the relationship of the *ayllus* with the state was mediated by coins in the form of tribute, and the tribute payment was an important ceremony. Indeed it is maintained to this day by some *ayllus* of Northern Potosí; in the Macha ceremony the stone used to hold down the money (banknotes these days) is even known as an 'inka' (Platt 1986).

This apparent division between the 'raw' and the 'minted' does not however exhaust the semantics of money in Laymi thought. Why does the ritual term *phaxsïma*, used above all in libations, refer in particular to *old coins*? Why is the 'best money' that of the Inka, stamped with the image of the long-haired Ferdinand VII? And what is the other 'money', said to be of the *chullpa*?

There was of course no money in the Inka economy; nonetheless the profound significance of gold and silver (the 'sweat of the sun and the tears of the moon') for the Inka cult, and indeed for all Andean civilisations is well-known. The Inka state controlled the production of metals which were paid as a form of tribute in kind by the mining nations (Garcilaso 1609; Murra 1955; Berthelot 1978). While in the Old World the important metallurgies established themselves in the domain of warfare, transportation and agriculture, in New World societies metals served mainly symbolic functions, communicating power, status and religious beliefs. As Lechtman's pioneering work has emphasized 'the most important property was colour, and the two colours that were paramount in the New World metallurgical spectrum were silver and gold' (1974: 630).[33]

Gold is still a significant attribute in ritual language. In Laymi libations the two words for gold (*quri, chukhi*) evoke strength and durability; on the other hand, the semantic identification of silver with money seems to outweigh all other associations for Laymi today,[34] though they still emphasise colour. The coins of the 'Inka Fernando' are said to be the best among other reasons because they are 'very white'. But why the emphasis on old coins, and why are *colonial* coins said to be *Inka* money?

There still exist in this region many colonial coins from the reign of Ferdinand VII, much sought after by metal dealers. But Laymi treat their old coins with great respect and refuse to sell them even for good prices;[35] people know which households own one and they are extremely reluctant to show them to anyone, particularly to an outsider. This emphasis on secrecy surrounding the old coins leads us closer to a full understanding of their significance. Some households own special amulets, carved or partially carved from stone, which protect the herds and ensure their increase. Known as *illa* they are surrounded with secrecy and no one outside the social group – nor ideally anyone outside the immediate family – should see them. The mystery that surrounds old coins closely resembles this secrecy, and suggests that they too are *illa* –

not for the herds but for money itself. The translations of *illa* in some Quechua dictionaries make this almost explicit. For Gonzalez Holguin in the *Vocabulario* of 1608 *illa* is 'whatever is very old and hidden away' (*todo lo que es antiguo de muchos años y guardado*). Lira's dictionary of 1973 defines *illa* as 'Brightness, transparency . . . Stone on which the lightning has struck, which is considered sacred . . . Precious coin.'[36] The mystery and reverence surrounding the old coins surely derives from this source; those families that own them must treat them with great respect and make them offerings so that they fulfil their function of creating wealth and prosperity.

The statement that the old coins are the 'best money' can now be more readily understood; they are the best because as *illa* they are the powerful *source* of money. What then is their relationship to the devils, to the other source of money which we have already discussed? The beginnings of an answer can be traced by turning to the third form of 'money', that of the *chullpa*, distinguished by Laymi both from Inka money and from that of the present day.

The word *chullpa* in altiplano mythology refers to the monumental tombs that dominate the landscape in some areas, built for the rulers of the pre-Inka kingdoms of the region. The same word is used also to refer to the pre-Inka population itself, which is mythically associated with the moon. They shrivelled up when the sun rose for the first time, heralding the new Inka age. The sun was for the Inka rulers their divine ancestor and was worshipped throughout the state. It was readily identified with the Christian God and is worshipped as God today. The *chullpa* on the other hand belongs to a shadowy world of half light associated with the dead and the devils.

There are many versions of what *chullpa* money is. Any interpretation is bound to be more schematic than is warranted by the medley of different and often vague beliefs held by people I have talked to, that accord well with the shadowy mythical status of the *chullpa* themselves. However for many people *chullpa* money is not money at all, but what they call 'treasure' (*tesoro, tapado*) and it is buried underground. (I have referred to it as 'money' because in both Andean languages and Spanish there is no lexical distinction between coins and the money-stuff – silver – from which they are ideally made.) In the month of August, which it will be remembered is the devils' month, people say that this treasure comes to the surface, and that those who are brave enough and who make a blood sacrifice – even a human sacrifice – will gain access to it.[37]

Chullpa 'money' then is also a primary source of money, but in this case it is not coins as currency that are emphasised, but rather the intrinsic value of the money stuff itself ('treasure'). Some beliefs surrounding *chullpa* money seem to link it directly with the veins of minerals hidden underground in the mines; in any event, the associations are close between the *chullpa* themselves and the sphere of the devils or *saxra*, between the 'buried treasure' of the *chullpa* which comes to the surface in August, and the buried riches of the mines which humans may extract with the generous aid of the *tio*, whose special month is August. And blood sacrifices, it will be remembered, are made only to the devils, not to the holy beings of God's sphere. Like the wealth bestowed by the *tio*, *chullpa* money is conceived as an unpredictable source of riches.

The way that Laymi distinguish present-day money from ancient money, then, suggests not so much a historical comparison between the present and the past as a means of conceptualising the ontological origins of money. As in so many aspects of Andean thought, the forces that engender money are located not in one past time but in two. The offerings of raw material belong to the *saxra*, while coins are in God's domain. In a parallel image, there are two sources of money: the most ancient which lies underground, and a less ancient which engenders the money of today. Both it seems are necessary to ensure the functioning of the economy.

Chullpa money, Inka money: the first is associated with the fertility of metal beneath the earth's surface, while the second, engraved with the 'head of the prince' and the insignia of the state, constitutes the mysterious and sacred source of actual currency. Andean cultures harness the powers of the past in this way: remnants of bygone eras are put to work for the living, and for the reproduction of the world.

Notes

1 The research in Bolivia on which this paper is based was carried out at various times between 1972 and 1983. In 1986 tragedy struck: the tin mines of Siglo XX, Uncia and Catavi were virtually closed down and the majority of the miners dismissed, victims of the present government's monetarist policies, pressure from the International Monetary Fund, and above all the great tin crash on the London Metal Exchange in October 1985 (Latin America Bureau 1987).

2 The circumstances were even more poignant, in that the previous two harvests had been disastrous due to the drought that had ravaged the highlands. If ever there was a moment for cutting back on festive expenditure, it was surely then.

3 Wallerstein makes the point in defining the modern world system in contrast to pre-modern empires: 'Capitalism . . . is based on the fact that the economic factors operate within an arena larger than that which any political entity can totally control.' (1974: 348).

4 Cited by Marx in Capital I (1976: 229). In the words of Pierre Vilar: 'It was gold which unleashed the conquest of America and ensured that it was carried

out in a rushed, haphazard and dispersed manner. As on other occasions, the myth of "El Dorado" played an important part' (1976: 66).

5 Such sentiments are the basis of the so-called 'black legend' of Spain's imperial role. It is worth remembering that at the same time that Phillips was writing, Cromwell was carrying out in Ireland similar policies to those of which the Spanish are accused in the Americas.

6 As Pagden notes, the great Spanish theologian Vitoria justified his argument that the Indians were men with reference to Aristotle's criterion of commerce, which he thought the Indians shared with Europeans. In contrast, the lack of iron, of writing, and of the arch, were for Vitoria more serious problems which required greater ingenuity to explain away (1982: 76–7).

7 The slippage was made easier by his wholehearted adherence to the exchange theory of money, and the liberal model of the independent producer exchanging his goods, which forms the basis of his concept of simple commodity production, as Bradby notes (1982: ch. 2).

8 The mystification surrounding the concept of barter has a similar origin. Either it is seen as the earliest – pre-monetary – form of exchange encroaching into a 'natural' economy (i.e., without exchange) or, since by definition it does not involve the use of money, it may be defined as based on principles antithetical to monetary exchange and profit-making. The apparent fascination of barter as exchange without the medium of money seems to lie in its being the negative signifier of money, either as temporal predecessor or as the mysterious other.

9 A similar slippage sometimes operates with regard to the concept of the 'moral economy'. In Thompson's original conception, it referred – like Aristotle's *oikonomike* – to the customary price, the just price (1971). However the phrase is then extended to refer to an economy from which money, *and therefore immoral behaviour*, is absent. The implication in such usage is that a 'moral economy' is one in which exchange is peripheral or absent altogether.

10 As, for example, in the Christian account of Christ throwing the moneylenders out of the Temple. As Crump notes, it is only the Judaeo-Christian tradition among world religions that treats money as antithetical to the sacred (1981: 17, 285).

11 Pol Pot's imitators in the southern Peruvian highlands, known as Sendero Luminoso (Shining Path), according to some reports have tried to abolish exchange entirely (see, for example, L. Taylor 1983: 29).

12 Platt 1982a; Godoy 1986. The spread of haciendas in the late nineteenth century and early twentieth centuries was limited in this region, and the Agrarian Reform Law of 1953 made little impact outside the haciendas (Platt 1982a; Harris and Albó 1975).

13 Bertonio 1612: I: 314: Mercader a nuestro modo: Mircatori, vel Tintani. Mercader a modo de indios. Haurucu, Alasiri. II: 125: Haurucu: El que va a rescatar comida a otros pueblos.

14 The same people would say a few sentences later without a trace of irony that the Indians are like savages or children, and do not understand the uses of money.

15 This excludes consideration of the *yapa*, the 'increase' given by one party to the other in a transaction. The amounts given in *yapa* are directly affected by the nature of the relationships between the parties.

16 This pattern is in sharp contrast to the neighbouring Jukumani *ayllu* (Godoy 1983). It was true for the decade of the 1970s, and it seems that the Laymi steered clear of mining from the beginning of the tin boom (Harris & Albó 1975). However, recently things have changed both because of the drought, and because the Chapare has become one of the main cocaine-producing regions. High rates of pay in dollars act as a magnet for migrant labour from all over the country.

17 One old woman told me in great detail how prosperous Laymi households used to be in her youth. In particular she emphasised all the bought food items that they consumed in greater quantity, e.g., bread, sugar, vegetables. Platt has emphasised the importance of the wheat trade for this region, until its destruction by the importation of cheaper Chilean wheat in the mid nineteenth century (1982). With the development of tinmining at the end of the century, Laymi say that they earned good money transporting the mineral. This source of cash presumably came to an end when the railway was extended to Uncia in 1921.

18 The metaphor of natural reproduction to signify monetary gain is of course not unique to the Andes. The Greek word *tokos* means both child and interest. Aristotle for example comments that 'interest (*tokos*) represents an increase in the currency itself. Hence its name (*tokos*) . . . currency is born of currency' (1962: 87). Marx, referring to interest-bearing capital, describes it as 'money which begets money' (1976: 256). But the imagery of these writers refers particularly to interest on loans and usury. As far as I know Laymi do not pay interest on monetary loans; their idea of money giving birth is more benign, denoting the legitimate profit made on a monetary transaction.

19 Bertonio 1612:
   II: 216 manusitha: Tomar prestado algo.
   I: 294 logro: Manusitha. Mirani chasitha.
   II: 222 Mira: Multiplico, y tambien logro.
         Mira marmi: Muger fecunda.
   II: 51 Collque miraatha: Gragear o tractar con la plata o dar a logro.
   II: 115 Hamacatha, miracatha: Multiplicarse assi la plata dandola a logro
   For a seventeenth-century English version of the same idea, see Bacon 'Money is like muck, not good unless it be spread' (1625, Essay 15 'Of Seditions and Troubles').

20 Ideas about the proper and improper uses of money and cloth given as *arkhu* prestations make this clear. It is significant that when people talk of *arkhu* gifts being squandered on personal consumption they talk of sweets, oranges, bread, and never, to my knowledge, of alcohol. I suspect that this is because although some people – particularly housewives – complain about the squandering of money on drinking, and recognise the personal pleasure involved, drinking is not viewed as an act of personal gratification since it operates to reproduce the *ayllu* through the offering of libations to the sacred powers.

21 The critique of the concept of exchange and its replacement by the idea of circuits, of circulation, of reproduction has been argued for the Melanesian context (the *locus classicus* of exchange in anthropological theory) by writers such as Weiner (1980) and Damon (1980).

22 As one miner told June Nash: 'The Tio is the real owner here. The administrators just sit in their offices and don't help us in our work.' The Tio according to Nash is now more important in relation to protecting miners from accidents than to the production of wealth itself. She associates this with the changed forms of remuneration for productivity (1979: 162).

23 Round La Paz, in fact, the month of August is apparently divided in two: the first half is particularly associated with the *pachamama* and the second (i.e. after the 15th) with the *tio*.

24 The term used by Laymi is *phiru*, from the Spanish *fiero* (wild).

25 The attention of Simon Patiño to the cult of the *tio* is well known, even after he had consolidated ownership of the whole mine and become wealthy.

26 This is the core of Taussig's argument (1980). The idea of contracts with the devil is mentioned in Nash (1979: 192–3), and I have heard townspeople talk of it. The stories told by Laymi seem to fit the same notion. However, the metaphor used is always one of feeding, and for Laymi feeding is emphatically not exchange. Feeding is the proper behaviour of human beings. You naturally expect that other human beings will feed you, but you do not offer food to visitors *in order* that they should reciprocate. Similarly, humans must feed the devils to assuage their voracious hunger; but their eating the food does not guarantee food or prosperity to their worshippers.

27 The name of the mining town itself – Llallagua – is obviously significant. Querejazu (1978) reports that the name was given because the shape of the tin mountain was like that of a *llallawa* potato: extraordinary and ritually important. I have been told that the name is in fact recent, and was given to the burgeoning town because of the mineral *llallawas* found there. Whatever reason is historically correct, the connection between the fabled wealth of the tin mine and the ritual significance of unusual tubers is made explicitly by local inhabitants.

28 Another symbolic reiteration of the same triad is found in the selection of saints for special worship (*milagros*) in the chapel of Muruq'umarka. During the patronal feast there are five different celebrations; the first is for God (*suwirana*), and the last for the ancestors in the form of a skull (*t'ujlu*). The three intermediate days are devoted to Saints Philip and James, the Virgin, and Saint Michael; they stand respectively for livestock, for crops and for money.

29 In 1572, according to Vilar, with a mint established seven years earlier in Lima. Benavides implies the Potosí mint was established earlier (1972: 11). With the replacement of silver by tin as the major source of mineral wealth, the direct connection between mining and money disappeared; however, in pouring libations, Laymi link the tin-mines directly with money. Apart from the obvious fact that the tin-mines are the source of monetary wealth for the whole region, raw metal can also form part of the miner's wage, either officially as in the *corpa* (Assadourian 1979: 268), or unofficially as in the

'robbery' to supplement the low mining wages known as *kajcheo* (Tandeter 1981: 134) or *jukeo* (Harris & Albo 1975: 17).

On the other hand, since 1869, when banknotes were introduced by President Melgarejo (Benavides 1972: 110), silver has gradually ceased to be the base of the currency. Today the Bolivian currency is based on the gold standard; coins are reduced to the status of small change, or, at moments of acute inflation, disappear from circulation altogether. Paper money has not replaced silver coinage in the symbolic discourse of money; however it does have its own metaphorical attribution. In particular, when money is given as ceremonial *arkhu* it is usually in the form of banknotes, placed in the hatband of the recipient and known as *phaqhara*, or flowers. This is the word used in libations to refer to livestock and their continued fertility; this connection is not accidental, since as we have seen, the proper use to which *arkhu* gifts of money should be put is to buy livestock. In fact, *arkhu* gifts as a whole are closely associated with livestock, to the extent that a synonym for *arkhuyana* (to make an *arkhu* gift), is *phaqharayaña* (to make flowers).

30 In economic theory there are fundamentally two theories for the origins of money. One is the state theory, according to which money was created and guaranteed by a political system and functioned as a 'token' or sign of the mutual obligations of the state and its citizens. The other is the commodity theory, which argues that the functions of money depend on its material form; in order to operate as a means of exchange according to this theory the money-stuff must have an intrinsic value (Bradby 1982; Hart 1986).

31 Platt (1978: 1097). Another link between mirrors and coins may be the image of the lake. Platt notes the symbolic connection between the lake and the mirror; while Tschopik relates that the Aymara of Chucuito used a silver coin to represent Lake Titicaca in certain rituals (1951: 244).

32 An observation made by Pablo José de Arriaga in 1621 suggests an interesting parallel. Commenting on the use of silver coins in offerings to the *huaca* shrines he writes: 'They also offer silver in *reales* (coins); and in some places, for example in Libia Cancharco, fifteen patacones have been found with other small coins, while in the town of Recuay Doctor Ramirez found two hundred patacones in a *huaca*. *They usually beat them and dent them so that you can barely make out the royal coat of arms, and it appears that they are spattered with blood and with chicha, placed around the shrine.* In other circumstances the priests of the shrine keep this money and collect it for meeting the expenses of their feasts' (1968: 43; my emphasis). One possible interpretation of such actions would be that the coins were offered to the gods whose cult at the beginning of the seventeenth century was already forbidden and operated in clandestinity; and that except for cases where they were used to cover ritual expenditure, the insignia of His Most Catholic Majesty were erased in order to make them acceptable as offerings to the indigenous deities.

33 Reichel-Dolmatoff discusses the significance of colours and their associations with minerals for indigenous cultures of Colombia. The Desana, for example, contrast white and yellow (silver and gold) as an invisible creative force and a material potential (1981: 21, N. W. Amazon. I am grateful to Warwick Bray for drawing my attention to this article). It should be noted that Europe had

its own tradition of hermeneutic interpretation of precious metals, in the science of alchemy.

34 Tschopik notes the frequent use of gold and silver in libations amongst the Chucuito Aymara (1951: 247). Bertonio's entry for gold indicates an association of this metal with love (1612: II: 89).

35 Laymi friends told me with glee how they had given short shrift to a Frenchman who had misguidedly gone walking through the area trying to buy antique coins.

36 Quoted in Flores (1977). This article is fundamental for understanding the importance of *illa* for Andean religion, and why they are secret. Another example of coins used as *illa* is the *qollque conopa* given to couples at marriage in Chuschi (Isbell 1978: 121). Using coins in this way as *illa* has the paradoxical consequence of protecting money from being 'sold'.

37 In some areas, buried treasure is explicitly identified with the gold of the Inka which, it is said, went underground when he was garrotted by the Spanish, and will only return to the surface when his decapitated head has grown a new body and the old order is renewed (e.g., the version of the myth recorded by J. Roel Pineda 1973).

References

Albornóz, Cristobal de 1967. 'La instrucción para descubrir las guacas del Piru y sus camayos y haziendas', *J. de la Soc. des Américanistes*, 56 (1): 7–39 (c. 1580), Paris, transcribed P. Duviols.

Aristotle 1962. *The politics*, London: Penguin Books.

Arriaga, P. J. de 1968 (1621). *The extirpation of idolatry in Peru* (trans L. Clark Keating), Kentucky: University Press.

Assadourian, S. 1979. 'La producción de la mercancia dinero en la formación del mercado colonial', ed., E. Florescano *Ensayos sobre el desarrollo economico de México y América Latina (1500–1975)*, Mexico: Fondo de Cultura Económica.

Assadourian, S. 1982. *El sistema de la economia colonial*, Lima: IEP.

Bacon, Francis 1625. *Essays*, London.

Bakewell, P. 1984. *Miners of the red mountain: Indian labour in Potosí 1545–1650*, Albuquerque: University of New Mexico Press.

Benavides M, J. 1972. *Historia de la moneda en Bolivia*, La Paz: Edn. Puerta del Sol.

Berthelot, J. 1978. 'L'exploitation des métaux précieux aux temps des Incas', *Annales ESC*, 33e année: 5–6, Paris.

Bertonio, Ludovico 1612. *Vocabulario de la lengua aymara*, Chucuito.

Bradby, B. 1982. 'Plan, market and money: a study of circulation in Peru', University of Sussex: Ph.D. thesis.

Burridge, K. 1969. *New heaven, new earth*, Oxford: Blackwell.

Casas, B. de las 1972 (1552). *The tears of the Indians* (Reprint of 1656 trans. by John Phillips of *Brevissima relación de la destruyción de las indias*), New York: Oriole Chapbooks.

Choque, R. 1978. 'Pedro Chipana: cacique comerciante de Calamarca', *Avances*, 1: 28–32, La Paz.

Clearman England, N. 1974. 'Verbal derivational suffixes', ch. 6, pp. 148–208 in, ed., M. Hardman, ed., *Outline of Aymara*.

Crump, T. 1981. *The phenomenon of money*, London: Routledge & Kegan Paul.

Damon, F. 1980. 'The Kula and generalised exchange', *Man* (n.s.), 15 (2): 267–92.

Espinoza, S. W. 1969. 'El "Memorial" de Charcas: "crónica" inédita de 1582', *Cantuta. Revista de la Universidad Nacional de Educación*, Chosica, Peru.

1981. 'El reino aymara de Quillaca-Asanaque, siglos XV y XVI', *Rev. del Museo Nacional*, 45: 175–274, Lima, Peru.

Flores, J. 1977. 'Enqa, enqaychu, illa y khuya rumi', ed., J. Flores, *Pastores de Puna*, Lima: IEP.

(ed.) 1978. *Actes, XLIIe Cong. Int. des Américanistes*: IV, Paris.

Foucault, M. 1970. *The order of things*, London: Tavistock Press.

Garcilaso de la Vega, El Inca 1609 (1943). *Comentarios reales de los Incas*, Buenos Aires: Emecé Edit.

Godoy, R. 1983. *From indian to miner and back again: small-scale mining in the Jukumani ayllu, Northern Potosí*, Columbia: Ph.D. thesis.

Godoy, R. 1986. 'The fiscal role of the Andean ayllu', *Man*, (n.s.), 21 (4): 723–41.

Gonzalez Holguín, Diego 1608. *Vocabulario de la lengua general de todo el Peru*, Lima.

Hardman de B., M. (ed.) 1974. *Outline of Aymara phonological and grammatical structure*, vol. 3, Ann Arbor: University Microfilms.

Harris, O. 1982a. 'Labour and produce in an ethnic economy', ed., D. Lehmann, *Ecology and exchange in the Andes*, Cambridge: Cambridge University Press.

1982b. 'The dead and the devils among the Bolivian Laymi', eds., M. Bloch and J. Parry, *Death and the Regeneration of Life*, Cambridge: Cambridge University Press.

Harris, O. & J. Albó 1975. *Monteras y guardatojos. Campesinos y mineros en el norte de Potosí*, Cuadernos CIPCA, 7, La Paz.

Harris, O. & T. Bouysse Cassagne, 1987. 'Pacha. En torno al pensamiento aymara', ed., J. Albó *Raices de América: el mundo aymara*, Madrid: Alianza Editorial.

Hart, K. 1986. 'Heads or tails? Two sides of the coin', *Man*, (n.s.), 21 (4): 637–56.

Humphrey, C. 1985. 'Barter and economic disintegration', *Man*, (n.s.), 20: 48–72.

Isbell, B. J. 1978. *To defend ourselves: a view through the Andean kaleidoscope*, Texas: University Press.

Latin America Bureau 1987. *The great tin crash. Bolivia and the world market*, London: Latin America Bureau.

Lechtman, H. 1974. 'Pre-Columbian surface metallurgy', *Scientific American*, 250 (6): 56–63.

Lira, J. 1950. 'El demonio en los Andes', *Tradición*, 1 (1): 35–40, Cusco.

Marx, K. 1976 (1887). *Capital*, vol. 1, London: Penguin.

Masuda, S., I. Shimada & C. Morris, eds., 1985. *Andean ecology and civilization*, Tokyo: University Press.

McLeod, M. 1984. 'The Atlantic trade, 1492–1720', *Cambridge History of Latin America*, 1: 34–88, Cambridge University Press.

Mitre, A. 1981. *Los patriarcas de la plata*, Lima: IEP.

Muelle, J. 1940. 'Espejos precolombinos del Peru', *Rev. del Mus. Nac*, 11 (1): 5–12.

Murra, J. V. 1972. 'El contról verticál de un máximo de pisos ecológicos', *Visita de la Provincia de León de Huánuco en 1562*, by Iñigo Ortíz de Zúñiga, Huánuco: Univ. Nac. H. Valdizán.

  1978. 'La correspondencia entre un "Capitán de la Mita" y su apoderado en Potosí', *Historia y Cultura* 3: 45–58 La Paz.

  1979 (1955). *The economic organization of the Inca state*, Greenwich, Conn.: JAI Press Inc.

Nash, J. 1979. *We eat the mines and the mines eat us*, Columbia: University Press.

Nock, F. & G. Armstrong 1985. *Devils and despachos in Oruro*, Talk at the Museum of Mankind, Latin American Seminar Series.

Orlove, B. 1986. 'Barter and cash sale on Lake Titicaca', *Current Anthropology* 27 (2).

Pagden, A. 1982. *The fall of natural man*, Cambridge: Cambridge University Press.

Platt, T. 1978. 'Symétries en miroir: le concept de yanantin chez les Macha de Bolivie', *Annales ESC*, 33e année (5–6): 1081–107, Paris.

  1982a. *Estado boliviano y ayllu andino*, Lima: IEP.

  1982b. 'The role of the Andean ayllu in the reproduction of the petty commodity regime', ed., D. Lehmann, *Ecology and exchange in the Andes*, Cambridge: Cambridge University Press.

  1983. 'Religión andina y conciencia proletaria. Qhuyaruna y ayllu en el Norte de Potosí, HISIA, 2: 47–74. Lima.

  1984. 'Liberalism and ethnocide in the Southern Andes', *History Workshop Journal*, 17: 3–18.

  1986. *Estado tributario y librecambio en Potosí siglo XIX*, La Paz: HISBOL.

Polanyi, K. 1977. *The livelihood of man*, New York: Academic Press.

Prescott, W. 1889 (1847). *The conquest of Peru*, London: Swan Sonnenschein & Co.

Querejazu, R. 1978. *Llallagua. Historia de una montaña*, La Paz: Amigos del Libro.

Reichel-Dolmatoff, G. 1981. 'Things of beauty replete with meaning – metals and crystals in Colombian Indian cosmology', *Sweat of the sun, tears of the moon; gold and emerald treasures of Colombia*, Los Angeles County: Natural History Museum.

Rivera C. S. 1978. 'El mallku y la sociedad colonial en el siglo XVII:el caso de Jesus de Machaca', *Avances*, 1: 7–27, La Paz.

  1984. *Oprimidos pero no vencidos. Luchas del campesinado aymara y qhechwa 1900–1980*, La Paz: HISBOL.

Roel Pineda, J. 1973. 'Versión del mito de Inkarrí', ed., J. Ossio *Ideologia mesiánica del mundo andino*, 222–3, Lima: Ignacio Prado Pastor.

Rostworowski, M. 1977. 'Mercaderes del valle de Chincha', *Etnia y Sociedad* Lima: IEP.

Sanchez-Albornoz, N. 1978. *Indios y tributos en el Alto Perú*, Lima: IEP.

Simmel, G. 1978 (1907). *Philosophy of money*, trans. T. Bottomore & D. Frisby, London: Routledge & Kegan Paul.

Tandeter, E. 1980. *La rente comme rapport de production et comme rapport de distribution. Le cas de l'industrie minière de Potosí 1750–1826*, Thèse de 3e cycle, Paris.

— 1981. 'Forced and free labour in late colonial Potosí', *Past and Present*, 93: 98–136, London.

Tandeter, E. & N. Wachtel, 1983. 'Conjonctures inverses. Le mouvement des prix a Potosí pendant le XVIIIe siècle', *Annales ESC*, 38e année, (3): 549–613, Paris.

Taussig, M. 1980. *The devil and commodity fetishism in South America*, Chapel Hill: University of North Carolina.

Taylor, L. 1983. 'Maoism in the Andes. Sendero luminoso and the contemporary guerilla movement in Peru', *Centre for Latin American Studies, Working paper no. 2*, University of Liverpool.

Thompson, E. P. 1971. 'The moral economy of the English crowd in the eighteenth century', *Past and Present*, 50: 76–136, London.

Tschopik, H. 1951. *The Aymara of Chucuito, Peru*, New York: Anth. Papers of the American Museum of Natural History, 44 (2): 137–308.

Vilar, P. 1976. *History of gold and money 1450–1920*, London: New Left Books.

Wallerstein, I. 1974. *The modern world system*, New York: Academic Press.

Waman Puma de Ayala, F. 1980 (1612). *Nueva corónica y buen gobierno*. Edición crítica de J. V. Murra & R. Adorno, México: Siglo XX.

Weiner, A. 1980. 'Reproduction: a replacement for reciprocity', *American Ethnologist*, 7: 71–85.

Author Index

269

General Index

272